Praise for *Learning Blender, Second Edition*

"Oliver Villar's book will give you a solid foundation in Blender and computer graphics in general. Filled with well-crafted examples and lessons, this book will give you the tools you need to succeed as an artist."

—*David Andrade, Producer, Theory Studios*

"The days are now over when beginners found learning Blender 3D difficult. Oliver Villar introduces to beginners the best of Blender's 3D features and 3D fundamentals in fun and exciting ways. His approach of completing a character from scratch, touching every aspect of 3D from Blender's point of view, is truly filled with explanations of techniques and important tools that will help readers to bring their ideas to life creatively while following professional workflows in 3D.

Starting with the fundamentals of 3D, this is a great resource for every beginner artist who is looking to learn Blender 3D. It's truly a book written with great dedication!"

—*Waqas Abdul Majeed, CG Generalist, www.waqasmajeed.com*

"I found Oliver Villar's book *Learning Blender* to be an essential tool in getting users not only acquainted with Blender but also in preparing them by explaining the history and the magic that has made Blender what it is now. His book also prepares users to be productive and informed by explaining the community and its various portals. His book is complete in explaining all the aspects of the UI and acquainting users with the classic G, S, and R. The exercises are perfect for getting users on the level to begin making their own worlds. I was even pleased to see him discussing F2, ripping with V, and even knife project, which are classics I usually consider to be more advanced. This book is a no-holds-barred approach to getting the most out of this capable little program. I must also add that the character created is attractive and well created and is a fine example of using the program for character modelling. Oliver is truly a skilled artist and that shines through in his use of this program. "

—*Jerry Perkins, 3D Conceptor, Fenix Fire*

Learning Blender

Second Edition

Addison-Wesley Learning Series

Visit **informit.com/learningseries** for a complete list of available publications.

The **Addison-Wesley Learning Series** is a collection of hands-on programming guides that help you quickly learn a new technology or language so you can apply what you've learned right away.

Each title comes with sample code for the application or applications built in the text. This code is fully annotated and can be reused in your own projects with no strings attached. Many chapters end with a series of exercises to encourage you to reexamine what you have just learned, and to tweak or adjust the code as a way of learning.

Titles in this series take a simple approach: they get you going right away and leave you with the ability to walk off and build your own application and apply the language or technology to whatever you are working on.

Make sure to connect with us!
informit.com/socialconnect

Learning Blender

A Hands-On Guide to Creating 3D Animated Characters

Second Edition

Oliver Villar

♦ Addison-Wesley

Boston • Columbus • Indianapolis • New York • San Francisco • Amsterdam • Cape Town
Dubai • London • Madrid • Milan • Munich • Paris • Montreal • Toronto • Delhi • Mexico City
São Paulo • Sydney • Hong Kong • Seoul • Singapore • Taipei • Tokyo

For information about buying this title in bulk quantities, or for special sales opportunities (which may include electronic versions; custom cover designs; and content particular to your business, training goals, marketing focus, or branding interests), please contact our corporate sales department at corpsales@pearsoned.com or (800) 382-3419.

For government sales inquiries, please contact governmentsales@pearsoned.com.

For questions about sales outside the U.S., please contact intlcs@pearson.com.

Visit us on the Web: informit.com/aw

Library of Congress Control Number: 2017931009

ISBN-13: 978-0-13-466346-3
ISBN-10: 0-13-466346-2

1 17

Editor-in-Chief
Mark L. Taub

Executive Editor
Laura Lewin

Development Editor
Michael Thurston

Managing Editor
Sandra Schroeder

Full-Service Production Manager
Julie Nahil

Project Editor
Thistle Hill Publishing Services

Copy Editor
Kathy Simpson

Indexer
Jack Lewis

Proofreader
Rebecca Rider

Editorial Assistant
Olivia Basegio

Cover Designer
Chuti Prasertsith

Compositor
The CIP Group

❖

*To Gosia, the strongest woman I've known, for being with me, for
her encouragement, and for helping me evolve.
To my parents and family, for their support in my journey.
To my friends, for their patience, happy moments, and encouragement.
To everyone who crossed paths with me at some point of my life;
I've been able to learn a lot from all of you.*

❖

Contents at a Glance

Preface **xxiii**

Acknowledgments **xxix**

About the Author **xxxi**

Part I The Basics of Blender **1**

1 What You Need to Know About Blender **3**

2 Blender Basics: The User Interface **11**

3 Your First Scene in Blender **31**

Part II Beginning a Project **53**

4 Project Overview **55**

5 Character Design **61**

Part III Modeling in Blender **77**

6 Blender Modeling Tools **79**

7 Character Modeling **111**

Part IV Unwrapping, Painting, and Shading **159**

8 Unwrapping and UVs in Blender **161**

9 Painting Textures **181**

10 Materials and Shaders **195**

Part V Bringing Your Character to Life **221**

11 Character Rigging **223**

12 Animating Your Character **263**

Part VI Getting the Final Result **277**

13 Camera Tracking in Blender **279**

14 Lighting, Compositing, and Rendering **291**

Part VII Keep Learning **311**

15 Other Blender Features **313**

Index **319**

Contents

Preface **xxiii**

Acknowledgments **xxix**

About the Author **xxxi**

Part I The Basics of Blender   1

1 What You Need to Know About Blender   3
What Is Blender?   3

Commercial Software Versus Open-Source Software   4

    Commercial Software   4

    Open-Source Software   5

The History of Blender   5

The Blender Foundation and Blender Institute   7

The Blender Community   9

Summary   10

Exercises   10

2 Blender Basics: The User Interface   11
Downloading and Installing Blender   11

Using Blender with Recommended Hardware   11

Navigating the Blender User Interface   13

Understanding the 3D View Editor   14

Navigating 3D View   18

Managing Areas   20

Working with Editor Types   21

Selecting Objects   24

Making an Active Selection   25

Using the 3D Cursor   25

Setting Blender's User Preferences   27

Summary   29

Exercises   29

3 Your First Scene in Blender   31

Creating Objects   **31**

Moving, Rotating, and Scaling   **32**

   Using Manipulators (Basic Mode)   **32**

   Using Keyboard Shortcuts (Advanced Mode)   **34**

   Arranging Objects in Your Scene   **35**

Naming Objects and Using Datablocks   **35**

   Renaming Objects   **36**

   Managing Datablocks   **36**

   Naming Your Scene's Objects   **38**

Using Interaction Modes   **38**

Applying Flat or Smooth Surfaces   **39**

Working with Modifiers   **40**

   Adding Modifiers   **41**

   Adding a Subdivision Surface Modifier to Your
   Object   **42**

Using Blender Render and Cycles   **44**

Managing Materials   **44**

   Using Blender Render Materials   **45**

   Using Cycles Materials   **45**

   Adding Materials to Your Scene   **46**

Turning on the Lights   **46**

   Light Options in Blender Render   **46**

   Lights Options in Cycles   **46**

   Adding Lights to Your Scene   **47**

Moving the Camera in Your Scene   **47**

Rendering   **48**

   Rendering in Blender Render   **48**

   Rendering in Cycles   **49**

   Saving and Loading Your .blend File   **49**

   Launching and Saving the Render   **49**

Summary   **51**

Exercises   **51**

Part II Beginning a Project   53

4 Project Overview   55
The Three Stages of a Project   55
  Preproduction   55
  Production   56
  Postproduction   56
Defining the Stages   56
  A Film Without Visual Effects   57
  A Visual-Effects Film   57
  An Animated Film   58
  A Photograph   58
Making a Character-Creation Plan   59
  Character Preproduction   59
  Character Production   59
  Project Postproduction   59
Summary   60
Exercises   60

5 Character Design   61
Character Description   61
  Personality   62
  Context   62
  Style   63
  Appearance   63
Designing the Character   64
  Silhouettes   64
  Base Design   65
  Head   67
  Details   68
  Refined Design   69
Adding Color   70
Finalizing the Design   71
Making Character Reference Images   72
Using Other Design Methods   74
Summary   75
Exercises   75

Part III Modeling in Blender   77

6 Blender Modeling Tools   79

Working with Vertices, Edges, and Faces   **79**

Selecting Vertices, Edges, and Faces   **80**

Accessing Modeling Tools   **80**

Making Selections   **81**

Shortest Path   **81**

Proportional Editing   **82**

Linked Selection   **83**

Loops and Rings   **83**

Border Selection   **84**

Grow and Shrink Selection   **84**

Limit Selection to Visible   **84**

Select Similar   **84**

Select Linked Flat Faces   **85**

Select Boundary Loop and Loop Inner-Region   **85**

Checker Deselect   **85**

Other Selection Methods   **85**

Using Mesh Modeling Tools   **86**

Bevel   **86**

Boolean Operations: Intersect (Boolean) and
Intersect (Knife)   **87**

Bisect   **88**

Bridge Edge Loops   **89**

Connect   **89**

Delete and Dissolve   **90**

Duplicate   **91**

Edge Offset   **91**

Extrude   **92**

Fill and Grid Fill   **93**

Inset   **94**

Join   **95**

Knife   **95**

Knife Project   **96**

Loop Cut and Slide   **97**

Make Edge/Face   **98**

Merge   **98**

Poke   **99**

Remove Doubles   **100**

Rip and Rip Fill   **100**

Screw   **101**

Separate   **102**

Shrink/Flatten   **102**

Slide   **102**

Smooth Vertex   **103**

Solidify   **103**

Spin   **103**

Split   **104**

Subdivide   **105**

Working with LoopTools   **105**

Working with F2   **107**

Using Other Interesting Blender Options   **108**

AutoMerge   **108**

Hide and Reveal   **108**

Snapping   **108**

Summary   **109**

Exercises   **109**

7 Character Modeling   111

What Is Mesh Topology?   **111**

Choosing Modeling Methods   **113**

Box Modeling   **113**

Poly to Poly   **113**

Sculpt and Retopologize   **113**

Modifiers   **114**

The Best Method   **114**

Setting Up the Reference Planes   **114**

Modeling the Eyes   **117**

Creating an Eyeball   **117**

Using Lattices to Deform the Eyeballs   **119**

Mirroring and Adjusting the Eyes   **120**

Modeling the Face   **121**

Studying the Face's Topology   **121**

Blocking the Face's Basic Shape   **122**

Defining the Face's Shapes   **124**

Defining the Eyes, Mouth, and Nose   **126**

Adding Ears   **128**

Building the Inside of the Mouth   **130**

Modeling the Torso and Arms   **131**

Modeling the Basic Shapes for the Torso and Arms   **132**

Defining the Arms and Torso   **134**

Detailing the Backpack and Jacket   **136**

Finishing the Belt and Adding a Neck to the Jacket   **138**

Modeling the Legs   **139**

Modeling the Boots   **141**

Modeling the Hands   **143**

Building the Basic Hand Shape   **143**

Adding the Fingers and Wrist   **145**

Modeling the Cap   **147**

Creating the Base of the Cap   **147**

Adding Details to the Cap   **149**

Modeling the Hair   **150**

Shaping Locks of Hair   **151**

Adding Natural Details to the Hair   **152**

Modeling the Final Details   **154**

Eyebrows   **154**

Communicator   **155**

Badges   **156**

Teeth and Tongue   **156**

Other Clothing Details   **157**

Summary   **158**

Exercises   **158**

Part IV Unwrapping, Painting, and Shading   159

8   Unwrapping and UVs in Blender   161

Seeing How Unwrapping and UVs Work   **161**

Unwrapping in Blender   **162**

Using the UV/Image Editor   **163**

Navigating the UV/Image Editor   **166**

Accessing the Unwrapping Menus   **166**

Working with UV Mapping Tools   **166**

Defining Seams   **168**

Considering Before Unwrapping   **169**

Working with UVs in Blender   **170**

Marking the Seams   **170**

Creating and Displaying a UV Test Grid   **171**

Unwrapping Jim's Face   **173**

Using Live Unwrap   **174**

Adjusting UVs   **174**

Separating and Connecting UVs   **174**

Reviewing the Finished Face's UVs   **175**

Unwrapping the Rest of the Character   **176**

Packing UVs   **177**

Summary   **179**

Exercises   **180**

9 Painting Textures   181

Defining the Main Workflow   **181**

Painting in Blender   **181**

Texture Paint Mode   **182**

Before You Start Painting   **183**

Conditions for Painting   **184**

Paint Slots   **185**

Limitations of Blender's Texture Paint Mode   **186**

Creating the Base Texture   **186**

Placing Texture Elements   **186**

Saving Your Image   **187**

Packing Your Images   **187**

Texturing in 2D Image Editing Software   **188**

Exporting the UVs as an Image   **188**

Loading the UVs and Base Elements   **189**

Adding Base Colors   **189**

Adding Details   **191**

Applying the Final Touches   **192**

Seeing the Painted Character in Blender   **193**

Summary   **193**

Exercises   **194**

10 Materials and Shaders   195

Understanding Materials   **195**

Materials Application   **195**

How Materials Work   **196**

Masks and Layers   **196**

Channels   **196**

Blender Render Materials   **198**

Cycles Materials   **198**

Procedural Textures   **198**

Shading Your Character with Blender Render   **199**

Setting Up Blender Render Materials   **199**

Applying Textures in Blender Render   **202**

Shading Jim in Blender Render   **205**

Making Render Tests   **211**

Shading Your Character with Cycles   **212**

Using Cycles Materials   **212**

Using Basic Shaders   **214**

Mixing and Adding Shaders   **215**

Loading Textures   **215**

Shading Jim in Cycles   **216**

Running Render Tests   **219**

Summary   **220**

Exercises   **220**

Part V Bringing Your Character to Life   221

11 Character Rigging   223

Understanding the Rigging Process   **223**

What's a Rig?   **223**

Rigging Process   **224**

Working with Armatures   **224**

Manipulating Bones   **225**

Working in Object, Edit, and Pose Modes   **227**

Adding Constraints   **227**

Rigging Your Character   **229**

Creating the Base Bone Structure   **229**

Rigging the Eyes   **231**

Rigging the Leg   **232**

Rigging the Torso and Head   **235**

Rigging the Arm   **235**

Rigging the Hand   **237**

Mirroring the Rig   **238**

Organizing the Rig   **240**

Skinning   **242**

Understanding Vertex Weights   **242**

Setting Up the Model for Skinning   **243**

Adding an Armature Modifier   **244**

Defining Weights   **245**

Creating the Facial Rig   **250**

Modeling Shapes   **250**

Creating the Face Rig   **252**

Using Drivers to Control the Face Shapes   **253**

Creating Custom Shapes   **255**

Making Final Retouches   **257**

Reusing Your Character in Different Scenes   **258**

Library Linking   **258**

Working with Groups   **259**

Protecting Layers   **259**

Using Proxies to Animate a Linked Character   **260**

Using Dupli Visibility   **260**

Summary   **260**

Exercises   **261**

12 Animating Your Character   263

Inserting Keyframes   **263**

Using the Manual Method   **263**

Using the Automatic Method   **264**

Using Keying Sets   **264**

Animating Properties in the Menus   **264**

xx   Contents

Working with Animation Editors   **264**

    Timeline   **265**

    Dope Sheet   **266**

    Graph Editor   **266**

    Non-Linear Animation (NLA)   **268**

    Common Controls and Tips   **268**

Animating a Walk Cycle   **269**

    Creating an Action   **270**

    Creating the Poses for the Walk Cycle   **270**

    Repeating the Animation   **272**

    Walking Along a Path   **273**

Summary   **274**

Exercises   **275**

Part VI Getting the Final Result   277

13 Camera Tracking in Blender   279

Understanding Camera Tracking   **279**

Shooting Video for Easy Tracking   **280**

Using the Movie Clip Editor   **281**

Tracking the Camera   **282**

    Loading Your Footage   **282**

    Studying the Anatomy of a Marker   **283**

    Tracking Features in the Footage   **284**

    Configuring Camera Settings   **286**

    Solving Camera Motion   **287**

    Applying Tracked Motion to the Camera   **287**

    Adjusting Camera Motion   **288**

Testing Camera Tracking   **289**

Summary   **290**

Exercises   **290**

14 Lighting, Compositing, and Rendering   291

Lighting Your Scene   **291**

    Analyzing the Real Footage   **291**

    Creating and Testing Lights   **292**

Using the Node Editor   **293**

    Compositing   **293**

    Understanding Nodes   **294**

    Studying the Anatomy of a Node   **295**

    Using the Node Editor   **296**

    Previewing the Result   **298**

Compositing Your Scene in Blender Render   **299**

    Setting Up the Scene   **299**

    Setting Up Render Layers   **299**

    Compositing Nodes   **302**

Compositing Your Scene in Cycles   **304**

    Setting Up the Scene   **305**

    Setting Up Render Layers   **305**

    Node Compositing   **306**

Rendering   **307**

    Render Settings   **307**

    Output   **308**

    Final Render   **308**

Summary   **309**

Exercises   **310**

Part VII Keep Learning   **311**

15 Other Blender Features   **313**

Particles   **313**

Hair Simulation   **313**

Cloth Simulation   **314**

Rigid and Soft Bodies   **314**

Fluids Simulation   **314**

Fire and Smoke   **314**

Grease Pencil   **315**

Pie Menus   **315**

Game Engine   **315**

Freestyle Rendering   **315**

Masking, Object Tracking, and Video
Stabilization   **316**

Sculpting   **316**

Retopology   **316**

Maps Baking   **317**

Included Add-Ons   **317**

More Add-Ons   **317**

Animation Nodes   **318**

Python Scripting   **318**

Summary   **318**

Index   **319**

Preface

Character creation is a big undertaking. It involves several very different skills, and that's what you're going to learn soon enough. In this preface, I quickly show you what this book is about and what you can expect from it. If you already have some experience with other 3D software, you've come to the right place, as you'll find some instructions on how to handle switching between different programs, which can be frustrating—and sometimes even more difficult than learning a program for the first time.

Welcome to *Learning Blender*!

Welcome to the second edition of *Learning Blender: A Hands-On Guide to Creating 3D Animated Characters*. In this book, you'll learn how to use Blender in a complete and complex project. You'll see every part of the process so that you can understand what is involved in the creation of a 3D character and decide which part you like the most afterward. In other words, this book is not a specialized book that will make you a modeling genius or an expert animator; instead, it helps you understand the basic concepts behind every part of the process. The idea is that when you finish reading this book, you'll have the knowledge you need to start any other project, from preproduction to the final result.

If you're a freelancer (or want to be), this book is tailored to you, as freelancers often get small but very different and varied jobs, and having basic or medium skills in different tasks can be more useful than being very good at a single specific thing.

If you want to work for a big company and prefer to specialize, it helps to understand the full process. If you're a modeler, for example, but you also understand how rigging works, when you create your models, you'll be able to recognize the possible issues that your rigger mates will encounter, which will make their work easier. When you work on a team, you'll work only on part of the project, but if you have at least a little understanding of what the rest of the team's job is, your work will be more valuable to them, and everyone will be happier!

Maybe you're already familiar with Blender and want to learn about 3D character creation. Very good. You can skip the first two or three chapters and go straight to the main part of the book—but do this only if you're sure that you understand the basics of Blender.

Finally, if you just want to get started in this amazing world of 3D and dive into the sea of vertices, this book will give you a good insight into how 3D projects are handled. If you have never used 3D software before, don't worry if it looks a bit overwhelming in the beginning. That's normal. The software has lots of options and crazy stuff that will be unknown to you, and we all tend to be afraid of what we don't know. If you keep going, however, when you start using and understanding Blender, you'll start enjoying the learning process, and your results will get better with time and practice. Good luck!

Do You Come from Another 3D Software?

I took this path myself years ago, so I understand what you will go through. That's why throughout the chapters, I share tips, keeping in mind the differences between Blender and other 3D software. I came to Blender after using commercial software such as 3ds Max, Maya, and XSI for years. Back then (version 2.47), Blender was less user-friendly, but it's been greatly improved since. It's still a little alien when compared to other software, though, and it may feel intimidating to you at first. Don't worry; that reaction is completely understandable. Just don't give up!

Learning Blender won't be easy at first. It took me three or four times checking different versions of Blender until I finally decided to start learning it for good. You'll see weird features, such as right-click selections (I go through this process in the early chapters) and the omnipresent 3D cursor, which you always see in the scene but apparently has no function. (I've heard someone say that it looks like a sniper's visor for shooting at your models.)

Also, you'll be forced to learn a lot of shortcuts. This requirement makes the learning curve for Blender difficult in the beginning, but when you get used to Blender, you'll love it, as shortcuts help you work a lot faster in the long run!

Before I used Blender, it was difficult for me to work with fewer than three 3D views on the screen at the same time, for example. Now I work in full-screen mode with only one view in a much more comfortable way; it's like using the expert mode in other software all the time! I even feel weird sometimes when I need two 3D views for some special reason.

I've taught a lot of people and talked with many others who came to Blender from other software, and usually, they kind of hate it at first. (That's why most people give up and stick with commercial software.) After a short time using it, though, they start loving Blender and get addicted to it. They find that a lot of tasks are easier or faster to do in Blender than in other software.

Blender has its limitations, of course, but for the general needs of most users, it's more than enough.

I really encourage you to keep exploring Blender and find out what it has to offer. I've learned to use a lot of different software and tools, and after repeating the learning process and switching software several times, I've found that Blender works best for me.

I'll share the method I've used with you. Maybe it'll help you too. The key to making a successful change (not only in software, but also in life, work, or whatever you want) is to *learn how to adapt yourself and be flexible*. You have to free your mind to some extent to leave space for the new situation, software, or anything else to get in. In these situations, a lot of people can only complain ("This software doesn't have that tool," "That was easier on the old one," and so on). Avoid this behavior at all cost, and *try to understand the new software*, as each program has different philosophies behind its development and workflow. Complaining is a waste of energy and time you could be spending on something much more useful, such as learning how to use the new software.

What is the best way to adapt? Force yourself!

Set a deadline (this way, you'll have a good or bad result, but at least you'll finish something), and decide what you're going to do. Think of an easy project, and go for it. Having a deadline keeps you from drifting around for days, going crazy over small details that make the process too long.

Usually, people start playing around with no purpose. They don't get a specific result, but something random. This doesn't motivate them and gives them the impression that they can't use the software.

Instead, if you propose a little project, you'll have a goal to work for, which allows you to find the tools you need to achieve that goal. When you finish, even if the project is not perfect, you'll have learned some tools and achieved a result, which will motivate you to do better next time or to start a different project so you can learn about other tools.

Keep in mind that you probably don't want to start very big or difficult. The key is to start learning little by little, taking small steps to keep yourself motivated. If you start with something big that involves a lot of steps, you may get stuck at some point, which will frustrate you. When you work on something small, even if it goes wrong, you won't have spent that much time, after all, so getting attached to the project won't be a real issue.

Over time, after you make a few small projects, you'll have a knowledge base, and you'll understand how the new software works. At that point, you can judge whether you're interested in learning more or whether you're more comfortable with the previous software.

A lot of software is out there, and each program is different, so depending on your work, style, taste, and personality, you may prefer one or another. What is intuitive and comfortable for some people isn't for others. Nonetheless, if you give the new software a good test-drive, even if some things that you're used to are missing, you'll learn about others that are really cool that you didn't see before!

In my case, I was very comfortable with 3ds Max, but after using Blender extensively for a few days (yes, only a few days; they were very intense, though!), I honestly couldn't go back. I missed some tools, of course, but I found that the advantages clearly surpassed the disadvantages for me, so I've used Blender ever since.

I hope that this book motivates you to try Blender and give it a chance instead of deciding that you don't like it because you can't master it in five minutes. (I'll bet you didn't understand any other software in five minutes the first time you used it!)

The essence of practicing to learn is to set a feasible goal, set a deadline (due date), and try your best to reach that goal. No excuses; no complaints! Discipline and not giving up are the keys.

My method is just a guideline. It may not be useful for you, or you may find a better approach. But if you don't know where to start and feel discouraged, just try it!

How to Use This Book

This book is divided into parts to help you to keep track of your progress:

- **Part I, "The Basics of Blender" (Chapters 1, 2, and 3):** Understanding Blender and learning the basics
- **Part II, "Beginning a Project" (Chapters 4 and 5):** Preproduction, project preparation, and character design
- **Part III, "Modeling in Blender" (Chapter 6):** Starting production, focusing on character modeling
- **Part IV, "Unwrapping, Painting, and Shading" (Chapters 7, 8, and 9):** Unwrapping, texturing, and applying materials
- **Part V, "Bringing Your Character to Life" (Chapters 10 and 11):** Rigging and animation
- **Part VI, "Getting the Final Result" (Chapters 12, 13 and 14):** Postproduction, Camera tracking, rendering, and compositing
- **Part VII, "Keep Learning" (Chapter 15):** Other Blender features

You can start with the part you're most interested in, of course, but if you're new to Blender, I recommended that you start from the beginning so that you understand the software before you jump into something as complex as the creation of a 3D character.

In each chapter, if some basic knowledge is required, I explain it before you dive into the real thing. You'll also find tips and useful shortcuts along the way to help you work faster and more efficiently.

If you're already familiar with Blender, you can skip the first three chapters and start reading about character creation.

Chapter 1, "What You Need to Know About Blender," talks about Blender, open-source software, how the development process works, its history, and what Blender is all about. You don't really need to know these things to use Blender, but it's interesting and gives you an overview of some of the strong points of Blender.

Chapter 2, "Blender Basics: The User Interface," takes you through the user interface, basic navigation, selections, and Blender's innovative nonoverlapping window system.

In Chapter 3, "Your First Scene in Blender," you learn how to create your first scene with Blender. This very basic scene lets you play with the main tools, as well as work with simple modeling, materials, and lighting, and it helps you understand the differences between rendering with Blender Render and rendering with Cycles.

After this introduction, you start on the main project: creating a 3D character. The reason you create a character as a project for this book is that it involves almost every part of the software to get it done: modeling, texturing, rigging, animation, and so on.

This part of the book explains everything you'll go through, talking about preproduction and how to get ready for any project. You'll learn that preparation is essential!

In the final chapters, you see how to track the camera of a real video and composite your character into that scene so that you end up with something cool you can show your friends, not just a character inside Blender.

I discuss some other features of Blender in Chapter 15, "Other Blender Features," so that you get a glance at them, including dynamic simulations, particles, smoke and fire, the Grease Pencil, and add-ons.

I encourage you to create your own stuff from scratch and use your own video to track the camera, but if you prefer to follow the book in detail (with the same material used in it) or want to skip some parts, you'll find all the material you need to start from any point of the book in the production files (at www.blendtuts.com/learning-blender-files).

- .blend files with different levels of progress so you can start from whatever part of the book interests you. You don't have to start from scratch.
- Texture images for the character
- Real video for camera tracking (and some alternative videos so that you can experiment with something different from the example used in the book)
- Final results
- Video tutorials of some parts of the book

What's New in This Edition

What you have in your hands is the second edition of *Learning Blender*. The whole book has been updated to be compliant with the latest Blender version (2.78b) and beyond. Most figures have been updated or reworked to improve readability. New tools have been discussed throughout the book, especially (but not limited to) selection and modeling tools. A lot of new tips and tricks have been added, and some chapters have been extended, based on feedback I got from the first edition. That said, I hope that you find these new additions interesting and that they make your experience with the book and Blender better.

Without any more hesitation, get ready to start learning. You have a long way to go!

Register your copy of *Learning Blender, Second Edition,* at informit.com for convenient access to downloads, updates, and corrections as they become available. To start the registration process, go to informit.com/register and log in or create an account. Enter the product ISBN (9780134663463) and click Submit. Once the process is complete, you will find any available bonus content under "Registered Products."

Acknowledgments

Although the author of a book usually takes most of the credit, a lot of people are needed to make it, improve it, and get it into your hands. Thanks to Laura Lewin and Olivia Basegio for giving me the opportunity to participate in this project; they were patient with me during the entire process and helped me with everything I needed. Thanks to Michael Thurston, who did a great job of cleaning up my non-native English and making sure that everything I wrote was consistent and made sense. Thanks to Daniel Kreuter, Mike Pan, and Tim Harrington, who did an amazing job of reviewing the manuscript and providing valuable feedback that definitely made the final result a lot better. Thanks to Andrea Coppola, David Andrade, and Aditia A. Pratama, who worked on the revisions for this second edition of *Learning Blender* and made sure that everything was up to date with the latest Blender versions. Thanks also to Angela Urquhart, Julie Nahil, Andrea Archer, and Kathy Simpson, who took care of the production of this second edition. Thanks to everyone else at Addison-Wesley who was involved in any way in the creation of this book.

This book wouldn't be possible, of course, without the work of the Blender Foundation, Ton Roosendaal, all the Blender developers, and the amazing Blender community. Thanks, everyone.

Special thanks to César Domínguez Castro, who filmed the footage used in the camera tracking and compositing chapters and other videos that you'll find in the bonus files (www.blendtuts.com/learning-blender-files), which will allow you to experiment with Blender tools.

About the Author

Oliver Villar, born in Galicia (Spain) in 1987, has been drawing since he was a kid. His interest in art brought him to 3D, which he's been studying since 2004. He used different commercial 3D software before stumbling onto Blender in 2008. Since then, he has used Blender professionally as a freelance 3D designer and tutor. In 2010, he founded blendtuts.com, a website to which he's devoted, which offers quality Blender training videos to the community. Currently, he's working as co-director of *Luke's Escape*, a 3D animated short film made with Blender, and teaching Blender for online schools in Spain as a Blender Foundation Certified Trainer.

The Basics of Blender

1 What You Need to Know About Blender

2 Blender Basics: The User Interface

3 Your First Scene in Blender

What You Need to Know About Blender

Blender has quite a remarkable story, as open-source software (OSS) works in a very different way from typical commercial software. It is helpful to know this if you intend to use Blender professionally, as it may give you insight into how powerful its concept is. In this chapter, you'll learn about how Blender was created, how the development process works, how it is funded, and what type of community surrounds the Blender world.

What Is Blender?

Blender is OSS that provides one of the most complete 3D-graphics creation suites. It includes tools for modeling, texturing, shading, rigging, animation, compositing, rendering, video editing, interactive content creation (Game Engine), and more. Since the development of version 2.50, which introduced a completely new user interface (UI), Blender's user base has grown significantly, and more professionals have started using it. It has reached animation studios and has been used for some purposes in top movie productions such as *Life of Pi, Spider-Man 2*, and *Red Riding Hood*, and in 2016, it was used to animate and compose a creature in *Warcraft*.

Its principal target audience is professional, freelance 3D artists and small studios, and Blender works very well for their needs. It still isn't widely used by big studios for several reasons. Larger studios typically have long-established software, and the commercial software they use often has impressive third-party plug-ins that have been developed over years for specific uses in production. Blender is still growing and lacks a lot of third-party support, but despite being relatively new to the professional landscape (initially, it was used mainly by hobbyists), it is overcoming those problems, and big productions have begun to use it for processes such as modeling and UV unwrapping—two areas in which Blender is particularly efficient.

Blender is known for being very different from other software, and that's why some people are hesitant to use it (although, as mentioned before, things have been vastly improved since version 2.50). It doesn't follow a lot of the same standards that other 3D software has been using for decades, and this is usually an issue for new users. That's also the charm of Blender; once you experience it, it is very possible that you'll love it because it is so different! Initially, you may find that a lot of features and techniques are difficult to understand, but once you learn the basics, it begins to seem very intuitive and sensible.

Blender, because it is open-source, doesn't need to sell licenses, so it can bypass the way other software works and go for something new and unique. In the words of Ton Roosendaal (Blender Foundation's chairman and the creator of Blender), "I would never look up to average; I want to lift up the average. It's not following conventions, it's following a vision."

Blender's development is funded primarily through voluntary donations from users. This should give you an idea of how a lot of people find it so useful that they donate to its continued development even when they can use it for free. This can be difficult to understand for people who use only commercial software, but it's something you often find with OSS: People are more willing to contribute voluntarily because it's free.

Popular OSS such as Blender can have lots of contributors and grow quite fast. This is very good for users because they get new features and tools periodically. It has a down side, though: It's difficult to stay abreast of everything new and be aware of updates to the latest versions. Also, instructional material has a short lifespan. Although this material can be used for years because general features and workflow remain the same, some options, buttons, icons, and tools will be replaced, improved, changed, or removed.

Commercial Software Versus Open-Source Software

You can't understand OSS from the point of view of the "usual" copyright and privacy system, in which you can't use something if you didn't pay for it. The business model is completely different as well.

Commercial Software

Usually, the business model for companies that develop commercial software is to sell the software license itself. If you want to use commercial software, you have to pay for a license, but you don't really own the software. Some software companies may not allow you to use the software for particular purposes (such as getting into its code to study or change it), and you may be able to use it for only a fixed amount of time before having to pay for an upgrade or a new license. In certain cases, you can use the software for free, but only for learning purposes; you need to purchase a license if you want to use it professionally to generate income. In other cases, what you get for free is a limited version of the software, and you need to purchase the full version to access all its features. Here's where piracy comes in: Some people can't afford the software, and others just don't want to pay for it, so they use illegal copies, which results in a negative economic effect on the commercial software developers.

You can't develop new features in commercial software if you're not employed by the company that owns the software, and even if you are, you have to follow that company's guidelines (and you're not allowed to copy your code or show it to the general public). Anyone may develop plug-ins, but you are not allowed to change the software core or its basic features.

Open-Source Software

Open-source software is usually misunderstood as being free-of-charge software. The word *free* has a double meaning here, however: Not only is the software free to use, but also, its source code is freely available to everyone. Some software can be free of charge (freeware) but not free in terms of liberty of use—that is, you can't access the core (the source code) and modify it to fit your needs.

What open-source means is that the user has the power to access the source code of the software and modify it at will. Developers also encourage you to check the code, use the software for commercial purposes, and even redistribute it. Basically, OSS is the exact opposite of commercial software. You can download this software and immediately use it commercially. The business model of a company that creates OSS is not to sell the software itself, but to sell related services such as instructional material, training, technical support, and merchandising. This type of company often relies on donations from the public as well.

The good thing about open-source is that anyone in the world can download the source code and develop a feature he or she likes, and other people can use that new feature later. You are free to modify the source code, copy it as many times as you want, learn from it, and give it to your friends or classmates. Sometimes, OSS is developed by an individual or a small team. Some OSS is, of course, quite complex and highly organized, and it may even have additional companies contributing to its development.

Another fact worth noting is that there are several types of open-source licenses, such as General Public License (GPL), Eclipse Public License (EPL), and Massachusetts Institute of Technology (MIT) license. Before using OSS, you should get some information about the terms of those licenses to make sure you understand what you are allowed do with that software.

The History of Blender

Lots of people think that Blender is relatively new, but that's not accurate. Blender was born in the early 1990s, making it more than 20 years old. Recently, Blender Foundation Chairman Ton Roosendaal found an "ancient" file—Blender's first bit of code—that dated back to December 1992. It is true, however, that the software became much more relevant to the public within the past few years with the release of version 2.50, which included a completely revamped, written-from-scratch interface and core that made it more user-friendly and powerful than previous versions.

In 1988, Roosendaal founded a new Dutch animation studio, NeoGeo. Not long after, the new studio decided that it had to write new software to create its animations; as a result, in 1995 it officially started to build Blender. In 1998, Roosendaal founded a new company called Not a Number (NaN) to further develop and market Blender. Due to difficult economic conditions at the time, NaN wasn't a success, and investors stopped funding the company, shutting down Blender's development in 2002.

Later in 2002, Roosendaal managed to build the nonprofit Blender Foundation. The users community donated 100,000 euros (an amazing sum, and raising it took only seven weeks) to get the previous development investors to allow for the open-sourcing of the software and to make it available for free. Finally, Blender was released under the terms of the GNU General Public License on October 13, 2002. Since that day, Roosendaal has led a team of enthusiastic developers who want to contribute to the project.

The first Open Movie project (*Elephants Dream*) was born in 2005, with the goal of gathering a team of artists who could use Blender in a real production and also provide developers with feedback that would ultimately improve the software significantly. The goal was not only to create the movie with open-source tools, but also to release the end result and production files to the public under a Creative Commons open license.

The project ended up being a great success, and Roosendaal created the Blender Institute, located in Amsterdam, the Netherlands, in the summer of 2007. The institute is now the core of Blender's development, and more Open Movies have been made there since, including *Big Buck Bunny* (2008), the video game *Yo Frankie!* (2008), *Sintel* (2010), *Tears of Steel* (2012), and *Cosmos Laundromat* (2015).

The development of Blender version 2.50 began in 2008. It offered a major improvement in the software's core, which was already becoming outdated. The final release of this version came in 2011. *Sintel* was made to put this new version to the test. It also helped improve the tools and brought back previous functionalities that were lost in the recent update. Since then, Blender has experimented with some other significant new features, such as Cycles, a new render engine that supports GPU real-time, pathtracing-based rendering, and more complex and realistic light and materials calculations.

Tears of Steel, one of the latest Open Movies, was made to implement and improve visual-effects tools such as camera tracking, compositing nodes improvements, and masks (to name a few), making Blender one of the most flexible tools in the 3D software panorama.

The latest Open Movie, released in 2015, was *Cosmos Laundromat* (see Figure 1.1), born to be the first full-feature film made by the Blender Institute. The crowdfunding campaign didn't reach the final goal, however, so the project turned into a very ambitious short film that has been awarded and praised in many festivals, including the Jury's Award at Siggraph 2016. During its creation, hair simulation, Cycles rendering capabilities, video editing options, and many more features were heavily improved.

Figure 1.1   *Cosmos Laundromat* (2015) was an Open Movie project, completely crowdfunded. The movie was made to achieve goals such as improving hair simulations, rendering capabilities, and other Blender features.

Blender's development process has been refined over time, and new versions are now being released every three or four months. As this book is being developed, the current Blender version is 2.78b, and in the last updates, many improvements were made, including faster rendering with Cycles, GPU volumetrics support, new modeling and selection tools, Freestyle nonphotorealistic rendering options, and OpenSubdiv initial integration. But the Blender 2.7X series is not really aimed at adding amazing new features; the goal of these versions is to improve current features, improve Blender internally to make it more stable, and set up the software for version 2.80. When version 2.80 comes around, it will be easier to implement new features and maintain the forward and backward compatibility of tools, add-ons, and numerous other features. Also, internal improvement will enhance performance, which is critically important for professional users.

The Blender Foundation and Blender Institute

The Blender Foundation is the corporation that organizes Blender's development and other projects related to the software, such as Open Movies, conferences, and training. The foundation operates from the Blender Institute, where the main infrastructure of https://blender.org is located.

The head of the Blender Foundation is Ton Roosendaal, who organizes and sets the goals for the software and anything else related to Blender. Everyone can make proposals about features they'd like to see added to Blender, and after the main development team analyzes them to see which of them are feasible, the team begins development. This system is very different from the development of commercial software, in which the company decides what needs to be done and developers have no say in what is added to the software.

In fact, Blender users don't even need to request new features; they can just develop a feature themselves and send it to the foundation afterward. If the feature is found to be useful and interesting, and if it fits the Blender guidelines (it has to be consistent with the rest of the software), the main development team will work on adding it to the official Blender version.

The Blender Foundation hires some full-time developers to complete specific tasks and reach the most important goals, but most developers are volunteers who lend their time to learn and practice using the software, or just to participate in its ongoing development. Some developers even raise their own funds to create and perfect the features they want to see in Blender.

Because it is OSS, Blender has public master versions and branches. The *master version* is the official version released at https://blender.org; it contains the stable features of Blender. *Branches* are development versions for testing new features or alternative features that may make it into the official master version at some point. (Commercial software also uses this method, but all the work is internal. You can't create your own branch or test development versions unless the company that owns the software releases a beta version to generate feedback before the software's actual release.)

Chaos would result if everyone could just step in and add ideas to the software, of course, so one of the Blender Foundation's main tasks is organizing all the developers in one place, defining priorities, and deciding what features should make it to the final official version. The foundation determines which features need branches and which branches should be removed. It also provides and maintains the platform for Blender and operates the bug-tracker system, in which users can report bugs that are then assigned to specific developers for correction (usually, really quickly).

> **Note**
>
> If you're interested in testing development versions of Blender, you can visit http://graphicall.org and https://developer.blender.org, where you can find the version for your system. Testing is not recommended if you aren't an experienced user, as these versions are experimental and unstable, so you must use them at your own discretion. The Blender Foundation also offers automatic daily builds. Go to the Download tab of https://blender.org, scroll to the Bleeding Edge option at the bottom, and download the latest additions to Blender's master version.

The Blender Foundation also decides how donations are spent. Above all, the Blender Foundation is the nerve center of Blender development, and the Blender Institute is its physical location.

The Blender Foundation also organizes Open Movies with several goals:

- **Raising money.** People pay for the movies in advance, so the movie and related contents fund their own development.

- **Testing Blender in production.** Making a movie is the best way to test how Blender responds in a production environment. It provides developers with an opportunity to fix issues and discover what features can be improved.

- **Improving Blender.** Usually, each Open Movie has a technical goal. The goal of *Sintel*, for example, was to test the new version of the software and make it stable and production-ready. *Tears of Steel* was made to improve Blender's visual-effects capabilities. *Cosmos Laundromat* helped improve hair simulation and rendering capabilities. Thus, each Open Movie has a list of features to add that ultimately improve Blender, and many users help raise money for the movie so they can also enjoy using these features in the future.

- **Generating content for the Blender Cloud.** Blender Cloud is a service that people can subscribe to (and that also helps raise money for Blender's development), through which the Blender Foundation publishes video tutorials and content created for Open Movies with educational purposes. Also, some external services to Blender are being added for Blender Cloud subscribers, such as adding textures to models directly from the cloud or directly uploading renders when finished.

- **Demonstrating features.** With these kinds of projects, the foundation demonstrates Blender's capabilities and shows the world that Blender is absolutely usable in a professional production environment.

The Blender Community

For every type of software, it's very important to have a community surrounding it to provide feedback and engage others in using the software. But in OSS, a community is even more important. The community not only provides feedback, but also proposes new features, discusses development, creates new features, organizes events, supports the projects, and donates money.

Open-source software communities are very open-minded and enthusiastic. Members are usually treated as "fanboys" or "fanatics" by users of other software, but once you are part of one of these communities, you understand why. Members are not only talking about a particular type of software, but also adhering to a set of ethics, and they're willing to contribute their help for free to improve the software or even to donate funds to have some features developed.

The Blender community includes everyone who uses Blender and shares his or her experience in forums, websites, blogs, podcasts, and videos. The community helps new users, provides tutorials, writes articles, and raises and donates money to the Blender Foundation. Although learning Blender is not an easy endeavor, its great community makes the process considerably less difficult, thanks to the huge amounts of free instructional content that users produce; you'll also find people who are willing to answer your doubts and inquiries in forums and on social networks.

Lately, a new feature has appeared in the community: content and add-ons stores. Some stores make it easy for content creators and developers to sell their creations (models, textures, materials, animations, and so on) and add-ons (external tools that add specific features to Blender). This development creates a new path for the community, as professionals can now pay developers directly for tools that make their jobs easier, and small studios can buy material made by others to quickly advance in their projects and meet the deadlines. (These possibilities are already widely available in other software.)

Following is a partial list of community forums and reference websites:

- www.blenderartists.com: A forum where you can show your work and get feedback, critique other artists' works, ask questions, or discuss any subject related to Blender and 3D

- www.blendswap.com: A website where you can share your models and assets and download those made by others to use in your projects

- https://blendermarket.com: A marketplace to sell and buy Blender add-ons; training material; and 3D assets such as models, materials, and animations

- www.blendernation.com: The main Blender news website, which you can visit daily for updates, new add-ons, interesting works, tutorials, and more

Summary

Blender has been around for many years. It's free to download and use, even for commercial purposes. The Blender Foundation organizes the software's development, and anyone can contribute to it by programming, reporting bugs, donating money, and purchasing the foundation's products. Two of the most attractive features of OSS are the ability to play with the core code of the software to make it fit your needs (or your studio's) and the opportunity to interact with its developers and its diverse, open-minded community.

Exercises

1. What is open-source software?
2. When did Blender's development start?
3. Do you need to buy a license to use Blender commercially?
4. What are the main functions of the Blender Foundation?
5. Can you sell the content you create with Blender?

Blender Basics: The User Interface

This chapter helps you begin to understand how Blender's user interface (UI) and main navigation features work. Blender has a distinct way of using windows and menus. You might have to rethink how you work with interfaces while you catch up, but don't worry; it'll be fun!

Downloading and Installing Blender

Before you start using Blender, you need to install it, of course! This is really easy: You need only an Internet connection and a visit to https://www.blender.org (Blender's official website). Once you're there, simply click the Download link on the home page or go to the Download tab. There, you will find a panel with the current official version. You have to select your operating system and specify whether you want an installer (for Windows only) or a portable version. (Yes, you can copy a portable Blender to your pen drive and use it everywhere you go.) You also select whether your OS is 32-bit or 64-bit. (If you don't know, check your OS version in Control Panel.)

If you use Windows and download an installer, execute it and follow the instructions. If you download a .zip (Windows and Mac) or .tarball (Linux) portable file, extract it; then select the executable file from the folder and launch it.

> **Caution**
>
> Before you download, read the information on the Blender website, as it provides instructions on packages or libraries you have to install in case Blender doesn't work:
>
> - Windows: Visual C++ 2013 Redistributable Package; Windows XP is no longer supported
> - Mac OS: Only Mac OS X 10.6 or later is supported
> - Linux: Requires glibc 2.11

Using Blender with Recommended Hardware

3D has some hardware requirements that other, more basic software (such as software for text editing or office work) doesn't. In this section, I recommend some hardware that you should have to get the most out of Blender, even though you can use it without this equipment in most cases:

- **A mouse with three buttons and a scroll wheel:** 3D software requires you to navigate a tridimensional world and usually takes advantage of the three buttons of a mouse for this purpose. Having a scroll wheel or a middle mouse button is very important. A scroll wheel is optional in Blender, as you can just drag while clicking the middle mouse button to get a similar effect. You won't be able to work without a middle button, however, so Blender offers you the option to hold down **Alt** and left-click to emulate a middle mouse button (you can find this option in User Preferences, as mentioned later in this chapter), but this process is more uncomfortable.

- **Numerical keyboard:** You can definitely work without a numerical keyboard, but Blender makes extensive use of it. Also, this type of keyboard makes working in a 3D world a lot easier, giving you access to camera controls and allowing to quickly jump to predefined points of view by pressing its keys. Blender offers you the option of using the alphanumerical keys (the numbers on top of the letters on your keyboard) instead, but this option limits functionality. I personally have a portable numerical keyboard (similar to a calculator) to plug into my small laptop so I can use it with Blender when I don't have access to a full keyboard.

- **CPU:** All computers and laptops have a CPU. Blender is quite lightweight, so any current computer should be able to run the software. Keep in mind, however, that Blender uses a CPU for most of its computing, and the more complex your scene is, the more powerful your CPU needs to be; otherwise, your computer will start slowing down as you work and decrease performance. I won't recommend a specific CPU here. Just keep in mind that the better your CPU is, the better Blender performs.

- **8GB RAM:** It's very important to have a decent amount of RAM installed, as Blender uses it for several purposes, such as storing the scene before rendering. (If your scene takes more memory than you have, you won't be able to render it.) Although you can use the software with a minimum of 1GB of RAM, I recommend having at least 8GB.

- **Graphics card with CUDA or OpenCL support:** If you're planning on rendering with Cycles, a good graphics card can help, as a GPU (Graphics Processing Unit) is much faster than the CPU. To use the GPU, your graphics card must be compatible with CUDA (Nvidia) or OpenCL (AMD) technology. OpenCL integration in Blender (as of version 2.78b) is still experimental, and not all Cycles features are supported, so Nvidia cards are currently recommended.

  To select an Nvidia graphics card, keep these specifications in mind (other specifications, such as speed, also improve render times, but the ones mentioned here are key): graphics memory (as with RAM, your scene needs to fit in the graphics memory, so the bigger, the better) and CUDA cores number (the more cores, the faster it renders).

Navigating the Blender User Interface

As mentioned before, Blender's UI is different from the UI in other software. The main thing you'll notice when you start using Blender's interface is that it is made up of what are called *areas*. You can split and join areas to create your own workspace, depending on what you feel most comfortable with or what task you need to accomplish. If you need further help with the interface, you can find a video tutorial on the book's companion website (www.blendtuts.com/learning-blender-files) with downloadable files that explain the basics of this chapter.

Each area can show different tool sets and views, called *editors*. Each part of Blender, or each task you can perform with it, is developed in a specific editor. 3D View, Outliner, Timeline, Node Editor, and UV/Image Editor are some of the various types of editors you will encounter.

At any time, you can split an area and decide which editor you want to use in it—a feature that provides you with great flexibility as you work. You can also save different workspaces so that you can load the one you need very quickly without the need to set it up again.

The following list describes what you will encounter the first time you use Blender (see Figure 2.1):

- **Info Editor (A):** This is the main menu, where you find typical options such as Save, Load, and Help. You also find two drop-down menus—Workspace (covered later in this chapter) and Scene (which lets you switch between 3D scenes you can store in the same file)—as well as the Render Engine selector and information about the scene in which you're working.

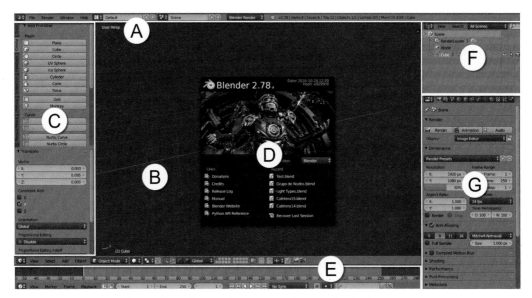

Figure 2.1   Blender's user interface and splash screen

- **3D View (B):** Here is where the magic happens. In this view, you can create your objects, model and animate them, and add lights, for example. By default, you see a grid that represents the floor and shows the colored axes (X is red, and Y is green), a light, a cube, and a camera—all you need to launch a render that turns your 3D scene into an image.

- **Tools region (C):** Some editors, such as 3D View (shown in Figure 2.2), have their own regions where you can see certain options relevant to that specific editor. Most editors have two types of regions: Tools and Properties. The one you see by default on the left side of 3D View is the Tools region, where you have access to common tools and actions.

- **Splash Screen (D):** This screen appears as you launch Blender. It shows the version you're using, interesting links about Blender, and options such as Help and Recent Files. If you just want to start using Blender, close the splash screen by clicking somewhere in the interface away from the splash screen.

- **Timeline (E):** This section represents the time dimension in your scene (by default, in frames) and allows you to watch the animation, see where you have set animation keys or time markers, and locate the start and end of the animation.

- **Outliner (F):** This area contains a schematic representation of the current scene similar to a tree that you can collapse and expand. Here, you can check a list of every object in the scene and its relationships with other objects, or you can quickly find and select the particular object you're looking for by typing its name.

- **Properties Editor (G):** This is probably one of the most important editors of Blender. Here, you find all the options you need for rendering. You can create materials, change the parameters of the selection, add modifiers or constraints, set up physics and particle effects, and do much more.

Understanding the 3D View Editor

In this section, I examine the elements of the 3D View editor, which is the main editor in Blender (see Figure 2.2). Some of these elements are also present in other editors. This section helps you understand what these elements do.

- **View Name (A):** In the top-left corner (by default), you see the name of the current view (such as User Perspective, Front Ortho, or Right Ortho). If you're not sure where the camera is located, a quick look at the view name will give you a clue.

- **Tools region (B):** Most of the editors have regions to the left and right of the view. You can show or hide the Tools region by pressing **T** on your keyboard. You can also adjust the region's width by hovering the cursor over its border and then clicking and dragging. If the Tools region is hidden, on the left border of 3D View, you'll find a little **+** button; click that button, and the Tools region reappears.

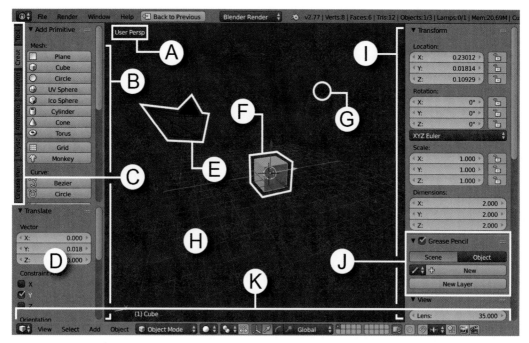

Figure 2.2   3D View in Blender—one of the most important editors

- **Tabs (C):** The Tools region has context-sensitive tabs that you can click to show different types of tools. In Figure 2.2, for example, the Create tab is selected; it shows buttons you can click to create different geometric shapes, curves, lights, and other objects. Hover your mouse cursor on top of the tabs and scroll with the mouse wheel, or middle mouse button click and drag to quickly navigate all the tabs.

- **Operator panel (D):** At the bottom of the Tools region is the Operator panel, which shows the parameters of the last action you performed. If you create a circle, for example, the Operator panel displays options such as the number of vertices or the circle's radius and whether the circle should be filled. You can experiment with those options and see their effects in real time. As an alternative (useful if you like to work in full screen with no menus), you can press **F6** to make the Operator panel appear over 3D View.

- **Camera (E):** You can't take a render (the resulting 2D image or animation generated from your 3D scene) without a camera in the scene. The camera defines the point of view, the field of view, zooming and depth of field, as well as other extra options that help you see in the viewport what will be rendered in the final image.

- **Default cube (F):** The first time you start Blender, a cube appears in the center of the scene, so you already have a geometric shape to start working with. You can delete it by pressing **X** or **Del** on your keyboard and confirming whether you prefer to start with a different object or a blank scene.

- **Lamp (G):** If you want your render to look nice, you need lights that illuminate your scene and generate shadows. By default, Blender has a Point lamp in the scene to provide basic illumination.

- **Grid (H):** The grid represents the floor of your scene, with the X (red) and Y (green) axes as references to the scene's orientation and size. By default, each square in the grid represents 1 meter, but you can use the Display panel in the Properties Region to customize the grid scale and number of divisions.

> **Note**
>
> For a lot of users, using realistic units of measure is relevant. Since Blender version 2.78, the units system has been improved, and it's now possible to work with different units easily. By default, Blender uses meters; you can go to the Scene tab in the Properties Editor, and below the Units panel, you find options to customize units. You can select the Metric or Imperial System, whereupon a series of presets for common measuring units becomes available, such as Meters, Centimeters, Kilometers, Inches, and Feet. At the bottom of this panel, you see the Scale value. 1.00 is 1 meter, and for the rest of units, this value is converted accordingly. (0.01 becomes centimeters, for example, and 0.0254 becomes inches.) The scene also scales to adapt to these changes. Don't forget that if you want the 3D View's grid to represent the same measuring unit, its scale must be the same as the value on the Units panel.

- **Properties Region (I):** Don't confuse this part of the interface with the Properties Editor; this region contains only properties and parameters that affect your interaction with 3D View. It's hidden by default, but you can show it by pressing **N**. This region contains options to transform objects, position the 3D cursor precisely, set view options (like the field of view), display options (such as the grid's scale), and open background images to use as references. It's also context-sensitive, so some options change depending on your selection or the mode in which you're working. You can adjust its width in exactly the same way as you do with the Tools Region.

> **Tip**
>
> In other 3D software, you usually work with several 3D views at the same time. In Blender, you have an option to make a Quad View in a unique 3D View Editor. In the Properties Region of 3D View, look for the Display panel, and click Toggle Quad View (or press **Ctrl+Alt+Q**). In the same menu, you find additional options for using Quad View.

- **Panels (J):** Blender menus, such as those in the Tools and Properties regions or the Properties Editor, are divided into panels. Each menu has different options and buttons for you to use. You can expand them or collapse them by left-clicking the small dark triangle to the left of the panel's title or the title itself.

  In Figure 2.3, you see a down-pointing triangle to the left of the title (3D cursor). When you click the triangle, it points to the right and the panel collapses to save space in your interface. You can also press **A** while hovering over any part of a panel to expand or collapse it. Also, if you click the little dots in the top-right corner, you can reorder the panels inside a menu by dragging and dropping.

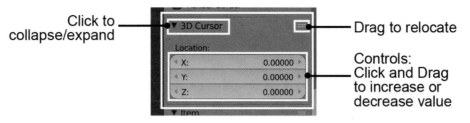

Click to collapse/expand — ▼ 3D Cursor

Drag to relocate

Location:
◄ X: 0.00000 ►
◄ Y: 0.00000 ►
◄ Z: 0.00000 ►

Controls:
Click and Drag to increase or decrease value

▼ Item

Figure 2.3   A panel from the Properties Region that controls the location of the 3D cursor

- **Header (K):** Every editor has a header—a horizontal bar at the top or bottom of the current view with menus and options for that view (see Figure 2.4). Hover the cursor over the header and press **F5** to switch its position from bottom to top or top to bottom.

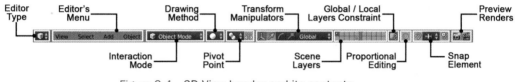

Editor Type   Editor's Menu   Drawing Method   Transform Manipulators   Global / Local Layers Constraint   Preview Renders

Interaction Mode   Pivot Point   Scene Layers   Proportional Editing   Snap Element

Figure 2.4   3D View header and its contents

Depending on your selection or the interaction mode you're using, you'll see different options. (The header is context-sensitive.) These are the main options that you generally find on the 3D View's header (other editors' headers are similar), from left to right:

- **Editor Type:** Selects the type of editor in the current area.
- **Editor's Menu:** Provides options you can use within a specific editor. In this case, for 3D View, you have the options View, Select, Add, and Object.
- **Interaction Mode:** Selects the mode in which you're working (Edit Mode, Object Mode, and so on).
- **Drawing Method Selector:** Toggles between the display methods in 3D View (such as Wireframe, Solid, Textured, and Rendered).
- **Pivot Point:** Provides a reference point in space for transforming an object.
- **Transform Manipulators:** Selects the manipulators, which show visual aids that serve to transform objects (Move, Rotate, and Scale).
- **Scene Layers:** The small blocks represent different layers in which you can store objects from the scene to keep everything organized.
- **Global/Local Layers Constraint:** Links the visibility of layers between the 3D View and the Scene Layers that you render. If you want a layer to be rendered but don't want it to be visible in 3D View, you can turn that layer on from the Render Layers tab (see Chapter 14, "Lighting, Compositing, and Rendering") and turn the Global/Local Layers Constraint off so that the visibility of layers in 3D View and in the final render is not linked.

- **Proportional Editing:** Lets you select different falloff methods that affect the objects surrounding your selection when you transform it. A circle around the selection indicates the range of the effect; you can modify its size with the scroll wheel of your mouse. The farther an object is from the selection, the less affected by the transforms it will be.
- **Snap Element:** Offers several options to snap the selection to other elements when you perform a transform operation.
- **Preview Renders:** Render OpenGL previews. The first button renders a still snapshot, and the second one renders the entire animation using the format and output folder selected in the Render Output options in the Properties editor. These renders are captures of what you see in 3D View.

> **Tip**
>
> If an area is too small for you to see all the options in the header, you can hold and drag the middle mouse button (**MMB**) over the header to the left and right to see the rest of the options.
>
> You can also right-click the top of the header to find some other options, such as collapsing the menus inside a single button to use less space, which is useful if you're working in a small area.

Navigating 3D View

Now that you know what's going on in 3D View, you're ready to see how to navigate it to check your scene and get in touch with the world you're creating. When your cursor is hovering in 3D View, you can perform a variety of actions to change your point of view (see Figure 2.5):

- **Pan (Shift+MMB):** This action moves the camera parallel to the current view.
- **Orbit (MMB or NumPad 4, 8, 6, and 2):** This action rotates the camera around the scene.

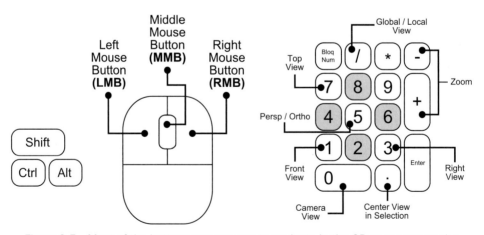

Figure 2.5   Most of the buttons you can use to navigate in the 3D scene are on the mouse and NumPad. Buttons highlighted in gray let you orbit the camera.

- **Zoom (scroll wheel or Ctrl+MMB drag or NumPad + (plus sign) and NumPad − (minus sign):** This action moves closer to or farther away from a point.

- **View Selected (NumPad .):** This action zooms and centers the camera in the selection.

- **Predefined (Front, Right, and Top) Views (NumPad 1, 3, 7):** This action changes the point of view aligned to one axis. Press **Ctrl** at the same time to get the opposite view (Back, Left, and Bottom). Combine the previous keys with **Shift** to align the view to the selection's orientation.

> **Tip**
>
> To use Blender's default navigation configuration efficiently, it is highly recommended that you use a keyboard with a NumPad and a mouse with a scroll wheel and middle button. If you don't, you can still navigate with other buttons by setting them up in User Preferences, enabling the Emulate 3 Buttons Mouse option (so **Alt+LMB** would act as a **MMB**), and by using the conventional number keys on the alphanumerical keyboard by enabling the Emulate Numpad option and Emulate Middle Mouse in User Preferences. You'll have limited functionalities, however, and navigation won't be as smooth.

- **Perspective/Orthographic Switch (NumPad 5):** This action switches between Perspective and Orthographic.

- **Camera View (NumPad 0):** This action jumps to the point of view of the active camera. Select a camera and press **Ctrl+NumPad 0** to make that camera the active one. Press **Ctrl+Alt+NumPad 0** to place the active camera in the current view. Keep in mind that with **Ctrl+NumPad 0**, you can turn any object into a camera, so don't worry if you accidentally had an object selected when you pressed that shortcut and suddenly see the scene from a strange point of view; this option is meant to help you orient objects in a different manner. You can use this feature to see the scene from the point of view of a directional light, for example, which will give you a better sense of what the light will illuminate.

- **Global View/Local View (NumPad /):** Local View hides everything except the selection so that you don't have other objects blocking your view while you work. Press **NumPad /** again to switch back to Global View. Select an object and press **M** to move it out of the local view if you don't need it anymore.

- **Walk Mode (Shift+F):** This action moves the point of view slowly around the screen. Use the arrow keys (**Up**, **Down**, **Left**, and **Right**) or **A, S, D,** and **F** to navigate through the scene as though you were moving in a video game. Use **Q** and **E** to move up and down. Use the mouse to rotate the camera. You can increase or decrease the moving speed with the scroll wheel. Press **G** to enable a gravity effect; the experience in Walk Mode is similar to playing in a first-person videogame, as the camera falls down to stay on top of the scene's geometry, allowing you to "walk" on the surfaces. You can press **Shift** to move faster and **V** to jump. Left-click to accept the movement and right-click to cancel it.

- **Fly Mode (Shift+F):** This action is an alternative to Walk Mode, letting you fly through the scene instead of walking. To activate this action instead of Walk Mode, set it as default on the Input tab of User Preferences. You can rotate the camera with the mouse, pan with a **MMB** and dragging, and fly forward and backward with the scroll wheel. Left-click to accept the movement and right-click to cancel it.

Tip

If you are familiar with other software, such as 3ds Max or Maya, you may find the main Blender controls for panning and orbiting the camera to be uncomfortable. You can customize these keyboard shortcuts on the Input tab of User Preferences, under 3D View/3D View. I use these shortcuts myself:

- Pan (referred to as Move View): **MMB**
- Orbit (referred to as Rotate View): **Shift+MMB**

Managing Areas

As you've seen, Blender's UI is made of areas. In this section, you see how to master them! First, you learn how to split and join areas; the key to performing these operations is in the bottom-left and top-right corners. Each area has little diagonal lines in those corners that you can click and drag. When you hover the mouse over these lines, your cursor turns into a cross.

You can work with those corners in the following ways:

- **Split:** Click **LMB** and drag inside an area to split it. Dragging vertically creates a horizontal split, while dragging horizontally creates a vertical split. Right-click before releasing **LMB** to cancel splitting (see Figure 2.6).
- **Join:** Click and drag an area's corner toward a contiguous area to darken that area and show an arrow that displays the direction in which the areas will be joined. The area from which you've dragged takes the space of the area into which you dragged. Keep in mind that you can join only areas with contiguous borders of similar sizes. Right-click before releasing **LMB** to cancel joining (see Figure 2.6).

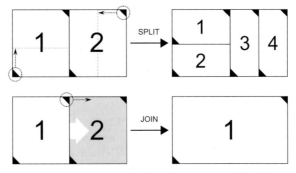

Figure 2.6   Splitting and joining areas in Blender

> **Tip**
>
> If you position the cursor on top of the border of an area and right-click while the cursor turns into a two-headed arrow, you get a pop-up menu with options to split and join. Decide where you want the split to be or how to join the areas; then left-click to accept or right-click to cancel.

- **Swap:** Press **Ctrl+LMB** in one of these corners and drag over a different area to swap the editors inside those areas.

- **Duplicate:** Press **Shift+LMB** and drag in the corner. The area is duplicated in a new window, which is useful if you are using a second monitor.

- **Full Area:** Hover the cursor over an area and press **Shift+Space** or **Ctrl+Up**. That area now occupies the entire interface to give you more space to work. Press one of those shortcuts again to return to the original workspace.

- **Full Screen:** Press **Alt+F11** to make the current workspace full-screen.

- **Resize:** Hover the cursor over the borders of an area. The cursor becomes a two-headed arrow. Click and drag to resize that area.

Workspaces

The Info Editor has a drop-down menu with stored workspaces. You can create your own workspace by clicking the **+** button near the selector. Customize these areas and editors as you prefer; then put a name to that workspace. Go to the menu or press **Ctrl+Left** or **Ctrl+Right** to navigate the saved workspaces.

Working with Editor Types

Now that you know how to use areas to shape your workspace, you're ready to look at what types of editors you can show in those areas. You can select the editor type for an area by clicking the icon to the left of the editor's header (see Figure 2.7). These are the different editors and what they're used for:

- **Python Console:** A built-in console that allows you to interact with Blender by using its Python application programming interface (API). This editor is mainly for developers.

- **File Browser:** A browser that allows you to navigate your system's folders to look for images, for example. Keep in mind that you can drag images to other editors, such as dragging an image to 3D View to use it as a background reference. File Browser is also useful when you're editing video and frequently need to access the video files and load them into the timeline.

- **Info:** The main menu, located by default in the top-left corner of the interface. If you drag down this area, you see a Python Console that shows you logs and error messages.

Figure 2.7   Selecting the editor type that will be shown inside an area

- **User Preferences:** A window with different tabs that allow you to customize Blender keyboard shortcuts and interaction options, change the interface's colors and theme, adjust performance settings, and manage add-ons.

- **Outliner:** A tree graph of every element in the scene that is very useful when you're looking for objects or navigating all the elements of a scene. You can select specific objects or groups in complex scenes or even search for them by name.

- **Properties Editor:** One of the most important editors in Blender, with different tabs for different groups of options you can access. (Depending on your selection, tabs may vary, as they are context-sensitive.) This editor is where you set up your render size and performance, add modifiers, set the object parameters, add materials, control particle systems, and indicate which measuring units you want for your scene (see Figure 2.8). These tabs are organized from most general to most specific.

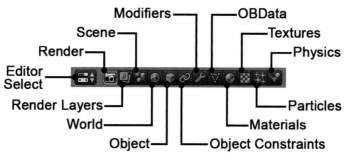

Figure 2.8   Properties Editor tabs

- **Logic Editor:** An editor that provides an interface to define behaviors and functions that control the objects in a scene. This editor is used to create interactive content and games inside Blender.

- **Node Editor:** An editor that lets you create node trees for final image compositing, textures, and materials.

- **Text Editor:** An editor that you use for scripting (you can even run Python scripts from it) or for adding text notes to the scene—especially useful if you work with a team and want to add information or instructions about how to use the scene.

- **Movie Clip Editor:** An editor that you use to load and analyze video footage and then use it for camera or motion tracking and stabilizing shaky footage. You can also create and animate masks that you can use in the compositor.

- **Video Sequence Editor:** An editor that you use for editing video inside Blender.

- **UV/Image Editor:** An editor that you use for loading images as a reference or to paint over them. It's also where you manipulate UVs and unwrap objects. You can use it to see the compositing result preview. Renders are also displayed in this editor.

- **NLA Editor:** An editor that is similar to the Video Sequence Editor but works with animations. In it, you can load different animations for an object or armature and mix them by using strips; you can even add transitions between animations.

- **Dope Sheet:** An editor to display objects in the scene and their keyframes, making it very easy to adjust the timing of your animations. (A *keyframe* is the state of an element in a given frame of the animation; see Chapter 12, "Animating Your Character," for more information about using keyframes for animation.) This sheet can also be used as an advanced timeline.

> **Tip**
>
> In other animation software, you can access the basic timing control of keyframes from the timeline. In Blender, you can replace the basic timeline for a Dope Sheet and enable the Summary and Selected Only options to display a summary of keyframes that belong to the selected objects. When you do, you have a timeline that allows you to control an animation's timing.

- **Graph Editor:** An editor that is similar to the Dope Sheet but also shows animation curves, which you can use to control how interpolations between keyframes work and to fine-tune your animations.
- **Timeline:** An editor that shows the time in the scene and lets you play the animation and select the frame in which you want to work. You can also add markers to easily designate important parts of the sequence and to set the start and end frames of the animation.
- **3D View:** An editor where you control the 3D world by modeling, animating, and adding objects to a scene.

> **Tip**
>
> In Blender, you can even zoom in and out inside menus. Hover your cursor over a menu, press **Ctrl+MMB**, and drag up and down to make menu items bigger or smaller.

Selecting Objects

To do anything in Blender, you need to select objects. What you'll notice first is that you select objects with the mouse's right button! Users often go crazy when they learn this fact because most programs use the left button to select. Blender has at least a couple of reasons (probably more) for the **RMB** selections:

- **It's ergonomic.** Research over several years has shown that about 90 percent of the time, you use only left clicks in most programs. Blender's right-click selections share the workload between two fingers, so in the long run, your hand is healthier and less subject to carpal tunnel syndrome.
- **Blender is different.** Blender doesn't follow conventional software standards, and that's why it does things in a new way. The Blender UI changes the paradigm other software uses. For some actions, such as selecting an object, you use a right click, whereas for confirming an action or clicking various buttons, you still use a left click. Also, you're supposed to work with shortcuts in Blender, so you have no need for a right-click menu. As a plus, left-clicking alone has another use in Blender: setting the 3D cursor location (which I discuss later in this chapter).

> **Tip**
>
> If you're still not convinced by the right-mouse-button selection, you can change it from **RMB** to **LMB** in User Preferences, below the Input tab. As **RMB** is the default in Blender, however, I assume throughout this book that you're using **RMB**.

Selected objects are highlighted with an outline. While you select, you can press **Shift+RMB** to add objects to or subtract objects from the selection. You can also use various tools to select a group of objects (see Figure 2.9):

- **Box Selection (A):** Press **B** and **LMB** drag to determine the size and position of the box. By default, any objects inside the box will be added to the current selection, but you can subtract them by dragging the box with **MMB** instead of **LMB**.

- **Lasso Selection (B):** Press **Ctrl+LMB** and drag to draw the lasso shape over the objects you want to select. The objects inside the lasso will be added to the current selection. Press **Shift+Ctrl+LMB** to deselect by using the lasso.

- **Paint Selection (C):** Press **C**, and a circle appears around the cursor. Move the scroll wheel to modify the size of the brush; then click and drag with **LMB** to add to the selection or drag with **MMB** to subtract it.

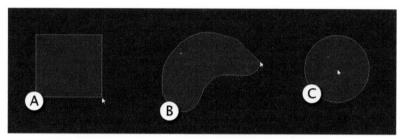

Figure 2.9   Methods for selecting groups of objects

If you want to select or deselect all the objects in the scene, press **A**.

Tip

In Blender, as in almost all software nowadays, you can undo and redo your actions:

- Undo: Press **Ctrl+Z** to go back to the previous scene state if you made a mistake or if you were just experimenting with something and didn't like the result.

- Redo: Press **Shift+Ctrl+Z** to reverse the effect of the Undo command.

Making an Active Selection

When you select multiple objects at the same time, the last object selected (and only the last object) becomes the active object and has a brighter highlight than the others. The active object has several uses, such as providing a pivot point or enabling you to copy its attributes to the rest of the objects in the selection. If you have multiple objects selected and apply a modifier, for example, the modifier is added to the active object, not to the whole selection.

Using the 3D Cursor

Something you may not understand when you first open Blender is why a circle always appears in the middle of the view. What is its function? This circle is the 3D cursor, and it's a special feature in Blender. Although this cursor can be a little disturbing initially, it becomes really useful when you learn how to use it.

Here are the main functions of the 3D cursor:

- You can use it to set the location where new objects will be created.
- You can use it to align objects.
- You can use it as a pivot point to rotate or scale objects.

Press **Shift+S** to reveal the Snap menu (see Figure 2.10), which includes various options that are primarily used with the 3D cursor. The menu is divided into two sections. The first section includes options that transform the selection, and the second section includes options that place the 3D cursor.

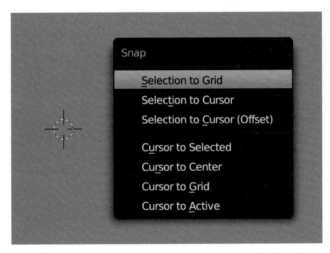

Figure 2.10   3D cursor and its Snap menu (**Shift+S**)

If you want to align an object to a specific place on the surface of another object, for example, you can select a vertex of that object, press **Shift+S**, and select Cursor to Selected. Then select the other object, press **Shift+S**, and click Selection to Cursor.

By pressing **,** (comma) or **.** (period) on your keyboard, you can switch between using the Box Center Pivot and the 3D Cursor Pivot. Sometimes, placing the 3D cursor and using it as a pivot to rotate or scale objects comes in very handy! Suppose that you want to pose a character. Thanks to the 3D cursor, you don't need a skeleton for simple posing; you can select the vertices of the leg, place the 3D cursor in the articulation, and rotate those vertices by using the cursor as a pivot point.

At this point, you may not understand some of these Blender terms, such as transforms, vertices, and skeletons, or know how to access them. Don't worry; you'll learn about them in the following chapters.

> **Tip**
>
> In Blender's User Preferences (press **Ctrl+Alt+U** or click User Preferences on the File menu), you can find the Cursor Depth option on the Interface tab. If you turn this option on, when you left-click over a surface, the 3D cursor is placed on that surface, making it easier to align objects to the surface.

Setting Blender's User Preferences

From the File menu, choose User Preferences (or press **Ctrl+Alt+U**). Blender's user preferences appear in a new window, which you can close when you're done selecting your preferences (see Figure 2.11).

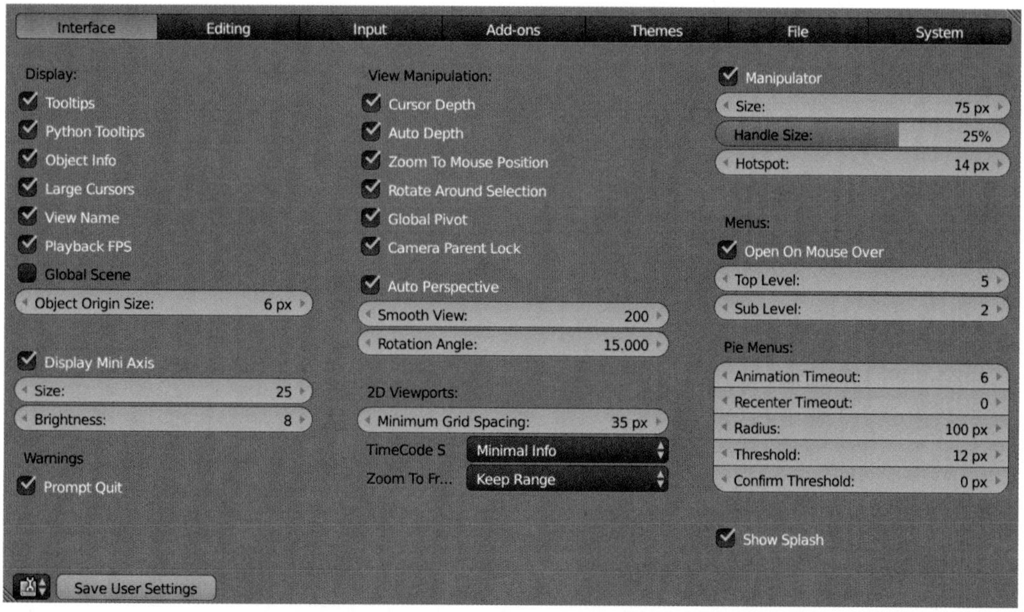

Figure 2.11   Blender's User Preferences (**Ctrl+Alt+U**)

This window has tabs across the top to divide preferences in different categories:

- **Interface:** Here, you find a lot of options for setting the Blender interface to your desired parameters so that you feel more comfortable while interacting with it.

- **Editing:** On this tab, you find options for editing things like materials, animation curves, and grease-pencil strokes. You can also adjust how objects are aligned when you create them or how duplicate objects should behave.

- **Input:** You can edit keyboard shortcuts on this tab, as well as set some other options that determine how you work with Blender by using your mouse and keyboard. This tab also lets you create, edit, export, and import custom keymaps. In fact, Blender comes with some predefined keymaps aimed to help you make the transition to Blender if you come from 3ds Max or Maya.

- **Add-Ons:** On this tab, you can manage extensions that come with Blender or install others that add new functionalities to Blender. Most of these extensions are disabled by default, but you can look for the ones you're interested in and turn them on to use them while you work.

- **Themes:** Here, you can create your own color schemes to make Blender more appealing or to fit your corporate color scheme.

- **File:** This tab defines general file paths, what external software to link with Blender (such as a default player for rendered animations or an image editor), and how Blender saves files. You can also set the Auto Save feature on this tab.

> **Caution**
>
> On the File tab, one of the file paths you can set is Temp. Temp is the folder in which Blender will write temporary files when needed, such as backups in case of a crash. Make sure to select the right folder, because in your OS and with your current settings, the predefined path may not exist or you may not have permission to write files to it, which can result in lost work.

- **System:** On this tab, you can set up performance options to improve how Blender works, depending on your computer, such as selecting your graphics card (useful when you want to work with GPU rendering with Cycles). Or you can change your own preferences for things such as the default lighting applied to objects in the solid view, as well as text size and font, or the method Blender should use when drawing 3D objects.

> **Tip**
>
> I highly recommend that you check out all these options. If you don't know what they do, hover the cursor over each of them to get a brief pop-up description. Some of these preferences may make your life easier when you use Blender, especially if you're coming to it from other animation software.

Click Save User Settings in the bottom-left corner of the User Preferences window to confirm your selections and make your new preferences appear the next time you open Blender. Keep in mind that you can save how your scene, workspace, and menus look when you open Blender. Just set everything up as you like (even replace that default cube with another interesting shape, if you want), and press **Ctrl+U** to save your selections as the startup .blend file.

.blend files

The Blender file format is .blend. If you have the Save Versions feature turned on, however (you can find this option on the File tab of User Preferences), Blender automatically generates backup files *.blend1, *.blend2, and *.blend3 (the asterisk represents the original filename) when you save. By default, Blender saves one backup file, but you can increase the number of versions saved from User Preferences. These backup files can be opened from within Blender like the original files; they just have a different extension so you can easily distinguish between the original files and those automatically saved by Blender.

Another option you can enable on the same menu is Auto Save Temporary Files. Set a timer in intervals of minutes, and Blender saves the file in the temporary folder when that interval passes. Usually, you access Auto Save files only when something goes wrong or you need to recover a file you've lost or didn't save.

Keep in mind that if you use images as textures or use any kind of external files inside Blender, they won't be inside the .blend file by default. You can pack them inside the .blend file if you want to, though. You see how to do this in Chapter 9, "Painting Textures."

Summary

At this point, you understand how Blender's interface works. You know how areas divide the interface and what types of editors you can display on them, and you know the shortcuts for navigating the 3D scene. You also know that you can perform easy, quick customization if you don't like the default interface. In Chapter 3, "Your First Scene in Blender," you learn how to manipulate objects and actually get the job done.

Exercises

1. Create a new workspace, splitting and joining areas to get a single area, and then delete the workspace.
2. What is the NumPad used for in Blender?
3. Select all objects in the scene and deselect them again.
4. Why does Blender use a right click to select objects?
5. What are the main functions of the 3D cursor, and how is it used?
6. Is it possible to change keyboard shortcuts in Blender? If so, how?
7. What format does Blender use for saving files?

Your First Scene in Blender

You've been introduced to the basics of Blender, and with practice, you'll have the interface under control. It's time to create objects; interact with them; add modifiers, materials, and lights; and then render your creation. This chapter presents a very simple exercise to help you better understand how to create your first scene. You also learn about Blender Render and Cycles, the two render engines included by default in Blender. In the associate files for this book, you'll find a video tutorial that explains the steps presented in this chapter to help you create your first scene in Blender. If you're using Blender for the first time, you'll find this chapter to be especially useful.

Creating Objects

When you open Blender, you'll find the familiar default cube sitting in the middle of the scene. You can use that cube to build your model, or you can delete it. To delete objects in Blender, just select them, press **X** or **Del**, and click **Delete** in the dialog box that appears to confirm the deletion.

First, you want to create an object. You have different ways to do it:

- In 3D View, in the Tools Region (press **T** if the Tools Region is hidden), and on the Create tab, click the object type you want to create.

- In the 3D View header, choose from the Add menu the object you want to create from the different object categories.

- With the mouse cursor in 3D View, press **Shift+A**. The same Add menu that you see on the 3D View's header appears. Choose the desired object from the list.

When you use any of these options, the object is created in the position of the 3D cursor inside the 3D scene.

After you create an object, the Operator panel at the bottom of the Tools Region lists parameters that you can use to modify it, such as adjusting the depth and radius of a cylinder. Make sure that you have made any adjustments you want to make in the object before moving it or performing any other action on it, because after you create the object, it is converted to a mesh, and you no longer have access to those parameters. The parameters of the last performed action appear in the Operator panel; pay attention to this area, as it provides really cool options. As an alternative, you can press **F6** with the cursor over the 3D View to see those options in a pop-up window.

Animation software often has a test object. In Blender, that object is the monkey head (called *Suzanne*), and you'll use it for the test scene in this chapter. Create a monkey mesh, using any of the three methods described earlier in this section. Then create a plane, as this plane later serves as the floor of your scene. Don't worry if the head and plane intersect in the middle of the scene and are not aligned; you'll correct that problem in a moment.

Moving, Rotating, and Scaling

After you create objects in your 3D scene, you need to be able to control where they are located, how they are oriented, and what size they are. In this section, you see how to do just that. Moving, rotating, and scaling are the three different transform operations you can perform on an object.

Using Manipulators (Basic Mode)

When you want to transform objects or elements in the 3D scene, Blender offers manipulators that help you control those transformations. Following are the different manipulators (see Figure 3.1):

- **Move (A):** Changes the position of an object in space
- **Rotate (B):** Controls the orientation of an object
- **Scale (C):** Manipulates the size of an object
- **All Transforms (D):** Provides the option to use more than one transform manipulator at the same time

In the 3D view header, you can select the type of transform you want to perform. If you press **Shift** while clicking different transform icons, you can perform multiple transforms at the same time. (In Figure 3.1, example D shows all three transform manipulators being used at the same time.)

Using the different manipulators, you can move, rotate, and scale objects. These manipulators appear at the pivot point of the object (marked as a little orange spot, called "origin" in Blender), and you perform an action with them by using the following controls:

- Left-click one of the axes to make the object move, rotate, or resize on that specific axis. (X is red, Y is green, and Z is blue.) Left-click again to confirm the transform. Or press **Enter** to confirm or **Esc** to cancel.

- To enable precision mode, press and hold **Shift** *after* you click to transform. This action makes the transform slower, allowing you to make precise adjustments.

- To lock one axis and manipulate the other two, press and hold **Shift** before you click the axis you want to lock. If you press **Shift** and then click the Z-axis to move it, for example, the object actually moves on the X- and Y-axes, as the Z-axis is locked. (This option works only for moving and scaling; it is not available for rotations.)

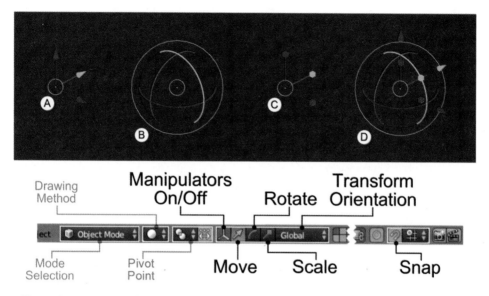

Figure 3.1   Manipulators in Blender and the transform controls in the 3D View header

- Each manipulator has a small white circle in its center. Click and drag that circle with the Move manipulator to move the object using the current point of view as a reference (dragging it parallel to the view). Click and drag the small white circle within the Rotation manipulator to enter orbit mode, which allows you to rotate on all axes at the same time. Click and drag the small white circle of the Scale manipulator to scale the object on every axis. The Rotation manipulator also has an outer white circle; click and drag that circle to rotate the object using the current point of view as the rotation axis.

- Hold down **Ctrl** while using these manipulators to switch between normal transforms and snap mode. This feature allows you to snap to several elements while you perform transforms. If snapping is enabled, holding down **Ctrl** frees the object when transforming; if it's disabled, holding down **Ctrl** enables the snapping. This feature is very useful because you won't need to continuously turn the Snap tool on and off by clicking the Snap icon on the 3D View header.

- In the 3D view header, you can select Pivot Point and Transform Orientation. The pivot point defines the point around which objects rotate and scale. By default, Transform Orientation (access this menu by pressing **Alt+Space**) is global, which means that it's aligned to the 3D World axes (default scene axes: X is left/right, Y is front/back, and Z is top/bottom). You can switch the Transform Orientation to the local axes of the selection to transform objects using their own orientation.

Tip

If you don't like the default behavior of transforms in Blender (click once to start transforming and click a second time to confirm), you can activate the Release Confirms option on the Edit tab of User Preferences. Release Confirms makes the transform behavior faster so that you can click and drag, and the transform is confirmed as you release the mouse button. This behavior is typical in other software. This feature affects only right-click transforms (clicking and dragging with **RMB**).

Using Keyboard Shortcuts (Advanced Mode)

Although you can use manipulators easily, the expert, really fast way to transform objects in Blender is to use keyboard shortcuts. Sometimes, the manipulators are useful, but most of the time and especially for simple transforms, using the keyboard is faster and more efficient. Here are some of the most relevant keyboard shortcuts that make transforms easier and faster:

- Press **Ctrl+Space** to show or hide the manipulators (or click the Manipulator On/Off icon on the 3D view header).

- Press **G** (Grab) to move, **R** to rotate, and **S** to scale. When you do these things to move and rotate the objects, they move and rotate according to the view. Left-click to confirm, and right-click or press **Esc** to cancel.

- After pressing **G**, **R**, or **S**, if you press **X**, **Y**, or **Z**, the selection transforms only on that global axis. Press **X**, **Y**, or **Z** twice to align to the selection's local axis.

- Press **R** twice to enter trackball rotation mode, which makes the object rotate in all axes following your mouse movements.

- As an alternative to the previous option, when you're transforming with no attachment to a given axis, you can press **MMB**. Lines for the axes appear, and if you move the object close to one of those lines, it is automatically locked to that specific axis.

- Precise transforms, snapping, and axis locking using **Shift** and **Ctrl** while transforming with manipulators also apply when you use keyboard shortcuts. Press **G** and then **Shift+Z** to translate the object in the X and Y axes at the same time, for example.

Numerically Precise Transforms

When you're performing a transform, Blender allows you to input numerical values. If you look at the 3D View header when you are rotating an object, you'll find that the header buttons disappear and are replaced by a display of the values of the transform in action. At this point, you can enter values directly from your keyboard, and Blender will use them for the current transformation. Here are two examples:

- To move an object 35 units on the X-axis, use manipulators and write the desired numerical value while dragging. Press **G** to move; then press **X** to snap the object's movement to the X-axis. Now you can drag the object through the X-axis. Enter 35 from the keyboard, and the object moves 35 units on the X-axis. Left-click or press **Enter** to confirm the operation.

- Press **R** to rotate, press **Y** to snap to the Y-axis, and enter **-90** on your keyboard to rotate an object -90 degrees on the Y-axis. (When you're writing a numerical value for a transform, you can add the negative value by pressing the minus key at any time, before or after the number. If you press the minus key again, the value becomes positive.) Left-click or press **Enter** to confirm the operation.

As you can see, using this method makes transformations really fast and easy to perform. The shortcuts are intuitive, and you can use them in most editors; **G**, **R**, and **S** always move, rotate, and scale, for example.

Arranging Objects in Your Scene

Now that you know how to transform objects, you can make your floor bigger and sit the monkey head on it (see Figure 3.2), as follows:

1. Right-click to select the plane, press **S** to scale, enter **5** from your keyboard to make the plane 5 times bigger, and press **Enter** to confirm. (Or use the manipulators if you feel more comfortable with them.)

2. Select the monkey head, moving and rotating it until it looks as though it's sitting on the floor. As a recommendation, you can switch the 3D View to a side view to see what's going on more clearly and transform the head there by using **G** and **R**. Keep in mind that if you're in a side view and rotate using **R**, the object will rotate on the X-axis.

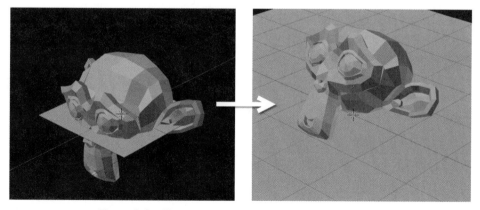

Figure 3.2   The scene before and after the transforms

Naming Objects and Using Datablocks

Before proceeding, you need to learn how to rename objects. This skill will come in handy when you're working in really complex scenes and want to recognize objects by their names. Otherwise, you'll find yourself lost in a sea of objects called Plane.001, Sphere.028, and other generic names.

If a Blender scene were a wall made of bricks, each brick would be a datablock. Every object in Blender has a datablock inside that represents its contents. Datablocks can be named and used in different ways that I talk about in the following section.

Renaming Objects

You have several ways of renaming an object:

- Locate the object in the Outliner. Right-click its name and choose the Rename option from the contextual menu. Alternatively, you can double click the name. Type in the new name and press **Enter** to confirm.

- In the 3D View Properties Region, you can rename the object in the Item panel. Left-click the text field, type the name, and press **Enter** to confirm.

- In the Properties Editor, go to the Object tab (the one with a yellow cube); type the new name in the text field in the top-left corner; and press **Enter** to confirm.

Managing Datablocks

Datablocks are the most basic Blender components. All the elements you can build—such as objects, meshes, lamps, textures, materials, and armatures (skeletons)—are made of datablocks. Everything in the 3D scene is contained in an object.

Whether you're creating a mesh, a lamp, or a curve, you're creating an object. In Blender, any object has object data (ObData) inside it, so the object itself acts as a kind of container for the data and stores information about its location, rotation, scaling, modifiers, and so on. ObData defines what's inside an object. If the ObData is a mesh, for example, you see a mesh with its vertices and faces inside the object. When you access the ObData, you can adjust its parameters. If you click the drop-down list of the ObData datablock, you can load a different ObData into the object. You could load a different mesh into the object's position, for example. Several objects can use the same ObData. (These objects are called *instances* or *linked duplicates*.) This means that even if the objects are in different positions in the scene, all of them synchronize their contents, so if you adjust the mesh vertices in one of them, the others reflect those changes. In this section, you look at a mesh and see the difference between the object and the object data.

Figure 3.3 shows how to check for an object's name inside the Properties Editor. The image to the right shows that the Mesh's Name is inside the Object's Name. In the image, the ObData is a mesh; if it were a lamp or a curve, the icon would change accordingly. The Properties Editor always shows information about the selected object, but if you click the Pin icon, the currently selected object's information is pinned, and even if you select a different object, the Properties Editor keeps displaying the pinned object's information.

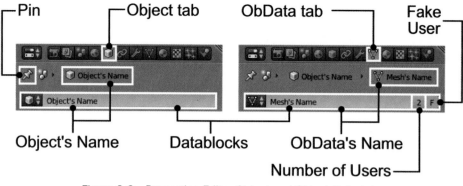

Figure 3.3   Properties Editor Object and Object Data tabs

Duplicates and Instances (Linked Duplicates)

You need to understand the difference between a duplicate and an instance. A *duplicate* is a new object created from an existing one so that it looks the same as the original but is independent, and no link exists between the new one and the original. An *instance* is also a new object; it can be in a different position, but its content (ObData) is directly linked to the original, so if you change the ObData in an object, the change also affects all its instances.

When you duplicate an object (**Shift+D**), some ObData is duplicated with it, and other ObData is instanced. You can define the default behavior on the Editing tab of User Preferences. If you duplicate an object, for example, by default Blender duplicates the mesh data contained in it, but it uses the same material data, so both objects use the same material datablock.

On the other hand, instancing (**Alt+D**) duplicates only the object; the rest of the ObData it carries inside is linked and synchronized with the original object. An alternative way to instance a mesh is to go to the Properties Editor's ObData tab and select a different mesh from the drop-down list in its datablock.

To the right of some datablock names, you find an F button as well as a number. The number indicates the number of users that the datablock has. In Figure 3.3, the mesh ObData has two users, which means that two different objects are using that mesh data. (The scene has an instance.) If you want to turn an instance into an independent, unique datablock, just click the number. Blender creates a duplicate and indicates a single user for the new one.

If at some point, a datablock (such as a mesh or a material) has 0 users, and you close the file, Blender cleans out the unused datablocks in the file, so you lose that great material you created but weren't using. That's why the F button exists; it creates a fake user of that datablock. Even if you're not using the datablock in the scene, that datablock has one user, which prevents the datablock from being deleted when you quit Blender. Datablocks that have zero users are called *orphan data*.

> **Caution**
>
> If you want to make sure that you keep a datablock in the file even if it's not being used (such as a material), click the F button next to the datablock's name to make Blender believe that the datablock is being used and to keep it.

Keep in mind that you usually work with the names of objects. Most of the time, you don't need to access the names of ObData like meshes inside objects, so if you are running low on time, you can generally skip ObData naming.

Naming Your Scene's Objects

After you understand what datablocks are and how to rename objects, you can name the objects in your scene accordingly. (You might name the plane Floor, for example.) Sometimes, you have to select a datablock's name from a list, so naming datablocks intuitively will help you find the one you're looking for.

> **Tip**
>
> When you have lots of objects in a scene, it can be difficult to select a specific one, as others may be in the way. If you right-click the objects in 3D View several times, the selection jumps between the objects under the cursor, and if you press **Alt+RMB**, Blender displays a list of objects under the mouse cursor, so you can select the one you need. This feature is useful only when your objects are named intuitively, of course.

Using Interaction Modes

Blender provides different ways to modify objects in your scene (such as modeling, texturing, sculpting, and posing), called Interaction Modes. By default, when you work in Object Mode, you are able to move, rotate, and scale; Object Mode essentially allows you to place objects in a scene. Probably one of the most useful modes is Edit Mode, which you use to edit ObData. You would use Edit Mode to model a mesh, access its vertices, edges, and faces, and change its shape, for example.

You can find the Interaction Mode menu on the 3D View header (see Figure 3.4); the options it displays depend on the type of object you have selected. For now, I focus on the Object and Edit modes. You'll learn about the other modes throughout the rest of the book.

You use Object Mode to create and place things in your scene (even animate them if you aren't using *armatures*, which are Blender skeletons used to animate characters and deform objects). In Edit Mode, you can perform modeling tasks on the mesh. You can quickly switch between these modes without having to access the selector by pressing the **Tab** key on your keyboard.

When you select an armature, you use Edit Mode to access the bones inside it and manipulate them. Pose Mode is available as well; it's the mode you'll use when animating a skeleton. (For more information, see Chapter 11, "Character Rigging," and Chapter 12, "Animating Your Character.") If you select a mesh, you have access to modes such as Sculpt, Texture Paint, and Vertex Paint, as shown in Figure 3.4.

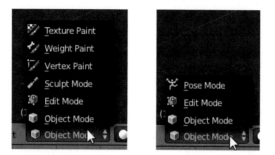

Figure 3.4   The Interaction Mode selector. On the left are the options available when a mesh object is selected; on the right are the options available when an armature is selected.

As you can see, a lot of options are available, and depending on what you want to do at any point in time, you just have to select the right Interaction Mode for the actions you want to perform.

Applying Flat or Smooth Surfaces

The monkey head looks weird with the rough edges and polygons that currently comprise its shape. This look is useful for some things, but for objects that should look more organic, you may prefer to have a smooth surface. This option only changes the surface's appearance; it doesn't add any geometry. You have several ways to smooth a surface in Blender:

- Select the object you want to smooth. On the Tools tab of the Tools Region is a Shading option with two buttons: Smooth and Flat. If you click one of those buttons when you're in Object Mode, every part of the object will use that shading method.

- In Edit Mode, select the faces you want to shade, and use the Smooth or Flat shading options on the Shading/UVs tab of the Tools Region.

- In Edit Mode, select the faces you want to shade with the smooth or flat method, and press **W** to display the Specials menu. From the Specials menu, choose the option you want: Shade Smooth or Shade Flat.

Figure 3.5 shows where these options are in Blender's interface.

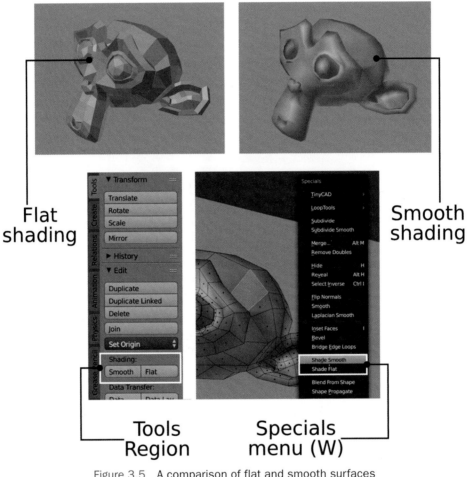

Flat shading

Smooth shading

Tools Region

Specials menu (W)

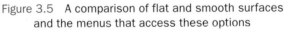
Figure 3.5   A comparison of flat and smooth surfaces and the menus that access these options

Working with Modifiers

Even though you used smooth shading in the mesh, the object still doesn't look just right, as it has very low resolution. You could use a Subdivision Surface modifier to add more detail to the surface and smooth it out (at the cost of adding more polygons to the object). A *modifier* is an element you can add to an object to alter it, such as a deformation, the generation of geometry, or the reduction of existing geometry. Modifiers won't affect the original mesh and adapt automatically to the changes you perform in the original mesh, which gives you a lot of flexibility, and you can turn modifiers on and off when you want. You should be careful, though, as adding too many modifiers may cause your Blender scene to operate slowly.

Adding Modifiers

Clicking the wrench icon in the Properties Editor opens the Modifiers tab, where you can add modifiers (see Figure 3.6). When you click the Add Modifier button, a menu displays every modifier you can add to the active object. (Not all the modifiers are available for every type of object.) The modifiers are listed in columns based on their functions: Modify, Generate, Deform, or Simulate. Left-click a modifier in the list to add it to the active object.

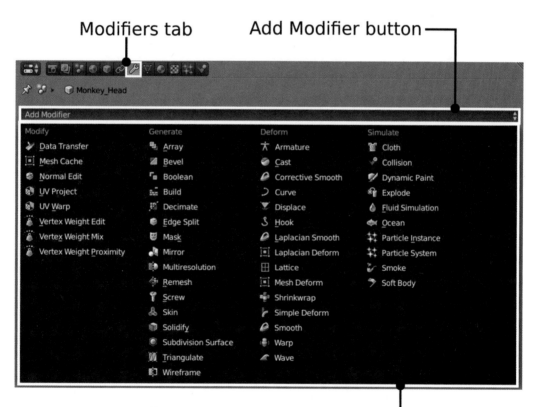

Figure 3.6   On the Properties Editor's Modifiers tab, you can add modifiers to the active object.

When you add a modifier, a node is added to the modifier stack, which works similarly to layers; if you keep adding modifiers, they add their effects to the previous modifiers. Keep in mind that the modifier stack works in the opposite order of layers in other software, such as Adobe Photoshop. In Blender, the last modifier you add is at the bottom of the stack, and its effect alters the effects of the modifiers above it in the list. The order of the modifiers is crucial in defining the resulting effects that the modifiers have on the object.

If you model one side of a mesh, for example, assign a Mirror modifier to generate the other half and then assign a Subdivision Surface modifier to smooth the result, the Subdivision Surface modifier should be at the bottom of the list. Otherwise, the object is smoothed before being mirrored, and you see the seam in the middle.

Copying Modifiers to Other Objects

When you assign a modifier, it affects only the active object, which is the last selected object (even if you have 20 selected objects). If you want that modifier to be applied to every object in the selection, you have two ways to do this:

- Press **Ctrl+L** to access a menu of linking options. In this menu, you'll find an option that lets you copy modifiers or materials from the active object to the rest of the selection.

- Activate the Copy Attributes add-on in User Preferences (this add-on comes bundled with Blender) and press **Ctrl+C** to access a special menu to copy attributes from the active object to the rest of the selected objects. You'll find the modifiers within those attributes as well.

Adding a Subdivision Surface Modifier to Your Object

The Subdivision Surface modifier is one of the most common modifiers used in models, because it allows you to increase the details and smoothness of a low-resolution model interactively. You can change the number of subdivisions at any time to display a smoother surface. The modifier basically divides each polygon and smoothes the result. As a rule of thumb, when you apply this modifier, the number of faces in your model is multiplied by 4 for each subdivision you apply; therefore, be mindful of the polygon count when setting high subdivision values. You can use this modifier to smooth your monkey-head object, as shown in Figure 3.7.

When you add a modifier, you get a panel in the modifier stack with options that are specific to the modifier you picked. Here are the main options you'll find with a Subdivision Surface modifier:

- In the top row of the panel that encloses the modifier, you can expand/collapse the modifier (by clicking the little triangle to the left), rename it (give the modifier an intuitive name when you have a lot of modifiers added to an object), and define the contexts in which this modifier should be visible. Two buttons with arrows pointing up and down allow you to change the order of the modifiers when you have more than one modifier in the stack. Clicking the X button deletes the modifier.

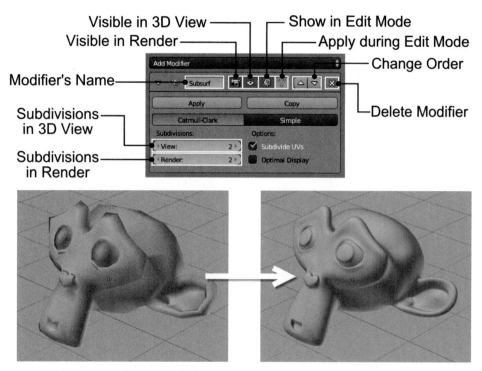

Visible in 3D View ———
Visible in Render ———
Show in Edit Mode
Apply during Edit Mode
Change Order
Modifier's Name ———
Subdivisions in 3D View ———
Subdivisions in Render ———
Delete Modifier

Figure 3.7   Before and after applying a Subdivision Surface modifier

- Next, you find two buttons: Apply and Copy. Apply transfers the effect of the modifier to the mesh itself. It deletes the modifier, but its effect on the mesh is permanent. Copy duplicates the modifier.

- In the Subdivisions section are two fields that let you define the number of subdivisions that the modifier will perform in 3D View and in the render. This option is very useful because when you're in 3D View, you usually want to save resources to ensure that this view is responsive but, in a render, you want a high-quality result. You can set a low number of subdivisions for the 3D View and a higher number for the render.

Tip

Subdivision Surface is a widely used modifier, so Blender comes with a keyboard shortcut that lets you add and control it. Press **Ctrl+1** (you must have a mesh selected in Object or Edit mode for this to work) to add a Subdivision Surface modifier with one subdivision. The number you press with **Ctrl** defines the number of subdivisions. If the object already has a Subdivision Surface modifier added, use this shortcut to change its number of subdivisions.

Using Blender Render and Cycles

Blender has two built-in render engines: Blender Render and Cycles (the new render engine). In the middle of the Info Editor (the bar at the top of the interface), you'll find a button that lets you select the render engine you want to use. By default, Blender Render is selected. If you click the button, you see two other options: Blender Game and Cycles. Blender Game allows you to play with real-time graphics as though Blender were a game engine. You can create games and interactive content that will run in the Blender Game engine.

Blender Render is the old engine, as it's not receiving further development, even though it's useful and can be used to create stunning results. (Cycles will replace it at some point in the future.) This engine allows you to set up materials that simulate reality, but it's just a simulation, so achieving realistic results can be difficult. Although Blender Render is not a realistic render engine, if you control its parameters, materials, and lighting correctly, you can achieve pretty realistic renders with good quality. Due to its nature and because it is not as realistically accurate, it's also a lot faster than Cycles, which makes it a nice alternative when you want to do nonrealistic rendering or when you're short on time.

Cycles is slower than Blender Render, but it's a physically based render engine, so light and materials behave realistically due to mathematical functions that simulate real light behavior. Light bounces off surfaces and generates indirect lighting, just as real light does. Getting a realistic result with Cycles is much easier than with Blender Render, but it requires different skills, because Cycles is designed to use materials built with nodes. When you're creating very basic materials, however, you don't really need to use nodes. Cycles also lets you render by using GPU, so if you have a good graphics card, you can speed your render times considerably.

You need to decide which render engine you want to use before you start building the materials for your scene. For the most part, the two engines are incompatible, and their lighting systems are quite different, so switching between the engines after you have your materials set up usually is not a good idea. You would have to rearrange your materials or even build them again from scratch.

Managing Materials

Materials define how an object looks, such as what its color is, whether the object is dull or shiny, and whether it is reflective or transparent. With materials, you can make an object look like glass, metal, plastic, or wood. In the end, both materials and lighting define how your objects look. In this section, you see how to add materials to your objects by using both Blender Render and Cycles.

On the Materials tab (the shiny red-sphere icon) of the Properties Editor, you can add new materials or select existing ones from the drop-down list shown in Figure 3.8. A single object can have multiple materials, and these materials appear in the list at the top of the material properties. You can add and remove new slots for materials by clicking the + and – buttons on the right side of the list, and you can assign each of those materials to a selection of faces when you're in Edit Mode.

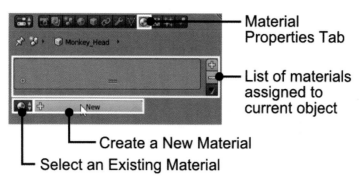

Material Properties Tab

List of materials assigned to current object

Create a New Material

Select an Existing Material

Figure 3.8   Use this menu on the Material Properties tab to add materials.

Using Blender Render Materials

In Blender Render, all materials are built in the same way: You have a set of parameters, and you can use them to build any kind of material. You can activate transparency and reflections (Mirror) to simulate materials such as glass or metal, for example. Each one of these attributes has different parameters, such as color, intensity, hardness, and glossiness. Here are brief descriptions of some of the main options:

- **Diffuse:** The main color of the material.
- **Specular:** The color, intensity, and hardness of a material's shine.
- **Shading:** The shadowing over a material. The Shadeless option makes the material completely unaffected by lights and shadows in the scene.
- **Transparency:** The transparency of the material. The basic attribute is Z Transparency, which is very fast to render because it just reduces the material's opacity. Raytrace is more accurate and offers some parameters for controlling the refraction to make it look more realistic, but it renders more slowly.
- **Mirror:** The reflectivity of the material. This option allows you to define the glossiness (roughness) of the reflections.

Using Cycles Materials

In Cycles, building materials is quite different from building them in Blender Render. You can use the Node Editor with Blender Render to achieve complex materials, but Cycles allows for the use of only basic materials if you're not willing to use nodes. Don't worry; for now, I'll keep things simple. Inside a Cycles material, you'll find the Surface panel, which includes various types of surface shaders:

- **Diffuse:** Creates a basic material with only color—no shine, reflection, or other special properties
- **Glossy:** Makes the material reflective and shiny
- **Emission:** Makes the material emit light into the scene
- **Transparent:** Lets light pass through the material

- **Glass:** Simulates a glass surface
- **Mix:** Mixes two shaders to achieve a more elaborate effect

Many surface shaders are available; these are just some of the main ones. Each of the shaders has different parameters to control how light affects that shader, such as color and roughness. Accessing nodes makes it easier to create complex and custom materials by combining the effects of some of the shaders and using textures. (See Chapter 10, "Materials and Shaders.")

Adding Materials to Your Scene

To add some color to your scene, add two new materials. This procedure is a very basic setup that you should be able to accomplish easily in both Cycles and Blender Render. Follow these steps:

1. Select the monkey head.
2. Click the Materials tab in the Properties Editor.
3. Add a new basic material, and set the diffuse color to red.
4. Repeat the process with the floor, but set the material to white.

Turning on the Lights

Now that you have materials set up, it's time to make the scene look more realistic with some light and shadows. Lights are compatible with Blender Render and Cycles, but given the different natures of these render engines, the lights have different effects, so if you switch from one render engine to another, you may need to adjust their parameters. Also, one of the benefits of Cycles is that because it is a realistic render engine, it allows you to use emissive materials, which can turn any mesh into a light emitter to illuminate the scene. This feature can simulate cool, very realistic effects that cannot be achieved with normal lights. In this first scene, you use only a couple of point lights. (Chapter 14, "Lighting, Compositing, and Rendering," provides more information about lighting.)

Light Options in Blender Render

In Blender Render, go to the Lamp tab of the Properties Editor. (The icon will change depending on the type of lamp that you select, but it will always be yellow.) You'll find options such as Color and Energy (Intensity). You can select the type of light as well. Also, in the Shadow panel, you can deactivate the shadows or control how they look. The Soft Size parameter makes the shadow softer, but you may need to increase samples to make it look better. Usually, 7 is adequate, but go higher if you need more quality; fewer samples result in a noisy shadow. Keep in mind that adding samples increases render time.

Lights Options in Cycles

When you access the same Lamp tab in Cycles, the options for light properties are different. You may need to click the Use Nodes button to activate all the options. You can also control the type of light. The Size parameter adjusts the softness of the shadows, and on the Nodes panel, you can set the light's color and strength.

Light options in Cycles may look rather simplistic because Cycles is a physically realistic render engine with no artificial settings such as shadow quality.

Adding Lights to Your Scene

Follow these steps to create a basic lighting scheme for your scene (and remember that you can access the menu for adding new objects to the scene by pressing **Shift+A**):

1. Select the light in your scene or create a new one if you don't have a light yet.
2. Duplicate the light, and place it on the other side of the scene to fill the shadow areas.
3. Arrange the intensity and colors of your lights so that the one on the right is brighter, while the one on the left is dimmer and a different color. You want the main light to come from the right, so that light should be brighter.

Moving the Camera in Your Scene

You need a camera in your scene, of course, so that Blender knows the point of view to look from when it takes the final render. Follow these steps to position the camera:

1. Select the camera in your scene or create a new one (**Shift+A**) if you deleted it previously.
2. Place the camera so that it focuses on the monkey head from a point of view that appeals to you. You can divide the interface into two 3D Views. In one of those views, you can look through the camera (**NumPad 0**), and in the other view, you can adjust the placement of the camera. Also, you can use Walk or Fly mode (**Shift+F**) to position and orient the camera while you're in Camera View.

Figure 3.9 shows what your scene should look like.

Real Time Preview Rendering

In Blender, you have options to see a rendered preview in 3D View while you work and adjust parameters. It's very useful to see what's going on in the scene and how the shadows and materials behave as you arrange them.

Real Time Rendering Mode, in this case, is not actually "real time"; it just means that you are performing the render interactively, and you can change things in the scene as you render it. The speed of the render depends, of course, on your computer's processing speed. If you are using Cycles and have a powerful GPU, you may want to use that GPU to increase the speed of the rendering.

To access Real Time Rendering Mode, just change the drawing method from the 3D View header to Rendered or press **Shift+Z**. When you're done, you can go back to Solid Mode or any other 3D View display mode. Keep in mind that when you use Real Time Rendering Mode, you won't see the selection highlights or manipulators, so you may want to keep a second 3D View open to manipulate objects.

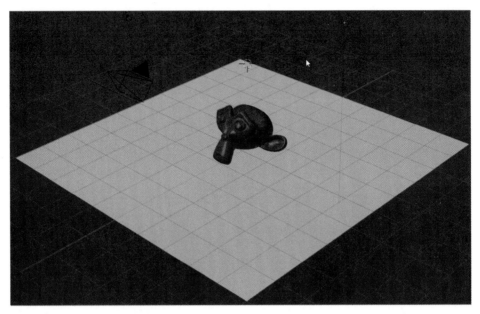

Figure 3.9   At this point, your scene should look something like this figure.
The monkey head is on the floor, the camera is pointing at it,
and two lights illuminate everything in the scene.

Rendering

Rendering is the process that converts your 3D scene to a 2D image or animation. During this process, Blender calculates the properties of materials and lights in the scene to apply shadows, reflections, refractions, and so on—everything you need to build your cool final result and turn it into an image or a video.

To set the resolution and format for the image, you need to go to the Render Properties tab of the Properties Editor (the camera icon). You can set the resolution in the Dimensions panel and the format in the Output panel. (The output is not needed for still images, as you can save them after the render, but you should set it if you're rendering an animation.) After selecting a resolution and format, click Render to complete this simple process. In the following sections, I describe the differences between rendering with Blender Render and rendering with Cycles.

Rendering in Blender Render

You can adjust a lot of options for the render, but Blender Render doesn't have many important options to configure. You can set up things like antialiasing samples to get a smoother render or improve the performance depending on your computer's specs, but for this basic scene, the render is adequate as it is.

Rendering in Cycles

If you render in Cycles, you'll probably need to change the samples number. Cycles uses samples (a sample is like an iteration on the image) to render, so if you don't use enough samples, you'll get a noisy image. Each sample refines the scene further, so with more samples, you get cleaner renders. This feature is handy for doing quick test renders and not spending lots of time on them. Even if a render is noisy, it gives you an idea of how everything will look in the end, so you can change the number of samples based on how much time you have.

On the Render Properties tab, look for the Sampling panel. If you're getting a noisy render, increase the Render Samples value, if not, leave it as it is or reduce it to speed the render. (The default Render Samples value at the time of this book's publication is 128, but it may change in future versions of Blender.)

Saving and Loading Your .blend File

Now you're at a good point to save your file. Rendering can take some time, and something can go wrong in the meantime (such as power failures or software crashes) that could cause you to lose your work. That's why it's recommended that you save your file often.

You can save your file by pressing **Ctrl+S**. If you're saving a file for the first time, Blender displays a menu where you can select the location where you want to store your file and name the file. If you've saved the file previously, press **Ctrl+S** to overwrite the previous version. If you press **Shift+Ctrl+S**, Blender displays the Save menu again so that you can choose Save As, which allows you to create a new copy of the file with a different name.

To open a file, press **Ctrl+O**. Blender shows you the folder navigation menu, where you can look for the .blend file you want to open. On the File menu, you can also access the Open Recent option, which shows you a list of the latest files you've worked on so you can open them quickly. You don't need to use those shortcuts, of course; you can always choose the Save and Load options from the File menu.

Tip

There's a little trick for saving different versions of a file really fast. Sometimes, you want to save your progress in a new file, so you'll have different files from different parts of the process and can go back to a previous version if necessary. Choose Save As from the File menu (or press **Shift+Ctrl+S**), and press the **NumPad +** key. Blender automatically adds a number to the filename. If the filename is already numbered, Blender adds 1 to it.

Launching and Saving the Render

You can start your render from the Render Properties tab of the Render panel, which has three options: Render (still frame), Animation (animation of several frames), and Audio (audio only). You can also use keyboard shortcuts. **F12** renders a still frame, for example, and **Ctrl+F12** renders an animation. (If you render an animation, make sure that you configure the output file path and format on the Render tab so the images are saved automatically where and how you want.)

When you start rendering, you see the process inside a UV/Image Editor, and when the render is complete, you can save the resulting image. Press **F3** to save, or go to the Image menu on the header of the UV/Image Editor to access the Save As Image option. Press **Esc** to return to 3D View.

Figure 3.10 shows the images that result from both engines' renders. It's clear that even with a really basic scene, Cycles produces more realistic results (but also takes more time to render).

Figure 3.10   The results of these very basic renders with
Blender Render (top) and Cycles (bottom)

Summary

In this chapter, you learned how to create and transform objects, add modifiers, lights and materials, and launch a render. This chapter gave you a lot to process, but I hope that you now know the basics of interacting with your scene. You're ready for the more extensive information in the chapters that follow.

Exercises

1. Create and manipulate a few objects.
2. Add some other modifiers, and play with them to see their effects.
3. Add more lights to the scene, and play with materials to improve the results.

Beginning a Project

4 Project Overview

5 Character Design

4

Project Overview

Every project has different steps you need to follow to be successful. The order in which you proceed through the steps to reach the final result can be called the *workflow* or *pipeline*. In this chapter, you learn about the process that you'll follow throughout the rest of the book to create a character from scratch. You gain basic knowledge of how to divide any project into stages and execute it.

The Three Stages of a Project

Usually, any project in 3D, graphics, or video goes through three stages: preproduction, production, and postproduction.

Preproduction

Preproduction is everything that happens before the actual production of a project, such as preliminary sketches, ideas, designs, and planning. It's probably the most crucial stage of any project, and a lot of amateur projects fail because of the lack of good preproduction. (Sometimes, people even try to start a project without any preproduction, which is usually a bad idea; the project will probably be unsuccessful.)

When you plan and organize what you need to do to complete a project, chances are that you're going to be better prepared for what's to come. If you skip preproduction and jump right into production because you can't wait to see the results, you'll likely encounter problems and issues you didn't anticipate. You'll have to redo a lot of work and lose lots of time. In the worst-case scenario, you'll give up.

Good planning allows you to anticipate any possible problems so you can prevent them from occurring. If you run into something you don't know how to do, you can make some quick, basic tests to find a solution *before* you get far enough into the project to discover that it doesn't work.

As a result of this preparation, the actual work during production will be a lot faster, easier, and more focused, as you'll already know how to proceed. Keep in mind that even with a good preproduction stage, you will still run into issues. This is how it goes, but at least a lot of those issues will be handled before they become bigger problems. The more preparation, the better.

Preproduction has another important advantage: It can motivate you during the production stage. When you think about everything you'll have to do and then define the process step by step, the work suddenly gets easier because you don't have a *big* project before you; instead, you have a list of small, manageable tasks. Go through this list, keeping track of your progress, and you'll always know what you have done so far, what you still need to do, and what may be missing.

A popular phrase sums up preproduction pretty well: "Think twice, work half." A great result doesn't come from working harder, but from working more efficiently. You need to think of efficient ways to work. Usually, you discover efficient methods only after you've done something wrong, but that's when you learn and gain valuable experience!

Production

When you have everything planned for a project, it's time to start the actual job, which is *production*. When you're making a movie, for example, production is the stage of the project in which the sets are built and the scenes are filmed with the actors and props in place as planned during preproduction. Thorough preproduction helps you complete production more easily and in a more straightforward manner.

Production is probably the hardest stage of a project because it's the point of no return. When production is complete, it's very difficult to change things. Suppose that you're building a house. During preproduction, it's very easy to change the design and plans of the house by using a computer or an architectural drawing, but it's really difficult and time-consuming to make changes after the walls are in place!

Preproduction is crucial because it helps you make sure that you're not going to make mistakes while you're developing the final product. Production is difficult enough, involving a lot of challenges. It's impossible to predict every possible problem until you're actually making the product, so any preparations you can make to smooth the process help a lot.

Postproduction

Postproduction is everything that happens between production and the final result. It's like putting the finishing touches on a new house with details such as painting the walls and adding interior decoration. In a movie project, postproduction is the stage at which you add final visual effects and retouch what was filmed during production.

Depending on the project, postproduction can be easy or hard, simple or complex, and it can involve minor details or really important things. Postproduction is when you decide how the finished project will look.

Suppose that you film two actors having a conversation. During postproduction, you can color-correct the scene, switch it from day to night, change what will be seen through a window, blur things, zoom in, or even add a new character. The possibilities are endless, and they define what people will see when you release your image, video, film, or whatever your project may be.

Defining the Stages

Now that you know the three main stages of a project, it's very important to know where each stage ends and the next one starts, as each project is different. This section presents some examples that illustrate these differences.

A Film Without Visual Effects

Today, almost every film has some visual effects, but consider a film that doesn't have any visual effects, which will help you understand the basic process of film production.

> **Note**
>
> Remember that visual effects are not just explosions, spaceships, aliens, and monsters. Many visual effects (commonly referred to as *invisible effects*) are much more subtle, and you may not notice them while you're watching a film. Set extensions, background replacements, and set cleaning, for example, are present in almost every movie made today, and they are also visual effects.

During preproduction, the filmmakers create the film's script and decide what will be the climax moments (and maybe even film them on their phones to test whether the scenes really work). Every film goes through *storyboarding*: the process of making quick drawings to define where the cameras will be placed and what will happen during each shot. Storyboarding helps the production team plan each shot, see what they'll need on set, know what type of lenses to use in the camera, and identify where the actors will be located and how they'll move through the set. Then the filmmakers search for the locations where they're going to film the scenes. They also have to create the costumes the actors will wear and all the props the actors will have to interact with. Then the filmmakers cast the actors and all the extras who will appear in the film. Finally, the filmmakers assemble the technicians who will film the movie and manage all the equipment, build the sets, and so on. Usually, composers begin to develop the music at this stage so that a rough edit of the film can be made by following the storyboard and the timing of each shot can be defined.

Everything is ready now, so production begins. At this point, the actors already know the script, and the team members know what they need to do on each shot and what has to appear on camera. Production usually is not a very long process; because all aspects of the project were organized during preproduction, the production stage (the most expensive stage) usually is as short as possible. When production is complete, the movie has been filmed according to the decisions made during preproduction.

When filming is complete, postproduction can begin. The film must be edited at this point, perhaps by using some color correction to make a scene look more vivid, warm, or cold, depending on the feeling the director wants each scene to convey. Perhaps the director decides that a shot would work better if the main actor's face were closer, so the video editor zooms in a little. Postproduction is the stage in which the last retouches are added to the film, the complete soundtrack and all the sound effects are included, and the final result is achieved.

A Visual-Effects Film

In this section, I analyze the differences between the preceding example and a film with complex visual effects.

During preproduction, the production team needs to think about what visual effects to use, how they're going to be filmed, and what is required to create them. Generally, the visual-effects team works closely with the director during preproduction to see what's possible, what's not possible, and how the effects will be achieved. (Usually, almost anything is possible with visual effects, but the effects may be way too expensive for a particular film's budget.)

During production, the visual-effects team may need to film some shots in special ways, using green screens or markers or puppets that the actors can interact with so that later, the team can add an animated character to the scene. Lighting in the sets has to be measured and recorded so that the team can simulate it later in the 3D world to make it match the lighting on the real set. Effects such as explosions may need to be filmed separately so that they can be integrated with the footage of the actors.

After the movie has been filmed, it's time to begin the postproduction stage, but because this film involves visual effects, the line between production and postproduction tends to blur, and sometimes, the stages overlap. The visual-effects artists probably work on some shots before production begins so that during filming, all the elements that comprise a scene fit together seamlessly.

The visual-effects team has its own preproduction, production, and postproduction stages. Team members plan the specific effects and determine how a shot will be accomplished. Then they proceed to production and work to create the elements of the visual effects. Finally, they combine those elements, adjusting colors, shapes, textures, and so on.

An Animated Film

The stages of an animated film are even more difficult to distinguish, as the entire film is computer-generated. The line between production and postproduction is not so clear.

During preproduction, all aspects of the film are planned and designed as usual, but production and postproduction tend to overlap because every aspect of these stages happens in 3D software. Usually, it's easier to divide the stages, with production creating the action (developing characters, sets, and animation), and postproduction creating the effects (water, splashes, particles, cloth, dust, smoke, fire, explosions, and other simulations). Then final compositing brings all these diverse elements together.

A Photograph

Yes, even something as simple as a photograph can be divided into three production stages. Even if photographers are not conscious of the fact, they're performing the three stages of production.

First, photographers complete the preproduction stage by thinking about what they're going to shoot and where. During production, they must go to the location, pose the subject, and take the photo. Then they can do some postproduction work such as adding an aging effect to the photo, increasing its contrast, or even changing it to black and white; sometimes, they can even do these things on their smartphones.

Making a Character-Creation Plan

This section introduces the process you'll follow throughout the remainder of this book to create a complete 3D-animated character.

Character Preproduction

Character creation starts, of course, with character design:

- **Character idea:** Design starts in your mind. Before designing a character, you must imagine it, think about its story and personality, the world it lives in, and so on.
- **Designing:** Make some drawings to define what the character will look like from different points of view, what clothes it will wear, and what features suggest its personality.

Character Production

This stage can be rather complex and extensive because it's the main part of the process that takes you from the design to the completed character.

- **Modeling:** Model the 3D character in Blender, following the design you created in the preproduction stage.
- **Unwrapping:** Unfold the 3D model into a 2D mesh internally (UVs) so that you can project a 2D image texture onto it.
- **Texturing:** Paint the textures for the various aspects of the 3D model's surface, such as clothing textures, skin, and hair color.
- **Shading:** Take texturing a step further by creating materials that define the surface properties of your character, such as how reflective or shiny they are and whether they are rough or smooth.
- **Rigging:** Add a skeleton to your character to define how it will work and how it will control the character.
- **Animating:** Pose the character, using keyframes at different times of an animation to make the character perform an action such as walking or running.
- **Video recording:** Record a video in which you'll place your character later.

Project Postproduction

When the character is finished, you still have some work to do to make it look pleasing or to put it in a scene.

- **Camera tracking:** Simulate the live video's camera movement so that you end up with a camera in the 3D world that moves similarly to a real camera and allows you to insert 3D elements into your video.

- **Lighting:** Add lighting to your scene to make the lights and shadows fit the video you recorded during the production phase. The addition of lighting is usually part of the production stage, but because this project's main goal is the creation of a character, lighting is considered part of postproduction.
- **Rendering:** Convert the 3D scene to a 2D image sequence with shadows and lighting.
- **Compositing:** Combine the video and the 3D objects, and make any necessary adjustments so that everything fits together and looks realistic.

Summary

After reading this chapter, you have an idea of the process you're going to go through to create your own animated character, and you understand the three main stages of any project. Preproduction is especially important—a fact that you have to keep in mind for future projects. A lot of people fail even after significant planning and preparation, so imagine the probability of failing if you don't make thoughtful preparations and design choices in preproduction. Almost every professional 3D artist has gone through this process and understands the importance of preparing and organizing projects. Learn from their experiences.

In the next chapter, you start working on the actual project.

Exercises

1. Think of a movie you recently watched, and imagine how it was divided into preproduction, production, and postproduction stages.
2. Have you ever had a project fail? Analyze where you failed, and think about how you'd do the project differently using the three stages discussed in this chapter.

5

Character Design

The first stage of your character-creation project is, of course, preproduction (discussed in Chapter 4, "Project Overview"). There are a lot of ways to design a character, and each artist uses a different method. In this chapter, you explore a common approach that you can later adapt according to your skills. I also note some other methods so that you can try them if they sound interesting to you.

You can use any medium to design your character, such as paper or software. In this chapter, the whole process is carried out with digital painting software and a pen tablet, but you can use any other painting medium.

Character Description

Before you start drawing or imagining what clothes a character will wear, how big its eyes will be, or what color to make its hair, you need to have at least a basic idea of who your character is. The design ultimately represents the character's personality, so understanding how that character thinks and acts will help you represent it. It's easier to know the type of clothes the character will wear if you know its profession. A knight or a soldier will wear armor or battle gear, for example, but it would make no sense at all for an accountant to wear armor or carry a weapon, no matter how cool it looks!

Also, the attitude of a character can define its looks. A dynamic character would be fast-moving, whereas a sad character would slouch and move slowly. A happy character would have a big smile and large, expressive eyes, whereas a sad character would have small, tearful eyes and a frown.

Developing a good description of your character helps you understand how it will behave. As a result, you can get into its head, imagining what it will wear and how it will walk, talk, smile, laugh, and cry. Different people can react in different ways to the same situation, and this also applies to the characters you create. Establishing personality traits helps you understand your character and define its lifestyle, for example.

You don't need to develop the character's complete history or personality if you don't want to go that far. A simple description of its personality and appearance may be enough.

In the following sections, you take a look at a brief description of the character you'll build in this book. The character is called Jim. From now on, you need to have a personal relationship with Jim so you can understand how he thinks and acts. Consider Jim to be a living being, not a thing.

> **Note**
>
> Learning about body language helps you determine how a character with a specific attitude would look, including the clothes it would wear. Reading a specialized book on the subject is highly recommended if you want to design great characters. I encourage you to take a look at *What Every BODY Is Saying: An Ex-FBI Agent's Guide to Speed-Reading People*, by Joe Navarro and Marlin Karlins (William Morrow Paperbacks, 2008).

Personality

Following is a description of Jim. The various aspects of his personality are related, and some of them are influenced by the others. A lazy person would never want to be an adventurer, for example, and if he isn't happy and doesn't love challenges, there's no way he would go into the unknown to discover new things. He needs lots of motivation to do that. The lesson here is that the aspects of a character's personality must be coherent (unless for some reason, the story requires it to be otherwise).

Jim is a 15-year-old kid. He is very active and participates in a lot of sports with his friends. He's always happy and positive, he likes challenges, and his dream is to become an adventurer and discover new things. His ambitions are motivated by his never-ending curiosity, and as a result of his curiosity, he pays a lot of attention to details. He also likes to be different from the rest of the kids his age. And…he manages to get himself into trouble quite often.

Context

You have a basic understanding of Jim's personality, but another very important thing defines a character: the story's context, or the world in which the character dwells. Check it out:

It's 2512, and humans have populated quite a few planets. Space exploration is the major topic in the news, and astronauts are treated as heroes. Cars fly and don't produce pollution. Robots are everywhere, making human life easier, and some even develop relationships with humans. A down side of this setting is that it's difficult for a person to stand out from the rest of the population. Everyone wears the same kinds of clothes, everyone owns similar cars, and everyone lives in buildings that look the same.

Can you see how this context could affect what Jim would look like? Also, humans living on several planets and space exploration being the focus of the news every day are good reasons to make a young boy dream about being an astronaut, right? If the context was prehistory, a kid's dreams would be very different; maybe he'd want to be a mighty hunter or a fearsome shaman.

Context (where the character lives, his culture, and his relationships) clearly defines your character's personality and his ways of thinking and acting. Jim's context encourages him to be an adventurer, explore space, and find new planets…or even aliens!

Style

Before you begin to imagine how your character would look, define the style you want to aim for. For this example, I'd encourage you to opt for a cartoony look. The reason is that although you'll explore the full animation process, you don't want Jim to be so complex that the character creation is hard to achieve. For learning purposes, Jim will have smooth shapes without too many details.

Although you'll keep Jim simple, you still want him to look cool. You can go for something more realistic, something dark, or even kind of abstract. Decide ahead of time and create some drawings, or find some photos or other reference materials to help you determine his style, which will be essential to how the character ultimately looks.

Something else you want to keep in mind while you define the style (and every other thing that has to do with the appearance of a character) is technical limitations. You may not want to have really long hair on a character, for example, because long hair would make the animation or simulations much more complex.

Also, style depends on the medium in which the character will be used. In movies, you can use more detail and complexity, as you have enough time and sufficiently powerful machines (even render farms) to render each frame. But if you're working on a videogame character, the limitations are greater, as the character needs to work in real time. You need to use fewer polygons, less resolution in textures, or less complicated effects to increase the performance and allow a computer (or a console) to render the images in real time.

Appearance

Now that you have Jim's personality, the context of his world, and his style, you can start thinking about his appearance. He lives in a futuristic environment, and when you think of futuristic worlds, you might picture plain-colored clothes with clean lines. White and blue clothes could look right.

Here, it's OK to use clichés because certain characteristics are embedded in people's minds and give them an idea about a character or theme. That's precisely why clichés work, so don't fear or avoid them.

Suppose that clothes in the future are tight and fitted to the body. Furthermore, Jim is healthy and active, and he plays sports, so he's in good shape. It wouldn't be a problem for him to wear close-fitting clothes, as he wouldn't be ashamed of his body. Also, he's an adventurer, so maybe he worries less about appearance and more about clothes that are functional as well as comfortable.

The character's description (refer to "Personality" earlier in this chapter) mentions that he likes to be different from everyone else, so if everyone wears similar clothes, he would surely add some unique details to his attire to represent that attitude. He might wear a pin, a jaunty hat (which would also help represent him as adventurous), or some kind of reference to space travel and exploration: the dream he's fighting for.

Designing the Character

In this section, you follow a typical process you can use to create a character. The process progresses from general forms to details. You start by creating the basic shapes; then, little by little, you refine those shapes and add color to get to the final result.

Silhouettes

It's a good idea to start with quick sketches and basic shapes that help you explore and find the right proportions for your character (see Figure 5.1). Then you can pick the ones you like and keep developing and adding details to them. Many artists use this technique in designing a character. Silhouettes are very important; a great character is recognizable by its silhouette. You can recognize Super Mario, Mickey Mouse, Sonic or Pikachu just by their silhouettes, because they have original, unique designs.

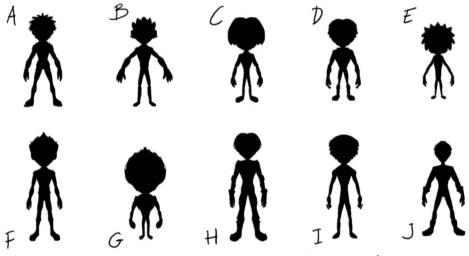

Figure 5.1   Silhouettes of Jim drawn for the purpose of studying the desired proportions and shapes

In this case, you're learning about 3D character creation, not designing the ultimate marketable character, so you don't need the whole world to recognize Jim by his shape. The goal is to design a character that looks cool and has personality.

Looking at the silhouettes in Figure 5.1, you can see how, from the character description, you can imagine completely different shapes for a character. Now you have to decide which one you like most or which one best fits the style you're looking for. Suppose that the silhouettes you like most for their shapes and proportions are A and F. They're kind of realistic but have big hands, feet, and heads. A big head (in comparison to the body size) helps identify Jim as a kid. J looks more like an adult, as its head is smaller, and E, which has a really big head compared with the body, resembles a child.

Figure 5.2 shows the final silhouette, which is a mix of the versions liked most, with a little more detail added. The first silhouettes are little thumbnails that gave you an idea for Jim's shape; the final one is bigger and has more detail, so it can be used as a reference in the next stage. The silhouette doesn't have clothing details or a hat; those items will be added over the base design. For now, all you need is the character's main shape.

Figure 5.2   The final silhouette is a mix of versions A and F.

Note

The silhouettes in Figures 5.1 and 5.2 were done in Krita, a free open-source painting software that you should check out. You can find more information at https://krita.org. You have many alternatives for painting, of course, and you can use any software you feel comfortable with, such as MyPaint, Painter, GIMP, Adobe Photoshop, or Manga Studio. A feature that is very useful for creating silhouettes is mirror painting, which allows you to mirror in real time what you're painting on the opposite side of the canvas. This feature really speeds the process, because you can see the full shape coming together while you're painting only one side of it.

Base Design

Next, you create your base design by taking your final thumbnail and turning it into a drawing. Just sketch some strokes around the borders and define some of the figure's interior shapes. At this stage, you need only a basic version of the character, so don't worry too much about details; you'll add those in the next pass.

You also add clothing at this stage. You can place as many variations as you want over the silhouette. It's OK to explore and create different versions of this base design so that later, you can choose the designs you like, mix them, and keep modifying them until you achieve the design you like best. Keep in mind, however, that you don't want to add things that will make the design too complex later, so you should avoid complex design elements and aim for something that is easy to achieve.

You don't need a really refined drawing at this point; a quick rough sketch will do, such as the one in Figure 5.3. This sketch helps you understand how the character may eventually look so that later, you can dive into the specific design of each of its parts and finally combine everything for a clean finished version. If something doesn't look great, don't worry; you still have a lot of time to change things.

Figure 5.3   Comparison between the final silhouette and the base design

As you can see in Figure 5.3, the hairstyle is not well defined. That part of the character will require some technical thinking, as hair is always a challenge. If you want to go for realistic hair, you can later use 3D particles to grow hair on a surface, comb it, cut it, and add the effects of gravity or wind to it. If you want to go that route, you need to have a detailed understanding of how hair particles function to make sure that the hair will work properly when designed using this method. (Otherwise, it's easy to screw things up.) If you prefer to go with a hand-modeled mesh, you have more options, but keep in mind the limitations of the mesh method.

For this character, you use a mesh for the hair, as it's easiest, and for this type of character design, it works just fine. If you don't have much drawing experience, keeping things simple by starting with generic geometric spheres helps you understand the volumes. The head can be a distorted sphere, for example, and arms and legs are in essence similar to cylinders. If you have difficulty coming up with the character's shapes, try starting with this geometric base and then draw the details on top.

Head

Now it's time to design the head, face, and hairstyle. Maybe now is also a good time to work on hats, as they affect the hairstyle. Figure 5.4 shows several sketches for Jim's face. Keep in mind that you probably won't come up with anything great during your first tries. (For this figure, I'm showing you only my best attempts.) You should keep drawing and designing until you're happy with the result. The process may take hundreds of drawings, or you may be lucky and find something you like on the first try, but don't count on that!

Figure 5.4   Different sketches for Jim's head and some studies with a cap

After you look at all the designs, you may opt for the one featuring a cap, as a cap gives Jim some personality and looks cool. It also covers a big part of the head, making hair creation a lot easier!

A typical baseball cap may not be common in 2512, because people in that future society may wear crazy stuff on their heads, but remember that Jim wants to be different. In this chapter, you're creating only Jim, but if you also had to depict the city where he lives and more of its citizens, he would surely look different just by wearing a baseball cap in 2512.

Details

You now have a base design for Jim's body and his head, so it's time to add the details. Maybe you don't know how to draw or paint, but don't worry! The goal of making these designs is not to make a perfect drawing. Designs are just sketches—quick drawings that help you understand the shapes of your character. Understanding the character and how its details are constructed allows you to translate everything into the 3D model.

Suppose that you are modeling a watch. If you start modeling right away, maybe you'll end up encountering some issues and failing. Maybe the watch won't look realistic or the gears won't fit, and the reason may be that you didn't study the shapes. It's always good to look for references and use them when designing. You can go ahead with only an idea in your head, but I recommend that you put the idea on paper (or a screen) so you can see and explore it before diving into the 3D modeling process.

Figure 5.5 shows some of the sketches I made to define Jim's clothing and the details selected for the definitive design, which were drawn from several points of view. The jacket, for example, has designs on its front and back. These features are important because you probably wouldn't need the back for a 2D drawing, but in a 3D model, every side is equally important.

The suit has rectilinear shapes that maintain the style and make the material look more elaborate than plain fabric. The shoulders, elbows, and knees have padding, which gives the clothes the look of a uniform and is just what you want for Jim, because everyone in the future Jim lives in is wearing the same kind of suit.

Jim is wearing an earpiece to listen to music or receive calls. The cap is a personal detail that distinguishes him from others, and he's going to wear it turned around, as a rebel would. His personality can be reflected in the colors of his clothes as well. Maybe some parts of the suit will be different colors to make them stand out from the clothes worn by the rest of the people in his world; you explore colors in the coloring stage (see "Adding Color" later in this chapter).

The back of the jacket has a small backpack where the suit's electronic systems may be stored. The cuts in the arms, above the elbows, seems to resemble the design of today's astronaut suits.

One other detail has been added to the suit. Jim put space-exploration symbols on the chest and on the front of the cap; these symbols, along with the uniformlike style of the clothes, make him look like an actual space explorer. For those symbols, I used Saturn, which is both a recognizable planet and a known icon of space exploration.

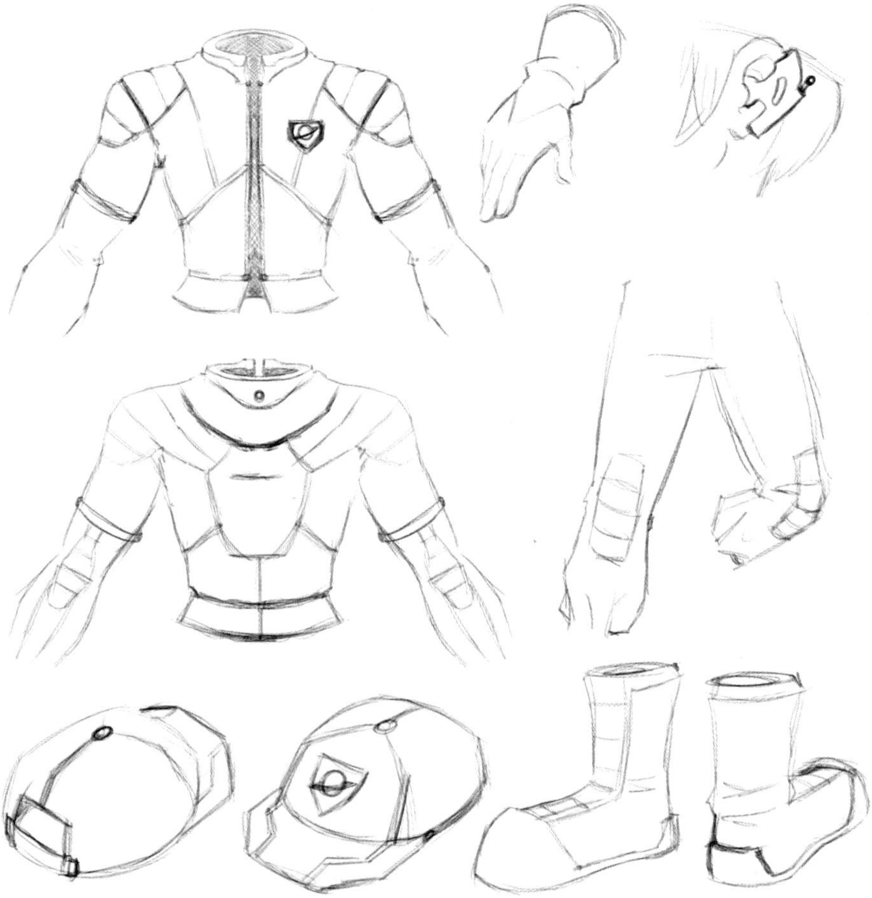

Figure 5.5   Sketches of character-design details, including clothes, earpiece, boots, gloves, and cap

Refined Design

At this point, you have a clear understanding of how everything looks: the face, hair, and clothes, as well as other details. Before you create the final artwork, get back to the base design and add more detail. Now is also a good time to sketch the character from the back (see Figure 5.6).

Everything is in place and looking good! In the next section, you do some color testing.

Figure 5.6   Refined design over the base design
and a design for the back of the character

Adding Color

Now that the base design is complete, it's time to add some colors to Jim and see how he looks with different color schemes. (If you have been working on paper up to this point, now is a good time to scan your design and start using a digital 2D image editor, as it allows you to test more than one color scheme for the same design and to make easy, fast retouches.) You need a version of Jim's front view with clean lines that allows you to use the color bucket tool in your editing program to quickly fill in areas with color (see Figure 5.7). Store each part of the character in a different layer, which lets you play with the skin-color values, for example, without affecting the rest of the colors. With this method, you can try several options.

When your colors are well organized by layers, testing a new color scheme may take only a couple of minutes. Figure 5.7 shows different hair colors so you can see how the process works. Suppose, though, that you already know that the hair is going to be blue, just like the eyes, as blue complements the bluish grays of the suit. You also need to pick a definitive color scheme for Jim's suit. Continue with the version in the middle, which already has the blue hair you chose, as the light tones of the suit have less contrast than the tones in the other two versions.

Figure 5.7   Testing different color schemes over the design

Finalizing the Design

At this point, making a final illustration of the character is possible, as you know how it's built, how it looks, and what its design details are. Figure 5.8 shows the final version of Jim. This level of quality is unnecessary for a preliminary design, but it helps you become familiar with the character so you can learn about him and understand his proportions and features. Also, the process of creating some final artwork sometimes even identifies potential problems in the character's design when you try to pose it and watch it from a particular perspective. Some pieces of the suit may not work properly in certain positions, for example. Usually, when they create a complex character, concept artists do a lot of illustrations like these to make sure that the character not only looks cool, but also has all its pieces working well together.

> **Note**
>
> In the associated files for this book, you can find a video showing the painting process for this illustration. I hope that this video will help you understand the steps I followed and motivate you to paint your own character.

Figure 5.8   Using the final design to create an illustration of Jim

Making Character Reference Images

You've designed your character. If you're an experienced designer, you can start modeling right away. But regardless of your expertise, you probably want to create some references to use in the 3D modeling program so that you have at least a general idea of the character's size and basic shapes, which will make the modeling process much faster. These images stay in the background of 3D View while you model, so you can model on top of them. The reference images should represent the character in a neutral pose, as that pose is what you'll need to model the character. Cool poses will come later.

For this example, you need six different reference images to place in 3D Views. You'll put these images in the background and place your model on top of them:

- Head, front view
- Head, back view
- Head, side view

- Body, front view
- Body, back view
- Body, side view

These reference images help you make your 3D model fit your original design. Design elements tend to change during 2D-to-3D conversion, as 2D and 3D are different worlds. But by using references, you get something in 3D that's close and proportionate to the 2D design you created.

For the head views, you don't need hair right now. You're modeling the head shape at this stage; you'll add the hair on top of that shape later (see Figure 5.9).

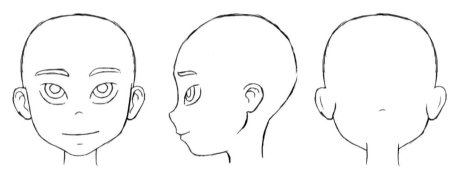

Figure 5.9   Head with front, side, and back views

For the body views shown in Figure 5.10, you can see that the side view doesn't have arms. This omission is intentional, as you don't want the arms to be in the way as you model the rest of the body. Later, you can model the arms from the front and back images. The side view would not have much relevant information about the arms, and they would cover the body of the character, which needs to be visible in the side view.

Notice the horizontal lines in the sketch. These lines serve as references so the character's features are in the same position in all the views so that later, you won't have trouble placing the characters in 3D. It's to be expected that your images won't be perfect; after all, they're hand drawings, and there will always be some errors, but the better aligned your images are, the easier they'll be to model later. If the reference images are not aligned, you'll have to do a lot of guesswork when modeling your character; you may even have to reinvent some areas while you model.

Note

Feel free to play with these designs and change them to something that looks better to you or has a style that you like more. The intention is to give you a good starting point if you've never done character design and need some initial guidance. This example should give you a base to start with and a method to follow, but you don't have to stick to it. Character design is a creative process, so don't be afraid to try new and crazy things!

Figure 5.10   Body with front, side, and back views

Using Other Design Methods

The method I just described isn't the only one available for designing a character. A lot of artists create their own methods and techniques over time. The following list provides some other options you might try:

- Use a simple 3D model made of spheres, cubes, or cylinders to explore the silhouette's basic shape and proportions. This method allows you to see how the character will look in 3D.

- Use random brushes in a painting program when exploring shapes. This method is likely to give you some unexpected results, and you may discover cool things that you would have missed by working with pencil and paper.

- Use vector imaging software such as Adobe Illustrator or Inkscape to test silhouettes. This method is similar to the simple 3D-model method, except that it's in 2D. This method is cool because it lets you scale and rotate parts of the body easily to try different proportions in your design.

- Use the Skin modifier in Blender for character prototyping. Basically, you draw a character's skeleton with vertices and edges and then use the Skin modifier to give it thickness and a solid mesh in which you can also control the thickness of each part. This modifier is intended to be used to create base meshes for sculpting, but you can also use it to test shapes for character creation.

- Use image compositing to pick parts of various photos or drawings and combine them to build your character's silhouette.

Summary

Character design can be quite complex, and you have to think about a lot of elements. You can dive into the modeling with just an idea in mind, of course, but that's probably going to be difficult, as you'll have to invent stuff on the fly. This design stage is crucial because it lets you define everything about your character: personality, attitude, looks, clothing, details, and so on. When you've done all that, you'll know your character very well, and you'll know for sure that it will look good when it's modeled in 3D. Otherwise, you may find that after all your time and effort, the idea you had in mind was not clear enough, and some things may not work as expected.

Design is a process of iteration, so it's important to keep in mind that not everything will work on the first try. You should be prepared to try, fail, and repeat parts of this process until you reach the point at which you're satisfied with your resulting design.

Remember: Preproduction is your friend!

Exercises

1. Starting with Jim's designs, add or replace elements to make the character look different.
2. If you're up for the challenge, design your own character!

Modeling in Blender

6 Blender Modeling Tools

7 Character Modeling

Blender Modeling Tools

Modeling is probably the most important stage in the character-creation process because it's when you generate the polygons that become the principal forms of your finished character. In this chapter, you learn the basics of modeling in Blender and see how to use some of the main tools you'll have at your disposal. As a result, when one of these tools is mentioned in the following chapters, you'll be familiar with it. You need to address three primary technical considerations before you can properly model in 3D: identify the elements that comprise a mesh, learn how to select them, and know what tools you can use to work with them. You learn about all these subjects in this chapter.

Working with Vertices, Edges, and Faces

Every 3D model is made out of the same three elements: vertices, edges, and faces. A *vertex* is a point in space. When you connect two vertices, you've created an *edge*, and if you connect three or more vertices in a closed loop and fill in the gap between the edges, you've created a face. A *face* is basically a polygon. You can see how these elements look in Figure 6.1.

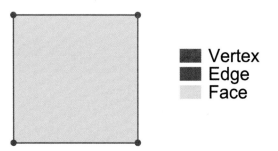

Figure 6.1   Vertices, edges, and faces: the elements that make up every 3D mesh

The three types of faces are triangles, quads (four-sided faces), and n-gons (faces with more than four sides). In 3D modeling, there is a rule: If you possibly can, use only quads when creating a model. There are different reasons for this rule, but mainly, if you're using subdivisions, the model deforms and can be smoothed better if it's made out of quads. Triangles and n-gons can be problematic at times because they can cause pinches in the mesh, especially if they are used in curved shapes or if the model is deforming because of animation.

In some situations, though, using a triangle or an n–gon is more beneficial for the mesh. In some complex formations, n–gons create better deformations and subdivisions than four–sided polygons do. It takes experience in modeling to discern those situations, and I encourage you to look into articles on the subject by experienced modelers (search online for topics such as 3D modeling topology), as this topic is beyond the scope of this book. The way vertices, edges, and faces are distributed to shape the surface of your model is called *topology*.

Selecting Vertices, Edges, and Faces

To access these mesh elements, first enter Edit Mode through the Interaction Mode selector on the 3D View header, or press **Tab** on your keyboard. When you're in Edit Mode, you'll be able to select vertices, edges, and faces. In Figure 6.2, you can see those elements' icons on the header.

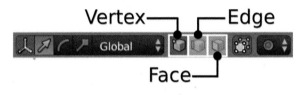

Figure 6.2   The 3D View header and its icons for
selecting vertices, edges, and faces

> **Tip**
>
> If you press **Shift** while you click the element icons on the 3D View header, you'll be able to select two types of elements at the same time. In Vertex selection mode, for example, hold down **Shift** while you left-click the Edge icon, and you'll be able to select vertices and edges simultaneously.
>
> A faster way to switch among Vertex, Edge, and Face selection modes is to press **Ctrl+Tab** while you're in Edit Mode. A little pop-up menu appears at your cursor's position, listing options that let you select a different element.

Accessing Modeling Tools

You have different ways to access the modeling tools in Blender. You can access all the tools from menus, but the most common tools also have their own keyboard shortcuts. You can access the modeling tools as follows:

- **Mesh Menu:** In this menu, located in the 3D View header, you'll find submenus for vertices, edges, and faces.
- **Tools Region (T):** Most of the main modeling tools are in the Tools Region when you're in Edit Mode.
- **Search:** In Blender, when you press **Space**, a Search menu appears. You can type the name of the tool you want to use and then choose it from the menu to apply it.

Following are the keyboard shortcuts you can use to access these tools while in 3D View:

- Vertices: **Ctrl+V**
- Edges: **Ctrl+E**
- Faces: **Ctrl+F**
- Special tools: **W**

Making Selections

In this section, you discover some tips for making selections when you're in Edit Mode. For the most part, selections work exactly the same way as they do in Object Mode (selection is covered in Chapter 2, "Blender Basics: The User Interface"), but in Edit Mode, they are applied to vertices, edges, or faces. You can add to a selection by pressing **Shift**, for example, or you can perform a box selection by pressing **B**. The following sections cover a few selection techniques that are available only in Edit Mode.

Shortest Path

If you right-click to select a vertex and then hold down **Ctrl** while you right-click a second vertex, Blender automatically selects the shortest path between the two vertices (see Figure 6.3). This selection method also works with edges and faces.

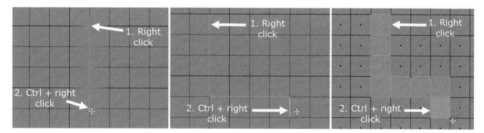

Figure 6.3   Some examples of how Shortest Path
Selections works with vertices, edges, and faces

If you keep pressing **Ctrl** and right-clicking, the new paths are added to the selection, making this method a very fast way to select a series of vertices that follow a path. (This technique proves to be very useful in Chapter 8, "Unwrapping and UVs in Blender," where it's used to mark seams in a model.)

The interesting features of Shortest Path Selection include the nth selection, skip, and offset options, which you can access from the Operator panel (or by pressing **F6**). These options let you change the values to deselect vertices in the path alternatively. Selecting one vertex every three vertices, for example, is possible thanks to this option, which in big models with many vertices can save lots of time. Shortest Path Selection's options include other interesting features, and you should take a look at those as well.

> **Tip**
> Another great use of this tool is to hold down **Shift** while using Shortest Path Selection to select a rectangular grid of faces that uses your first and last selected faces as opposite corners.

Proportional Editing

Proportional editing is a very useful feature, especially when you're working on organic modeling. Basically, you select an element (vertices, edges, faces, or objects), and when you transform it, the surrounding elements follow the selection, depending on the falloff type and radius of influence you define (see Figure 6.4).

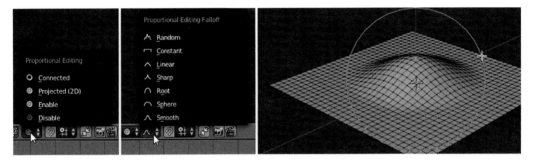

Figure 6.4   The proportional editing menu on the 3D View header (left), the falloff types (middle), and the effect of the proportional editing tool on a mesh when moving a single vertex (right)

Using proportional editing is very easy: Just find the icon on the 3D View header and select one of the methods to enable it. Alternatively, you can press **O** on your keyboard to turn it on and off. If proportional editing is enabled, when you perform a transform, a circle appears around the selection that indicates the radius of influence. You can roll the scroll wheel of your mouse up and down to increase or decrease the size of the circle.

When you enable proportional editing, another drop-down menu appears next to the proportional editing icon, allowing you to select different falloff types. Here are the proportional editing methods you can use (see Figure 6.4):

- **Connected:** This option affects only the vertices, edges, or faces that are directly connected to the selection. It won't affect parts of the same mesh that are separated.
- **Projected (2D):** This option's effect depends not on the mesh, but on the point of view from which you're looking at the mesh.
- **Enable:** This option activates the effect of the proportional editing tool on the mesh surrounding the selection inside the radius of influence, even if the vertices are disconnected.
- **Disable:** This option disables proportional editing.

> **Tip**
>
> In other software, this feature is called falloff selection, soft selection, smooth selection, or other names with a similar meaning. These features may work in slightly different ways, but they're basically the same as Blender's proportional editing.

Linked Selection

A mesh can be made of different parts that are not connected by edges, and you may want to select some parts without selecting the others. These isolated parts of a mesh are also called *islands*. You have two quick ways to select those linked parts:

- Select one of the mesh's vertices, edges, or faces, and press **Ctrl+L**. All the elements of that island are selected.

- With nothing selected, place the cursor on top of an island and press **L** to select it. Press **Shift+L** to add to and subtract from the selection.

Loops and Rings

The shape that edges follow along a surface is usually called *edge flow* or *mesh flow*, and it's very important in modeling (as you learn in Chapter 7, "Character Modeling"). In any mesh, you can find loops and rings. A *loop* is a series of connected edges that follow a path. A *ring* is a series of parallel edges along the surface of a mesh (see Figure 6.5).

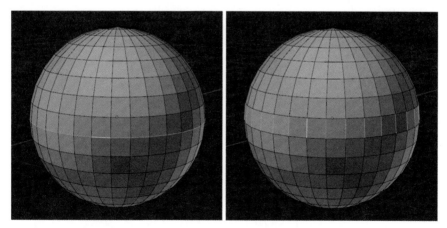

Figure 6.5 An edge loop (left) and an edge ring (right)

You can quickly select loops or rings with two keyboard shortcuts:

- **Selecting loops:** Place your cursor on top of an edge, press **Alt**, and right-click to select the whole loop.

- **Selecting rings:** Place your cursor on top of an edge, press **Ctrl+Alt**, and right-click to select the whole ring.

Hold down **Shift** combined with either of these shortcuts to add to the selection.

This technique works with vertices, edges, and faces, but in the case of faces, selecting a loop or a ring returns the same results.

Border Selection

A *border* is the series of edges that define the limits of a mesh that is not closed. Take a plane, for example. A plane's four edges are open, and that's a border. A cube, on the other hand, is closed.

To quickly select a border, hold down **Alt** while you right-click the outer edges of the mesh twice.

Grow and Shrink Selection

When you have a selection of vertices, edges, or faces, you can press **Ctrl+NumPad +** (plus sign) or **Ctrl+NumPad –** (minus sign) to grow or shrink the scope of the selection through the connected elements.

Limit Selection to Visible

When you have the display mode in Wireframe (**Z**), you can select vertices, edges, or faces that are in front of the model, as well as those that are behind it. This selection is not possible with the Solid display, which lets you interact only with the parts of the model that are facing you.

In Edit Mode, when a mode other than the Wireframe display is active, right next to the icons on the 3D View header for selecting vertices, edges, or faces, you'll find an icon with a little cube that has marked vertices. If that option is turned on, you see only the parts of the model that are facing you, but if you disable the option, you can see any of the elements behind the model—and also select them. Sometimes, you want to select a large portion of an object. If the model has holes and cavities, it's useful to be able to select all the vertices at the same time. Most of the time, however, you probably want to select only elements that are visible and in front of the model so that you don't accidentally select something behind it. You need to turn this option on or off depending on the situation and your preferred working method.

Select Similar

After making a selection, pressing **Shift+G** shows different options depending on the type of element that you just selected. When you select an element, such as an edge, and use the Select Similar tool, for example, you can select all the similar edges in that mesh automatically. You can select by length, face angles, direction, and several other parameters.

Pay attention to the Operator panel, as it gives you options for modifying the selection. An especially useful option is the threshold, which lets you define the amount of similarity with the original selection, which requires a certain value for the other elements to be selected.

Select Linked Flat Faces

This keyboard shortcut is quite tricky, but here it goes: **Shift+Ctrl+Alt+F**. This shortcut selects all the faces around the selection as long as they are on a flat surface. The sharpness value in the Operator panel lets you tell Blender how big the angle between faces has to be to limit the selection.

Select Boundary Loop and Loop Inner-Region

You can find options for selecting the boundary loop and the loop inner region in the Select menu of the 3D View header and in the Edges menu (**Ctrl+E**).

When you have a selection of several faces on a surface, you can use the Select Boundary Loop tool. This tool leaves only the boundary loop selected on the borders of the previously selected faces (see Figure 6.6).

The Select Loop Inner-Region tool is exactly the opposite of Boundary Loop. This tool allows you to select a closed loop on a surface and to select all elements inside that loop (see Figure 6.6).

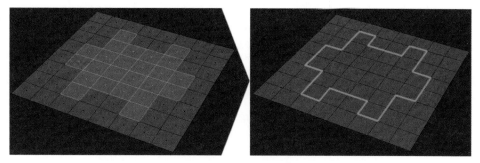

Figure 6.6   The effect of the Inner-Region selection (left).
Boundary Loop selection has the opposite effect (right).

Checker Deselect

The Checker Deselect tool is actually a reverse take on selections. First, you select an area; then you use Checker Deselect to deselect given elements, thus ending up with the desired selection. You can access this tool from the Select menu on the 3D View header.

Basically, this tool generates a pattern based on three values that you set up in the Operator panel: nth selection, skip, and offset. Then you use this pattern to deselect some of the elements in the selection you made.

Other Selection Methods

In the 3D View header's Select menu, you'll find all the selection methods previously discussed, as well as several others. The methods mentioned in this chapter generally are the ones that are used most often, but I encourage you to check out the rest of them, as you may find some that are useful. Also, keep in mind that you can always go to the Select menu in case you don't remember the keyboard shortcut for any of the methods. (Note that the Proportional Editing option cannot be accessed from the Select menu; it's accessed from the 3D View header.)

Using Mesh Modeling Tools

This section provides a reference for the main modeling tools (alphabetically ordered) that are available in Blender. You'll learn how to use them, see what options they have (on the Operator panel of the Tools Region in 3D View), and know what their effects are. Test them and learn them, as they will be used a lot in the following chapters. Don't worry if you don't remember all their features, however; you can come back to this chapter whenever necessary.

> ### Note
> All the tools discussed here can be found in the menus explained in the previous section, but in this section, I specify only the keyboard shortcuts for them. Also, with many of these tools, you can drag things with your mouse to move them. Remember that you can use the keyboard shortcuts to aid the transform: Press **Shift** to move things precisely; press **Ctrl** to snap; or enter numerical values and then use the **X**, **Y**, and **Z** keys to constrain the movements to their respective axes.

Bevel

Bevel is a very useful tool, especially for technical and inorganic models; it is used to create bevels and chamfers. It can be used with vertices, edges, and faces. (The Bevel tool works with vertices only when you enable the Only Vertex option in the Operator panel after invoking the tool.) You can see how it's used in Figure 6.7.

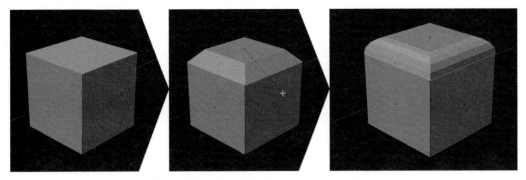

Figure 6.7   Using the Bevel tool over a face

To use the Bevel tool:

1. Select the element you want to bevel.
2. Press **Ctrl+B** and drag your mouse to increase or decrease the bevel size.
3. Roll the scroll wheel to increase or decrease the bevel divisions (segments). Alternatively, press **S** and move the mouse or enter a number to define the segments amount.
4. Press **P** and move the mouse to change the profile (shape) of the bevel. (Numerical input of a specific profile value is allowed.)
5. Left-click to apply or right-click to cancel.

In the Bevel tool options of the Operators panel, you'll find the size calculation method, the size of the bevel, the amount of segments, and the bevel's profile (in or out), as well as an option that lets you apply the bevel only to vertices. (You can launch the Bevel tool in vertices-only mode directly by pressing **Ctrl+Shift+B**.)

> **Tip**
> Blender's Bevel tool is similar to the Chamfer tool in 3ds Max.

Boolean Operations: Intersect (Boolean) and Intersect (Knife)

The Intersect (Boolean) and Intersect (Knife) tools let you use two parts of a mesh and cut new edges in their intersections (see Figure 6.8). There are some differences between the tools, both of which you can find in the Face menu (**Ctrl+F**). Keep in mind that these tools work only when elements of a mesh (inside the same object) intersect.

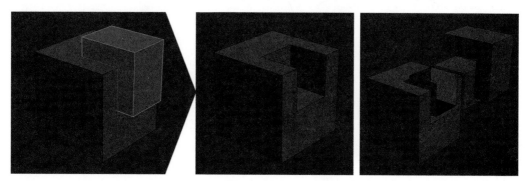

Figure 6.8   The selection of one cube inside another (left), the result of the Intersect (Boolean) tool in Difference mode (middle), and the effects of the Intersect (Knife) tool (right)

Intersect (Boolean)

The Intersect (Boolean) tool acts similarly to a Boolean modifier operation. Booleans let you subtract volumes from and add volumes to a mesh by intersecting it with another mesh. In Blender, you do this by using the Boolean modifier, but you can also do it in Edit Mode with the Intersect (Boolean) tool.

To use the Intersect (Boolean) tool:

1. Select the part of the mesh that you want to use as a cutter.

2. Press **Ctrl+F** and select Intersect (Boolean).

3. Select the type of Boolean operation that you want to apply from the Operator panel.

Intersect (Knife)

Intersect (Knife) works similarly to the Intersect (Boolean) tool, but instead of subtracting or adding volume, it cuts the mesh and generates new edges on the surface. It also separates the different intersecting meshes through those edges. This tool is very useful when you need to perform a cut with a given shape on a mesh. Just model a cutter mesh and use this tool to generate such a cut.

To use the Intersect (Knife) tool:

1. Select the part of the mesh that you want to use as a cutter.

2. Press **Ctrl+F** and select Intersect (Knife). The meshes are cut but kept in their positions.

3. Remove any parts that you don't need.

Bisect

The Bisect tool lets you create a line across a selection and project it to generate an edge loop that divides the mesh. After that, you're able to leave only one side of the mesh from that division visible, which is useful for creating cross sections of objects (see Figure 6.9).

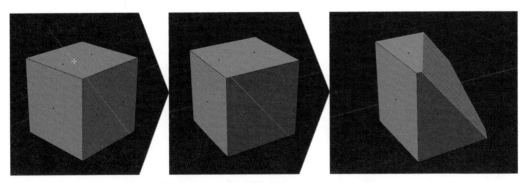

Figure 6.9   Using the Bisect tool on the default cube

To use the Bisect tool:

1. Select the part of the mesh you want to divide. (Sometimes, you want to divide the entire mesh, which you can select by pressing **A**.)

2. Select the Bisect tool from the Tools Region or the Mesh menu in the 3D View header. (This tool has no keyboard shortcut.)

3. Left-click the first point of the line you want to draw, and drag to indicate the line's direction.

4. Release the mouse button to apply.

Bridge Edge Loops

The Bridge Edge Loops tool works well to join a series of adjacent edge loops. It's like an advanced Face tool (covered later in this chapter), but instead of creating one face at a time, it creates a group of them, joining two selected edge loops (see Figure 6.10).

Figure 6.10   Using the Bridge Edge Loops tool to connect two separated edge loops

To use the Bridge Edge Loops tool:

1. Select a string of edges (edge loop).
2. Select another edge loop in a separate part of the model. (For optimal results, both edge loops should have the same number of edges.)
3. Press **Ctrl+E** to access the Edge menu, and select the Bridge Edge Loops tool.

The options for this tool let you control the type of connection that is made between the loops, twist the resulting geometry, and apply some merging options (but only if the edge counts are the same in both edge loops that you're trying to connect). These options also include several features that allow you to control the number of segments (cuts) in the new geometry, as well as its shape.

Connect

The Connect tool joins two vertices with a new edge across a face or a series of faces. For this tool to work, a face must exist between the selected vertices (see Figure 6.11).

To use the Connect tool:

1. Select two vertices.
2. Press **J** to connect them.

Figure 6.11   Using the Connect tool to join two vertices sharing a face with a new edge

> **Tip**
> If you select a series of vertices (assuming that there is a face between one and the next),
> when you press **J**, Blender connects them in the same order in which you selected them,
> so you don't need to connect them one at a time.

Delete and Dissolve

In Blender, when you have some of a mesh's elements selected and you press **X**, a menu
appears that gives you several options. You can use Delete to remove vertices, edges, or
faces. This tool has a variety of effects. If you select one of the other options, such as Only
Faces, only the faces are deleted; the edges and vertices remain.

You also see the Dissolve tool, which is similar to Delete except that instead of making elements disappear, it replaces them with a single n-gon. This tool comes in handy when you're
working on complex surfaces and need to adjust the way in which the edges are placed. You
can dissolve the faces and then reconnect the remaining vertices manually (see Figure 6.12).

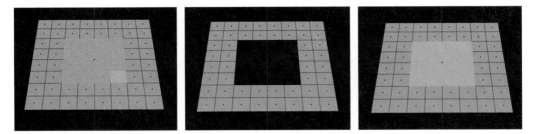

Figure 6.12   The selected faces (left), the effect of deleting those
faces (center), and the result of dissolving those faces (right)

To use Delete or Dissolve:

1. Select a set of adjacent vertices, edges, or faces.

2. Press **X** and select Delete or Dissolve from the pop-up menu to delete or dissolve
   the selection.

When you use the Delete tool, depending on the option you select, Blender presents another set of options that let you control the degree of deletion for that particular tool. With the Limited Dissolve option, you have control of the angle at which the dissolved faces are joined.

Tip

To save some time when dissolving faces, you can select the faces you want to dissolve and press **F**. The **F** key usually generates faces between vertices and edges, but when it's used on faces, it replaces all the selected faces with a single face (which is the same effect as Dissolve).

Duplicate

Duplicate is as simple as it seems. This tool lets you duplicate a piece of the mesh and place it somewhere else very quickly.

To use the Duplicate tool:

1. Select one or more vertices, edges, or faces.
2. Press **Shift+D**.
3. Drag your mouse to move the selection. You can use the **X**, **Y**, and **Z** constraints while moving, just as you would in a normal transform.
4. Left-click to confirm.

Duplicate is quite a simple tool, but it gives you a lot of options. From the Operator panel, for example, you can control the offset of the duplication, constrain it, and even access the proportional editing features.

Edge Offset

The Edge Offset tool is especially useful for defining corners while using a Subdivision Surface modifier. It creates two parallel edges, one on each side of the originally selected edge (see Figure 6.13).

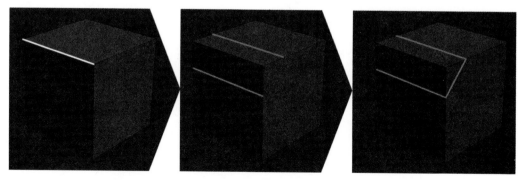

Figure 6.13   The original selection (left), two new parallel edges (middle), and the effect of the Cap Endpoint (right)

To use the Edge Offset tool:

1. Select one or more edges.
2. Press **Ctrl+Alt+R**.
3. Slide the generated edges. You can press **E** to make the separation from the original even instead of calculating that separation automatically by averaging the distance from the next edge.

In the Operator panel, you can define the slide amount, as well as cap the endpoints (Blender connects the ends of both new edges if possible), even the distances, and set other parameters.

Extrude

Another useful modeling tool is Extrude. To understand how it works, imagine the floor of a house. You select the floor, and when you extrude it, you move it up as though it were a duplicate to create a ceiling; then Blender generates the walls to join the floor and ceiling (see Figure 6.14). You can use Extrude for vertices, edges, and faces. Blender provides different methods for extruding and a few Extrude options, such as Extrude Region and Extrude Individual. The first option extrudes the entire selection at the same time, and the second extrudes each face individually.

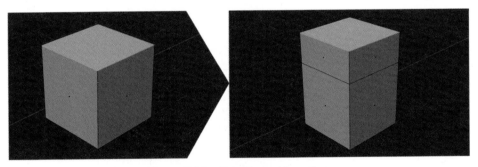

Figure 6.14   Extrude tool in action

You have three methods for using the Extrude tool. Here is the first method:

1. Select one or more vertices, edges, or faces.
2. Press **E** to extrude.
3. Drag your mouse to move the new geometry. You can press **X**, **Y**, and **Z** to constrain it. (If you extrude a face, by default, it is constrained according to the orientation of the face.)
4. Left-click to confirm the extrusion.

This is the second method:

1. Select one or more vertices, edges, or faces.
2. Press **Ctrl** and left-click where you want the extrusion to go. Blender extrudes automatically.

And here is the third method:

1. Select one or more vertices, edges, or faces.
2. Press **Alt+E** to bring up a menu of extrude options, and select one.
3. Drag your mouse to adjust the height of the extrusion.
4. Left-click to confirm.

Within the Operator panel for an extrusion, you'll find options to change the extrusion's direction and size or constrain it to an axis, as well as some proportional editing features.

Fill and Grid Fill

With the Fill and Grid Fill tools, you can select a part of the mesh where you have a hole, and Blender fills it. Generally, Grid Fill provides better results and cleaner geometry (see Chapter 7, "Character Modeling," for more information about clean geometry and topology) than Fill does (see Figure 6.15).

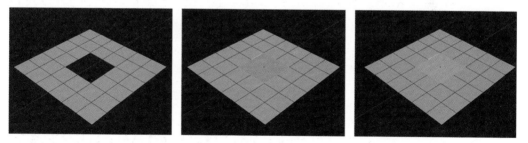

Figure 6.15   Mesh selection (left), Fill (middle), and Grid Fill (right)

To use the Fill tool:

1. Select the borders of the hole. (Sometimes, you can select them as a loop by pressing **Alt** and right-clicking.)
2. Press **Alt+F** to fill the hole with new geometry.

The Fill tool has a few options, such as Beauty, which tries to give you a better result when generating the new geometry.

To use the Grid Fill tool:

1. Select the borders of the hole.
2. Press **Ctrl+F** to access the Face menu (Grid Fill doesn't have a keyboard shortcut by default), and select Grid Fill to fill the hole with new geometry.

Grid Fill tries to create a new geometry made of four-sided faces (a grid). It gives you a couple of options to rotate the pattern and get a cleaner geometry, depending on the shape of the hole that you're filling. It also has a Simple Blending option that relaxes some of the grid's surface tension.

Inset

The Inset tool is similar to the Extrude tool, but the new faces it creates are on the surface of the selection and do not change the surface's shape. This tool generates a copy of the geometry that is an inset of the original selection; you can also use it to add height to the new geometry. This tool works only with faces (see Figure 6.16).

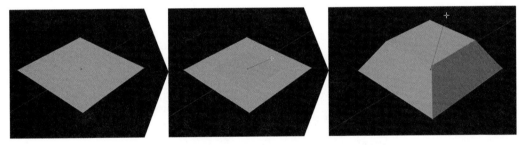

Figure 6.16   The Inset tool used in a face, with the
inset amount defined first and then its height

To use the Inset tool:

1. Select a face or group of faces.
2. Press **I** to create an inset.
3. Drag the mouse to increase or decrease the inset's thickness. Press **Ctrl** while dragging to change the height of the inset.
4. Left-click to confirm the operation.

You'll find several interesting options for this tool. Boundary (press **B** while using the tool to enable or disable it), for example, takes into account the borders of the mesh when applying the inset. This option is very useful when you're working on a mirrored mesh and don't want the faces in the mirror's plane to be affected by the Inset operation.

Other options allow you to change how the thickness is calculated and define both the amount of the inset's thickness and its height (press **M** while using the tool). You have some options to outset instead of inset (press **O** while using the tool) or to apply the inset to each face of the selection individually (press **I** while using the tool). You can also select the outer or inner part of the inset after applying this tool, depending on which part you prefer to work with.

Tip

It may be confusing, but Inset in Blender is similar to Bevel in 3ds Max, while Bevel in Blender is similar to Chamfer in 3ds Max.

Join

The Join tool is used in Object Mode, not Edit Mode. With this tool, you can select two objects and join them so that they become a single object. This tool is the opposite of the Separate tool (discussed later in this chapter).

To use the Join tool:

1. In Object Mode, select two or more objects. Determine the object you want to keep as the primary one and select it last to keep it as the active object. Attributes such as the center of the resulting object or its modifiers will be taken from the active object before you use the Join tool.

2. Press **Ctrl+J** to join the objects into a unique mesh.

Tip

Join and Separate (explained later) are similar to the Attach and Detach tools in 3ds Max.

Knife

Knife is a useful tool that allows you to cut through the surface of a mesh to divide it into faces and edges and to generate new geometry (see Figure 6.17).

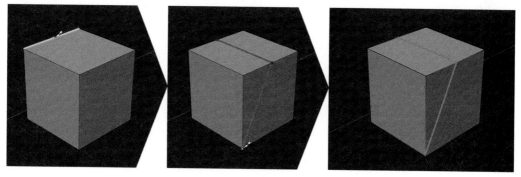

Figure 6.17   Using the Knife tool to cut through faces

To use the Knife tool:

1. Press **K** to start the Knife tool. Alternatively, press **Shift+K** to affect only the selected geometry.

2. Left-click, move your mouse to define the cut line, and left-click again.

3. Repeat Step 2 until you're happy with the cut. The knife will show the points on-screen where it will add a vertex to the cut and, by default, the Knife tool will snap to vertices and edges. Press **Shift** to avoid snapping to vertices and edges and to do a free cut. Press **Ctrl** to snap to the center of the edges.

4. When you're done with the cut, press **Enter** to confirm and apply the cut.

> **Tip**
>
> While using the Knife tool, you can click and drag to quickly cut through geometry. If you want to perform different cuts before applying the effect, you can press **E** to start a new cut.

Knife Project

Knife Project is similar to the Knife tool, except that it uses another mesh to project the shape of the cut on a surface. That cutter shape is projected from your point of view onto the mesh and creates new edges (see Figure 6.18).

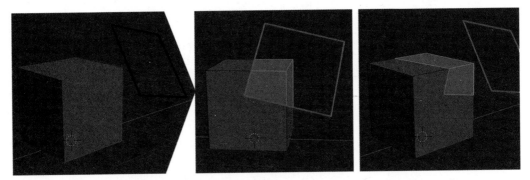

Figure 6.18   Model and cutter mesh (left), Knife Project operation from a given point of view (middle), and result from a perspective where you can see the resulting edges created on the surface (right)

To use the Knife Project tool:

1. Create a mesh with the shape you want to cut.

2. Hold down **Shift** and select (to add to the selection) the mesh in which you want to use the tool.

3. Change the point of view so that you can see the cutter mesh where the final cut should be.

4. Select Knife Project from the Tools Region. (This tool has no keyboard shortcut.)

The options for this tool let you make the cut go through the mesh, not just the side that is facing you.

Tip

You can select another object when in Edit Mode. Hold down **Ctrl** while right-clicking the other object, and that object is added to the selection as though you selected it before the current object. You can use this trick to select the cutter mesh even though you are in Edit Mode.

Loop Cut and Slide

The Loop Cut and Slide tool creates a cut through the entire loop you select, generating one or more new loops; then you can slide the new loop between the two adjacent loops (see Figure 6.19).

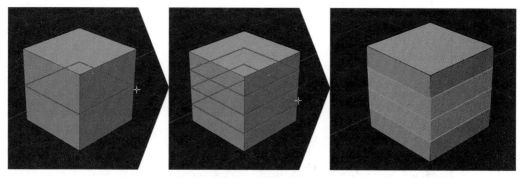

Figure 6.19   The Loop Cut and Slide tool used on the default cube

To use the Loop Cut and Slide tool:

1. Press **Ctrl+R**.
2. Move your cursor around the model to select where you want to add the new loop. A preview appears in pink.
3. Place your cursor on top of an edge to detect the edge's ring, and place the new loop across that ring.
4. Roll your scroll wheel up and down to increase and decrease the number of loops to add.
5. Left-click to accept where you want the new loop.
6. Drag your mouse to slide the new loop along the edges.
7. Left-click again to confirm and apply the new loops. If you right-click instead, you cancel the sliding, and the new edge loop is perfectly centered when it is applied.

The Operator panel provides some cool options for this tool. After you apply it, you can change the number of cuts and even their smoothness, as well as the falloff type of the smooth feature, to create curved shapes with the new geometry. Also, you can control the Edge Slide factor.

> **Tip**
>
> While you use the Loop Cut and Slide tool, the new edge loop average sits positioned between the previous and next loops. If you don't want the new loop to be averaged, but to adapt its shape to one or the other, press **E** (even) while sliding. A yellow line appears perpendicular to the edge that you're sliding to show you the direction and limits of the slide, and a red dot marks the side to which the new loop's shape is adapting. Press **F** (flip) if you want it to adapt to the opposite side.

Make Edge/Face

The Make Edge/Face tool is very valuable because it lets you select two elements (only vertices or edges) and create an edge or face between them (see Figure 6.20). This tool has different effects, depending on the elements you select. If you select two vertices, the tool generates an edge between them. If you select three or more vertices (or two or more edges), the tool creates a triangle, a face, or an n-gon, according to your selection.

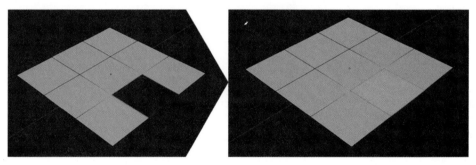

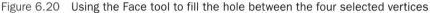

Figure 6.20   Using the Face tool to fill the hole between the four selected vertices

To use the Face tool:

1. Select two or more vertices or two or more edges. The vertices or edges need to be on the borders of the geometry; on the side where the face will be generated, no geometry should be connected to those elements.

2. Press **F** to create the edge or face.

Merge

With the Merge tool, you can select two or more elements and merge them into a single element. This tool is similar to the welding tools in other software. Merge can be used with vertices, edges, and faces.

To use the Merge tool:

1. Select two or more vertices, edges, or faces.
2. Press **Alt+M**, and select one of the options.

Blender offers several Merge options that have different results. With vertices, for example, you can usually decide where to merge: in the position of the first selected one or the last selected one, at the center of the selection, or at the point of the 3D cursor.

Collapse merges each of the groups of connected elements individually, so if they're not connected, they won't be merged. This option is useful if you want to get rid of a loop; you can select an edge ring and collapse it so that each edge is turned into a vertex. If you select two faces in different parts of a mesh and collapse them, for example, each of the faces is converted to a single vertex at its center.

After you merge elements, you can still change the merge type and where the elements are merged from the Operator panel. This feature is useful for experimenting, as it allows you to see the effects of the merge types. It's also useful if you selected the wrong type accidentally, as it allows you to easily fix the mistake.

Poke

The Poke tool is simple enough and can be valuable. It creates a vertex in the center of each selected face and then creates an edge between that central vertex and all the vertices of the face (see Figure 6.21).

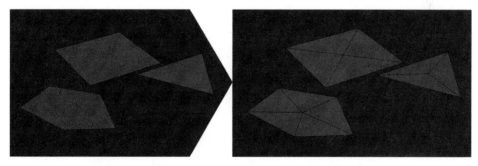

Figure 6.21   Using the Poke tool on different faces

To use the Poke tool:

1. Select one or more faces.
2. Press **Alt+P** to create the vertex.

In this tool's options, you can define the height of the generated central vertex and define how that center is calculated.

Remove Doubles

Sometimes, you accidentally end up with duplicated vertices at some points of your mesh. Remove Doubles lets you automatically merge all the vertices that are very close to one another inside a range you can define.

To use the Remove Doubles tool:

1. Select the part of the mesh from which you want to remove double vertices. Usually, you want to remove them from the entire mesh, which you can select by pressing **A**.

2. Press **W** to access the Specials menu, and select the Remove Doubles option (which lacks a keyboard shortcut). In the Info area, usually at the top of the interface, you get a notification displaying the number of vertices that you removed.

After using this tool, you can go to the Operator panel and change the merge distance. At minimum (values close to zero), Merge tool merges only the vertices that are in the same position, but you can increase the merge distance to merge vertices that are close to each other but not exactly in the same location. Remove Doubles is applied only to the selected vertices, but you can activate the Unselected option to include the unselected vertices that are very close to the selected ones.

Rip and Rip Fill

The Rip tool works only with vertices; it lets you rip apart the selected vertex or vertices and create a hole in the mesh. Rip Fill automatically fills the hole that you created (see Figure 6.22).

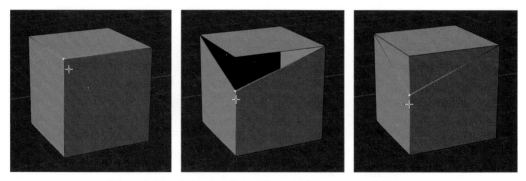

Figure 6.22   Selection (left), Rip (middle), and Rip Fill (right)

To use the Rip or Rip Fill tool:

1. Select one or more vertices.

2. Place your cursor on the side of the vertex you want to take apart. That action defines the resulting vertex you'll displace after the rip.

3. Press **V** to use Rip or press **Alt+V** to use Rip Fill.

4. Drag your mouse to move the ripped vertex or vertices around.

5. Left-click to confirm the operation.

Screw

The Screw tool lets you add a screwing or spiral effect around the 3D cursor. You can select the number of turns and segments, as well as the height of the generated screw (see Figure 6.23).

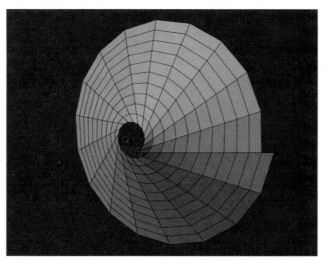

Figure 6.23   Result of using the Screw tool with an edge

To use the Screw tool:

1. Select a string of vertices or edges. (This tool doesn't work with faces.)

2. Place the 3D cursor where you want the center of the screwing effect to be.

3. Place your point of view in the direction in which you want to apply the effect. The center position is defined by the 3D cursor, and the orientation is determined by your point of view.

4. Access and launch the Screw tool from the Tools Region.

After you perform the Screw operation, some options are available to you in the Operator panel, such as adjusting the center of the screw effect, its orientation, and the number of turns and steps (segments) it has.

Tip

Keep in mind that when you modify the options in the Operator panel for an action, the next time you perform that action, those modifications will be its default values. If you turn on the proportional size for an extrusion, for example, the next time you extrude, you'll be using that same proportional size.

Separate

You can select a part of the mesh and separate it into a different object with the Separate tool.

To use the Separate tool:

1. Select the parts of the mesh you want to separate.

2. Press **P** to display a pop-up menu.

3. Choose the Selected option if you want to separate the selection, the By Material option if you want to separate the mesh into parts that use different materials (only if you've applied different materials to parts of the mesh), or the Loose Parts option if you want to separate the disconnected parts of the mesh. (You don't need to make a selection to use the Loose Parts option.)

Shrink/Flatten

Very simple but frequently very useful, the Shrink/Flatten tool scales the selected vertices, edges, or faces depending on their normal. (A *normal* is what the orientation vector of a face is called in 3D.)

To use the Shrink/Flatten tool:

1. Select the parts of the mesh you want to modify.

2. Press **Alt+S** (similar to scaling) to launch the tool.

3. Drag your mouse to adjust the Shrinking value.

4. Left-click to confirm the operation.

This tool also has some very simple options that allow you to adjust the shrinking or flattening value; it has some proportional editing options as well.

Slide

With the Slide tool, when you select a vertex, an edge, or a loop, you can slide the selection along the adjacent edges. Although you can use this tool with faces, it's usually more intuitive to use it with vertices and edges.

To use the Slide tool with vertices:

1. Select one or more vertices. (As a rule of thumb, use this tool with only one vertex at a time, as having more vertices selected makes the sliding unpredictable.)

2. Place your mouse near the edge where you want to slide the vertex.

3. Press **Shift+V** to launch the tool.

4. Drag your mouse to slide the vertex. Blender displays a yellow line to let you see where you can move the vertex.

5. Left-click to confirm the new vertex position.

To use the Slide tool with edges:

1. Select the edge or edge loop you want to slide.
2. Press **Ctrl+E** to access the Edge menu, and choose the Edge Slide option.
3. Drag your mouse to slide the edge or edge loop.
4. Left-click to confirm the operation.

The options in the Operator panel for the Slide tool are very simple. They allow you to adjust the distance and direction in which the selected elements slide along their edges.

> **Tip**
>
> A quicker way to slide, whether you're working with vertices, edges, or faces, is to press **G** twice. The same options are available as when you slide the Loop Cut and Slide tool, such as pressing **E** and **F** to adapt the shape to the adjacent edge loops.

Smooth Vertex

Smooth Vertex does just what its name tells you: smoothes the selected vertices' shape. This tool is useful when you have some unwanted bulges or just want to distribute in a more uniform way the vertices that you created in a mesh.

To use the Smooth Vertex tool:

1. Select a group of vertices, edges, or faces.
2. Select the Smooth Vertex tool from the Tools Region. (The tool has no keyboard shortcut.)

The options for this tool let you control different parameters to control how the smoothing is performed.

Solidify

The Solidify tool adds thickness to the selection. It works only with faces.

To use the Solidify tool:

1. Select the faces to which you want to add thickness.
2. Press **Ctrl+F** to access the Face menu, and choose the Solidify option.

When you apply Solidify to a face or group of faces, you can use its options in the Operator panel to adjust their thickness.

Spin

The Spin tool lets you pick a vertex, edge, or face (or a group of these elements) and extrude them around the 3D cursor from the current point of view (see Figure 6.24).

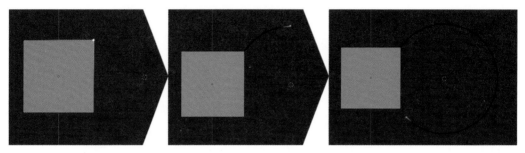

Figure 6.24   Using the Spin tool with a vertex around the 3D cursor

To use the Spin tool:

1. Select one or more vertices, edges, or faces.
2. Place the 3D cursor where you want the center of the resulting circle to be.
3. Position the point of view to define the orientation of the spin.
4. Press **Alt+R** to use the Spin tool.

Spin gives you options for defining the angle of the spin and the number of steps (extrusions during the spin) and for adjusting the center and axis from which the spin takes place. Also, the Dupli option makes duplicates of the resulting geometry instead of extrusions.

Split

The Split tool disconnects a selected part of the mesh from the rest of the mesh (see Figure 6.25). It works best with faces. (With vertices and edges, the effect is similar to duplicating them if they are parts of a face.) When the selected part is disconnected, you can move it freely to any other location. Split is different from the Separate tool in that Split keeps the mesh in the same object rather than creating a new object from it.

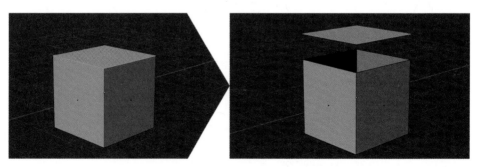

Figure 6.25   Splitting a face from the default cube

To use the Split tool:

1. Select the faces you want to disconnect.
2. Press **Y** to use the Split tool.

Subdivide

As its name implies, the Subdivide tool subdivides geometry. It works with edges and faces. With this tool, an edge is divided in half, generating a new vertex right in the middle. A face is divided into four new faces, and if you select an edge ring, Subdivide generates a loop that divides all the edges of the ring right through the center of each edge. You can also increase the number of divisions (cuts) when using this tool (see Figure 6.26).

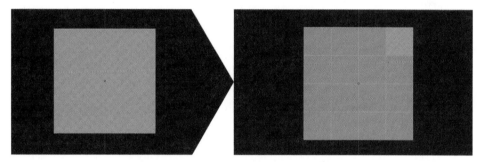

Figure 6.26   Subdividing a face with three cuts

To use the Subdivide tool:

1. Select the geometry you want to subdivide. (The minimum is two connected vertices that are equal to one edge.)
2. Press **W** to access the Specials menu, and choose the Subdivide option.

You can define the number of divisions and their smoothness, depending on the surrounding geometry. You can also generate triangles around the subdivisions to prevent the creation of n-gons and apply fractal noise patterns to the resulting geometry.

Working with LoopTools

LoopTools is an add-on that's built into Blender but not active by default. You can go to User Preferences and activate it within the Add-Ons tab. When it's active, LoopTools is accessible from the Tools Region in 3D View and from the top of the Specials (**W**) menu in Edit Mode (see Figure 6.27).

Figure 6.27   LoopTools add-on in the 3D View Tools Region

This add-on provides some interesting and useful modeling tools that I encourage you to check out. These tools speed the modeling process. Here's what they do:

- **Bridge:** This tool was present in the LoopTools add-on before it was implemented in Blender. The version included with Blender (called Bridge Edge Loops) is not exactly the same; its options are slightly different, though they provide similar results. The Bridge tool lets you select edges or faces and create new geometry that forms a bridge between them.

- **Circle:** This tool places your selected elements (vertices, for example) in a perfectly circular disposition.

- **Curve:** Select an edge or a face and then use this tool to convert the straight edge loops to smooth curves. Use the Operator panel in the Tools Region to control the effects of this tool.

- **Flatten:** Select faces, edges, or vertices (a minimum of four), and this tool moves them to the same plane. Suppose that you created a surface mesh that's not planar. With this tool, you could select the entire surface and use the Flatten tool to make the surface flat.

- **Gstretch:** When you use the Grease Pencil to draw a curve, this tool distributes your selection along that curve.

Grease Pencil Basics

To use the Grease Pencil (which is mainly used for annotations in 3D View), press and hold down **D** while you left-click; then drag to draw. Press and hold down **D** while you right-click; then drag to erase the strokes. In the 3D View Properties Region, you'll find options for deleting or changing the parameters of the Grease Pencil layers. You can also access Grease Pencil tools from the Grease Pencil tab of the Tools Region in 3D View.

- **Loft:** This tool is very similar to the Bridge Edge Loops tool but goes a little further: It allows you to bridge more than two edge loops. Suppose that you have three circles. With Loft, you can select all of them and create a bridge from the first to the last, passing through the middle circle. The tool gives you the chance to control the shape in the middle of a bridge operation.

- **Relax:** This tool smoothes the selection and prevents sharp shapes. It's similar to the Smooth Vertex tool, but it respects the position of the border elements and relaxes only what's inside.

- **Space:** This tool spaces your selection so that the distances between all the selected elements are the same. Space is useful for technical modeling when you have several divisions made by hand and need them to be equally spaced.

Working with F2

F2 is a simple but useful add-on that comes bundled with Blender but needs to be enabled in User Preferences. This add-on adds some functionalities to the **F** key to increase the speed at which you can create new faces.

One of those functionalities allows you to select a corner vertex and press **F** to generate a new face from that corner. A different use is tricky to explain, but you can see it in Figure 6.28: Select two vertices and press **F** repeatedly to create new faces very quickly and fill the holes.

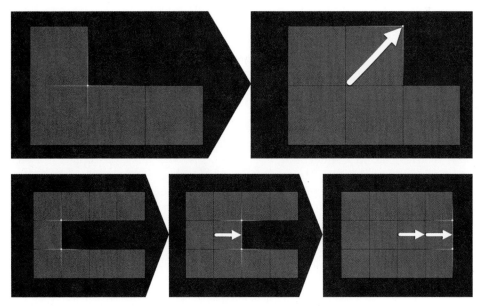

Figure 6.28   Each arrow in the image represents a press of the **F** key, and each row of images indicates the effect of the F2 add-on, depending on the selection and surrounding elements to which you apply it.

> **Tip**
>
> When you enable the F2 add-on in User Preferences, expand its menu, and you'll be able to activate the Auto Grab option. When Auto Grab is enabled, creating a face from a corner vertex automatically selects and grabs the generated vertex, allowing you to quickly relocate it. This option is especially handy when you're retopologizing a model.

Using Other Interesting Blender Options

In this section, you learn three tricks that make dealing with models simpler. You may not realize that these tools and features are available, but Blender provides them for you to work faster and more comfortably.

AutoMerge

The AutoMerge feature is very helpful in modeling. When you activate it, if you place a vertex in another vertex's location, AutoMerge automatically merges those vertices.

   If you activate the Snapping tool as well (or just set it to Vertex Snap and press **Ctrl** when you want to merge), when you move one vertex near another one, the vertex you're moving snaps to the second vertex's location, making merging very fast and straightforward.

   This technique is similar to using welding tools in other 3D packages. You can activate AutoMerge from the Mesh menu and in the 3D View header.

> **Tip**
>
> While in Edit Mode, you can find the option for Doubles Threshold inside the Options tab of the Tools Region. This distance is the minimum distance at which you need to drop a vertex from another to make the vertices merge when AutoMerge is enabled. Increase that value if you want to AutoMerge vertices without using the snapping tools; the vertices will merge when you drop them at a distance smaller than the threshold.

Hide and Reveal

Hide and Reveal is very useful. You can select a part of your mesh and press **H** to hide it so that it's not in the way while you work on other parts of the model that may be hidden. When you're done, press **Alt+H** to reveal all the parts of the model that you've hidden. Also, you can hide what is unselected by pressing **Shift+H**.

   This feature is not only helpful for hiding certain parts or making them visible, but it also allows for selective adjustments. Suppose that you want to create a loop cut. Normally, doing so affects the entire edge ring. But if you want the loop cut to affect only part of the edge ring, you can hide some of the ring's parts, and the tool affects only the parts that remain visible. Hide and Reveal also works this way with most of the modeling tools, so take advantage of it!

Snapping

Just as in Object Mode, you can activate the snapping tools on the 3D View header and select the type of snapping you want: Vertex, Face, Increments, and so on. If the Snap tool is active, when you move things around, they snap to close elements, which is really useful when making alignments. In addition, while pressing **Ctrl**, you can move the selected elements freely. Alternatively, if Snap is disabled when you press **Ctrl**, things snap while you move them.

Summary

In this chapter, you learned about the main Blender modeling tools: what their effects are, how to use them, and how to adjust their options when they are applied to your mesh. This information should give you a head start on modeling, and you should be able to create simple models and use these tools to modify and shape your meshes. You also learned that you can perform almost all these actions by using keyboard shortcuts. (You can also access these tools through the menus and reference their keyboard shortcuts from those menus.) Remembering all the shortcuts may be difficult at first, but in the long run, you'll be thankful for knowing them, because they allow you to work a lot faster!

Exercises

1. Try every modeling tool in this chapter on some simple objects.
2. Model a very simple object that Jim can use in his adventures (such as a flashlight). Figure out which tools to use, how to use them, and in which order.

7

Character Modeling

It's finally time to start modeling Jim! In this chapter, you learn about topology and some of the most popular modeling methods; then you'll set up the reference images you created so that you can model over them. Finally, step by step, you model every part of Jim's body. This phase is one of the most crucial phases of the project because it defines the shape and look of the character with which you're going to work in the chapters to come.

What Is Mesh Topology?

Mesh topology is the way in which edges are distributed along the surface of a model. Two surfaces can have identical shapes but different topologies. Topology is important because it affects how the mesh subdivides (using a Subdivision Surface modifier) and deforms. It is especially critical for animated characters. When a character moves, the model is deformed. A good topology ensures that deformations look natural; otherwise, the mesh will pinch, stretch, or just deform incorrectly and look weird.

In Figure 7.1, you see two topology examples, one good and one bad. (These examples are exaggerated and are meant just to illustrate how a shape can be created with a badly distributed topology.) In the example on the left, the topology is poor: Most of the edge loops run only vertically and horizontally, and they don't really adapt to the face's shape, which will certainly cause problems when, for example, you want to make the character open its mouth. In the example on the right, the topology is much better: Edge loops flow with the face's shape and define it correctly.

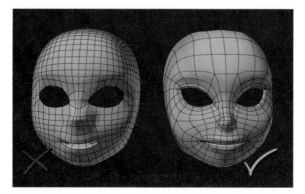

Figure 7.1 An example of poor topology (left) and good topology (right)

Think of *topology* as being the skin and the muscles of a face or other body part. Depending on how they will deform, they need to follow the shapes of the model; otherwise, the skin will have serious problems.

Here are some things you should keep in mind to make sure that you have a good topology:

- **Use four-sided faces (quads) as often as you can.** Avoid the use of triangles or n-gons unless you really have a good reason to use them. Triangles and n-gons, when used carelessly, can generate pinches in the surface when the model is subdivided and deformed. This doesn't mean that you can't use triangles and n-gons—just that you need to know where they can be used without causing problems. These elements tend to be problematic on curved surfaces, but on a flat surface, you generally can use them without issues.

- **Use squares rather than rectangles.** Overall, if you're working with organic shapes, four-sided faces won't have the same length on all four sides, so try to avoid using really long rectangles, as they'll be difficult to manage during deformations and other stages of the animation process that follow modeling. Try to keep your topology as uniform as possible.

- **Keep an eye on areas that require complex deformations.** Some parts of a model are more complex than others, not just because of their shape, but because when they're animated, you'll probably need a wide range of movement for them. The edge flow should be especially good in those areas to make sure the model will deform correctly later. The eyelids, shoulders, knees, elbows, hips, and mouth are some areas to which you should pay close attention to a good topology and perhaps even include more faces to provide additional geometry for more-defined deformations. Generally, for simple characters, using three edge loops in the articulations works quite well: a loop for the articulation itself and one on each side of it.

- **Keep a low poly count.** *Poly count* refers to the number of polygons (usually measured in triangles, as any polygon can be divided into triangles) that form a model. More polygons mean more work in all the stages of modeling, which could result in difficulties if you have to change something. As a rule of thumb, keep the number of polygons to the minimum needed to achieve the shape and the level of detail you want for your model.

- **Pay attention to density and tension.** When you're using a Subdivision Surface modifier, it's very important to keep an eye on density and tension. Subdivisions tend to smooth the surface, but sometimes, you want to create a corner. In that case, you need to add more density (more geometry). If you have low density, you have more tension; the shape becomes stretched when subdivided because there's not enough geometry, so the edge loops move further from their original positions. Use density and tension to your benefit. Remember that more density defines the shape better because it reduces tension (but also requires more geometry).

- ▪ **Follow the shapes.** Your edges should flow with the shapes. Around the mouth, for example, you should have circular loops that create a smooth deformation when the character opens its mouth or talks. If those loops are vertical and horizontal lines, chances are that your character will look cubical and quite strange when it opens its mouth—the usual pitfall when you start modeling and don't yet have control of your edge flow.

> **Note**
>
> Topology is a complex subject, and an entire book could be written about it. Techniques for achieving good edge flow and using n-gons and triangles correctly would fill hundreds of pages. If you're interested in learning more about mesh topology, look for resources on the Internet. A lot of great articles and websites are available to you!

Choosing Modeling Methods

Modeling can seem rather technical (as it really is), but it offers a lot of freedom and creativity. Quite a few methods and techniques are available to explore and use as you need them. Some of them may be more comfortable for you to work with than others, or you may want to pick a method based on the type of model you're working on. This section presents some of the most popular methods you can use.

Box Modeling

Box modeling is based on the premise that you can model anything from a simple primitive, such as a cube, sphere, or cylinder. Don't be fooled by its name: The *box* in *box modeling* means only that the most essential shape can be the base for any kind of object. The idea behind this method is that if you start from a primitive, you can divide it, extrude it, and otherwise modify it to reach the shape you want.

With box modeling, you start from something very basic and, little by little, add details to it. From the beginning, your model has the basic shape it needs, so you have to add only as many details as you want. You can compare box modeling with sculpting in mud; you start with a raw general shape and then gradually add details. You move vertices around, add modifiers to achieve various effects, and smooth the surface with a Subdivision Surface modifier.

Poly to Poly

Poly to poly (also called poly2poly) is about drawing a shape one polygon at a time. You create vertices and edges, extrude them, and join them to make faces, constructing the model as though you were building a brick wall. Again, you add a Subdivision Surface modifier to smooth the geometry you created.

Sculpt and Retopologize

Although box modeling and poly to poly are probably the most traditional modeling methods, sculpting came to the 3D just a few years ago and is now widely used, especially for organic models. With sculpting, you create a basic shape; topology doesn't matter much. Then you sculpt it, adjust the shape, and add a lot of detail to it. After that, you can use the *retopo* (short for *retopology* or *retopologize*) process, which involves creating the final topology for the model with a poly-to-poly method, but the new geometry snaps to the shape you sculpted initially.

This method is by far the most creative modeling method, and artists love it. It allows you to focus on the shapes of your model and not have to think about a lot of technical stuff. Only when you're happy with your shapes do you worry about topology, which you create very easily because you don't have to think about whether the shapes will look right as you already have them covered in your sculpture!

Modifiers

Using modifiers is not a method in itself, but modifiers play a big role in modeling in a lot of cases. Suppose that you're modeling a character. You can model one side of it and use a Mirror modifier so that the opposite side simultaneously builds itself, mirroring the one on which you're working. You can speed your work by using modifiers. If you have to work on a complex curved model, for example, make it in a plane and then deform it along a curve with a modifier. Modifiers help a lot, and in some cases, they're essential to the construction of your model, so they deserve a mention here.

The Best Method

If you thought that this section would tell you the best method to use in modeling, I'm sorry: There is no *best* method. Each person is more comfortable with certain methods than with others, depending on his or her skills and spatial vision, the particular project, and so on. Some people switch among methods as needed. Are you modeling a car? Use box modeling. Creating a monster? Try Blender's Sculpt and Retopo features.

The most powerful thing to keep in mind is that you can mix all possible methods (only some of the most popular ones for character creation are mentioned here) in the same model! You can model one part with box modeling, another with poly to poly, and the most organic parts with sculpting. You can even adjust the shapes of your character by using Sculpt Mode when you have the basic topology in place and then go back to working with box modeling.

The possibilities are endless, and that's why 3D modeling—even though it requires some technical knowledge—can be a very enjoyable and creative process.

Setting Up the Reference Planes

Before you start modeling, you need to load into your scene the character designs you created in Chapter 5, "Character Design," as background images to use as references while modeling. This design definitely helps you define the right proportions of your character, Jim.

Some people prefer to load references in planes that they can see when they rotate the camera around the scene. You can do this by adding planes in the views you need to show and then adding the images to those planes as a texture. This technique can be a little tricky (especially before you learn to use materials in later chapters), but Blender offers easier ways to use reference images:

- Open the folder in which you store your images, and drag them into 3D View. When the images are loaded into the scene, you may need to adjust them a little. You can go to the Background Images menu in the 3D View Properties Region to make any necessary adjustments.

- Go to the 3D View Properties Region, scroll to the Background Images panel (see Figure 7.2), and turn the feature on to load your images.

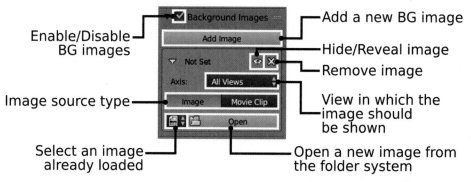

Figure 7.2   Background Images panel in the 3D View Properties region

- Create an empty in your scene (select the type Image for your empty). Then, on the Empty tab of the Properties Editor, load an image, and control its size and transparency as needed. (This option is great because it allows you to see the image even if you are in wireframe display mode.)

From the Background Images panel, you can load an image and decide the view in which it will be visible. After you load your image, you'll be able to adjust its position, size, and opacity.

Note

These background images in 3D View are visible only when you're using a predefined orthographic view, such as Front, Right, Back, or Top; they won't work if you're in a Perspective View or a random orthographic point of view. If you have a NumPad, press **5** to switch between Perspective and Orthographic views; otherwise, you can switch views from the View menu on the 3D View header.

Load the reference images for the front, side, and back of the head into their corresponding views so that you can see them in the background while you're building Jim's head (see Figure 7.3).

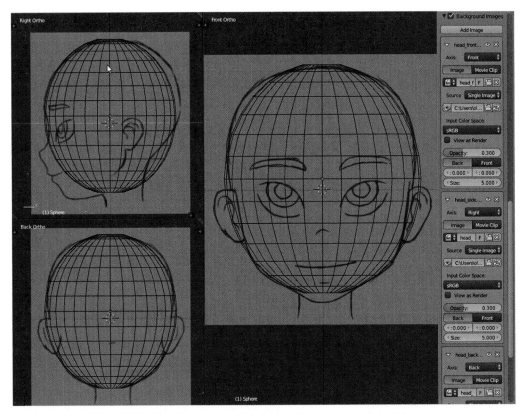

Figure 7.3   The three views with their reference background images

Caution

It's very important for the reference images to be properly aligned. In this case, all the images have the same height, and the front and back images are centered. In some cases, however, the images can have different sizes or margins, so you may need to adjust the scale and position from the Background Images menu in the 3D View Properties Region. To help with those adjustments, you can use a very simple mesh that allows you to compare the size and position of the images with those of the 3D model. In Figure 7.3, you can see that a sphere was used to make sure that Jim's head references are properly aligned. Remember that the drawings are not physically accurate, so leave some space for modifications to the images, as it's very difficult to make the 3D model fit the 2D images perfectly.

2D Versus 3D

Keep in mind that 2D drawings have incongruences in volume and shape, so it's perfectly normal for the 3D model not to totally fit the image references, or at least not to fit all views. 2D references are just that: references. Don't stress if your 3D model doesn't fit the references in all the views. The most important thing is to focus on the shape of the 3D model and whether it looks good, regardless of its accuracy with the reference images.

Modeling the Eyes

Each person is most comfortable beginning to model in a different way. Some people prefer to start with the face; others, with the body. For Jim, start with the eyes, because that way, you'll be able to use them as references when modeling the rest of the face—especially the eyelids, because you'll be able to align those features with the eyes.

Creating an Eyeball

Jim's eyes are drawn in an animation/manga style (not completely round). The eyes are basically spherical, but to make them a little more realistic, you can create the cornea with the pupil beneath it. Figure 7.4 shows the process step by step, and an explanation of what happens in each step follows:

1. In Object Mode, create a UV Sphere, and in the Operator panel, set it to have 16 segments and 16 rings.

2. Rotate the sphere 90 degrees on the X-axis so that the poles are positioned at the front and back. This way, you'll be able to use the circular edge loops on the front pole to build the pupil.

3. Enter Edit Mode by pressing **Tab**. Select the two edge loops of the front pole and the pole vertex. A quick way to do this is to select the vertex in the pole and then press **Ctrl + NumPad +** to grow the selection twice.

4. Press **Shift+D** to duplicate the geometry you selected in Step 3, and move the new geometry out a little (or, for now, hide it by pressing **H**). Later, this geometry will become the eye's cornea.

5. Select the same geometry you selected in Step 3 from the sphere and extrude it into the eye by pressing **E**.

6. Scale the selected geometry to invert its curvature by pressing **S**, pressing **Y** to scale on the Y-axis, and then typing **–1**. Press **Enter** to confirm. Then adjust the position of this geometry on the Y-axis so that it fits into the eye in case the geometry moved out of alignment when you inverted it.

7. Select the outer edge loop of that inverted circular area and bevel it (**Ctrl+B**) to add some density and create a defined corner when you add the Subdivision Surface modifier later.

8. Press **Alt+H** to unhide everything and see the cornea you previously detached. Move it back to its place and scale it up a bit if needed to cover the gaps that you made when beveling the borders of the pupil.

9. Add a Subdivision Surface modifier with two divisions. Go to Object Mode, and in the Tools Region, click the Smooth option so that the eyeball doesn't show the edges of all the flat faces.

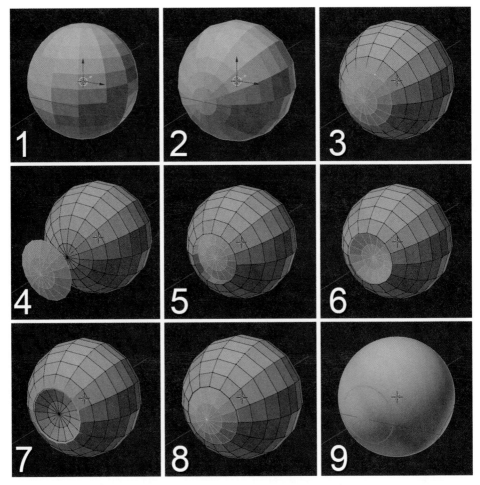

Figure 7.4   Steps for creating the eyeballs

Note

For this exercise, the lamp and the camera are on different layers. Press **M**; select one of the squares; and then, on the 3D View header, turn those squares (layers) on and off. You learn more about layers in future chapters. Alternatively, you can delete the lamp and the camera to get them out of the way. If you do, though, you'll need to re-create them when you need them again.

Using Lattices to Deform the Eyeballs

Now you have one eyeball, but it's completely round; in the reference designs for Jim, the eyes are more oval. Fortunately, Blender has a tool called Lattice that lets you deform geometry and then maintain that deformation when you rotate the geometry, which is exactly what you need for these eyeballs. You could go ahead and scale the eye on the Y-axis to make it flatter, but when the eye moves during animation, it won't fit the eye socket. Figure 7.5 shows the effects of the Lattice modifier.

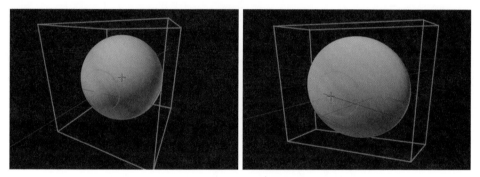

Figure 7.5   A lattice (left) and how it squeezes the eyeball when its points are moved (right)

Follow these steps to apply a Lattice modifier to the eyeball:

1. Press **Shift+A**, and create a lattice.
2. Scale up the lattice so that it covers the entire eyeball.
3. Select the eyeball, and add a Lattice modifier to it. It's best to add it on top of the Subdivision Surface modifier; that way, the lattice will deform the low-resolution mesh and the deformed mesh will be subdivided afterward so it works more smoothly.
4. From the Lattice modifier options, in the Object field, select the name of the lattice you created in Step 1.
5. Select the lattice; press **Tab** to enter Edit Mode; and see how, as you move its vertices, the eyeball deforms accordingly.
6. Select all the vertices (press **A**), and scale them down on the Y-axis.

7. Pick the outer side's edges to better align the eye with the side view.

8. Exit Edit Mode, and rotate the eyeball object. It should rotate while keeping the lattice deformation in place, which is exactly what you need.

Mirroring and Adjusting the Eyes

You've made one eyeball, but Jim needs two! First, you need to align the existing eyeball with one of the eyes in the background image. Keep in mind that because the lattice is now deforming the eyeball, you need to select both eyeball and lattice to move them together. To create the second eyeball, duplicate and mirror the first one (see Figure 7.6).

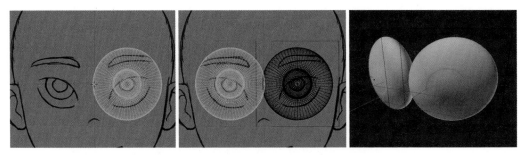

Figure 7.6   Aligning the eyeball (left), mirroring a second
eyeball (center), and the result in 3D (right)

Here are the steps to adjust and mirror the eyeball:

1. Select the eyeball and the lattice.

2. Move and scale the eyeball and lattice to adjust them to the shape and size of the drawn eye in the front view. Adjust their positions in the side view as well. Don't worry if they don't fit perfectly.

3. When the first eyeball is aligned, make sure to place the 3D cursor in the center of the scene. You can press **Shift+S** and select the Cursor to Center option, or you can press **Shift+C**.

4. Press **Shift+D** to duplicate the eyeball and its lattice. Right-click to cancel the movement and leave the new eyeball and lattice in the same exact locations as the originals.

5. Press **.** (period) on your keyboard to set the pivot point in the 3D cursor.

6. Press **Ctrl+M** to enter Mirror Mode. This mode makes the current pivot point the mirror plane (which is why you should use the 3D cursor for mirroring; otherwise, you'd be mirroring from the selection's origin).

7. Press **X**, **Y**, or **Z** to select the axis of the mirror. In this case, press **X**; the new eyeball and its lattice should move right into place (refer to Figure 7.6). Press **Enter** to confirm this action. Remember to set the pivot point to Median Point (**Ctrl + ,**) or to Bounding Box Center (**,**) before you continue working.

> **Caution**
>
> When using this mirroring method (**Ctrl+M**), you may find that sometimes, it gives you unwanted, weird results, such as not mirroring in the expected way. Usually, you've rotated or negatively scaled that object, and its axes are not correctly aligned with the world space. If you find yourself in this situation, select the object before mirroring, press **Ctrl+A** to apply Rotation and Scale, and try again. This technique should solve the problem.

Modeling the Face

Now that Jim has a good pair of eyes, it's time to start modeling a cool face to support those eyes! Throughout this stage, you use box modeling to create the face so that you can get a good idea of how this method works.

Studying the Face's Topology

You may remember from Chapter 4, "Project Overview," how important the preproduction phase is for a project. It's also important for any modeling task, and the face is one of the trickiest parts of the body to model, so it needs really good preparation. It's useful to look at the reference drawings you created and study the topology that could work for the face so that you'll have an idea of how to model before you begin, which is a much better approach than modeling on the fly! Figure 7.7 shows a topology study for Jim's face, with quick sketches over the reference drawings.

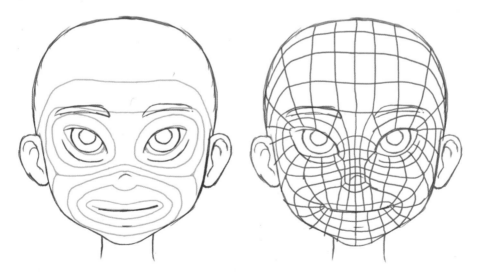

Figure 7.7   A representation of the edge flow around the main areas of the face, such as the eyes, nose, and mouth (left), and a drawing of a possible topology (right)

> **Note**
>
> Modeling a face is one of the most difficult topics discussed in this book and one of the most difficult parts of the character-creation process. Don't worry if you don't get it right on the first try; modeling takes practice, determination, and skill. Also remember that the following steps represent the key moments of the modeling process. Between steps, when you're modeling something organic, like Jim's face, you need to move vertices to make the new geometry define the correct shape. Organic modeling requires constantly adjusting the positions of vertices. Vertices won't magically snap to where they should be; it's your task to tell Blender where you want them.

Blocking the Face's Basic Shape

In this section, you start by blocking the face. Blocking is the first stage of creating a model, animation, painting, or any other artistic endeavor. It is the stage in which you define, quickly and roughly, how something will look; you're not paying a lot of attention to detail, just defining the base. In this case, for example, blocking consists of creating the basic shape and geometry of the face to which you'll add definition in later steps.

Blocking is useful because it's the part of the process in which making substantial changes is easier and faster, so during this stage, you can experiment with different modeling ideas.

> **Tip**
>
> Remember that keeping your scene organized is important. Now that you'll start creating a lot of new objects, it's a good idea to name them intuitively so that the names actually represent the objects that they belong to and generally avoid default names such as Plane.001 and Sphere.013.

In Figure 7.8, you see the first steps for modeling the face, which you use to create the basic shape. Explanations of the steps follow:

1. Create a cube, go to Edit Mode, and use Loop Cut and Slide (**Ctrl+R**) to divide the cube as shown in the first image: three vertical divisions for the front of the face, one horizontal division through the front and sides of the face, and one vertical division for the sides of the face. These edge loops will help you set the basic shape of the face in the first stages. The reason for three vertical lines in the front is that you need additional details for the mouth and the eyes.

2. Select all vertices by pressing **A**, and select the Smooth Vertices tool in the Tools Region or the Vertices menu (**Ctrl+V**). When smoothing is applied, increase its iterations in the Operator panel. The idea is to get a more spherical shape. Now scale the entire shape to make it approximately fit the size of the head in the reference images.

3. From the front view, select the vertices of the left section of the mesh (negative X) and delete them so that you're left with only half of the face model. Next, add a Mirror modifier; the default settings should be enough to make the mirroring work. Activate the Clipping option in the modifier so that the vertices in the middle are prevented from jumping to the opposite half of the mirror center. At this point, you can work on half of the face, and those changes will automatically be reflected on the other side.

4. Use proportional editing (press **O** to enable/disable it) to adjust the shape of the geometry to fit the reference images of the head. The eyes should be placed on the horizontal line in the front. At the bottom of the head, the faces in the back will be the base for the neck.

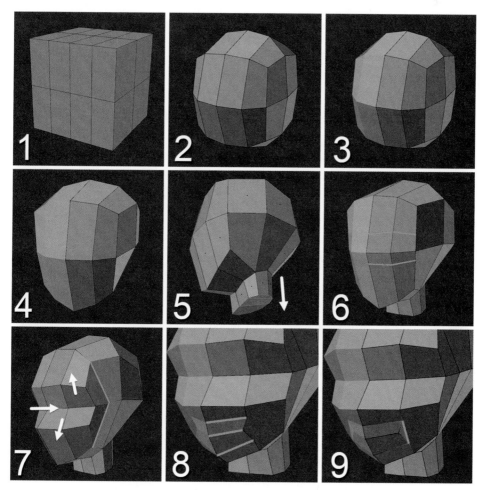

Figure 7.8   First steps of modeling Jim's face

5. Select the faces in that back area and extrude them to create the neck. To form the neck, adjust the vertices so that they look round. At this stage, you'll be defining the basic shape, so avoid cubic shapes. Otherwise, as you start adding details, those cubic shapes will be more noticeable, and it will be more difficult to arrange them properly at that later stage.

6. With the Knife tool (**K**), make a couple of cuts in the front, as highlighted in the sixth image in Figure 7.8. You're left with three edge loops.

7. Move the three edge loops to fit Jim's face. The top one will define the eyebrows, the middle one will determine the center of the eyes, and the bottom one will establish the nose and cheeks. After that, using the Knife tool again, make the cuts highlighted in the seventh image in Figure 7.8 to end up with a round face loop that surrounds the face.

8. Perform three cuts in the mouth area, and move them as needed. The middle one will establish the mouth, the bottom one can help define the chin, and the top one will mark the area of the mouth near the nose.

9. Join the side vertices of the edges above and below the mouth to form a triangle in the corner of the mouth.

Defining the Face's Shapes

After completing the blocking stage, in which you created the face's basic shape, you add some definition to the geometry.

Figure 7.9 shows the next steps of the face's modeling process, with a step-by-step explanation following:

10. Using the Knife tool, cut the triangle generated in the mouth's corner in Step 9, and create two new edge loops to connect the mouth with the cheek and the jaw. Now the loop around the mouth is composed of quads (four-sided faces).

11. Select the mouth's edge, bevel it just a little (**Ctrl+B**), and delete the new geometry so that you can make the mouth's opening and the area surrounding it with circular loops formed of quads.

12. Select the vertex in the middle of the eye, and bevel it with the Bevel Vertices tool (**Shift+Ctrl+B**). Then move the resulting vertices to make a shape similar to the eye in your reference images.

> **Tip**
>
> When you're adjusting your mesh to the reference images, it's best to overestimate the shapes' sizes and make them a little bigger. The reason is that as you add more and more details, some of those vertices will be divided, causing the shapes to shrink. The same thing can happen when you apply a Subdivision Surface modifier; when you smooth shapes, they shrink.

13. Perform several cuts around the eye with the Knife tool, as highlighted in the corresponding image. This step gives you more vertices to define the eye's shape, as well as some additional cuts to start defining the nose's geometry.

14. A side of the eye was not cut in Step 13, so cut it now. Keep the cut going to the top of the head, and end it with a corner pointing toward the mirror center. You only need the loop in the front of the head; this way, you can end the loop where it's no longer needed.

15. Using the Loop Cut and Slide tool (**Ctrl+R**), add a new loop from the mouth corner all around the face, and adjust its shape and the surrounding vertices.

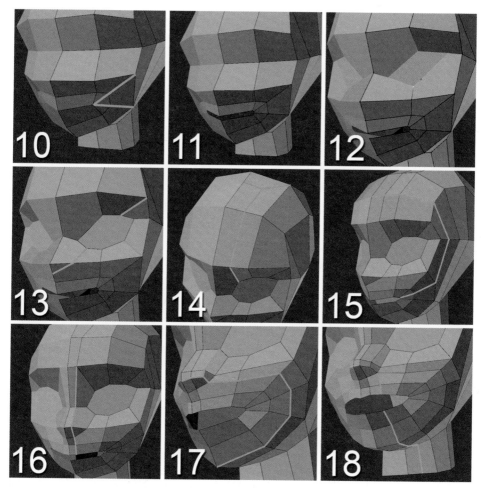

Figure 7.9   Continuing with the face modeling

> **Tip**
>
> When you add a new loop to an organic shape with the Loop Cut and Slide tool (**Ctrl+R**), you can take advantage of the Smooth option in the Operator panel to make the new loop less rigid and flat between the two existing loops. Also, when you have an area with quite a few vertices, you can select all of them and use the Smooth Vertices tool to smooth all of them at the same time.

16. Cut a line from the eyebrow to the mouth, and define the nose a little more.

17. Make a new cut from the eye down to the nose, and join it with a new loop around the mouth area. Adjust the shapes, and you have the geometry necessary to create the nostrils.

18. Create some new edges from the bottom of the neck to the mouth and then from the nose to the mouth. (This cut turns the n-gon between the nose and the mouth into two quads.) Move things around a little to adapt the new vertices to the reference images. Then you're ready to add some more details and create the lips.

Defining the Eyes, Mouth, and Nose

Little by little, Jim's face is starting to take shape! The next steps, shown in Figure 7.10, add definition to the eyes, mouth, and nose:

19. Select the mouth's loop, extrude it, and adjust the vertices to get the lips' shapes, according to the reference images.

20. Press **Ctrl+R**, and add a new loop to the lips to add more detail to that area. You can probably inflate the lips by adjusting the Loop Cut and Slide Smooth options in the Operator panel. At this point, you can add a Subdivision Surface modifier to the mesh and enable it from time to time to make sure that the geometry is behaving correctly when it's smoothed.

21. Select the outer loop of the lips, and press **Ctrl+B** to add a bevel to it. Then slide the vertices near the mouth's corners to separate them a little more than the other vertices in those loops. This step adds density and defines a corner at the border of the lips when you add a Subdivision Surface modifier. Separating the vertices near the mouth corners makes those areas smoother, and the central area of the lips has more definition, as its loops are closer together. (Remember that if the vertices are close together, the subdivisions look more like corners, whereas if the vertices have more space between them, subdivisions are smoother.)

22. Select the n-gon of the eye, and press **I** to inset and create the base of the eyelids.

23. Unhide the eyes, and adjust the eyelids' geometry to the eyeball's surface. Proportional Editing can help with this task. Leave a space between the eyelids and the eyeball. To do this, you can move the camera around and keep adjusting the vertices from different points of view until they look good.

24. Select the inner loop of the eyelids, and extrude it to fill in the space between the eyelid and the eyeball.

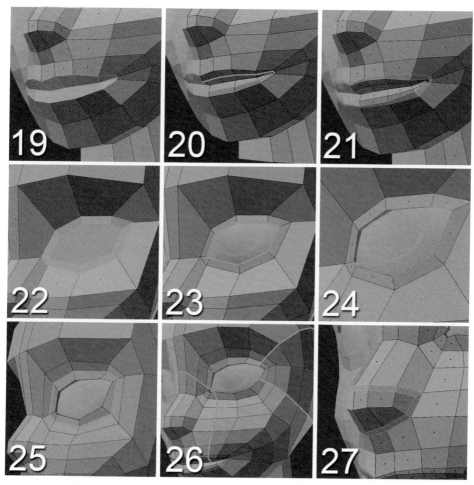

Figure 7.10   Adding more definition to the eyes and the mouth

25. Select the outer loop of the eyeball, and slide the vertex out to make some space for a new loop to help define the eyelids a little more.

26. In the eye area, add some more loops by pressing **Ctrl+R** to define the section between the nose and the forehead, the corner of the eye to the mouth, and from the eye toward the side of the head. Then adjust the vertices to the reference images, and make sure that the shape blends smoothly with the rest of the head (with no unwanted bulges or holes).

27. Select the bottom of the nose and the nostril faces. Inset them and turn the Boundary option off (you'll find it in the Operator panel) so that the nose's front faces don't inset in the center.

> **Tip**
>
> While you model, try to plan how you'll perform the next steps. If you have in mind what the final topology will look like, you can add loops and vertices to achieve that specific goal. Modeling blindly is possible, but you'll probably lose some time figuring things out. Sometimes, you'll have to delete certain parts and rebuild them to create a better topology.

Adding Ears

The face is almost done! Figure 7.11 shows steps that add more details to Jim's face. At this stage, you add the ears and define the neck and head a little more.

28. Move the nose vertices to define the shape of the nose. Turn on the Subdivision Surface modifier to see how the model looks when subdivisions are enabled. You may want to play with the nose geometry; in this case, as the design presents a pretty stylized character, you're not going to model the nostrils.

    > **Note**
    >
    > While you are working on the model, it's useful to enable the Subdivision Surface modifier from time to time to see whether the geometry behaves correctly when subdivided. Also, this modifier provides several display modes (the four buttons located at the top of the modifier panel), and the last two are really helpful for this stage. One of these modes allows you to see the subdivided model in Edit Mode while you keep working on the original mesh as though it were a cage for the subdivided model. The last mode lets you work on the subdivided model without displaying the original mesh cage (an option that, in some situations, can be useful and intuitive).
    >
    > You can also switch among the subdivision levels of the selected objects very quickly by pressing **Ctrl+1**, replacing the number 1 as needed with any other number to define the subdivision level. If you press **Ctrl+0**, you get 0 subdivisions, so this keyboard shortcut is the equivalent of disabling the modifier if it gets in the way while you're modeling. Press **Ctrl+2** to display two subdivisions.

29. Go to the side of the head, and create a new loop from the neck to the top of the head. The highlighted faces are going to serve as a base from which to extrude the ear. Ears are quite tricky, but in this case, you're making an anime design, so create a simple ear—one that is not very realistic but fits the overall look of the character.

30. Inset the selection to create the base for the ear.

31. Extrude the shape, and adjust it to resemble an ear.

32. Make an inset within the ear.

33. Extrude and shape the highlighted areas to define those parts of the ear.

34. Add a new extrusion to create the ear canal, and arrange those vertices a little. Don't worry if the geometry looks weird; just keep an eye on the subdivided mesh, because when it's smoothed, it will look quite different.

35. Cut a new loop in the neck to create a bit more geometry between the torso and the base of the head.

Tip

In the images that accompany the modeling steps, you're seeing the low-resolution mesh so that you can get a clear idea of how the polygons and vertices work. At this point in the process, however, you should be working with the subdivided mesh to get a peek at how it looks (even if you enable it only from time to time).

36. Keep adding more loops in the areas where you'd like to have more detail. In the image for this step, the two loops that were added to the mesh are highlighted. One loop is at the bottom of the neck, and it's extruded so that later, you won't see an empty space under Jim's jacket. Also, a clean loop surrounds the entire face, which you can think of as being a division to extract a mask from the face.

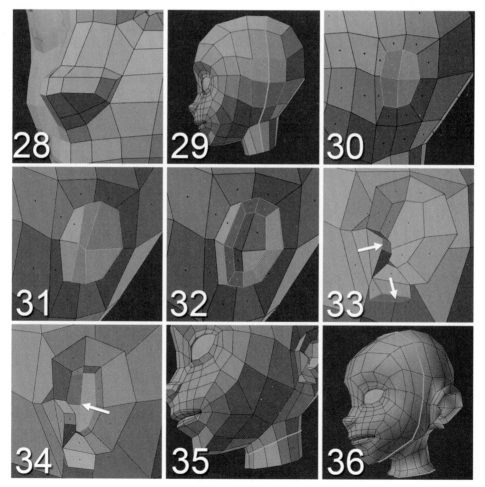

Figure 7.11   More adjustments and details to create the ears

Building the Inside of the Mouth

In this section, you add the final details to Jim's head. The face is looking good, but you need to create the interior of the mouth so that when Jim opens his mouth, you won't see empty space or the back of his head! Look at Figure 7.12, and follow these final steps:

37. Select the inner lips' loop, and extrude it into the head.

> **Tip**
>
> Remember that you can select what you want to keep in the view and press **Shift+H** to hide the unselected geometry. In these images, the rest of the head has been hidden so that you can clearly see what's going on.

38. Add some loops to better define a rounded area inside the mouth. Most important, add a loop near the inner lips; otherwise, they'll lose some shape when subdivided due to high tension in the geometry. Don't worry if the geometry overlaps a bit in the inner-lips area.

39. Close the back of the hole, and refine the shapes a little. You can add another loop near the inner lips so that the inside of the mouth in that area is more vertical; this addition creates some space for the teeth later.

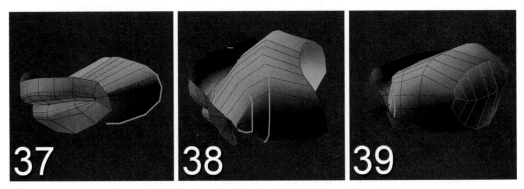

Figure 7.12   Creating the inside of the mouth so that
it isn't empty space and Jim can open it

You're done modeling Jim's face! In Figure 7.13, you see the result. The face is often one of the trickiest parts of modeling a character. You get used to seeing faces, and a character's face immediately looks wrong if something is out of place, so achieving a pleasing result can be difficult.

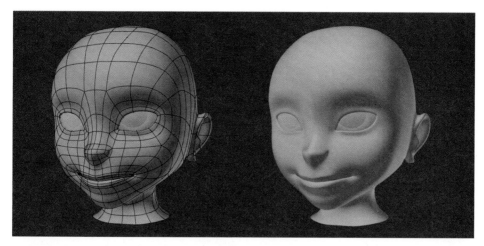

Figure 7.13   The topology for Jim's face (left) and the final subdivided result (right)

Modeling the Torso and Arms

Up to this point, you've been working on the face, but now you switch to the body, which means that the face's reference images in the background are not useful anymore. You can go to the Background Images panel in the 3D View Properties Region, delete the images, and load the full-body references; alternatively, you can replace the head references with the full-body references. But this time, you do something different: In the side view, modify the reference image so that the feet are touching the floor (increase the Y position value), and copy that Y value to the front and back reference images (see Figure 7.14).

The first thing you notice is that the face is really big and out of proportion, so select everything you created so far (face, eyes, and lattices), move them, and scale them to make them fit the new references. The head should now be in place, and you should have space to start working on Jim's body.

There is another problem you'll have to work out, which I created on purpose so you'd have an opportunity to play with your imagination a little and confront a situation you may encounter at some point in your own projects. Jim's designs show the character's arms in a pose slightly different from what you're actually going to model. Sometimes, arms are modeled in what is often called a *T pose*: completely extended and parallel to the floor. Although the T pose is appropriate for modeling purposes (if everything is aligned to one of the 3D world's axes, it's easier to manipulate), it may not be the best thing for the model in future stages. If you create the arms completely extended and parallel to the floor, when they are deformed, you could have issues with the shoulders due to their large rotation range.

In Jim's case, the shoulder area has some details in the jacket, so you should create the arms slightly flexed at about 45 degrees or so. Whether you rotate the arms up or down, the deformation won't be really big, and Blender will keep those details. So in this situation, the reference images show something a little different. As a result, you'll have to create your model in a slightly different pose, but don't worry; during the process, you'll learn a couple of useful tricks that will help you do this.

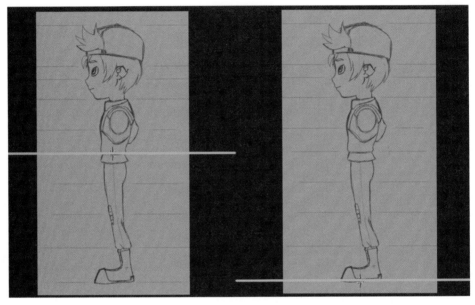

Figure 7.14   Jim's side reference floor position after you import it (left) and after you slide it up until the feet are touching the floor (right)

Modeling the Basic Shapes for the Torso and Arms

To start, block the shapes for Jim's torso and arms. In Figure 7.15, you see the first steps of the process. Because the face was modeled with box modeling, you have a chance to see how poly to poly works at this stage, even though it will be combined with box modeling at some points.

1. Create a circle with 12 vertices, delete the left half, add a Mirror modifier to it (similar to what you did when you started working on the face), and place it in the base of the neck area. Enabling the Clipping option of the Mirror modifier helps keep the central vertices of the torso in the mirror plane and prevents them from crossing to the reflected side.

2. Perform three extrusions (**E**), each one using two edges of the circle (two edges at the front, two at the back, and two at the side). The two frontal edges define the front of the torso, the two side edges draw the trapezoids that go to the shoulders, and the two edges in the back extend to the hips and define the back.

3. Use the Loop Cut and Slide (**Ctrl+R**) tool to divide the trapezoid; then select the front and back outer edges, and extrude them down. Next, select the four vertices that have an empty space between them, and press **F** to create a face in that space. Do the same with the empty spaces in the front and the back.

4. Select the side middle vertex of the shoulder, extrude it down to the hips, select the vertices, and press **F** to fill the vertices with faces. At this point, you have the envelope of the torso.

5. Make three horizontal loop cuts through the torso, and adjust the shapes to the reference images. Keep an eye on the highlighted faces; you should be giving them the shape from which the arm will be extruded.

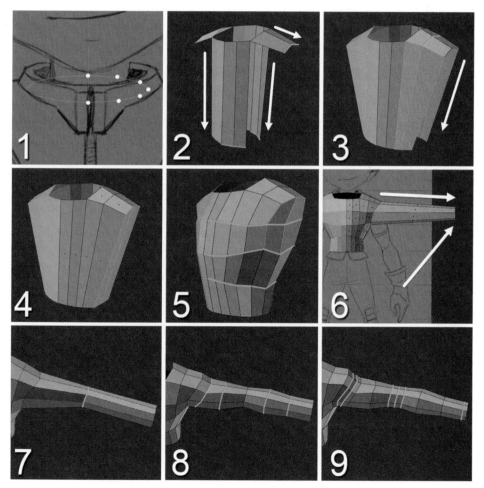

Figure 7.15   First steps in modeling Jim's torso and arms

6. Select the faces you highlighted in Step 5, and extrude them horizontally to create the entire arm down to the wrist.

> **Tip**
>
> Even if you extrude the arm completely horizontally (on the X-axis), use the arm in the reference as a guide. Imagine where the wrist would be if the arm were extended in a T pose. Later, you'll pose the arm better, but now it's easier to work with it aligned to one axis (X, in this case). Also, the shape of the wrist will be a little irregular, so after the extrusion, you can scale its vertices to 0 on the X-axis; from the front view, it now looks flat.

7. Cut a new loop in the middle of the arm, and adjust it a little to define the elbow. From the top view, move the loop back just a bit, as though the arm were slightly flexed. This step helps you achieve the arm's shape. Keep in mind that you should rarely have the arms extended completely straight at 90 degrees, as that would look unnatural.

8. To continue defining the arm's shape, add some new loops (**Ctrl+R**) in the biceps and forearm areas. Each time you add a loop, move the vertices around a little; if you add a lot of loops and try to modify the shape later, the process will be more difficult.

> **Tip**
>
> You have a lot of ways to model shapes like arms or legs. One good way is to extrude (in the case of an arm) from the shoulder to the wrist and then cut the elbow, divide the biceps and forearm, and keep dividing until you're happy with the result. This way, first you'll have the general shape of the arm and then you'll define the main articulation, which will have two divisions, then four, and then eight. This method is easiest for me to use in modeling and it's better for developing details little by little than extruding the shape piece by piece.

9. Add more loops in the articulation areas, such as the shoulders and the elbow. It's important to have enough geometry in those areas that they can deform correctly later. Remember that three loops in each articulation are often enough (at least for simple characters). You should also add another loop near the wrist to define the shape better when it's subdivided. As with the face, now is a good time to add a Subdivision Surface modifier and start checking on how the subdivided model will look.

Defining the Arms and Torso

In this section, you add more definition to the arms and torso, and you begin to add Jim's backpack. Continue with the next steps, shown in Figure 7.16:

10. Add some more loops and definition to the arms.

11. Select the faces surrounding the elbow area. You want to add some definition to the elbow to make sure that when Jim flexes his arm, the elbow responds accordingly.

12. Make an inset (**I**) in those faces, and use the sliding tools (select a vertex or edge and press **G** twice) to make the loops around the elbow rounded. Also, select the face in the middle of the elbow loops (the one highlighted in the image) and move it out a little bit to give the outside of the elbow a little bulge.

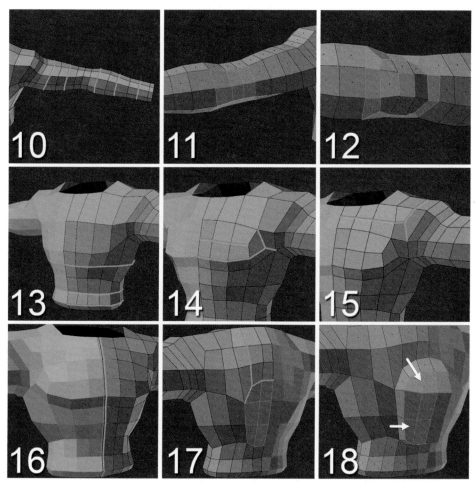

Figure 7.16   Continuing with the torso-modeling process

13. Go back to the torso, and add some loops to define the waist area.

14. Using the Knife tool (**K**), make a few cuts similar to those shown in the image, and adjust the new geometry to define the pectoral area.

> **Tip**
>
> If you really want a character's model to be awesome, work on the topology for the muscles in the arms and torso as you did for the face. In this specific model, the muscles are not very defined, and the jacket deformations will be pretty simple, so you can get away with topologies that are less complex.

15. With the Knife tool, cut some new edges around the neck and near the shoulder to add a new loop in that area. (In the image, you can see only the front part of the torso, but the cut is exactly the same as the one you use to model the back of the torso.)

16. Make two cuts vertically near the frontal mirror plane to create the zipper for the jacket. Pull the inner cut and the mirror vertices in to create that indentation.

17. Jump to the back side of the model. If you haven't done anything to it yet, adjust the shape of the vertices there according to the reference images. Create the cut indicated in the image, and adjust the highlighted faces, which will serve as a base for the backpack.

18. Extrude the selected faces for the backpack, and adjust the shapes.

Detailing the Backpack and Jacket

Next, you add detail to Jim's jacket and backpack. Continue with the steps, shown in Figure 7.17:

19. Select the edges that comprise the corners of the backpack, and bevel them (**Ctrl+B**). Some triangles may appear (they're marked with red circles in the image); you have to get rid of them. Two of the triangles are easy to remove; they are triangles with an adjacent n-gon, generated because more than four faces shared a vertex.

20. Select the edge between one of the triangles and the n-gon and simply collapse it, so that the resulting geometry is an edge instead of a triangle (marked with light green circles in the image). The third triangle is a little trickier, because if you take it out, you also take out some of the detail added by the bevel. In this case, add a new loop to the side of the triangle that is facing the beveled faces, and slightly move the fourth vertex created with the new loop. This way, adding a few more faces to the model, you end up with a quad instead of a triangle.

21. Select all the arm's vertices except those near the shoulder. Place the 3D cursor in the shoulder, and use the Proportional Editing tool to rotate the arm to relax it a bit. Also select the four faces at the end of the arm (the wrist), and delete them. These faces won't be visible and won't be useful later, so it's a good idea to get them out of the way now.

> **Note**
>
> This step uses a very nice utility of the 3D cursor that allows you to pose characters that don't yet have a skeleton! Just place the cursor in the articulation and select the part of the body you want to move, and with the help of the Proportional Editing tool, you'll be able to pose your character pretty well. (Keep in mind, though, that you may need to adjust the vertices around the articulations after these operations.)

22. Create a few extrusions to make up the shape of the flap at the bottom of the jacket.

23. With all the faces of the flap selected, press **Ctrl+F** to access the Face menu, and use the Solidify tool to add some thickness to the flap. In the image, the thickness is highlighted.

24. The thickness you added using Solidify in the previous step also created faces at the top of the flap that are not very useful and can even cause some problems when the mesh is subdivided, as they're welded onto the backs of other polygons. Delete those faces now. In the image, the faces are highlighted in a view from the jacket's

interior, looking down. Also, Solidify doesn't recognize the mirror's clipping in the back part of the jacket's flap, and it generated a few faces that crossed the mirror plane and created some intersections. Get rid of those faces as well.

25. Add a new loop at the bottom of the flap so that when the model is subdivided, it has more density and is more defined. You can merge (**Alt+M**) the bottom vertex of the zipper with the top vertex in the same area that the Solidify tool created so that you don't have an empty area.

26. Select all the faces around the waist to create a new object for the belt. Press **Shift+D** to duplicate, and right-click to leave the duplicated faces in their original positions. Next, press **P**, and choose the Selected option; this option sends those duplicated faces to a new object that you'll be able to modify.

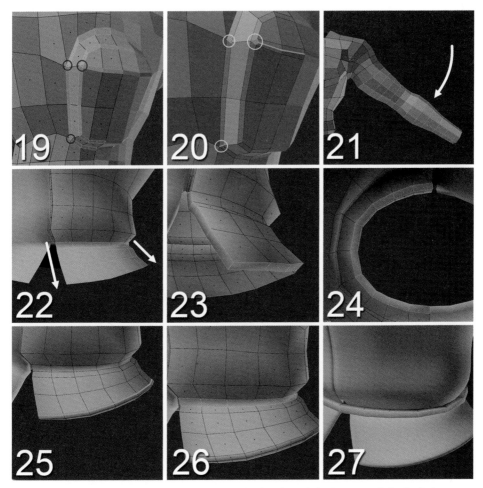

Figure 7.17   Adding some details to the back and the bottom of the jacket

27. Select the new object, and in Edit Mode (**Tab**), select the edge in the middle at the front and move it to the left until it attaches to the other side of the belt. Select all the object's faces, press **Alt+E** to extrude, and select the Region (Vertex Normals) option.

> **Note**
>
> When you duplicate an object or use the Separate tool to move a set of polygons from one object to another, the new object keeps the original object's modifiers.

Finishing the Belt and Adding a Neck to the Jacket

The jacket is almost finished, but you have to add a little more detail to the belt, and the jacket needs a neck. Follow these steps to model these features, as shown in Figure 7.18:

28. Select the top and bottom edges of the belt, and bevel them so that they'll look sharper when you subdivide them.

> **Tip**
>
> If you want to focus only on these details, you can hide the jacket itself so that it's not in the way while you work. Just select it and press **H** to hide it. Press **Alt+H** to unhide everything when you've finished.

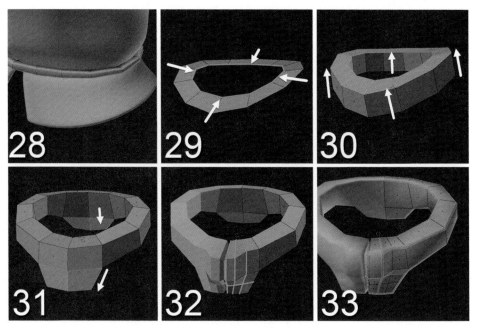

Figure 7.18   Modeling the jacket's neck details

29. Place the 3D cursor in the neck area, and create a circle. (Even though you could create the circle inside the jacket itself, for now, it may be better to create a new object so that you can treat the jacket and its neck separately.) Similar to what you did when you started modeling the jacket, make it with 12 vertices, delete the left-side vertices, and add a Mirror modifier to the object with the Clipping option enabled. Then move the vertices to form the shape of the jacket's neck. Select all the edges of that circle, and extrude them in.

30. Select all the faces, and extrude them up. You have the base shape of the jacket's neck.

31. Temporarily unhide the jacket and the head to adjust the shape of the jacket's neck to them, and perform the two extrusions shown in the image to add details to the neck.

32. Add a few loops to create the neck's front shape and the zipper.

33. When you add the Subdivision Surface modifier (which you can always add and enable/disable at any time to start checking the shapes), bevel the borders of the shape so that they are more defined. Also, watch the subdivided model, and adjust the shapes to make them fit Jim's head and body.

Modeling the Legs

Modeling the legs is pretty easy compared with everything you've done so far. The process is similar to the one you used for the arms, but you need to create the hips first, with a base from which you can extrude the legs. Figure 7.19 shows the steps you need to follow to model Jim's legs:

1. Create another circle with 12 sides, delete the left half of the circle, and add a Mirror modifier with the Clipping option enabled. Make two extrusions, and shape the model to look like hips.

2. Select the middle edges in the bottom of the model at the front and back sides of the hips, and create a face between them by pressing **F**. From this face, you'll create the crotch.

3. Divide the face you created in Step 2 by using the Loop Cut and Slide tool (**Ctrl+L**), and add three divisions. Move the divisions down, and adjust them to shape the crotch. At this point, the model should resemble underwear.

4. Select the loop around the hole that should be the top of the thigh, and extrude it down to the tops of the ankles, where the boots will start. The same adjustments you made in the arms apply here. Instead of following the legs' current orientation exactly, make them a little more perpendicular to the floor (more vertically aligned).

5. As you did to define the elbow, cut a loop for the knee, and adjust its vertices according to the reference images.

6. Add some more loops to the leg, and keep adjusting their shapes. Remember to add at least three loops for the hip and knee articulations so that you can deform them properly later when flexing the legs.

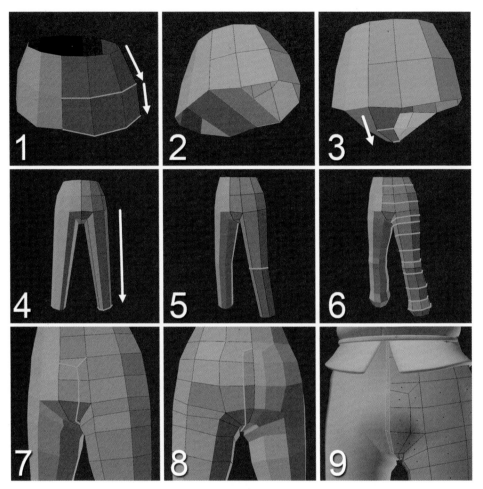

Figure 7.19   Steps for modeling Jim's hips and legs

7. With the Knife tool (**K**), cut a shape similar to the one displayed in the image, both to add some definition to the crotch area and to add some geometry there to make sure that it will deform properly, as that area is very close to the articulations of the legs.

8. Do something similar for the back of the trousers, but give this area a slightly different shape to resemble the buttocks.

9. Create a new loop in the center of the pants to make up the seam in the cloth. This step can be a little tricky, and you can use either of two methods.

   The first method is to press **Ctrl+R** to cut a new loop and then slide the vertices near the mirror plane. At the bottom of the crotch near the legs, the new loop is very close to the others surrounding it; at the front, the loop is farther from the others, as there is more space. You could always press **E** when using the Loop Cut and Slide tool to even the distances to the mirror plane edges.

The second method is to disable the clipping option for the Mirror modifier, move the central vertices apart, activate the mirror clipping again, and extrude those vertices to the middle. This way, both loops are completely vertical and become welded into a single loop at the center. Then pick the central loop and scale it (**Alt+S**) slightly to the inside, but very subtly.

At this point, unhide the rest of the objects, and make sure that the trousers fit well inside the jacket's bottom flaps.

Tip

Sometimes, when you model using the poly-to-poly method, you may see some faces that are darkened or have edges with strange dark and light colors. When that happens, the normals of those faces usually are looking in opposite directions. Remember that a face's normal determines the direction in which the face is oriented, and it's important for all connected faces to be facing the same direction. You have two options to solve the issue. First, from the Face menu (**Ctrl+F**), select Flip Normals to invert the normal of the selected faces. Second, if you select several faces, you can press **Ctrl+N** to let Blender automatically calculate the direction in which all the normals should be facing; it conforms all of them to look in the same direction.

Modeling the Boots

Jim needs some feet to stand on, of course. In this section, you model the boots. Figure 7.20 shows the steps for doing so. At this point, you should be getting up to speed, and you're probably becoming more proficient with modeling and using Blender's tools, so the boots should be an easy task! Follow these steps:

1. Create an eight-sided circle at the top of the boots, as shown in the reference images. Keep in mind that you need two boots. You can add a Mirror modifier to get the second boot (place the origin of the boot in the center so both boots will be aligned), or you can manually duplicate and mirror the first boot.

   ### Tip

   You can use a little trick to save some time: Select the bottom loop (**Alt+RMB**) of the trousers where they meet the boots, duplicate it (**Shift+D**), and separate it (**P**) into a different object that will become the boots. This way, you'll already have the Subdivided Surface and Mirror modifiers added to the new object, and you also have a shape to start modeling from.

2. Extrude (**E**) all the edges down to the ankle, and perform a couple of loop cuts to define the shape.

3. Select all the edges from the circle at the bottom except the two in front, and extrude them down to the heel. Then select the two in front, and make two extrusions to create the toe shape.

4. Create a face in the empty space at both sides of the boot.

5. Fill the sole of the boot with quads.

> **Tip**
>
> One reason why you should work with even numbers (such as eight sides for the initial circle) is that you can usually fill empty spaces with quads quite easily. On the contrary, if you start with uneven numbers, you'll end up being forced to use triangles to fill the holes.

6. Add some loops to start defining the boot's shape.

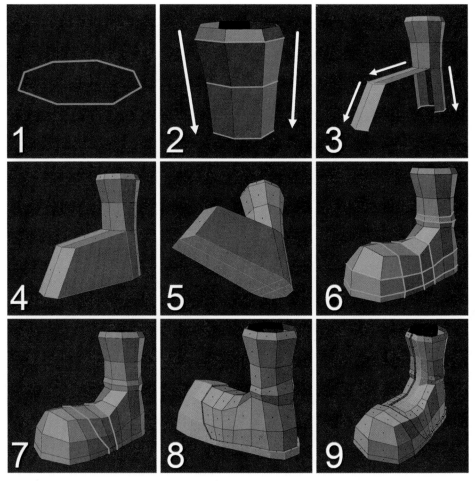

Figure 7.20   Steps for modeling Jim's boots

7. Perform a couple of loop cuts (**Ctrl+R**) to add definition in the articulation of the foot (recall that you added several loops at the knee and ankle articulations) so that deformations will work well later. One of these loops also helps you create the shapes of some of the details in the next step.

8. Select the area highlighted in the image (leave the sole of the boot unselected), extrude it (**E**), right-click to cancel the movement, and scale in the normal with **Alt+S**. You can also extrude by pressing **Alt+E** and selecting the Extrude (Vertex Normals) option, which draws the boot's details.

9. Finish the details with a few minor operations. Select the two central face loops that go from the top almost to the toe, and create an inset (**I**) there; then extrude the inset in to define the area where the shoelaces will be once the textures are in place. (See Chapter 9, "Painting Textures," to learn how to paint textures.) Also, when you extrude, two faces will be generated at the top of the boot with the same thickness as the extrusion, and you can delete them. As a finishing touch, add some loops to the thickness of the seams and small features to make them much more defined when subdivided. Last but not least, adjust the shapes of the boots where they meet the trousers. Some deforming may be needed; don't hesitate to use the Proportional Editing tools for that purpose.

Modeling the Hands

Hands are quite difficult to model, but I keep this example simple so that you can learn an easy method. (If something goes wrong, don't worry; just start again. Sooner or later, you'll get it right!)

Building the Basic Hand Shape

Figure 7.21 shows the modeling process for a hand. You can model it wherever you want and move and scale it later to fit the rest of the model.

1. Start by creating a cube.

2. Make the cube narrower, and move one of the edges to the middle of what will be the palm of the hand. The diagonal face left there will serve as the base for the thumb.

3. Add two loop cuts, one near the wrist and another one near the fingers. The fingers will be in the top part of the shape.

> **Tip**
> Remember to keep adjusting the vertices as you add them. The sooner you make adjustments, the easier the modeling process will be when you add vertices.

4. Select the base face, and extrude it to create the preliminary shape for the thumb.

5. Select everything, and from the Specials menu (**W**), select the Subdivide Smooth tool to add geometry. Notice that in the figure, the vertices have been distributed in a way that forms the four finger bases at the top of the palm.

> **Caution**
>
> People commit two major errors when modeling hands at this stage: They model so that the thumb grows from the side of the hand instead of partially from the front, and they make the other four fingers all start at the same height instead of having an arch in the knuckles area. Both of these errors can make the hand look very unnatural.

6. Delete the top faces (the base for the fingers), and on the back of the hand, add two cuts so that you end up with the same four bases for the fingers.

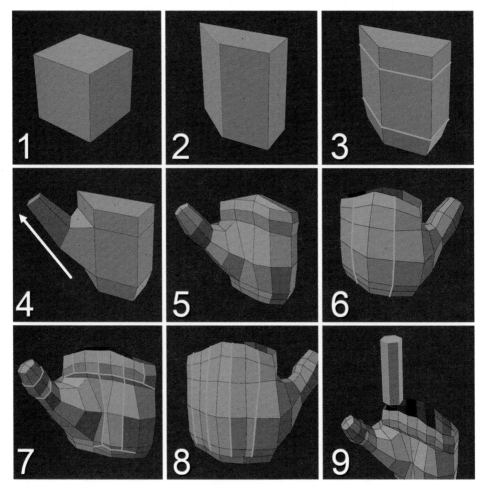

Figure 7.21   Steps for modeling Jim's hand

7. Make some cuts, as shown in the image. The purpose of these cuts is to create two edges on each side of the hand to prepare the geometry for connecting the fingers later. The outer cuts are made in such a way that they stay at the top of the hand; the central cuts go almost to the wrist to help define the shapes of the palm. Also, add a couple of loops to the thumb to give it some detail.

8. Make some similar cuts on the back of the hand to help define the tendons and knuckles. Look at how the cuts end before reaching the wrist, which allows you to extrude the flap of the glove with fewer edges later and then arrange the topology with the Knife tool.

9. On the top of the hand, create a cylinder with six vertices (and fill the top with an n–gon). This cylinder will serve as a preliminary shape for the fingers. You'll model one of the fingers and then duplicate and modify those duplicates to create the other fingers.

Adding the Fingers and Wrist

As you've realized by now, modeling hands is quite challenging, and it's difficult to get them right. Follow the steps shown in Figure 7.22 to add the fingers and wrist, and to finish the hand modeling. From time to time, it's a good idea to add a Subdivision Surface modifier to take a look at the smooth shape that results.

10. Make a few cuts in the finger to define the articulations. Join two vertices at the top to convert the n–gon to two quads. You can delete the n–gon at the bottom, as you won't need it.

11. Add some more loops to the finger, and define its shape.

12. Select the entire finger (you can select groups of connected faces by pressing **L**), and duplicate it three times. Move, scale, and adjust the duplicates to fit on the hand.

13. Activate AutoMerge (on the 3D View header near the Snapping options or in the Mesh menu), and use the vertex snapping tools to drag the vertices at the bottom of the fingers to the corresponding vertices at the top of the hand. Then adjust the vertices to make the fingers look natural. Also, add another loop at the base of the thumb.

14. Extrude the base of the hand down to create the shape for the glove's wrist flap.

> **Tip**
>
> The extruded edges may not be as circular as they should be. If you activate the LoopTools add-on, you can use the Circle tool to select that loop and converted it to a perfect circle. Then you can scale it and adjust it to become an oval that is more typical for a wrist.

15. Add two loop cuts to the flap to define the shapes a little more.

16. Remember those unfinished cuts from Step 8? Use the Knife tool (**K**) to arrange them, making some cuts similar to the ones shown in Step 16's image. Then, if the shape gets a little messy, you can select the entire area and use the Smooth Vertices option.

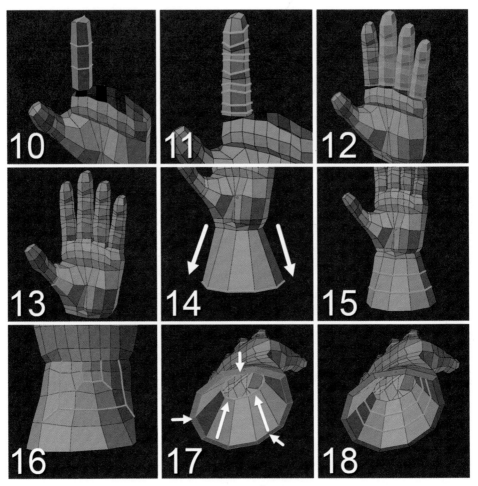

Figure 7.22   Final steps in modeling Jim's hand

17. Select the bottom loop of the flap, extrude it slightly to add some thickness to the glove, and extrude it up again to the interior of the wrist. This step prevents an empty space between the arm mesh and the glove.

18. Add a couple of divisions to the interior of the flap so that if you need to deform it, you'll have enough geometry.

At this point, you may want to adjust the overall shape of the hand. Unhide the rest of the models (if you hid them previously); scale, rotate, and move the hand to place it where it needs to be according to the arm; and make sure that it has the right scale. When the hand is in place, you can mirror it on the other side. You can use the same procedure you used for the eyes. Select the hand (in Object Mode; you can also press **Ctrl+A** to apply the rotation and scale to ensure that the hand mirrors as expected), press **Shift+C** to place the 3D cursor in the center of the model, press **.** (period) to set the pivot point to the 3D cursor, press **Ctrl+M** to mirror, and press **X** to select the mirror axis. Finally, press **Enter** to confirm. Figure 7.23 shows the results up to this point.

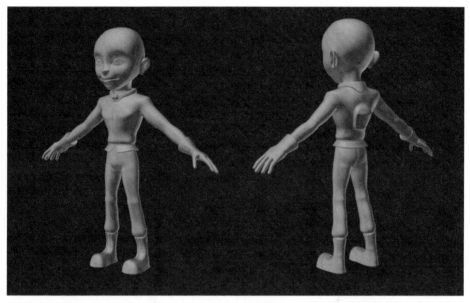

Figure 7.23   This is what Jim looks like so far. Only a few more details are needed.

Modeling the Cap

Next, you create Jim's cap. Modeling the cap should be easy, but it involves a few tricky steps.

Creating the Base of the Cap

Here are the first steps in building Jim's cap (shown in Figure 7.24):

1. Create a UV Sphere with eight vertices and six rings. Delete the bottom and left sections of the sphere, and add a Mirror modifier. Scale the object on the Z-axis so that it's no longer perfectly spherical.

2. Convert the selected faces from triangles to quads by using the Dissolve Faces tool (**X**). Repeatedly select two adjacent triangles and invoke the Dissolve Faces tool until all the triangles are converted to quads. (You can also press **F** for a similar effect.) You can also add a Subdivision Surface modifier.

3. With the Knife tool (**K**), make two cuts through the cap, similar to those in the image. The two cuts should be very close to each other so that when the model is subdivided, the seam will be sharp. At the top of the cap, the inner line touches the center of the mirror, and the other line continues through the cap's center to its other side.

4. Perform a loop cut, and adjust the resulting vertices to smooth the cap's shape.

5. On the back side of the cap, delete the two central faces at the bottom.

6. Go back to the front side, and extrude the front edges at the bottom to create the cap's visor.

7. Move the central faces of the cap up a little to make the visor bend up in the middle. Also, add a new loop near the bottom all around the cap's body. Add a Solidify modifier before the Subdivision Surface modifier in the stack, and adjust its thickness until it looks right to you.

8. Select the visor's faces, and press **P** to separate them from the cap's body. Doing this after adding the modifiers to the original model gives you the modifiers in this new model as well.

9. Add some new loops near all the visor's borders to help define its shapes.

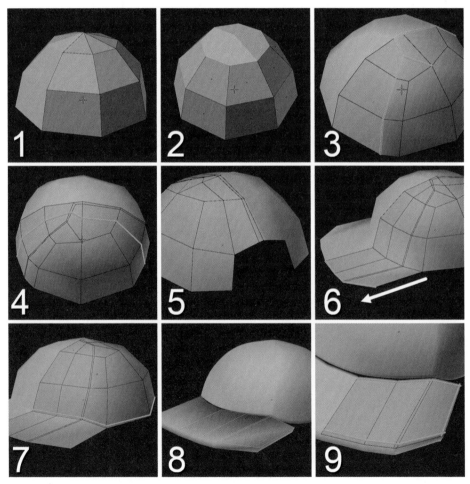

Figure 7.24   The first steps in modeling Jim's cap

Adding Details to the Cap

Now that you have the cap's base and visor, keep going and add some details to them. Follow these steps (shown in Figure 7.25):

10. Move the sides of the cap's visor back until there is no empty space between them and the cap's body.

11. Create a little sphere, scale it on the Z-axis, and place it at the top of the cap.

12. Go back to the cap's body, and use the Knife tool (**K**) to create a new loop around the hole at the back of the cap. If you have to create some triangles to perform that cut, do so, and merge the vertices afterward to leave only quads. Also, create a new loop at the bottom of the cap.

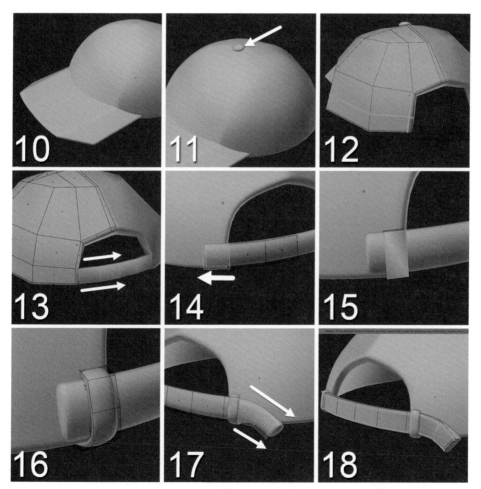

Figure 7.25   Adding some cool details to Jim's cap

13. Make an extrusion to create the strap on the back of the hat, and divide it once to give it more definition.

14. Select the two strap faces, and separate them to a different object by pressing **P** and choosing the Selection option. Make one extrusion to the left, adjust it to the cap, and cut a loop very close to the outer edge so that the shape will become more defined when you subdivide it.

15. Select one of those outer faces of the strap, duplicate it (**Shift+D**), and separate it to a different object (**P**). You'll use this face as the support for the strap.

16. Make some extrusions and cuts to create something similar to what you see in the image. You may also need to adjust the Solidify modifier's thickness.

> **Tip**
>
> Keep in mind that in the modifiers' options, you can activate the Subdivision Surface and the Solidify modifiers to see their effects while you're in Edit Mode, which gives you instant feedback while you're modeling.

17. Make one side of the strap a little loose. If you're in Edit Mode, switch to Object Mode by pressing **Tab**, and apply the Mirror modifier. (You can apply modifiers only when you're in Object Mode. After a modifier is applied, its effect is part of the object's original mesh.) After you apply the Mirror modifier, return to Edit Mode, and perform some extrusions on one side of the strap. Move and rotate the extrusions so that they hang down a bit.

18. At the top and bottom of the strap, add two loop cuts (**Ctrl+R**) so that the shape is much more defined when subdivided. Another thing you can do at this point is select every object that will be part of the cap and then select the cap's body. Press **Ctrl+P**, and choose Object from the pop-up menu. This step connects all the objects to the cap's body in a parenting operation. Now you need only select and move the cap's body; the rest of the pieces follow.

The cap is finished, so you just have to move it, scale it, and place it on top of Jim's head. Follow the reference images to do that, or at this advanced point of the modeling process, ignore the references and place the cap where you think it fits best!

Modeling the Hair

Modeling hair is very complex. You have a lot of ways to create hair, each one of them producing different results. You can model hair with flat surfaces, each one of them representing a lock of hair, perhaps with a texture applied to them. Another option, which is the most realistic, is to use locks of hair. Select the areas of the head that you want to have hair, and Blender generates hair that you'll be able to comb, cut, and style. After that, you can even simulate the effects of gravity or wind on hair, which is a pretty complex operation (and one that requires a powerful computer).

In this case, you'll be creating a mesh hair—basically, modeling the hair shapes manually with polygons and adapting the meshes to the character's hairstyle.

> **Tip**
>
> In 3D, there is a rule: If it won't be seen, don't create it! If Jim is always going to wear a cap, why should you create the hair under the cap? In this section, you create Jim's hair—but only the parts that will be visible.

Shaping Locks of Hair

In Figure 7.26, you see the basic steps to follow to start creating locks of hair:

1. Select the top faces of the head; the hair will be created from them. Duplicate them (**Shift+D**) and separate them into a new object (**P**). When the object is separated, apply the Mirror modifier (click the Apply button in the modifier's options), as from this point on, you'll be doing different things on each side of the head to make the hair look more realistic.

2. Delete some of the faces from the sides of the head to prevent every lock of hair from extruding from the same height on the scalp. (In the image, the Subdivide Surface modifier has been temporarily disabled so that you can better see what's going on, but it is enabled again in the following steps.)

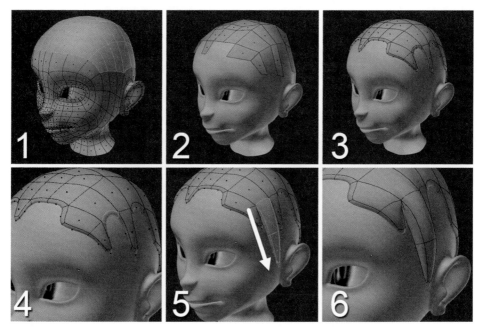

Figure 7.26   The first steps in creating Jim's hair

> **Tip**
>
> At this point, to make things a little easier, you can send all the objects you've cre-ated in the scene to one layer (press **M** and select one of the squares), the cap to a second layer, and the hair to a third layer. This technique allows you to work on the hair and show or hide the components of the cap very quickly (by pressing **Shift** to add a layer to or subtract a layer from those that are visible on the 3D View header). Keep in mind that you have to be in Object Mode to enable or disable layers, and you can use the numbers on your keyboard—not those on the NumPad—to show or hide layers quickly.

3. Select all the faces of the scalp, go to the Faces menu (**Ctrl+F**), and choose Solidify. Adjust the Solidify options. You may want to select everything again (**A**) to scale the new model up or down as needed to give the hair just enough thickness to stay on the head's surface.

4. Select some of the faces created by the thickness of the Solidify tool. You'll be extruding the locks of hair from those faces.

5. Make a couple of extrusions, and scale the final face down a lot so that it will look like a spike when subdivided. Adjust the vertices to reflect how you want the lock of hair to look. The lock in the image is adjusted to the face's surface.

6. Add some thickness to the lock by moving the edges that are on the lock's outer side.

Continue to do the same thing all around the head. Turn on the visibility of the cap layer now and then to see how the hair fits with it.

Adding Natural Details to the Hair

To make the hair look even more natural, take the locks of hair created in the preceding steps, and adjust their vertices and edges to make them overlap other locks of hair (see Figure 7.27).

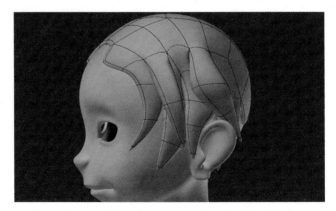

Figure 7.27   Overlapping locks make the hair look a lot more natural.

When you've created and overlapped locks of hair all around the head (which may take a while), you'll probably have some empty areas. To fill those areas, select a lock of hair, duplicate it several times, and adjust its vertices to layer it over other locks of hair, placing it above or below them (see Figure 7.28). Figure 7.29 shows you how the geometry of the hair looks so far.

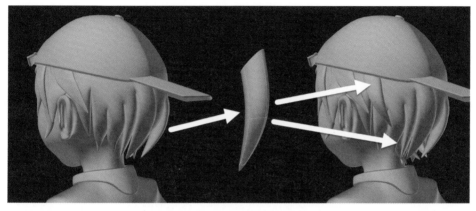

Figure 7.28   Duplicating locks of hair and placing them to cover empty spaces

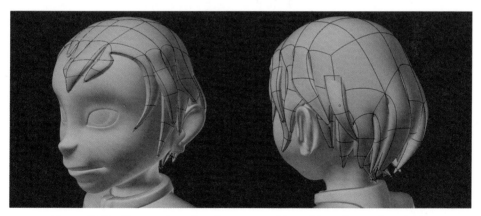

Figure 7.29   The result so far gives you an idea of how the vertices look.

Recall from the reference images that the cap is on backward, and the hair at the front of Jim's head that protrudes from the cap's hole will be a little tricky to model. You can select a lock of hair, similar to the one you duplicated before, and place it on the cap's hole. Add some loops to it, adjust it to fit the shape you want it to have, and make the lock large enough for its base to cover a good portion of the hole. After that, you can duplicate, scale, and rotate to adjust the lock of hair and cover some of the remaining parts of the hole, this time making the lock much smaller. Try to cover the hole with the big lock of hair and two or three of the smaller locks. In Figure 7.30, you see the result of adding that aspect of the hair.

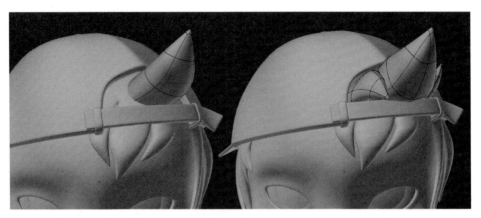

Figure 7.30   Adding the hair that will protrude from the hole in the cap

As you can see, modeling hair is not an easy task, especially because hair needs a lot of adjustments to fit to the head and the cap. But now it looks quite natural, so you're ready to move on and add the final details.

Modeling the Final Details

After all you have done throughout this chapter, you should already know how to use the modeling tools and should interact pretty well with meshes. In this last section, I briefly explain how I modeled some of these final details and added them to the previous models, but I don't provide any step-by-step instructions. The images show the results so that you can check them out and get ideas about other ways to work. Consider this section to be an exercise: Study the results, try to use your acquired knowledge about Blender modeling tools, and figure out how to model these final details on your own.

The details that are modeled in this section (and of course, you can create more if you want to) are the eyebrows, the communicator in Jim's ear, the badges for the chest and the cap, Jim's teeth and tongue, and a couple of details in the clothing.

Eyebrows

Creating the eyebrows was pretty simple. I selected three edges on top of the eye that had the eyebrow shape. I duplicated and separated them in a new mesh. I extruded the edges up to have some shape and thickness, and I moved the vertices around a little to create the eyebrow's shape. Then I applied a Solidify modifier with a little thickness before adding the Subdivide Surface modifier. It's important to keep an eye on the modifiers' order. If you apply Solidify after the Subdivide Surface modifier, the result will be different. In Figure 7.31, you can see what the eyebrows look like.

Figure 7.31   Jim's eyebrows added

> **Tip**
>
> For this detail and some of the details that follow, mixing several modifiers is quite helpful for achieving the results you need easily and quickly.

Communicator

The communicator earpiece was modeled from part of the ear. When you need to make one object fit another one, as in this case, it's a good idea to create the second object from a part of the first one, which ensures that the geometries fit together. Just select the faces of the ear that can be useful for the communicator and then duplicate and separate them, as you've already done several times. From the new object, model and give shape to the communicator, extruding, beveling, and using every kind of tool you need. The antenna (see Figure 7.32) was created with two cylinders.

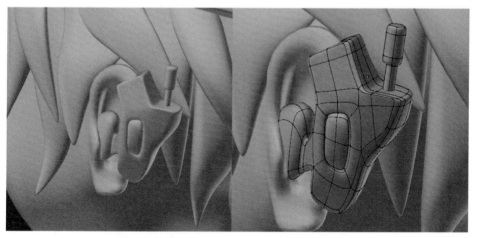

Figure 7.32   Communicator added to the ear

Badges

The badges take advantage of another modifier, Shrink Wrap, which lets you project an object over the surface of another object. Just add the modifier, and in the object's name field, select the one over which you want to project the Shrink Wrap modifier. (Alternatively, click the eyedropper next to the text field and then click the object to select it.)

Before doing that, move the badge, which is a simple flat object, to the surface on which you want to project it, such as over the chest. Play with the options for the Shrink Wrap modifier until you're happy with the projection, and then apply a Solidify modifier. What's cool about this feature is that if you applied thickness to the model, it would be lost in the projection with Shrink Wrap, but because the Solidify modifier adds thickness after the projection, it works perfectly!

Finally, add a Subdivision Surface modifier. Mixing modifiers to achieve a particular effect is a very powerful technique, as you see in Figure 7.33.

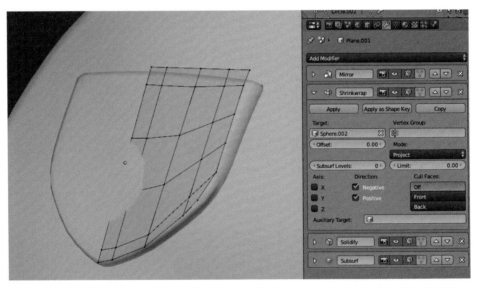

Figure 7.33   I used several modifiers to simplify the process of modeling the badge.

Teeth and Tongue

The teeth and the tongue are simple objects to model. Two curved surfaces with thickness will do for the teeth, and the tongue is also a very basic shape. In Figure 7.34, you see these features and their basic topology. In the figure, the teeth are apart so that you can see the tongue, but they're really touching inside Jim's mouth.

You should be able to do something similar with the skills you've learned so far. These features are not very complex, but are stylized to fit the rest of the character, so when Jim opens his mouth, you see something inside. When you are working on these models, you may want to adjust the shape of the inner mouth so that it doesn't cover the teeth or create other problems of intersecting geometry.

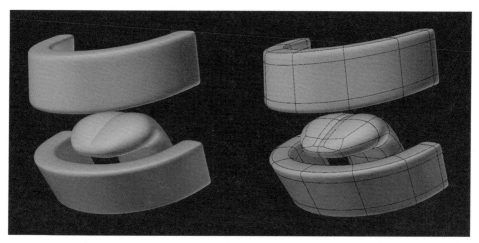

Figure 7.34   The teeth and the tongue, ready to go into Jim's mouth

Other Clothing Details

In the reference images, some details were added to the clothing. The technique I used was similar to the one I used for the eyebrows: duplicating and separating parts of the clothes, adjusting them, and applying modifiers such as Solidify to add some thickness.

In Figure 7.35, you see Jim up to this point. Looking good!

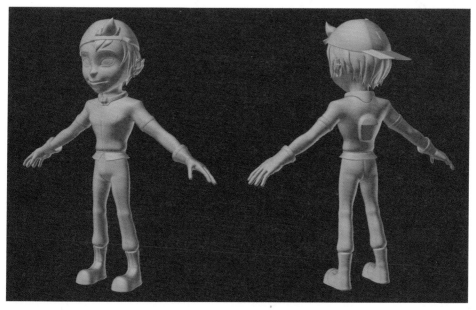

Figure 7.35   Jim is looking pretty cool!

Summary

Wow! This chapter was tough, but if you've come through it, you've learned a lot, for sure, and you should have your finished model. You know how to model the different parts of a character step by step, and (I hope) you've developed some insights into how to use Blender's modeling tools. Also, if you followed the instructions and tried to use the keyboard shortcuts, you may already be more efficient and able to remember a lot of the keystrokes for the basic tools. Modeling with polygons may be a technical task when it comes to topology, but if you find it interesting, it can be a very enjoyable experience. When you're done and see the finished model, of course, modeling is quite rewarding.

Exercises

1. Take the model further by adding some more details, such as lines on the cap or more details in the clothes.
2. Explain why having a good topology is essential for an animated model. List some rules to follow to ensure that you have a good topology.

IV

Unwrapping, Painting, and Shading

8 Unwrapping and UVs in Blender

9 Painting Textures

10 Materials and Shaders

8

Unwrapping and UVs in Blender

Unwrapping is a fundamental step in animation that comes before adding textures to a 3D model. Without it, the software wouldn't be able to get information to determine position, rotation, and scaling of the texture. *UVs* (the 2D counterparts of XYZs in 3D space) are the internal 2D positions of the vertices of a 3D mesh; they define how a 2D texture will be projected on the mesh's surface. One way to think of the unwrapping process is to visualize a globe. Imagine taking the Earth's surface and flattening it into a map. This process of converting a 3D shape to a 2D surface is referred to as *unwrapping*.

Unwrapping may look a little odd, and it's a task a lot of people dislike or fear, but that's usually due to their lack of understanding of how it works. Sometimes, unwrapping can indeed be a little tedious, but if you learn to like it, unwrapping can be a fun part of the process! Watching how everything starts to make sense and work properly can be a rewarding experience, but be aware: You'll need some patience.

Fortunately, Blender provides some helpful tools to unwrap your models, and people who come from other software usually love the way that the unwrapping process works in Blender. (There are even glowing reports from professionals working on Hollywood films who use Blender for UVs.) But as with almost everything else in Blender, unwrapping is done quite differently, so if you come from other software, forget the way you worked before, and open your mind for a little while!

Seeing How Unwrapping and UVs Work

Something tricky happens with textures, which define the colors of your models' surfaces: You have a 3D model, but the image texture is 2D. How do you "paint" a 3D model with a 2D texture? The answer is that you use UVs. The 3D model has its vertices located on the X, Y, and Z axes, but for Blender internally, they're on the U and V axes as well, and the U and V axes are 2D positions, made to be used for texture projection. In the UV/Image Editor, you can access those UVs and adjust them to define how a texture is projected onto a 3D model.

Unwrapping (also called *UV mapping*) is the process of adjusting an object's UVs so that the texture projection on the 3D model works properly. The process is probably easier to understand if you see how it works.

When you were a kid, did you take a piece of paper and, by cutting and folding it in a certain way, end up with a 3D shape, such as a cube? Unwrapping can be explained with that example, only in reverse order: You unfold a 3D model into a 2D shape by using the UV/Image Editor and then convert it to a plane. (Unwrapping won't affect the shapes in your 3D model at all; the process happens under the hood.) Figure 8.1 illustrates this procedure.

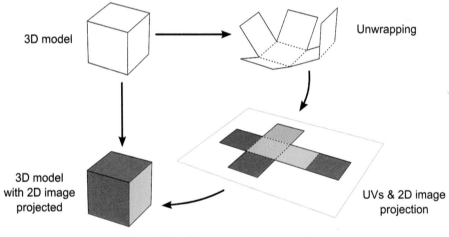

3D model

Unwrapping

3D model
with 2D image
projected

UVs & 2D image
projection

Figure 8.1   The unwrapping procedure

As you can see in the figure, unwrapping is like unfolding the 3D model and converting it to a 2D mesh. You can project an image onto that bidimensional mesh, and that projection will affect the 3D model itself.

Unwrapping in Blender

Now that you understand how unwrapping works, you can explore the tools that Blender provides to use unwrapping and the basic workflow of unwrapping.

To begin unwrapping in Blender, select the part of the model you want to unwrap, and access the unwrapping options (which I describe in the next section). When you unwrap the selection, it appears unfolded in the UV/Image Editor, where you can adjust the UVs, weld them to other parts of the model you've unwrapped before, or place them where you want them to be in the image.

Keep in mind that after unwrapping a model, you usually create textures tailored to those specific UVs. Sometimes, however, you're in a hurry, and you need to display part of an image in a specific position of the 3D model. In that case, you can adapt the UVs to the given image, not the other way around.

In the next section, you look at the different tools and find out how to use them. Then you see how to unwrap a basic model to understand the unwrapping procedures.

Using the UV/Image Editor

The UV/Image Editor is the part of the Blender interface where you can see and adjust the UVs. It's also useful when you want to load an image and use it for reference. Figure 8.2 shows an overview of the UV/Image Editor.

Tip

Loading an image into the UV/Image Editor can be as easy as dragging it from a folder on your hard drive. Drag the image file over the UV/Image Editor and drop it. Blender should load it immediately.

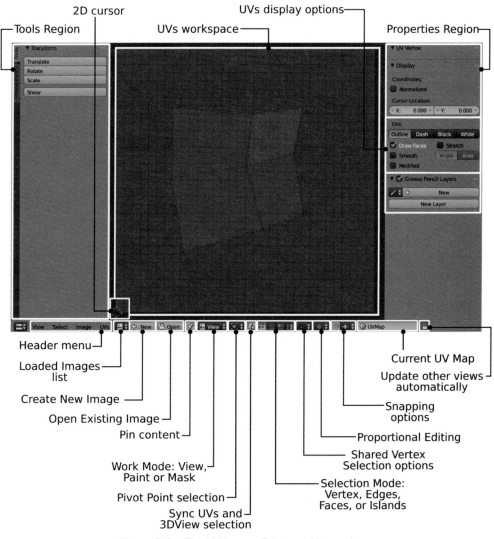

Figure 8.2   The UV/Image Editor and its options

The list that follows explains some of the main options available in the UV/Image Editor:

- **Interface:** This editor is basically a normal Blender editor. It has its own Tools and Properties regions on the left and right sides, the workspace in the center, and a header on which you can find buttons and menus for most of the options you need while arranging the UVs.

- **2D cursor:** The 2D Editor has a cursor that is similar to the 3D cursor; you can use it to align vertices or other UV elements. Place it with a left click and press **Shift+S** to see the snap options you can use with the 2D cursor.

- **Display panel:** In the Properties Region, you see the Display panel that lets you customize how you see the UVs. This panel even has a Stretch option, which shows the distortion using colors based on the angle or area of faces in the UV map compared with the 3D model—quite useful for identifying distortion in complicated areas. If the faces are very stretched (a blue face is good, and a turquoise face is not bad, but you should avoid green and yellow faces), the texture will probably look distorted or be of poor quality when you project it onto that part of the surface.

The header provides quite a few options:

- **Header menu:** View, Select, Image, and UVs menus are available. The UVs menu is especially important, as it provides most of the unwrapping tools.

- **Loaded Images List, Create New Image, and Open Existing Image:** You can load images, choose some that are already loaded from the drop-down list, or create new ones inside Blender (such as a solid-color image or a UV test grid, which I discuss later in this chapter).

- **Pin:** If you click the Pin icon, the current image is pinned and always shown independently of other objects you select. This tool can pin only images, however, not UVs. Remember that the UV Editor always shows the UVs of the selected elements while you're in Edit Mode. This option comes in handy when you want to display reference images in the UV/Image Editor.

> **Tip**
>
> Continually switching between UVs and reference images doesn't sound like a good time, and for sure, it's not efficient. You don't need to decide between adjusting your UVs and loading an image for reference; in Blender, you can do both! Divide your interface, and use two UV/Image Editors at the same time. In the editor that you're using for a reference image, make sure to click the Pin icon on the header. When you do, it doesn't matter what you select or what you're doing, because that editor will keep showing that image.

- **Work Mode menu:** In the Work Mode menu, you can choose among View, Paint, and Mask modes. View is the mode you usually use to adjust UVs and view images. Paint Mode allows you to paint directly in the 2D image when you're in Texture Painting Interaction Mode in 3D View as well (see Chapter 9, "Painting Textures"). Mask is a special mode in which you can create masks that you can use in the Node Compositor to isolate parts of an image.

- **Pivot Point:** The Pivot Point option works exactly the same as in 3D View. You can select the pivot point from which to rotate or scale objects; that's how you can use the 2D cursor as a pivot point. As in 3D View, you can press **.** (period) and **,** (comma) on your keyboard to switch between the 2D cursor and the center of the selection for the pivot point.

- **Sync UVs and 3D View:** The tool that synchronizes the UVs selection with the 3D model can be useful in complex models to find out where a specific vertex or face in the model is located on the UVs. Keep in mind that using this mode all the time may not be a good idea, as it limits some options for unwrapping. Island selections (explained in the next paragraph) don't work in this mode.

- **Selection Mode:** In the UV/Image Editor, you can switch among Vertices, Edges, Faces, and Islands selection modes. (An *island* is a group of connected faces.) You can also select an island by pressing **L**.

- **Shared Vertex:** Shared Vertex options are interesting. Suppose that on the UVs, Blender treats each of the faces separately but allows you to select vertices depending on certain conditions—such as the vertices sharing their X, Y, and Z positions—in the actual 3D model. When this option is disabled, and you select a vertex or a face, that vertex or face moves alone; the connected vertices or faces stay in their current places. If they are overlapped in the UV/Image Editor, the Shared Location option treats them as though they were welded on the UVs, but only if they share the same location in the 3D model. The Shared Vertex option selects the vertices that share the position in the 3D model, even if they're separated on the UVs. The best way to understand this option is to try it out.

  > **Note**
  >
  > To better understand the Shared Vertex options, you have to know how Blender treats UVs. Vertices in a 3D mesh are positioned on X, Y, and Z axes, whereas vertices in a UV layout are positioned on the U and V axes. The difference is that whereas one face in a 3D mesh typically is connected to another, faces in the UV space can be freed from their neighboring faces, so you can apply a different texture to a different part of the model, even though the parts may be adjacent in the 3D model.

- **Proportional Editing and Snapping:** You also have Proportional Editing and Snapping tools in the UV/Image Editor to help you manipulate UVs.

- **Current UV Map:** Current UV Map is pretty important because in Blender, a single object can have multiple UV maps that you can use independently when building complex materials. So you can use various textures that are differently distributed depending on the UV map they use. UVMap is the default name, and most of the time, you'll use only a single map. If at some point, you want to create other UV maps, you can go to the Properties Editor and look for the UV Maps panel on the Mesh tab.

- **Update Other Views Automatically:** The last icon you see on the header is a lock. This option, when enabled, makes other views in Blender show real-time updates while you adjust UVs. If you're using an old or slow computer, you may prefer to turn this feature off and save resources.

Navigating the UV/Image Editor

Navigation in the UV/Image Editor is pretty simple: Press **MMB** and drag to pan, and use the scroll wheel or drag with **Ctrl+MMB** to zoom in and out. A left click positions the 2D cursor. Apart from that, controls are exactly the same as in 3D View: Right-click to select; **RMB** drag to move; and **G**, **R**, and **S** to move, rotate, and scale the selections.

Certain features from other editors work in the UV/Image Editor as well, such as the Hide and Unhide feature (**H**, **Shift+H**, and **Alt+H**) or the ability to switch selection modes by pressing **Ctrl+Tab**.

Accessing the Unwrapping Menus

Blender provides some unwrapping menus that you can find within the interface:

- Select some faces in Edit Mode (usually, when unwrapping, you work with faces), and press **U** to display the UV Mapping pop-up menu.
- Marking Seams is one of the key unwrapping tools. You can access it from the Edge menu (**Ctrl+E**) after selecting one or more edges. (I discuss seams later in this chapter.)
- In the Tools Region of 3D View, the Shading/UVs tab provides the UV Mapping and Seams options.
- On the 3D View header, you can access the UV Unwrap menu from the Mesh menu.

Working with UV Mapping Tools

In Figure 8.3, you see the UV Mapping menu (press **U** in 3D View) and the Edges menu (**Ctrl+E**), showing the Mark Seam and Clear Seam options that are essential for unwrapping in Blender.

In this section, I cover the UV Mapping tools briefly so that you have an idea of what they do when you start using them later in this chapter. The following list describes the main UV Mapping tools and how they work:

- **Mark Seam and Clear Seam:** From the Edges menu, select one or more edges; press **Ctrl+E** to access the Edge menu; and choose Mark Seam. This option shows those edges in 3D View with a red outline. To clear the seam mark, select the edges you want to clear, press **Ctrl+E**, and choose Clear Seam.
- **Unwrap:** This option is the main unwrapping tool in Blender. Press **U** to access the UV Mapping menu, and select Unwrap. This option unfolds the model, taking into account the mesh's borders and seams, and usually gives good results if the seams are placed correctly.
- **Smart UV Project:** With this option, you don't need to mark seams. The option can work nicely for simple objects. It unwraps your object, separating parts of it depending on parameters you define in a pop-up menu, such as the angle between faces.
- **Lightmap Pack:** This option is not recommended unless you want to create UVs in an automatic way, which can be useful for complex objects that don't need to be very accurate or for objects you texture via automatic methods (such as texture baking,

which projects details from one model onto another using textures). This option separates all faces and arranges them in order to use the most space possible in the image.

- **Follow Active Quads:** This option provides a very technical result (everything is aligned in vertical and horizontal lines), but it works well only with small selections and when there is an active element. As the name implies, the option doesn't work with faces that are not four-sided, so triangles, for example, are excluded when you use this tool.

- **Cube, Cylinder, and Sphere Projections:** These options are basic tools, but they can be useful. These projections use the pivot point of the object and the view angle to work. They unwrap the object by using a geometric shape (as their names imply). After using them, you can find some options in the Operator panel that may be useful for adjusting the results.

- **Project from View:** This option is quite interesting, as it takes the selection and unwraps it in the UV/Image Editor while you see it in 3D View. Your point of view is key, of course, and perspective is maintained as well. If you select the Project from View (Bounds) option, Blender scales the resulting UVs to the borders of the UV workspace.

- **Reset:** This option takes every selected face and returns it to its original state, occupying the entire UV map.

Tip

To better understand what these unwrapping tools do, try them, and see the results for yourself. Some of them may seem to be more efficient or easy to use than others, and it's very difficult to clearly understand their effects just by reading an explanation. As with every part of the learning process, trial and error are the best teachers!

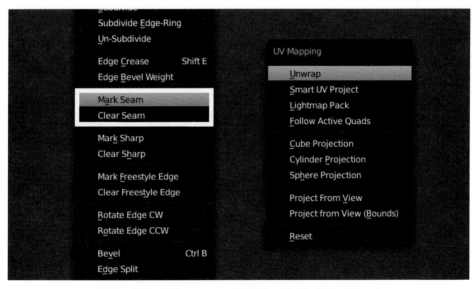

Figure 8.3   Edges menu (**Ctrl+E**) with Mark Seam and
Clear Seam options, and UV Mapping menu (**U**)

Defining Seams

Seams are the borders of an unwrapping operation. When the cube in Figure 8.1 (earlier in this chapter) is unwrapped, the black continuous lines are the seams. You can also think of seams in clothing. Before a shirt is made, it's just a series of flat pieces that are later joined into a 3D garment by stitching them together at their seams. In 3D, the most popular unwrapping method involves seams. First, you define the seams in the 3D model; then you unfold the UVs according to those seams.

Keep in mind that seams are not desirable in visible areas of a model, but they're needed to prevent distortion in the projection of textures. Seams usually are placed in areas where they're less visible. The reason is that when you apply a texture, in the seam area, you see a cut in the texture. That cut happens because where you have a seam, it appears as a border on the UVs. Even though you make the texture continuous, without any cuts, the sizes of the seams on the UVs may not be exactly the same, causing the resolution of the image to change and make the seam visible because of a resolution difference between its sides.

In UVs, the bigger a polygon is, the more resolution it requires in the image. Therefore, the texture displayed in the 3D model is sharper. This density of pixels per polygon is referred to as *texel density*. It's important to know which parts of your model need more detail in the textures and therefore need more space on the UVs.

In Figure 8.4, you see the effects of seams and how the size of the UVs affects the projected texture. The sizes of the faces on the UVs (left side of the image) and in the actual 3D model (right side of the image) are independent, but the size of UVs defines the resolution of the texture in the 3D model.

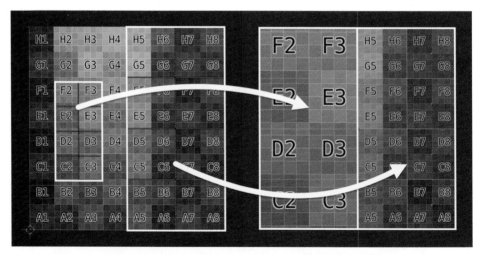

Figure 8.4   The UVs placed on the image (left) and how they
affect the projection's resolution in the geometry (right)

Considering Before Unwrapping

Not all the objects you've created for Jim's character have the same properties, so you need to make some decisions before jumping into UV mapping. The list that follows describes some things you need to keep in mind:

- **Meshes that don't need UVs:** If an object is supposed to look like a flat material, with no changes in its surface (which is not usual in realistic models but can happen in simple models for animations), you won't need to unwrap it. Unwrapping defines how an image is projected onto the surface of a model. But if you just need to add a flat color, a material with no texture will do, as is the case for Jim's hair.

- **Meshes with modifiers:** Some of the meshes that comprise your character may have modifiers applied. When a mesh is using modifiers that change its geometry, they affect the UVs as well. Take Jim's badges as examples. The badges are made with a Solidify modifier that adds thickness to the model; the UVs are available only for the original geometry, however, so the polygons generated by the modifier won't be able to display the texture properly. In the case of the Solidify modifier, the thickness polygons display the color of the texture's borders in the front, and the back side displays the same as the front side (which shouldn't matter in this case, because the back side is hidden). In such a situation, you must determine whether you'll get the correct unwrapping result without applying the modifiers or whether you need to apply the modifiers and then unwrap all the geometry. The answer depends on the amount of detail you're looking for and on where you need to display the textures accurately.

- **Mirrored meshes:** Mirror is a modifier, and it's especially important when it's used with UVs. If you do the UVs unwrapping, and you're using a Mirror modifier, the mirrored geometry uses the same UVs as the side you unwrapped. Sometimes, you want to have asymmetric textures for an object, so you should apply the Mirror modifier before unwrapping. In other cases, a mirrored texture could work nicely, which means two things: You need to unwrap only half the object, and you need less space in the image to texture that object. In yet another case, you need an asymmetric shape, but the texture could be symmetric, so you could work with a symmetric shape, perform the unwrap operation, apply the Mirror modifier, and make any adjustments to the shape. This way, you have mirrored UVs but an asymmetric shape. (The topology should be the same on both sides of the mesh. If you add or subtract geometry, UVs are broken.) The examples in the next sections, using Jim's face and jacket, will help you understand this option better.

Note

You need to determine whether it's more efficient to do the UVs and then keep adjusting your model, or whether it's better to apply modifiers and do the UVs afterward. The answer depends on your model, what you need to do to it, and what's most comfortable and efficient for you.

Working with UVs in Blender

In this section, you go through the process of unwrapping Jim's head step by step, and you learn how to use the basic unwrapping tools. Then, with some basic instructions, you'll be ready to unwrap the rest of the objects for your character. In this case, you won't use a mirrored texture for the face, so you'll need to unwrap the full face at the same time. To do this, select the face and apply the Mirror modifier in Object Mode.

Marking the Seams

The first step in unwrapping is marking the seams to tell Blender how you want your UVs to be unfolded. In Edit Mode (**Tab**), select the edges shown in Figure 8.5. You don't need to mark them all at the same time; you can mark some of them now and then mark seams in other areas as you proceed. To mark edges as seams, press **Ctrl+E** to access the Edge menu and select Mark Seam.

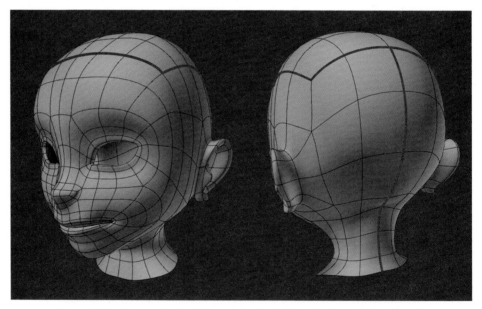

Figure 8.5   Seams marked to unwrap Jim's head (edges shown in red)

Pay attention to how the edges selected to be the seams of the UVs are placed in areas that won't be very visible. Those edges appear on the back and sides of the head and over the forehead, where they'll be almost completely hidden by the hair. The closed seam selected at the top of the head is there to make that part an isolated UV island. After all, that part will always be hidden under Jim's cap, so it doesn't need a lot of definition. As a result, you can use more space in the UVs for the areas that matter and need more resolution in the texture.

Also, although you can't see it in Figure 8.5, a loop is marked as a seam in the inner part of the lips so that on the UVs, the geometry of the face's interior is separated from the face's exterior. Remember that you can press **Alt+RMB** to select edge loops.

> ### Tip
>
> For marking seams, the Shortest Path option is a useful selection method. When you need to select multiple edges on a single line, select one and press **Ctrl+RMB** on another edge. The edges between the two edges you've selected are also selected, allowing you to select long lines of edges very quickly. You can press **Ctrl+RMB** again and again until you have the entire desired edge loop selected. This method also works in vertex selection mode.
>
> To speed things even more, go to the Options tab in the Tools Region of 3D View; then choose Edge Select Mode and Tag Seam. Thereafter, when you use the Shortest Path selection, those edges are automatically marked as seams. Remember to set this option back to Select when you're done with the seams!

Creating and Displaying a UV Test Grid

At this point, you could start unwrapping, but instead, you're going to create a UV test grid so that you can see how applying a texture to the face will look before unwrapping. Using the test grid helps you visualize how unwrapping affects the projection of the texture.

A UV test grid is a basic image made exclusively to test how the UVs of a mesh work. It's an image with a grid that, when it's projected on the 3D model, provides a lot of information. The size of the grid shows you which parts of your object are using more of the texture; the smaller the grid, the more resolution the texture has in that area. Using the test grid, you can adjust the size of every part of the object to be more or less consistent, and you can set a smaller grid on those parts where you need more details. It's also useful to see the grid's distortion. If you notice that at some point, the grid is becoming heavily distorted, you can try to solve the problem by adjusting the UVs. Using a UV test grid, you can also see where the seams are and how well they work, and you can make sure that they're barely visible.

The UV test grid can display colors as well as letters or numbers. This feature tells you which part of the UVs is being shown on a specific part of the model by the color, number, or letter it displays on its surface.

Creating a New Image for a UV Test Grid

Blender has two types of UV test grids that you can generate and use in your models: a UV grid (a chessboardlike grid) and a color grid (a grid that includes colors and letters to help you spot which part of the texture you're using when you see it projected). To create these grids, click New Image in the UV/Image Editor header; choose New Image from the Image menu; or press **Alt+N**.

In Figure 8.6, you see the New Image menu, which allows you to create images to paint on or UV test grids. You can set the image's name (Untitled by default), its resolution, and its color. The color applies only when you select Blank as the Generated Type. If you select one of the UV test grids as the Generated Type, Blender ignores the color setting.

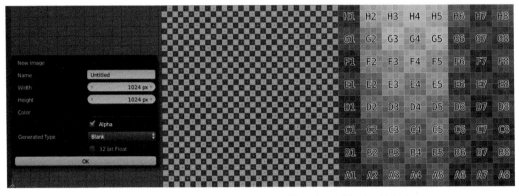

Figure 8.6   Generating a new image in Blender, with the New Image
menu (left), a UV grid (center), and a Color grid (right)

When you've made your selections, click OK to generate the image. You can change the image's name from the header and save it from the Image menu. If you open the Properties Region (**N**), in the Image panel, you can rename the image and access its parameters. Because the image is generated by Blender, you can change its type even after it is created and also switch between a UV grid or a color grid (or a blank image, or course).

Displaying the UV Test Grid in Your Model

How you show the image you're using in a 3D model in 3D View depends on which render engine you're using. In this section, you see how to display an image in both Blender Render and Cycles.

Both render engines let you display a texture by applying it to a material and switching the display mode of the 3D View to Textured or Material. Blender Render offers another method that doesn't require you to create a material, but you need to have UVs in your mesh to use it.

Go to the UV/Image Editor, and load the image while the UVs are displayed. This image is called a *texture face*—the texture that is applied to a UV map. Now, in 3D View, you can display that texture face even in the Solid display mode; open the Properties Region (**N**), and enable the Textured Solid option in the Shading panel.

Cycles offers a better method that uses a material. Create a new material from the Material tab in the Properties Editor, and call it something like uv_test_mat; this way, you'll always have a UV Test material in your scene, ready to be applied to the object with which you're working. Inside the Material options, in the Color parameter, click the button that has a little dot at the right of the color selector, and select Image Texture from the list. Select the UV test grid you just created from the drop-down list. Now go to 3D View and use the Textured or Material display mode to see how the UV test grid looks.

Unwrapping Jim's Face

Unwrapping Jim's face is fairly simple. Select Jim's face, and in Edit Mode (**Tab**), select all the faces (**A**). Press **U**, and select the first option, Unwrap. What you see should be similar to Figure 8.7.

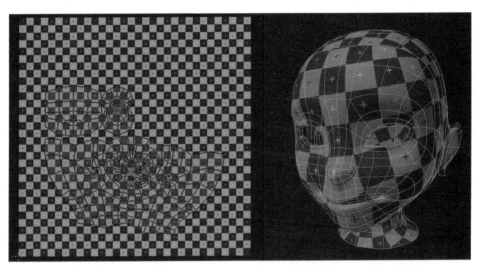

Figure 8.7   After unwrapping Jim's face, you see the UV map in the UV/Image Editor (left), and the UV test grid looks much more uniform (right).

After unwrapping the model, you see how the UVs have been unfolded. The face is flat, and you see the other two islands: the top of the head and the mouth's interior, as you defined them previously with the seams. Also, the face has been unfolded by using the seam from the back of the head.

When you have a test grid or an image in the background of the UV/Image Editor, it may be difficult to see the UVs accurately. When an image is loaded in the UV/Image Editor, on the right side of the header, you see three little buttons. Two of these buttons provide options to display the image, and the third one shows the current UV Texture Alpha channel (image transparency), or a white background when there is no Alpha to display, letting you see the UVs better. Another way to improve UVs visualization is through the Properties Region, where you can find some display options that may help.

Note

Remember that the UV/Image Editor shows only the UVs of the parts of your model that are selected in 3D View, and only while you're in Edit Mode. At first, this situation can be confusing for people who come from other software and are used to always seeing all the UVs. If you activate the sync between the 3D and UVs selection, you'll be able to see all the UVs, but if you want to see all the UVs without the sync option, go to 3D View and select all by pressing **A**.

Using Live Unwrap

Live Unwrap is a cool tool that lets you pin vertices in the UVs and move them to unwrap the mesh in real time. It allows you to adjust the UVs very quickly without having to unwrap again and again or to move them vertex by vertex.

In the UV/Image Editor's UVs menu on the header, activate the Live Unwrap option. To pin the vertices that you want to place in fixed positions, press **P**. Keep in mind that you have to pin at least two vertices. After pinning those vertices, which can be the reference points or the corners of the mesh, move some of them (pinned vertices are marked in red) to see how all the UVs adjust to fit your moves. In this mode, move only the pinned vertices. If you move any other vertex, when you move a pinned one, the unpinned vertices are reset; only pinned vertices are fixed during the live unwrap.

When you're done, you can unpin the pinned vertices by selecting them and pressing **Alt+P**. Make sure that you deactivate Live Unwrap before further adjusting the UVs.

Adjusting UVs

You can adjust vertices on the UVs to make sure that they look right in the 3D model, of course, and you see real-time feedback in the UV test grid of the 3D model as you make those adjustments.

Remember that you also have Proportional Editing tools at your disposal to move groups of vertices subtly, and you can move, rotate, and scale them. Try to adjust the grid for the face so that you have smaller squares in the face than on the back of the head. This practice helps you optimize the texture size and create more detail in the face, which is where you need it, instead of on the back of the head, where you don't need it.

You also have alignment tools for the UVs. Look at the options on the UVs menu on the header and try them out. Maybe you'll find something interesting. (Press **W** to get the Align and Weld options.) Also, when you use a tool, you may need to make an adjustment to its effect before you confirm it. In such a case, the header shows information with instructions you need to follow to use that tool as well as its current parameters, so keep an eye on that header!

You can use the Snap tools, which are useful when, for example, you want to align one vertex on top of another. Snap tools work the same way as in 3D View.

Separating and Connecting UVs

Blender offers unusual ways to separate and connect parts of the UVs, but when you get used to them, they're quite useful.

Separating UVs

The quickest way to separate UVs is to use the Select Split tool. Select the faces you want to separate, and press **Y**; the faces are separated, so you can move them independently of one another. You can also access this option from the Select menu on the header.

On the UVs, Blender shows only the faces you've selected in 3D View. But here's an interesting fact to keep in mind: When you select only a face (or a group of faces) in 3D View and move it on the UVs, it moves independently and becomes separated from the rest of the UVs. You can manipulate only the visible UVs, and when you do, they are separated from the UVs that are currently hidden.

Another way to separate UVs is to unwrap again the faces you want to separate. Select them from the 3D model, and unwrap them to separated them.

The last way to separate UVs is to use the Hide and Unhide features of Blender (**H**, **Shift+H**, and **Alt+H**), which are also available in the UV/Image Editor. Select the faces you want to separate, press **Shift+H** to hide the unselected faces, and transform the selection. Press **Alt+H** to reveal all the UVs, and you see that those faces are separated.

Connecting UVs

Sometimes, it's easier to unwrap a complex mesh by its parts and then join them as needed to create the least distortion possible.

Blender has a rule: Only vertices that are welded in the 3D mesh can be welded on the UVs. This means that you can snap or even weld (with the Welding tool from the **W** menu) two vertices, and they'll be in exactly the same place, but they won't actually be merged if they're not in the 3D mesh. Thus, when you move them, you actually move only one of them.

That said, to merge vertices on the UVs that are also welded in the 3D model, you have to put them in the same place by welding or snapping them.

One way to find out exactly which vertices are adjacent is to use the Sync selection mode between the UVs and the 3D mesh. With this method, if you select a vertex in the mesh or on the UVs, Blender shows the shared vertices that should go with it in other UV islands as well. Another option is to temporarily activate the Shared Vertex selection to see which vertices are in the same place in the 3D model.

Stitch is a tool that can be very helpful for connecting UVs. You can find it on the UVs menu on the header; its keyboard shortcut is **V**. Select some vertices on a border of a UV island, and press **V**; a preview shows you where those vertices should go to be joined to other vertices on the UVs. If you like what you see, left-click or press **Enter** to apply; otherwise, right-click to cancel the stitching.

Reviewing the Finished Face's UVs

In Figure 8.8, you see how the UVs for the head look after some adjustments. The UVs are nicely aligned, the top of the head and the mouth's interior now take less space in the texture, and the face portion has been enlarged so that it has more detail. The ears were separated to have some more space outside the head's UVs, but this separation is optional, as the ears in this particular model don't need that much detail in the texture.

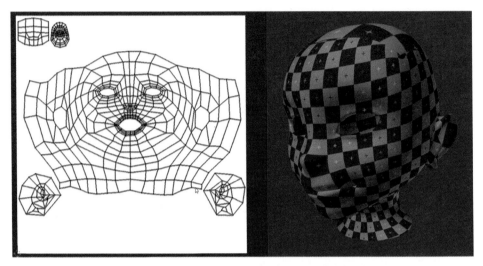

Figure 8.8   The UVs for Jim's face are finished!

Unwrapping the Rest of the Character

Unwrapping the rest of the character is pretty straightforward. First, I briefly explain the most important parts of the process so that you can understand what to expect. Figure 8.9 gives you an idea of what you'll be doing in this section and shows the objects to be unwrapped: the glove, the boots, the pants, the jacket, the cap, and the neck detail.

Unwrapping most of these objects should be fairly quick and easy. The pants, for example, need only a simple seam along the inner leg, just like a pair of real trousers, and the unwrap should work nicely. Keep in mind that the Mirror modifier does its part as well.

For the hand, a seam is marked all along the palm, passing through the bottom part of the fingers. The resulting UVs are adjusted with the Live Unwrap tool, especially the island that represents the top of the hand; it has the sides of the fingers in it, so its shape is somewhat spherical.

> **Note**
>
> Figure 8.9 shows only one hand because you modeled only one in Chapter 7, "Character Modeling," and didn't apply a Mirror modifier to it. Instead, you duplicated and mirrored it. It was made on purpose because it was helpful to show you a result with two hands, but it's better to unwrap the hand and duplicate it afterward so that you don't need to unwrap both hands separately.

The elements of the cap are basically unwrapped just as they were. No seams have to be used; just select all of the cap's faces and unwrap them.

The piece at the neck should be simple, too. It just needs a loop all around the interior bottom section so that Blender can unfold it properly.

Figure 8.9 The meshes that needed to be unwrapped, with their seams marked in red

The jacket can be a little trickier. First, unwrapping it in three pieces would be easier: the body, the arms, and the flaps. Later, after adjusting the UVs a little by using the Live Unwrap and Proportional Editing tools, you can join the arm to the side of the jacket, first using the Stitch tool and then snapping and moving some vertices around. The purpose of this junction is to have no seam in the shoulder, as the jacket will have the shoulder pads painted in the texture for that area, and a seam in the middle would not look good.

If you want to see what the UV maps look like, see the next section, "Packing UVs." Right now, each UV island takes the entire space, and showing the islands together would be rather abstract. That's why packing is important!

Packing UVs

After the objects are unwrapped, you have to pack them, which is the process in which you put all the UVs together in a single workspace so that they don't overlap. That way, instead of having a different texture for each object, you can have the entire character textured with a single image so that each part of it will occupy a part of the UV map.

Figure 8.10 shows what the finished UVs look like.

With all these objects in one place, a single texture is used for the entire character. As you can see in Figure 8.10, the face takes most of the texture space. There are also some spaces between objects. You can spend more time filling the entire texture space to have a more efficient texture, but you should always leave a little space between UV islands so that when you paint, they can bleed a little. Otherwise, you may see areas adjacent to the seams that weren't painted.

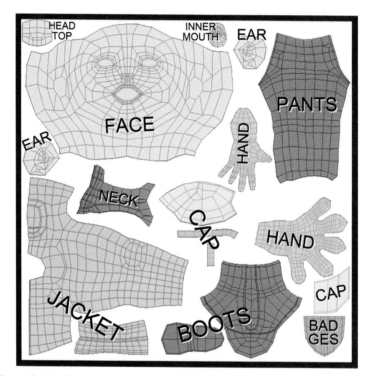

Figure 8.10   The packed UVs for Jim, shown with different colors for each object so you can see how the objects are distributed

You can pack UVs in several ways. In this section, I discuss a few of the most popular methods.

The easiest way to pack UVs is to have everything inside the same mesh, so you can take islands, move them, rotate them, and scale them very easily to make them fit together in the same texture space. You can do this with models that are made of numerous objects with no modifiers (such as Mirror or Solidify) applied; otherwise, you lose the modifiers' effects in the process. If there are no modifiers, you can select all the objects, press **Ctrl+J** to join them in the same mesh, and then start packing their UVs. When the packing is done, you can export the UVs (you learn how to do this in Chapter 9, "Painting Textures") and separate them again if necessary.

A down side of this method is that when you join meshes and separate them again, you lose their origins (pivot points), and they'll all be in the position of the active mesh's origin when you join them. In Chapter 11, "Character Rigging," you learn how to change the origin of an object.

> **Tip**
>
> Blender provides tools for packing UVs when they're all together in a single object: Average Islands Scale and Pack Islands. Average Islands (**Ctrl+A**) scales the selected islands so their sizes are relative to the sizes of the faces in the 3D model. Pack Islands (**Ctrl+P**) scales and places the selected islands automatically so that they take the largest space possible inside the UV's space.

Another packing method uses a feature of Blender that allows you to see the UVs of other meshes in the UV/Image Editor, even though you can adjust only the UVs of the active object in Edit Mode. Here's how it works:

1. Select several objects by pressing **Shift+RMB**. The last object selected is the active one.

2. In Edit Mode, adjust the UVs.

3. In the UV/Image Editor's header, activate the Draw Other Objects option in the View menu. Even though you can adjust only the UVs for the active object, the rest of the selected objects' UVs are shown over the workspace.

The quickest way to switch between objects is to press **Tab** to exit Edit Mode, press **Shift**, and right-click the next object you want to adjust. Enter Edit Mode again, and that adjusted object is the active object while keeping all the objects selected.

This method is probably the most popular method of packing when you have objects with modifiers that you can't join, and I used it to do the packing for Jim's UVs.

> **Tip**
>
> If you're working on the UVs in Edit Mode and want to see another object's UVs in the workspace, you can do so very quickly by holding down **Ctrl** and left-clicking that object without exiting Edit Mode. This technique adds that object to the selection, so its UVs become visible in the UV/Image Editor (only if Draw Other Objects is enabled).

Summary

You have Jim unwrapped with proper UVs, and he's ready to be textured! As you may have noticed, unwrapping can be tricky, and you need patience for it. Unwrapping is a mandatory step in building quality characters, however, because you have to properly define how the textures will be projected onto the model in the most efficient way. Proper definition is especially important if you're working on video games, in which everything needs to be optimized (including textures) to work smoothly in real time. Some software packages and tools support UVs that are almost completely automated, and that's cool for some specific situations. Usually, however, you want to have control of how UVs are unfolded so that it will be easier to paint your character's textures later.

Exercises

1. Unwrap a cube, and add a texture to it. This exercise helps you understand how UVs work.

2. Add a photo to any model (even Jim's face), and try to unwrap it in such a way that the seams are hidden as much as possible and the texture is not distorted.

3. Unwrap an object, and pack its UVs to use all the space you can from the texture.

9

Painting Textures

Textures are simply images that give color (or define other parameters, such as the amount of reflection or shininess an object has) to your models when projected onto their surfaces. In Chapter 8, "Unwrapping and UVs in Blender," you unwrapped the parts of Jim that need textures. Now it's time to use those UVs to paint a texture and give your character a layer of paint to move your project closer to the final result. Textures usually are created with 2D software such as Adobe Photoshop, GIMP, and Krita, and these programs are outside the scope of this book. This chapter briefly explains the workflow and texture-painting process in Blender.

Defining the Main Workflow

You have two main workflows for painting textures on 3D models:

- **Texturing before unwrapping:** Sometimes, depending on your needs, it's easiest to create a texture and then adapt the UVs to fit that texture. In this case, of course, you need to create the texture before you start unwrapping. A good example of this method is a wooden floor. You may have a photo of wood, and to apply it to the surface, you load that photo and adapt the UVs so that the wood in the photo has the right size and position on your surface. This method works best in simple models; in complex models, the projected image needs to be adapted to the model.

- **Texturing after unwrapping:** This method is the usual texturing method for characters or complex objects because it specifically tailors textures to that model. First, you unwrap the model; then you export the UVs as an image to use for a reference when painting and adjusting your textures to make sure that they fit the faces in your model. You'll use this method to texture Jim.

The second workflow in the preceding list is discussed in Chapter 8, "Unwrapping and UVs in Blender," but it's worth noting here so that it will be fresh in your mind.

Painting in Blender

Yes, you can paint textures right inside Blender and directly on the 3D model! In the Mode selector of the 3D View's header, choose Texture Paint Mode. In the Tools Region (press **T** if it's hidden), you see a lot of options that control how you paint, and you can select the brush you'll use.

Texture Paint Mode

Before you actually paint (several more steps are needed before you begin), I'll briefly describe how Texture Paint Mode works. In Figure 9.1, you see how the main interface in 3D View and the Tools Region changes substantially in Texture Paint Mode. In that mode, the cursor is circular and resembles a brush, and the Tools Region options are completely different from those in other modes.

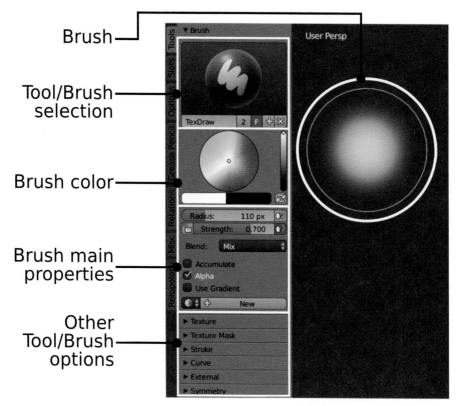

Figure 9.1   Texture Paint Mode and its options in the Tools Region

You can choose from among a variety of tools (brushes), such as Fill, Clone, Smear, and Soften (similar to a blur). With the options available to you, you can adjust settings for a brush/tool at the bottom of the Tools Region. You can adjust its radius and strength (its opacity), its texture, and its profile curve; you can even use the Smooth Stroke feature to stabilize the stroke while you move the brush. You can also create your own tool presets for fast access to them, as well as pick a color for your brush.

For the radius and strength of the brush, it's worth noting that you can quickly change those two values in 3D View. Press **F**, move the mouse to define the radius (you see a preview of the resulting brush radius as you move your mouse), and confirm with a left click to change the radius. Press **Shift+F**, move the mouse, and confirm with a left click to change the strength of your brush.

In Chapter 8, "Unwrapping and UVs in Blender," you learn a lot about the UV/Image Editor. As described in that chapter, a button on the header lets you change among View, Paint, and Mask modes. Well, when you're working in Texture Paint Mode in 3D View, if you switch to Paint Mode in the UV/Image Editor, you'll also be able to paint over the 2D image.

It's important to know that in 3D View, you can paint on only the selected object. If more than one object is selected, you paint only on the active one. To paint on a different object, you have to switch back to Object Mode, select another object, and go back into Texture Paint Mode.

Before You Start Painting

Before you begin painting, you must make sure of a couple of things:

- The object to be painted on is unwrapped. Otherwise, you won't be able to paint on it or (in the best-case scenario) it will look weird.
- The object has to have at least one texture and/or material.

In the latest versions of Blender, the workflow to start painting has been heavily improved, and if you don't fulfill these two conditions, Blender gives you options to create UVs and images or materials very quickly. I go through this process in the next section.

If you've followed along with the previous chapters, Jim's textured parts have a material applied, and they're displayed in the UV test grid. When you're done unwrapping, you might go to Texture properties and change from a UV test grid to a Blank Image; you can even change the texture's name to something like texture_base. Also, for the resolution, use a minimum of 2048 × 2048 pixels so that you have a black texture to start with.

Tip

When you change the image from UV test grid to Blank Image in the UV/Image Editor's options inside the Properties panel (**N** key), you can define its color in the same menu. Usually, you'll want to set the color to white when you want to draw details. Alternatively, you can use the Fill tool to fill the entire mesh with a single color by clicking the surface. The Fill tool paints only those parts that cover the image in the UVs, though, and leaves the rest in the original color. Using the Fill tool in the UV/Image Editor instead of the 3D model allows you to fill the areas between the existing UVs.

When you're set up, you can start painting! Move the camera as you normally would, but if you left-click and drag over the object you selected before entering Texture Paint Mode, Blender places a stroke in that part of the texture. If you go to the UV/Image Editor and set the mode to Paint, you'll be able to paint there as well.

Resolution

Texture resolution should be squared with a power-of-two number (8 × 8, 16 × 16, 32 × 32, 64 × 64, 128 × 128, 256 × 256, and so on). The reason is that these resolutions use the resources on your computer a lot better than rectangular images with random sizes. They're called power-of-two because to jump from one resolution to the previous or the next one, you must divide or multiply by 2. Usually, you should work in a pretty high resolution, because you can always scale it down if needed, but you'll lose detail and your model won't look right if you have to scale up. The size you finally use depends on the amount of detail you need for your model. If the model is high-resolution and will be seen from a great distance in certain shots, having textures with very high resolutions is unnecessary and would needlessly consume important resources. It's good practice to use high-resolution textures only while they're close to the camera and the details are visible. After you create a texture, it's best to make different sizes of it that you can use depending on the object's distance from the camera.

Conditions for Painting

As mentioned earlier, Blender has improved the texturing workflow in recent versions. These improvements include options in Texture Paint Mode that can be used when the selected object is not ready to be painted on (see Figure 9.2):

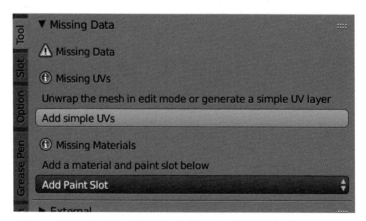

Figure 9.2   The Tools Region in Texture Paint Mode when you don't have UVs or images assigned to the object

- Blender detects whether the object has UVs. If not, Blender displays the message "Missing UVs" in the Tools Region and instructs you to unwrap the object before painting. Also, a button automatically generates quick UVs for the selected object. These UVs won't be perfect, but sometimes, they are good enough for quick tests or for simple objects.

- Blender detects whether the object has an image or material to paint on. If not, Blender gives you an option to quickly create a painting slot and start painting. I talk about slots later in this chapter.

If the active object has a UV and an image or material to paint on, painting tools appear in the Tools Region. If not, Blender gives you options to solve the problem and start painting as fast as possible.

Paint Slots

You'll often have different textures in your objects (see Chapter 10, "Materials and Shaders"), each of which uses a slot. Texture Paint Mode has a new Slots tab in the Tools Region. This tab has options that let you specify which texture you want to paint on. At the top of the menu are the two most important options:

- **Material:** When you select Material in the Slots tab, you can paint on the available textures inside the material that you assigned to the active object. All the textures are listed inside the Available Paint Slots section of the panel, which allows you to switch among them quickly (see Figure 9.3). If you add a new image inside the material, it automatically shows up in the slots list. A button also lets you save all the images in that material at the same time (the alternative is to save them one by one in the UV/Images Editor) after you've made some edits.

- **Image:** If you select Image, you gain access to an image selector from which you can select any image that you created in the file. This image is projected onto the active object, allowing you to paint on it. Below the selector are several other options. You can create a new image, select the UV map on which you want the image to be projected (this option is not available when working with Material Slots, as images inside materials have their UVs already defined), and save all the images.

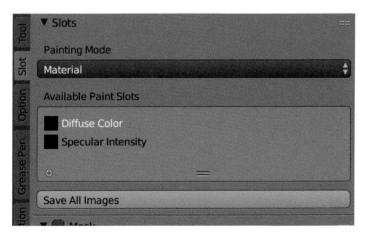

Figure 9.3   The Slot tab in the Tools Region, where you can select the image you want to paint on

> **Caution**
>
> Whether you're working in Material Slots or with Images, the Save All Images option works only if those images have been saved before and have a file path in your computer. After that first save, the Save All Images option updates the files correctly.

Limitations of Blender's Texture Paint Mode

Although Blender's Texture Paint Mode is quite powerful and has a lot of options (which you should explore further, as I discuss the basics in this chapter), it does have limitations. The mode has no layers, for example, which is a basic and useful feature for texture painting. Add-ons are available that provide Blender with some layering capabilities that you can explore, but they're not nearly as good as the layers you can work with image-editing software such as Photoshop, Krita, and GIMP. Also, painting over the 3D model can be a little slow sometimes, depending on how powerful your computer is.

Blender isn't a substitute for proper 2D image-editing software, of course, but it does provide a set of tools that allow you to do basic texture painting. (Some people have taken Blender's painting options to the extreme and made impressive artworks with them!)

You can use Texture Paint Mode to texture an entire character, but the decision depends on the character, of course, and whether you feel comfortable texturing it in 3D. Instead, you might try working with 2D image editors, loading textures, using layers, making color corrections, adding effects, and applying masks—things that you have no access to inside Blender's Texture Paint Mode.

That said, Texture Paint Mode proves to be really useful for a lot of things. It works well for creating the base for textures, for example. Sometimes in the UVs, when you're working only in 2D, it's difficult to see where a detail should be placed, so you have to find where it's supposed to go in the 3D model. But because you can paint in 3D inside Blender, you have a good opportunity to start your texture by painting where the details should be on the surface of the 3D model and then using the resulting image as a reference for your final texture.

Creating the Base Texture

It's time to paint the details over Jim's model. You won't do anything fancy for the base texture—just a quick black-and-white drawing that you can use later as a base in your 2D image editor of choice.

Placing Texture Elements

Using the character's reference images to see where to place the basic texture elements, start painting over the 3D character. This time, the reference images are not the ones in the background of 3D View (by the way, at this point you can turn them off in the Properties Region inside the Background Images panel), but you can divide your interface to have a UV/Image Editor display them. If you happen to have a second monitor, you can use it to see the references at all times without having to use space in your main workspace. When you have all the basic texture elements in place (see Figure 9.4), you need to save the image so that you can keep working on it in your 2D software.

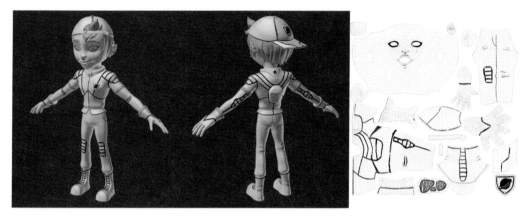

Figure 9.4   The positions of the basic texture elements have been set into a rough painting.

> **Tip**
>
> Drawing smooth lines can be tricky. For some elements, you may prefer to have steadier lines. To draw steady lines, go to the Tools Region, and activate the Smooth Stroke option in the Stroke panel. Now when you paint, the brush follows your strokes at some distance and smoothes them, providing very clean and steady lines.

Saving Your Image

Blender tells you when you have made changes to an image that you haven't yet saved. The Image menu on the UV/Image Editor header shows an asterisk (*) that indicates unsaved changes. Open the Image menu, and you see the save options. Also, pressing **Alt+S** inside the UV/Image Editor saves the image. Pressing **F3** performs a Save As... operation for the image.

Packing Your Images

In this case, packing has nothing to do with the packing in UV maps. Blender has another packing feature that allows you to include external files (such as images) in the .blend file itself. This feature is very useful when you work on multiple computers or you are collaborating with other people. Suppose that you loaded some textures from your hard drive into your model, and you want to send that model to a friend. If you send the model as it is, your friend won't see the textures because he doesn't have them on his computer, where Blender will look for them. In this case, you can pack the images. The images will be incorporated into the .blend file, and your friend will be amazed by your textured model!

To pack an image into the .blend file, go to the Image menu, and select one of the Packing options at the top. If you want to pack every single external file into the .blend file, go to the File menu, select External Data, and click Pack All Into .blend.

Keep in mind that saving all these files in the .blend file increases the file's size, which continues to multiply if you like to save your files in different versions as you progress.

Texturing in 2D Image Editing Software

Now you can take the base texture elements you just created and keep working on them in your image-editing software. I used Photoshop for the examples in this chapter, but you can use any software you want, of course.

Exporting the UVs as an Image

It's important to see the UVs while you work on the textures so that you can make the textures fit the model and make sure that they will project correctly onto the model later on. Here are the steps you need to follow to export Jim's UVs to an image file:

1. Select the object.
2. In Edit Mode, select everything (**A**).

   > **Caution**
   >
   > When you have UVs of different objects, as in Jim's case, the exporting procedure is a little different from the procedure for exporting a single object: You need to select all those objects first and join them (**Ctrl+J**). This action will probably mess up your model, so make sure that you only do this for the purpose of exporting the UVs. When you're done, without saving your changes, reload the file to its state before you joined the objects. When you join all these objects, if you jump to Edit Mode and select everything (**A**), you should see all the UVs together.

3. Open the UV/Image Editor.
4. On the UV/Image Editor header, click the UVs menu, and select Export UV Layout.
5. In the interface for saving the image, in the bottom-left corner of the screen, you need to adjust a few options. Select the Modified option to display the meshes with their modifiers applied, such as Subdivision Surface. (This is important because it allows you to see how the final mesh, in which the textures are going to be projected, will appear.) The All UVs option ensures that every UV is shown in the image, so enable it as well. For the resolution, 2048 × 2048 could work, but increase it to 4096 × 4096 so that you have enough room for details. As for the format, select .png. (You can also export vector images in .svg format.)
6. Select where you want to save the image, and click Export UV Layout.
7. In this case, and whenever you're working with similar characters, close your file without saving to prevent Blender from keeping a version with all the objects merged and their modifiers messed up.
8. Open the last saved version again. You should end up with an image similar Figure 9.5.

In the next section, I describe one of the typical methods you can use to create your texture.

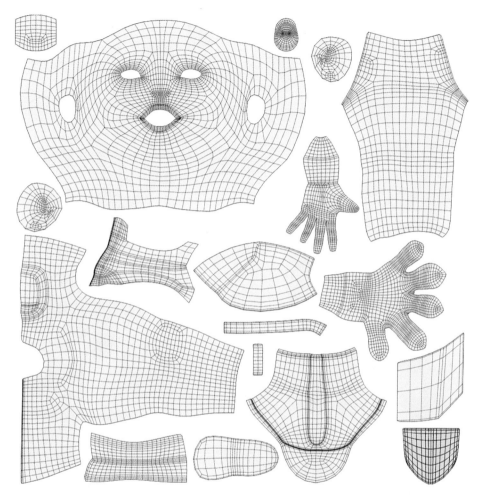

Figure 9.5   Jim's exported UV layout, which you can use as a reference to paint textures

Loading the UVs and Base Elements

First, load the reference images: the base elements you painted inside Blender and the UVs. Place these images on the top layers, using the Multiply blend mode (which makes only the dark areas visible and leaves the rest of the image transparent), so that you can turn the images on and off over your texture to check that everything is in place.

Adding Base Colors

The next steps are refining and cleaning the lines you painted in Blender. Then you can start filling the areas with colors. You can pick these colors from the color-scheme images you created during the character's design process. In Figure 9.6, you see how the texture looks at this point.

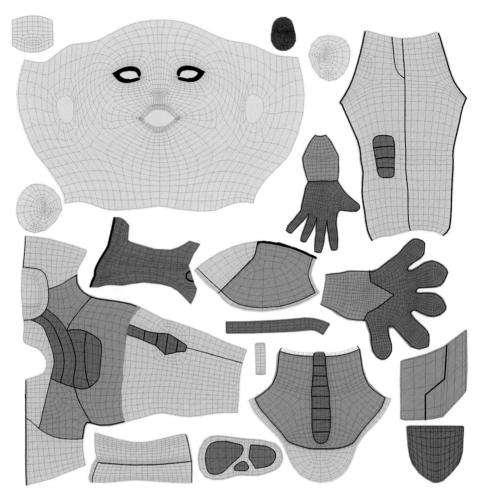

Figure 9.6   The base of the texture with the UVs
on top to help you see what's going on

Tip

At this stage, you can load the texture in Blender to make sure that everything looks right.
If you're working with Photoshop, Blender supports .psd files, so you can load them with no
conversion. If you load the image in an UV/Image Editor, you can update it quickly by pressing **Alt+R**. Also, if you save a new version of the texture, you can choose Replace Image from
the Image menu in the UV/Image Editor. This option replaces the old version everywhere you
were using it in Blender with a new version. Sometimes, after painting the basic details, you
can see that the texture looks a bit off in some areas of the 3D model, so you can go to the
UVs and adjust them slightly to get the desired result.

Adding Details

When you're done with the texture's base colors, you can start painting the details. This example is pretty simple, with flat colors, but you can add as much detail as you want (depending on what you want to achieve in terms of the character's style).

If you look at the texture in Figure 9.7, you see that some details have been added, such as thick gray lines in the clothing seams, a symbol on the badge, a darker lip color, and a little blush on the cheeks. You can also add soft shadows, wrinkles in the cloth, and other small details.

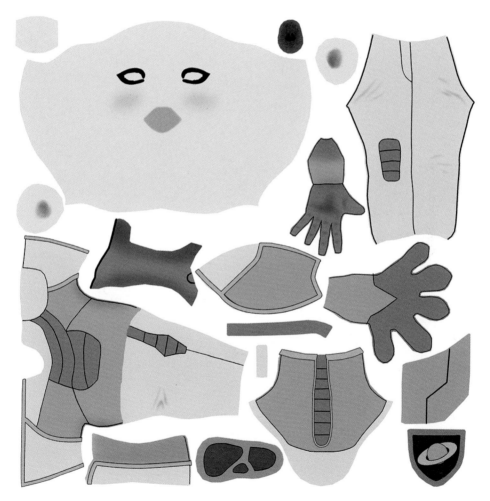

Figure 9.7   Some details have been added. (The UVs and references have been turned off to help you see those details.)

Applying the Final Touches

Finally, add a little more life to the texture by overlaying a photo of some noisy texture or perhaps painting with a brush that uses a texture. You can also define certain parts a little more. This is the stage where you finish the texture. In Figure 9.8, you see that the seams of the suit have been brought to life a little more by the addition of lines with darker and lighter colors around them, creating the impression that the clothing has a little volume.

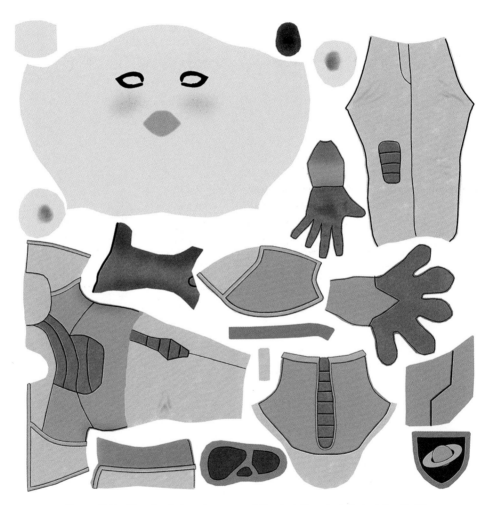

Figure 9.8   The final changes are subtle, but they help bring Jim to life.

Seeing the Painted Character in Blender

If you haven't done so already, it's time to load the texture in Blender to see how it looks on the various parts of the character. Don't hesitate to go back and forth between your 2D editing software and Blender to refine the texture as needed and to test it on your model. Figure 9.9 shows Jim's model with the texture projected onto it.

Some parts still have the mesh color without texture or anything else on them. Those parts will get their color from the Blender material that you apply to them in Chapter 10, "Materials and Shaders," so they don't need textures.

Figure 9.9   Jim is starting to look a lot more like the character you designed.

Summary

Texturing can be a lot of fun; it's a very creative process, and you can take it as far as you want. Applying the textures is the point in the process where you have the opportunity to make a character realistic. If you want realism, I recommend that you use photos to create your textures (skin, wood, grass, sand—virtually anything) instead of painting them manually. In Jim's case, the style is not photorealistic, so using basic textures to define the colors and adding some details is fine.

Depending on the requirements of the texture, its effects can be very different. If the texture is a diffuse color texture that will be mixed with other textures to define a surface's shine or reflectivity, for example, it needs to have only color information. If you're working on a video game in which lighting is more technically limited, however, the texture should include highlights and even some shadows.

If you're interested in creating really cool textures, you may want to learn how to use a 2D image editor such as Photoshop, Krita, or GIMP. These programs are really powerful, allowing you to create awesome textures that bring your characters to life!

Exercises

1. Use the method of unwrapping after texturing by loading the texture from this book's downloadable files on the companion website and making the UVs fit that texture.

2. Compose photos of skin or cloth in your image editor to make the texture look more realistic.

10

Materials and Shaders

You now have textures that define the color of the surfaces, but something's still missing: materials! *Materials* are sets of components and values that determine how the light is diffused, absorbed, reflected, or transmitted by a surface when you launch a render. A material can be reflective, may be transparent, and can even emit light. You have to set up these properties for materials. They're also called *shaders* because a shader (internally, through programming) tells the software how to draw an object on your screen. (There are even shading languages to program how these shaders work.) Hence, the process of adding materials is called shading. First, you learn about the main workflow and how to use materials. The rest of the chapter is divided into two parts so that you can see how to use materials in Blender Render and Cycles, as they're quite different when it comes to materials.

Understanding Materials

Before you get into using materials, you should get an idea of how they work and understand the differences between Blender Render and Cycles materials.

Materials Application

The process for adding materials follows:

1. Select an object.
2. On the Materials tab of the Properties Editor, select a material or create a new one to be applied to the active object.
3. Tweak the material to achieve the result you want. It's useful to add some basic lighting and take some test renders to see how the materials are behaving. Using the Rendered display mode in 3D View is a great help at this point.

> **Tip**
>
> If you want to apply the material to more than one object at the same time, select all the objects, and apply a material normally. The material will be used in the active object (the one selected last). Then press **Ctrl+L** and link the materials; they'll be applied to the entire selection from the active one.

How Materials Work

In the real world, materials on the surfaces of objects have different properties that make the light that hits them react in specific ways. Glass, for example, lets light go through it; metal shines; and wood absorbs light (doesn't reflect it). Depending on the roughness of the surface, the light is reflected, and the reflection may be blurry if the surface is rough. Something that is hot enough (like tungsten or hot metal) can even emit light itself.

In 3D, you can control some parameters that make virtual light act in ways similar to how it behaves in the real world. You can define the reflectivity, shininess, surface color, transparency, refraction coefficient, and more. With different configurations of those values, you can imitate real-world materials inside the 3D world.

Masks and Layers

Materials can be very simple … or very complex! You can have different properties of materials working together in different areas. Using masks (black-and-white images in which white means full effect and black means no effect), you can tell Blender where you want each parameter of the material to act. You can set specific parts of the material to be reflective and shine, for example, by using masks. This technique would be useful for rusty metal; the rusty parts would have no reflectivity, whereas other parts of the metal would be shiny and reflective. You can control those properties by using textures to act as masks.

Materials can be made of several layers. You can stack textures and shaders or parameters to get complex layered materials. Suppose that you have your car paint material on your car model, and you want to add some nice stickers to the model. You can use layers to put those sticker images on top of the base car paint material.

Channels

Materials can have different channels (usually, textures are loaded to affect each of those channels and control specific properties of a material), which matter during the compositing stage as well as during rendering, as they affect different characteristics of the materials. Some people find it hard to understand what those channels are, so here are brief descriptions of some of the most used channels:

- **Diffuse Color:** This channel defines the surface's base color.
- **Transparency/Opacity:** This channel sets the parts of the surface that should be transparent or opaque. Usually, you use a grayscale image or an image in a format that supports alpha (RGBA). Depending on the render engine, black is transparent, and white is opaque (or the other way around).
- **Emission:** Usually, this channel is a black/transparent image with some colored parts. From those colored parts, the software takes the color as the light emission color and the alpha value as the emission intensity. (Usually, it's possible to define only the color and use a different texture or numerical values for the intensity.)

- **Specular:** This texture defines the parts of the surface that are more or less shiny. Black is no shine, and white is full specularity. If you use colors, they indicate the colors of the shine.

- **Reflection:** This image makes some parts reflective. Again, black is no reflection, and any other colors define the color of the reflection. The lighter the color is, the greater the reflection.

- **Roughness/Glossiness:** This black-and-white texture tells the software how rough the surface is, diffusing and blurring shines and reflections in areas in which the surface is rougher. Roughness and glossiness are opposites, and different software uses one or the other. To convert roughness to glossiness and the other way around, invert the map.

- **Bump:** This channel is a black-and-white image that lends some bumpiness to the surface. The software uses this feature to change how light reflects on the surface and makes the surface look more detailed. Bump is useful for small details that are not big enough to be modeled, such as scars and scratches.

- **Normal:** This channel is like an advanced bump—an RGB (red, green, blue) texture in which each color tells the software the direction in which light should be reflected in the surface. This channel is widely used in videogames nowadays to make objects appear much more detailed than they really are. Normal maps (also called normal bumps) can be hand-painted with specific software or image-editing tools or created from two versions of a model: one with a high resolution and one with a low resolution. Normal maps are generated by baking the details of the high-resolution model into a texture for the low-resolution model.

- **Occlusion:** Occlusion is a channel that can greatly improve results at a very low cost. The channel usually is automatically generated or baked from the model into a texture (not painted, although you can paint it). Occlusion is like a soft shadows pass in which holes and cavities are marked, as this map shows proximity between geometries. If a part of the object is very close to another, that part gets shadows and then fades off. Occlusion is widely used to make shadows look more realistic, as it's not a real lighting effect.

You can use this key for most of the channels: Black and white define values, and colors define the colors. Black is no effect, and white is 100 percent effect. This key can also apply to specularity, reflection, emission, and so on.

Note

Not all software uses the same names for these channels, and even in Blender, they're named differently. The terms used here are the ones usually used. Consider these terms common names, but understand that different programs refer to them by different names.

Blender Render Materials

Blender Render is not a realistic renderer. Even though you can achieve realistic results with it, you have to work very hard to emulate manually how real-world light works. Blender Render renders a lot faster than Cycles does, however, making it a good candidate for a cool alternative if you don't need a lot of realism (for motion graphics and so on).

Materials in Blender Render have a lot of parameters. Every material has the same basic parameters, and by tweaking them, you can emulate the properties of real-world materials.

Emission is not actually supported, as Blender Render doesn't use bouncing light or mesh lights. In Blender Render, objects become bright if they have an emissive material, but they won't cast light over the scene.

Although you can use nodes to create very complex materials, in Blender Render, you usually work in the Properties Editor, on the Material and Texture tabs.

Cycles Materials

Cycles is a realistic render engine, meaning that light behaves in it in a way similar to how it does in the real world. Materials in Cycles are set up very differently from how they're set up in Blender Render. Although you can access basic properties in the Properties Editor, for slightly complex materials, you have to use the Node Editor to mix different shaders to achieve the result you need.

Cycles materials are made of shaders. Different kinds of shaders represent different types of surface properties: Diffuse, Glossy, Glass, Emit, Transparent, and so on. Sometimes, using one shader will do, but to create cool, good-looking materials, you have to mix several shaders.

Shaders are pretty simple, and each one only has a few properties, but the complex thing about them is that you have to mix them, and mixing can get very interesting!

In Cycles, you get a realistic result quite easily, but it costs you more render time than it would in Blender Render, and you need a powerful machine to work with it comfortably.

Procedural Textures

Procedural textures are widely used in computer graphics. Even procedural modeling exists. But what does *procedural* mean? It means anything that a computer program can generate mathematically through algorithms using a set of parameters that the user can input to control the result to some extent.

Suppose that you want to build a city. You can create a few buildings, but then you want to populate your city with them. You can do the job manually, duplicating those buildings one by one and placing them where you want them to be. For a big city with thousands of buildings, of course, this method wouldn't be very productive, which is why software offers you ways to do the job procedurally. Using different tools and giving you some level of control, the software can populate the city for you randomly.

What is a procedural texture? It's a texture that the software generates automatically to fit any surface. These kinds of textures are like patterns that repeat randomly, and you have some level of control over their features.

Blender has several procedural-textures options. For the texture type, instead of selecting Image or Movie, you can select any other type to create procedural textures. (I discuss this option later in this chapter.) Clouds is one of the types, for example; it generates a noisy pattern, which is useful for giving a surface variations in color. When you select a type, the Image panel is replaced by specific options for the type of texture you selected.

Blender has a lot of procedural texture types (Clouds, Blend, Wood, Checker, and so on), each with its own properties and uses. Make sure that you check them all out!

Shading Your Character with Blender Render

In this section, you dive into the Blender Render materials and learn about their properties. The Properties Editor has a Material tab and a Texture tab. In the Material tab, you edit the surface properties like color, reflection, roughness, and such; in the Texture tab, you load textures, and you tell Blender how to project them over the material and what channels they will be affecting.

Caution

You have to decide whether you want to work with Blender Render or Cycles before you start shading. Select the desired engine in the main menu (Info Editor) at the top of the screen. In the center of that menu is a button that you click to display a drop-down list of render engines. Choose the one you want, and carry on. You can always change your choice later, but materials are not completely compatible between different engines, so if you change later, you may need to rework some materials.

Setting Up Blender Render Materials

First, you learn how to set up materials. In Figure 10.1, you can explore the Material tab of the Properties Editor. To make Blender display these options, you need to create a new material or select an existing one from the list.

The following list describes each of the panels in Figure 10.1 so that you have a better understanding of how to use them and know their basic options:

- **Current selection:** At the top of the Material tab are symbols and names of the object and material for which the settings are being displayed. As always, clicking the pin on the left side pins those options and keeps them visible even if you select a different object with a different material, which is handy if you want to compare two materials (remember that you can have two or more Properties Editors in Blender) or if you're working on a material but want to move things around without losing sight of it.

Current selection

Materials list

Current material

Material preview

Material color

Material shininess

Light effect on material

Material transparency

Material reflectivity

Subsurface Scattering

Hair Particles rendering

Material options

Shadows options

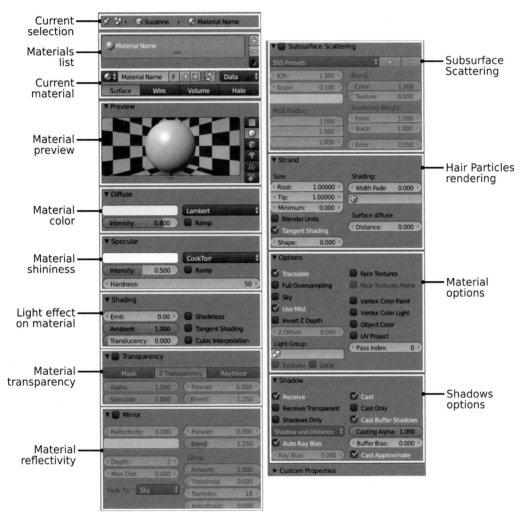

Figure 10.1   The Material tab of the Properties Editor and its panels

- **Materials list:** The Materials list is a list of the materials that is assigned to the selected object. (Yes, it is possible to assign more than one material to a single object; you learn how in "Shading Jim with Blender Render" later in this chapter.) This list has different slots. When you select a slot, you can see the material that has been used in that slot and replace it with another material.

- **Current material:** Below the Materials list is the current material's name. You can rename your materials in that box. If you see a number at the right side of the name, that number is the number of objects using the current material. Click that number to duplicate the material so that you can tweak it as a new material for the selected object alone. You can also duplicate the material by clicking the + button.

If you want to discard the material for that object, select a different one from the list or click the **X** button to discard it.

Near the name is a button that you click to enable or disable nodes. If you want to use nodes for this material, activate that option in the Node Editor to make nodes available.

Right below the material's name are four buttons that indicate the type of material you're working with. Surface is the usual material type; Wire shows only the wireframe (edges) of the mesh; Volume emulates volumetric objects such as clouds and smoke; and Halo makes the vertices of the object shine, producing a halo effect.

- **Preview:** The Preview panel shows a real-time visualization of what the material would look like with the current settings. On the right side of the panel, you can select the shape in which you want to see the preview of the material.

- **Diffuse:** This panel is where you set the base color of the material. If you activate the Ramp option, you can describe a gradient. The drop-down list lets you select the shader type you want to use (Lambert, by default), which affects the algorithms that Blender will use when computing the surface of the material.

- **Specular:** The Specular panel is where you tell Blender whether you want your material to be shiny, as well as where you indicate the shine's color, intensity, and hardness. You can also use a gradient for the shines if you enable the Ramp option.

- **Shading:** Here, you can set how the surface of the material reacts to light. Emit makes the object look as though it is emitting light. Shadeless makes the material be unaffected by lights or shadows (you see only the original color), which is very useful when you want something to appear in the render just as you colored it (such as background images or videos that you use as textures in the scene).

- **Transparency:** The name says it all! When Transparency is enabled, your material becomes transparent. Mask mode lets you display the background image where the material is shown. Z Transparency is basic transparency; it renders fast and is simple. Raytrace is the most realistic option; it provides an IoR (Index of Refraction) option that makes the material refract light and distort everything that is behind it. This feature is useful for emulating glass, for example.

- **Mirror:** This panel defines the reflectivity of your material. You can increase the amount of reflection and its color and set some options to make the material look better (such as Fresnel, which smoothes the effect toward the parts of the object that are not facing the camera). If you have a lot of reflective materials in your scene, you may want to increase the Depth value, which defines the number of times a reflection can be reflected in another reflection—which sounds crazy but is useful for preventing infinite reflections that would take a long time to render. Max. Dist (Maximum Distance) controls how much distance the material can reflect; anything farther than that distance fades to the material or background color. Gloss, when set to less than 100 percent (its default value), shows a set of options for making the reflections blurry and for controlling their quality. For Samples, the higher the number, the less noise reflections have, but also the longer they take to render.

- **Subsurface Scattering:** This panel lets you achieve some realistic complex materials such as skin, rubber, jade, and wax. The setting here computes the light passing through the object, so the surface depends on the thickness in that part of the object. Imagine a face. If you put a light behind it, you see the light passing through the ears and getting red because of the blood under the skin. You can achieve that kind of effect with the help of these options.

- **Strand:** This panel offers a group of options to set up the material when you're rendering strands of hair generated with hair particles.

- **Options:** Here, you'll find options for the material. These options are usually used for more advanced purposes, so you may want to check Blender's official documentation for details. An interesting option is Traceable; when it's disabled, the material won't cast shadows or be visible in reflections and refractions (anything that uses raytracing methods).

- **Shadow:** You use this useful panel in upcoming chapters. The Shadow panel allows you to tell Blender how you want the shadows to act with the material. If you have transparent materials, for example, they cast transparent shadows only over those materials that have the Receive Transparent option enabled (to save render time). The Shadows Only option makes the object transparent, but when rendering, you see the shadows cast over it, making this option useful for composing objects with their shadows on top of a photo or other image.

As you can see, you can manipulate a lot of options to get the desired result. And these options are only the tip of the iceberg; when you mix all these properties with textures, you get even more options and really nice-looking materials.

> **Caution**
>
> Remember that if a material is not being used by any object when you close Blender, it is removed and won't exist when you open the file again. If you really want to keep a material, be sure to click the F button next to its name (Fake User) to prevent Blender from deleting it.

Applying Textures in Blender Render

This section discusses the Texture tab of the Properties Editor. Figure 10.2 shows the Texture tab and its panels.

The following list describes these panels:

- **Current selection:** Like the Material tab (refer to the preceding section), this panel lists the active object, material, and texture you're working on. You can use the pin exactly the same way as in other editors. At the bottom of this panel are three little buttons to select the type of texture you want to work on. The button with the World icon (the first one) uses a texture; the second button allows you to work on the textures for the current material, and the third button lets you create textures for things like brushes.

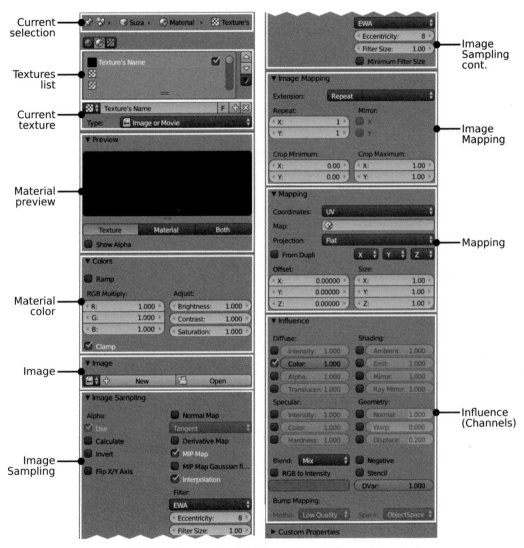

Figure 10.2   Texture tab of the Properties Editor and its panels

- **Textures list:** The Textures list is similar to layers. You can select one of the slots and then create or load a texture for that slot. You can load another texture in the next slot and make it transparent; then you see the first one behind it. As with modifiers, the layers at the top are below the ones at the bottom. This panel is used for more than just different layers of the same texture; you might have different textures affecting different channels or parts of the material, for example.

- **Current texture:** The current texture's name and drop-down list work exactly the same as any other datablock, allowing you to select the type of texture you're going to be using. In Figure 10.2, Image or Movie is selected, as it's the one you'll need when you load your own images to use as textures for the materials. The others are, for the most part, procedural textures. The texture type you define in this panel changes the next panels to show the parameters and options for the selected texture type.

- **Preview:** In the Preview panel, you can see how the current texture looks and decide whether you want to see the texture, the material, or both.

- **Colors:** This panel shows several options that change the image colors, such as Brightness, Contrast, and Saturation.

- **Image:** The Image panel is specific to the Image or Movie texture type. It gives you some options to load an existing texture or to create one generated by Blender as discussed in earlier chapters (such as a UV test grid).

- **Image Sampling:** This panel provides options that tell Blender how to interpret the image you've loaded. How to interpret the alpha of an image, for example, is one of the things you indicate with the Image Sampling options.

  > **Tip**
  >
  > If you want to use Normal maps, you should activate the Normal Map option of the Image Sampling panel, and select the type of normal map you're using. (The most common normal map type is Tangent.)

- **Image Mapping:** Here, you can offset, resize, and crop the image you've loaded into Blender. You can also specify whether you want the image to be repeated beyond its boundaries, like tiles in a wall.

- **Mapping:** Not to be confused with Image Mapping, this panel lets you define how the image is mapped (projected) onto the object. If you've unwrapped the model to which you're applying this material, you should choose UVs from the Coordinates drop-down list.

- **Influence:** As mentioned in the "Channels" section earlier in this chapter, this panel is where you select which channels of the material are affected by the current texture and the amount of effect the texture has on them. By default, Influence affects only the Color (Diffuse) channel. If you have a normal map loaded, for example, you should disable Color and enable Normal in the Geometry section to define its effect. If you have a black-and-white image to define the reflectivity of the material, turn on Ray Mirror.

  Suppose that you want to mix two images. You can load them in different Texture slots and adjust the influences in their respective channels. Also, you can change the blending mode (Mix, by default), which is similar to using the layers-blending modes in Adobe Photoshop or GIMP.

  Alternatively, you can use a mask. If you enable the Stencil option, the current texture is used as a mask for the previous slot in this Editor. Combinations really give you a lot of options!

Tip

Usually, you want to load a texture that has an alpha (such as a .png image), and you want to use that alpha as the transparency in Blender. The process is kind of tricky when you aren't sure how to do it. Here's how:

1. Activate Transparency for the material (Z Transparency or Raytrace in the material properties), and to give the control of the alpha to the texture, set the Alpha of the material's Transparency option to 0.

2. Load your image, including its alpha, in the Textures tab, and apart from the Color channel, enable its Alpha influence and set it to the maximum. Now the material will use the alpha from your image.

Shading Jim in Blender Render

Now that you know how materials work in Blender Render, you're ready to start shading Jim!

Setting Things Up

Before you start shading your character, however, make sure that you have a few things set up so you can see what's going on when you start adding materials. Follow these steps:

1. In the 3D View Properties Region (**N**), find the Shading panel, and select the GLSL shading method (the one that Blender uses to display materials in the view).

2. On the 3D View header, set the display mode to Texture or Material so that Blender shows textures and materials in the 3D preview.

3. If you have no light in your scene, add one. I usually add a Sun light, which is directional and illuminates the entire thing. An Omni light illuminates only the area around it, and you need to keep moving it around to see what's going on in different parts of the model. If you don't add a light, everything is black unless you set the materials to shadeless, which is useful for testing your textures but not for setting material properties such as shininess.

Note

Even though you set everything up correctly, keep in mind that in 3D View, you won't see all of the properties of the material: reflections, transparencies, shadows, refractions, and so on. Such properties work correctly only in the final render, and even though you can preview things like transparencies and shadows in certain situations, they won't be good-quality. In 3D View, you get a basic preview of what the material will look like. That's why when you work on a complex material, you should do test renders now and then to see how it behaves. You can also use the visualization's Rendered mode, which is slower but produces more accurate results.

Adding Basic Materials

To start, add a basic material, as follows:

1. Select Jim's face.

2. On to the Material tab of the Properties Editor, create a new material, and name it Jim_mat (material for Jim).

3. Jump to the Texture tab of the Properties Editor, create a new texture, and set the texture type to Image or Movie.

4. Inside the Texture properties, search the Image panel, and load the texture you've created for Jim. At this point, you should see the texture weirdly shown over Jim's face. Obviously, the UVs are not working yet.

5. To set the texture to be projected by using the UVs, scroll down to the Mapping panel of the Texture tab, and set Coordinates to UV. Now you should see the texture of Jim's face properly projected.

6. Select all the objects that will use the textures you've made, such as the jacket, cap, boots, gloves, and pants. Select the face so that it becomes the active selection. Then press **Ctrl+L**, and select Materials from the list to make all those objects use the same material as the face, and they'll use the part of the texture that their UVs indicate.

7. Select the hair objects and the eyebrows, and add a new material to them, which you can call hair_mat. In the Diffuse panel, choose the blue color that you used in the designs.

> **Tip**
>
> Keep in mind that you can load the designs into an UV/Image Editor. When you need to use a specific color that is present in an image, just click the color selector, pick the Eyedropper tool, and then click anywhere in Blender (like in the image reference) to select that color.

8. Repeat the process in Step 7 with the rest of the objects that still don't have materials. Add materials to them as needed, and set their colors. You'll refine those materials in the "Refining Materials" section later in this chapter. Leave the eyes alone for now.

You should see something similar to Figure 10.3 after adding materials.

Figure 10.3   Jim looks like this after you add a few basic materials to him.

Adding Several Materials to a Single Object

Jim's eyes are different from the other objects. Although they're a single object, they have different materials to define the pupil, iris, eyeball, and cornea. Figure 10.4 provides a reference of the materials you'll be using. Pay attention to the Materials list in the Properties Editor.

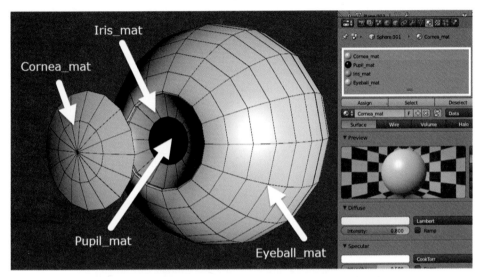

Figure 10.4   The eye object's materials (The cornea has been separated so that you can see what's going on inside.)

Here are the steps for adding materials to the eye:

1. Select the eyeball, apply a material to it, and call the material Eyeball_mat.

2. Enter Edit Mode (**Tab**), add a new material slot to the list, and create a new material in the slot. Call that material Cornea_mat. Select the cornea (**L**). Make sure that you have Cornea_mat selected in the Materials list, and with the cornea selected in the model, click the Assign button to assign that material from the list to the selected faces. With the cornea selected, press **H** to hide it so that you can work on the faces inside it.

3. Using Figure 10.4 as a reference, repeat the process in Step 2 to create two new materials called Iris_mat and Pupil_mat, and assign them to the iris and pupil faces. Pupil_mat should be black, and Iris_mat should be the same blue color that was used for the hair. Then press **Alt+H** to unhide the cornea.

4. Unfortunately, you have to repeat the entire process with the other eye or delete the second eye and duplicate the one you just worked on by mirroring it.

For now, the materials are basic. In the next section, you learn how to tweak them to make them look better and use more advanced properties.

> **Tip**
>
> You can quickly add different materials to a single mesh as you did for the eyeballs, using basic materials that are correctly named. After the materials are assigned to the faces of the mesh, you can select them from the list to tweak them and make them look cooler, even in Object Mode. You won't need to select the faces for any reason after the materials have been assigned.

Refining Materials

It's time to start tweaking the details of the materials to achieve a better result. First, you retouch the objects that are using materials without textures, such as the hair and the eyes. By working on these objects, you learn the how the properties of the materials work and get a taste of what you can achieve. Follow these steps:

1. Select any object with the hair material on it (eyebrows or the hair itself), and jump to the material Properties Editor. Reduce Specular Intensity to 0.3 to reduce the shininess. Set Specular Color to the same blue you used for Diffuse Color, and give Specular Hardness a value of around 100 to make the shines a little sharper.

    > **Tip**
    >
    > If you hover the mouse over a parameter (even a color) on the menus and press **Ctrl+C**, you copy it to the clipboard, and by hovering the mouse over another color selector and pressing **Ctrl+V**, you paste that parameter. This technique is useful for things like copying the diffuse color and pasting it on the specular color.

2. Next, arrange the eyes' materials to give Jim some life. Usually, you use textures for the iris and such, but in this case, to keep thing simple, you'll be playing only with material values. Select the eyeball to gain access to the four materials that the eyes own.

3. First, work on the cornea, as you need to have it transparent to show the iris and the pupil. Scroll down within the Properties Editor; activate Raytrace Transparency; and set Alpha to 0 (to make the material completely transparent), Specular to 1 (to make the shines visible even though the surface is transparent), and IOR to 1.5 (to refract light inside the cornea, distorting the pupil and the iris in an interesting, realistic way so that these objects don't look like they're inside a hole). At this point, you may want to have a small render preview (or use Rendered display mode in the viewport) to see how things look as you tweak the materials.

4. To make the shines in the cornea crisper, go to the Specular panel again, and set the Specular mode to Toon. This setting gives the shine a toon effect, making it very sharp. Set Intensity to 0.3, Size to 0.07 (to prevent the shine from covering the entire cornea), and Smooth to 0 (to make it sharp).

5. Next, you work the pupil. You may want the pupil to be absolutely black, which is simple enough. Select Pupil_mat from the Materials list. In the Shading panel, enable Shadeless so that lights and shadows won't affect the pupil anymore and it'll always be pure black (its base color).

6. For Iris_mat, you may want to do something similar, but you still want to capture little shadows and shines. Set Specular Intensity to 0.2 so that the shines are more subtle. Turn Specular Hardness up to 100 to make the shines sharper. In the Shading panel, set the Emit value to 0.05; this setting is similar to the Shadeless option, but you can set the amount of the effect. With these settings, the iris won't be affected much by the shadows. Don't turn Emit up a lot, though; otherwise, the iris will look like a lamp when the eye is in a dark environment!

7. The material for the eyeball is quite simple, so increase the hardness value to make the shines more defined.

Using Textures to Control Material Properties

Go back to the material that has the textures in it (Jim_mat), because now you use textures to control the material's properties. Right now, it shines and has a very bright, plastic-like appearance. You'll solve that issue by using textures in the appropriate channels. When you have a surface that is made of a single material, you can add a material to it and set the properties, and that's it! But when you have an object or character made of several materials with different properties, textures are the way to go, as they allow you to control different parts of the material to give each part different property values. Also, most materials have some variation across their surface, and you can achieve that effect by using textures.

Using Jim's texture as a base, I turned it to black-and-white and added some layers on top to darken some areas and brighten others. I came up with the two textures that you see in Figure 10.5.

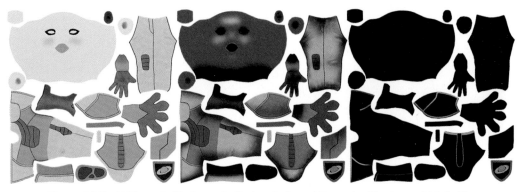

Figure 10.5   Diffuse (left), Specularity (center), and Specular Hardness (right). The textures in the middle and right were created from the texture on the left.

Follow this process to set up textures and make them control the material's channels and appearance:

1. Select Jim's material (the one to which you added the main color texture). In the Texture tab, select a new slot from the list; name it Specular; and switch its type to Image or Movie.

2. In the Image panel, load the texture for the specularity.

3. In the Mapping panel, set Coordinates to UV. This step is where the magic happens. (You can turn on Textured display mode in the view to see the difference.)

4. In the Influence panel of the Texture tab, turn Color off so that Jim doesn't appear to be black-and-white ... and weird. Turn on Specular Color, and leave its value at 1. Now Jim should look a lot better, and if you orbit the camera around him, you see that the darker parts of the texture don't shine, giving it a more natural look.

5. Pick a new slot from the Textures list, create a new texture, call it Hardness, and load the other picture. This texture usually needs to be really dark to work properly, and the darker it is, the softer the shines are. In some areas, however, you don't want the shines to be too soft, so leave light colors in those areas' texture. Set Coordinates to UV again. In the Influence panel, disable Color, and enable Specular Color and Hardness. As this texture is on top of the Specular one, the Specular Color overrides it, but if you decrease the influence of this texture, the previous one gains some effect, and the one on top loses some.

6. Another thing you can do to add some detail is select the Diffuse slot (the one for the base color texture), go to the Influence panel, and enable the normal channel. Set its value to something really low, such as 0.1, so that it's not very visible. Usually, you'd create a separate grayscale for the bump effect, but sometimes, using the diffuse texture for adding some subtle bumping to the surface works just fine, so if you're short on time, you may try doing that.

Making Final Adjustments

Some little tweaks are still needed, such as adding the materials for the small details of the clothing. Follow these steps:

1. For the clothing details, adjust the material's Specular value and Hardness so that they fit the rest of the character.

2. Repeat Step 1 for the communicator.

3. The teeth and the tongue are hidden, but of course, you have to add materials to them as well. Add a white material to the teeth and a reddish one with a bit of specularity to the tongue.

Making Render Tests

You've probably made a few render tests during the process to see how everything looked so far. Now you make a more elaborate render test to get a taste of how the character could look in a final render with some shadows and such (see Figure 10.6). Follow these steps:

1. Create a couple of lights, and set their type to Sun. Rotate one of the lights as the main lighting, and rotate the second so that it comes from the back of the character as a rim light to illuminate the borders or the parts of the character that are in the shadows and hidden from the main light. You can also reduce the intensity and change the color of the second light.

2. Enable the suns' raytrace shadows. You can increase Samples to around 8 and increase Soft Size as well.

3. In the World tab of the Properties Editor, tweak a few settings to make your render look better. You can change the background color, for example.

4. In the World panel, change Horizon Color to show the desired tonality.

5. Enable Ambient Occlusion, and set it to multiply; this setting creates a soft shadows effect and multiplies it over the image, giving it more realistic lighting. (If you want to clearly see the effect of ambient occlusion, use it in a scene that has only white materials.) You may get a little noise in the result. If so, in the Gather panel, increase Samples to 10 or more. Keep in mind that few samples render faster, but more samples produce a better and less noisy result.

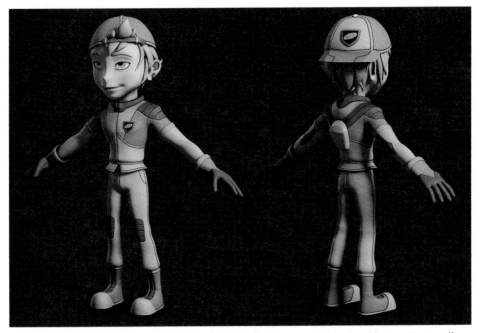

Figure 10.6   Final test render with Blender Render materials. Looking pretty good!

6. Enable Environment Lighting to add light coming from everywhere. Use a low value to prevent the shadow areas from becoming completely black, which looks very unnatural.

7. Create a plane on the floor, and add a material to it. In the Shadow panel of the Properties Editor, turn on Shadows Only to display the floor shadows in the final render and let the camera see the background color through it.

Shading Your Character with Cycles

Now that you have Blender Render under control, you should see how Cycles works, as it's pretty different. In Cycles, materials and lighting are based on reality, and the material properties are very different from those in Blender Render. Also, the way in which you build materials in Cycles has almost nothing to do with the way materials are created in Blender Render.

> **Caution**
>
> Make sure to choose Cycles from the render-engine selector on the main menu at the top of the interface. Otherwise, you won't see the options that are explained in the rest of this chapter.

Using Cycles Materials

First, you need to understand that in Cycles, a material is made up of shaders. You have various shaders to choose from, each with different properties from real materials, and you'll have to mix them to create your own materials. Before you start diving into shaders, review Figure 10.7 to see what the Material tab looks like when you use the Cycles render engine.

This menu may look simpler than Blender Render's at first sight, but here's the difference. In Blender Render, you see everything that is available in Blender Render. In Cycles, you can add shaders, mix them, nest them, and so on, so the material and menu can become really complex. Here are some of the panels you'll find in this menu:

- **Current selection, Materials list, and current material:** The first three parts of the menu are exactly the same as they are in Blender Render. They show the current selection; a Materials list that allows you to use different materials inside the same object; and a drop-down list that allows you to select an existing material, rename it, or create a new one. (The menu shown in Figure 10.7 is the one you see after clicking the button to create a material.)

- **Preview:** The Preview panel is almost the same as the one in Blender Render, though you'll notice that this one updates little by little. In the first stages, you may get some noisy results because the material is being rendered by Cycles, which works differently from Blender Render. In Cycles, the render is calculated through samples—the more samples, the cleaner and less noisier the result.

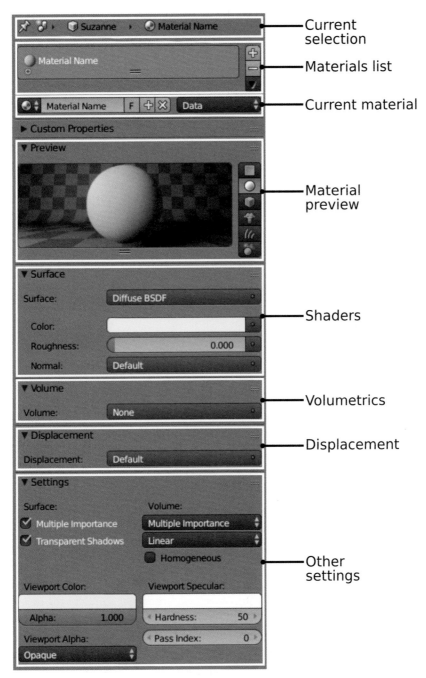

Current selection

Materials list

Current material

Material preview

Shaders

Volumetrics

Displacement

Other settings

Figure 10.7   Material tab of the Cycles Properties Editor—
very different from the one in Blender Render!

- **Surface:** This panel is the main panel of Cycles' Material tab. Here is where you select the type of shaders you're going to use and set their properties. You learn about shaders in the next section, "Using Basic Shaders."

- **Volume:** This option allows you to use volumetric effects with the objects that use this material. Volumetrics is the technology that simulates fog, smoke, and gasses— very useful for adding ambience to a scene. Volumetrics let light pass through and create cool effects. Unfortunately, even though they've been improved in recent versions, volumetrics are still complex and slow to render. If you want to use these effects, you usually want to add a shader (Volume Scatter or Volume Absorption) in this panel and have nothing on the surface (as Volume represents what's inside the object, and the object would be covered if something was on its surface).

- **Displacement:** This technology allows you to use a grayscale (height map) texture to deform the surface of a mesh so that it has much more detail. Although it's possible to use this feature, Displacement is still under development in Cycles. Alternatively, you can apply a modifier to the mesh to use Displacement, but it's really heavy, as you have to subdivide the mesh a lot to make it work properly.

- **Settings:** Here, you find some more options to set how the material interacts with certain ray types (make it invisible for reflections or shadow casting, for example).

Using Basic Shaders

Cycles materials are made of shaders. How can you add shaders to a material? When you add a new material, inside the Surface panel, you see a Diffuse BSDF shader. Clicking the shader's name displays a list of shaders. Following are some of the most-used shaders (but I recommend that you try the rest of them, as you may find them useful):

- **Diffuse BSDF:** This shader is the basic shader—just a colored surface.

- **Transparent BSDF:** This shader makes the surface transparent.

- **Glossy BSDF:** This shader is shiny and reflective, and by controlling its roughness, you get more blurred shines and reflections.

- **Hair BSDF:** This shader is specially tailored to be used with hair-strand particles.

- **Refraction:** This shader adds a refraction effect to the surface.

- **Glass:** This shader is a glass effect, including refraction, transparency, reflection, and glossiness.

- **Anisotropic BSDF:** This shader is very useful for simulating metallic pieces. On top of the effects of the Glossy shader, it adds anisotropic shines to the surface.

- **Volume Scatter and Volume Absorption:** These two shaders are used exclusively in the Volume part of a material. They're made to represent a volumetric effect, such as fog, smoke, or some phenomenon that happens inside transparent objects such as glass.

- **Emission:** Probably one of the coolest shaders, Emission allows you to convert any mesh into light! This shader emits light, and you can control its intensity and color. Although you could light a scene with objects that use this shader type, I recommend using lights when possible, as emissive materials can make your render slower and noisier.

Cycles has more shaders, but you'll probably use these most often. Each of them has a couple of options that you can tweak to control its properties (color, roughness, intensity, and so on).

Mixing and Adding Shaders

Shaders can't do much on their own. That's why inside the Shaders list are two special shaders, which are not shaders at all: Mix and Add.

A Mix shader lets you mix two shaders and adjust the influence of each of them on the result. Suppose that you want a simply colored surface with some shininess. You can use a Mix shader, and in its two slots that show up, you can add a Diffuse BSDF and a Glossy BSDF. Then adjust the properties and colors, and tweak the Mix Shader Fac (Factor). A value of 0 shows only the first shader, whereas 1 shows only the second one, as though the shaders were layers; values between 0 and 1 blend the shaders.

An Add shader, instead of letting you set the blending value between the two shaders, allows you to add colors; it generally gives you brighter results. Be careful with the Add shader, especially when using it with materials that reflect light, as it can generate noise in the render. Cycles is a physically based render engine, so one of the rules of reality applies: energy conservation. Materials you create should never reflect more light than they receive, which is something that can happen with an Add shader, as it sums the reflections of both materials connected to it. The Add shader is especially useful if you want to add reflections from a Glossy shader on top of a Diffuse shader, for example, but it must be used carefully. For most shader mixing, however, I recommend the Mix shader.

You can add Mix shaders inside Mix shaders (nesting) to get even more complex shaders. Do you see how complicated Cycles materials can get?

Tip
The Add shader doesn't have a Mix Factor parameter, like the Mix shader. Still, you can control the intensity of the mix by making the added materials darker or brighter. If you're adding a Glossy shader on top of a diffuse one, for example, you can control the amount of reflections by making the Glossy shader's color darker or brighter.

Loading Textures

Loading textures in Cycles is easier than in Blender Render. Take the Diffuse BSDF shader, for example. To the right of each of its properties is a button with a little circle. Clicking one of these buttons shows you a list of options. In that list, select Image Texture, and Blender displays below it the options for loading and controlling the image. A new parameter called Vector shows up as well. Vector is similar to Mapping Coordinates in Blender Render. If your object has UVs, the texture will use them by default. If you want to make sure that your texture is projected correctly, select the option Texture Coordinate | UV from the Vector list.

> **Note**
>
> You won't be using the Node Editor to create materials in Cycles at this time except for a couple of little tweaks, mainly because the materials you're going to create for now are basic. In Chapter 14, "Lighting, Compositing, and Rendering," you learn how to use the Node Editor. After that, you'll understand how nodes work, and you'll know how to use them for materials creation. This knowledge is important, as you'll have more control of Cycles materials when you work on them in the Node Editor.

Shading Jim in Cycles

Now that you understand how Cycles materials work, you can jump into using shaders to make Jim look good.

Basic Shading

Before you start, you may want to add one or two lights to the scene. Also, be sure to switch to Rendered mode from time to time to see how everything's looking. Keep in mind that staying in Rendered mode constantly could make working with materials a slower process, depending on the complexity of the scene and the power of your hardware.

Follow these steps to create Jim's basic shading in Cycles:

1. Select Jim's face, and add a new material called Jim_mat. Add a Mix shader to it, and for the first slot, pick a Diffuse BSDF shader. In the color field, load Jim's textures as an image, and make sure that Vector is set to Texture Coordinates | UV. The material may look a little dark, but don't worry; that's because the other half of the material is still empty.

2. Select all the objects that use the textures; then select the one that you just added the material to. Press **Ctrl+L** and select Materials to make all those objects use the same material.

3. Add a material to the hair elements called Hair_mat, and set Surface as a Diffuse BSDF with the blue color from the designs.

4. Select an eyeball, and follow the same steps you followed to add materials to its parts with Blender Render: Create four material slots in the list, and call them Eyeball_mat, Cornea_mat, Pupil_mat, and Iris_mat. For the pupil and iris, add Diffuse BSDF shaders with black and blue colors, respectively.

5. The cornea and eyeball are a little trickier. For the eyeball's material, add a Mix shader. Select a white Diffuse BSDF in the first slot and a Glossy BSDF in the second slot. Turn the roughness of the Glossy shader to 0.5 so that the shines are more blurred.

6. For the cornea, add a Glass BSDF shader. Give the Glass shader's color a light blue tone; increase the IOR (Index of Refraction) to 1.7 (similar to what you did in Blender Render); and set Roughness to something very low, such as 0.03, to make sure that the lights provoke some kind of reflection in the material. (Lights are not visible in reflections if there is no roughness.)

7. The cornea is really dark, because even though it's mostly transparent, it's creating a shadow in the eye's interior. To solve that problem, go to the Object tab of the Properties Editor (the one with the yellow cube), and in the Ray Visibility panel at the bottom, turn off Shadow. This feature prevents the eyeball from casting shadows. The cornea will look transparent, and light rays will go through it as though it didn't exist.

Advanced Shading

A few steps are needed to finish the shading of Jim in Cycles. You need to tweak the material that uses the textures so that it works properly. Follow these steps:

1. In the preceding section, you added a Mix shader to the parts of Jim that were half empty. To work on that shader now, in the second slot, pick a Glossy BSDF. This material causes some parts to reflect light.

2. Load a couple more textures to control the effect of the shaders' properties. Figure 10.8 shows the textures you are loading. The one that controls Mix Shader Factor is the same one used for Specular Intensity in Blender Render: a grayscale image in which the white areas are shiny and the black ones are not. Finally, you'll use another texture to control the Roughness value. Roughness in Cycles is exactly the opposite of the Hardness in Blender Render: black would define a sharp reflection, while white would be a totally blurred reflection. Notice in the figure that the texture on the right has some darker marks: Those marks have sharper shines.

   At this point, the textures are not yet working. You need to tweak the nodes in the Node Editor to arrange them. Unfortunately, when you load these types of textures from the Properties Editor, they automatically pick their Alpha values, but you need to use their color, and the only way to change it is to use nodes. For that task, you have to perform some basic adjustments in the Material nodes.

Figure 10.8   Diffuse color (left), Specularity (center), and Roughness (right)

3. Select an area of the interface, and switch it to a Node Editor. You should see the current material nodes. If not, select the object with the material you're tweaking. Look in the Node Editor's header for three buttons that show a sphere icon for

materials, a checkerboard icon for textures, and a layers icon for compositing. Switch to materials. On the same header is a material list, select Jim_mat.

4. Next, arrange the nodes, which may be a bit overlapped (a side effect of working in the Properties Editor with Cycles materials, all of which are created in the same place). Left-click and drag them around until you see the tree clearly. Figure 10.9 gives you an idea of how the tree should look.

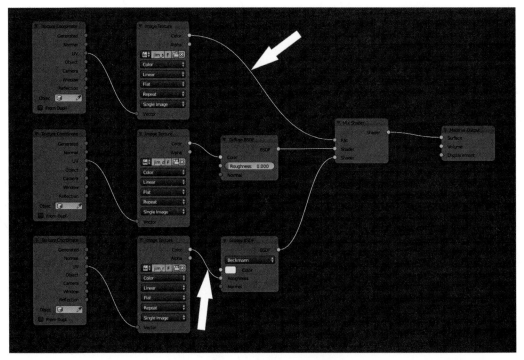

Figure 10.9   Jim's material node tree. Make sure that you reconnect the marked nodes correctly. (The connections between nodes have been highlighted to improve their visibility.)

5. When you see all the connections in a structure similar to the one shown in Figure 10.9, reconnect the marked lines as shown in the figure so that the color of those two textures is used instead of their alpha. Left-click and drag over the little dots at the sides of each node (input and output noodles) to reconnect them. (When you add shaders from the Properties Editor, another side effect is that this method creates a Texture Coordinate node for each texture. You could connect the same Texture Coordinate node for all three of the textures, as it tells them only that they should use the UVs to be projected.)

6. Adjust the material for the clothing details. Add a Glossy BSDF to the second slot, set Roughness to 0.15, and then reduce Mix Shader Factor to 0.1. This step makes those pieces of cloth look similar to the other details that are inside the textures.

Running Render Tests

Jim is shaded, so it's time to do some cool test renders. In Blender Render, you have to activate some stuff to get a better and more believable result, but in Cycles, which has a more realistic approach, the default settings and results are already pretty good by default. Add a couple of things, though, by following these steps:

1. Create a light setup similar to the one used for the Blender Render scene. Create two suns: a main one and a secondary one used as a rim light, with less intensity and warmer color.

   Unfortunately, having a material that only receives shadows is trickier in Cycles than in Blender Render (you have to do it through compositing, which you'll learn to do in the final chapters), so instead, you'll add a sky to the background.

2. Go to the World tab of the Properties Editor, and in the Surface panel, you see that Sky is similar to other materials. By default, Sky should have a background shader. Click Color to select a texture, and select Sky from the list. Then arrange the settings until they look good to you. If you click and drag over the sphere, you change the sun's direction.

The result should be similar to Figure 10.10.

Figure 10.10   Result of rendering Jim in Cycles

Summary

You should understand the clear differences between Cycles and Blender Render, both in the results and in the workflow required to build the materials. At this point, you know how to create basic materials by using textures in both render engines. (You'll understand nodes better when you get to Chapter 14, "Lighting, Compositing, and Rendering." Jim should look quite similar to your concepts.

Exercises

1. What's the advantage of using textures that control material properties?
2. What are some of the differences between the Blender Render and Cycles render engines?
3. Can you make a mesh emit light in Blender Render? Can you make a mesh emit light in Cycles?
4. What's the point of increasing Samples in the illumination options for Blender Render? What the point of doing the same in Cycles?

V

Bringing Your
Character to Life

11 Character Rigging

12 Animating Your Character

11

Character Rigging

Rigging is probably the most technical and complex part of the character-creation process. Your character exists, but it's static: It needs a skeleton that moves and deforms the mesh properly so that you can animate it and bring it to life. In this chapter, you learn the basics of creating skeletons, rigging them (which means setting your skeleton up so that it works as expected and can be used intuitively and comfortably), and skinning them (which is the process that makes the skeleton deform the mesh as though it were skin). You also learn how to use Drivers to control the facial expressions of your character. When everything is ready, you set the character up to be reused in other scenes via linking or appending.

Understanding the Rigging Process

In this section, I talk a little about the rigging process so that you have a better understanding of how everything works.

What's a Rig?

In Blender, rigs are called *armatures*. An armature is a container inside which you have the bones that conform to the rig. The purpose of a good rig is to make it easy and comfortable for an animator to control the character. Here is a list of the things that make up a rig:

- **Bones:** Everything inside a rig is made of bones, and the bones can have different uses, depending on how you set them up.

- **Deform bones:** These bones deform the character model. Their purpose is to deform the mesh, so usually they're hidden and moved by the control bones.

- **Control bones:** When you are posing the character, it's very helpful to have a set of bones that are made exclusively for controlling the entire rig. The leg is made of several bones, for example, but you can move them all with a single control bone. Control bones are what you'll animate later—the ones you can select and transform.

- **Helper bones:** These bones are very important, as they actually make the rig work. They exist only to help the rig behave as you'd expect, although they're hidden, and you should not move them by any means. They're also moved by control bones. You can consider them to be the engines of the rig; they make it function, but they're under the hood.

- **Constraints:** Constraints define what bones do. You can tell a bone to follow the position of another bone, copy its rotation, limit its movements, or do other cool things such as looking at another bone (which is how eyes are rigged). You can think of constraints as modifiers that tell the bones what to do. Inverse kinematics is one of those constraints, and you see how useful it is later in this chapter, in the "Rigging the Leg" and "Rigging the Arm" sections.

- **Custom shapes:** Control bones themselves are not self-explanatory, as they're just bones; that's why you can assign custom shapes to them and give them a nicer, more intuitive look, which is how you customize the visible part of the rig. Thanks to custom shapes, you can make a bone look like an arrow, a circle, or any other shape that represents the function of a particular bone.

Note

In other software, each bone is a different object, and dummies or helpers (called *empties* in Blender) are also objects that are used by a rig. That can make it difficult to control the full rig at the same time and can mess everything up when you want to scale your character up or down, or duplicate it if need be. In Blender, on the other hand, a character's rig is a single object, which makes it really easy to place it in the scene, scale it, or duplicate it. Inside that object are only bones, to which you can add custom shapes to make them look better, more intuitive, and easier to select.

Rigging Process

Here is the usual workflow that you need to follow to rig your character so you have an overview of what you'll do in the rest of this chapter:

1. Create an armature.

2. Enter the Edit Mode of that armature, and create the main bone structure.

3. In Pose Mode, add constraints to set up the rig, and jump to Edit Mode as needed to add helper bones.

4. When the rig is working, add custom shapes to it, organize the bones in layers, hide the bones that are not meant to be seen, and add anything else that will help you control the rig later.

5. Skin the meshes to the skeleton so that it deforms, and through weight painting, define the influence that each bone has over the vertices of the model. Your character is ready to animate!

Working with Armatures

In this section, you learn how to create and edit armatures so that you know how to do things when you start working in the actual character rig. You also learn how to access the armature or bone's properties and add constraints.

Manipulating Bones

You create an armature by pressing **Shift+A** in Object Mode and clicking Armature/Single Bone. To create a skeleton and modify the shape of the bone structure, switch to Edit Mode (**Tab**). In Figure 11.1, you see the elements of a bone.

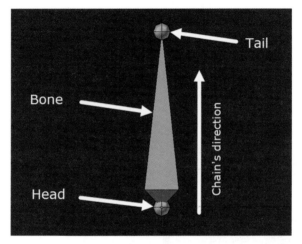

Figure 11.1   The elements of a bone

When you have a series of bones connected in a line, that line is called a *chain*. A bone's direction goes from its head to its tail, which is important because the bone's direction defines the bone chain's direction as well. A bone connected to the tail of another bone follows the movements of the latter and is its child. You learn more about parenting and hierarchy later in this chapter.

Here are some of the things you can do with bones:

- Select them with **RMB**, and move, rotate, and scale them the same way you do everything else in Blender (**G**, **R**, **S**). Bones are made of the bone itself and the spheres at the top and bottom, which are the bone's head and tail. (Those are their names in Blender; other software calls them joints or other names.) You can transform the entire bone or just the head or tail to adapt the bone to the shape you need.

- To create a chain of bones, you can select the tail of a bone and extrude it by pressing **E**, or by pressing **Ctrl+LMB** in the position where you want the new bone to end, just as though you were extruding vertices. When you extrude a bone from the tail of another, the new one is a child of the existing one. If you extrude from the head, Blender creates a new bone, with no parenting applied to it.

- In the Tools Region's Armature Options panel, you can activate the X-Axis Mirror option. If you do, mirrored parts of the skeleton mirror the transforms you do on one of the sides. To use this option properly, from a bone that is situated in the middle (the mirror plane), press **Shift+E** to extrude, which creates a first mirrored extrusion. Keep extruding and transforming the bones from that bone chain normally, and Blender mirrors them on the other side.

- You can duplicate bones by selecting them and pressing **Shift+D**.

- You can name bones in the Properties Region's Item panel. Keep in mind that armatures have two fields: the armature's name and the bone's name inside that armature.

  If you look at the Properties Editor, you'll notice that the tabs are slightly different: Object, Constrains, Armature, and Bone. When naming the selected bone from the Properties Editor, be sure to do so in the Bone tab; otherwise, you'll be renaming the armature object itself (the object that contains all the bones).

- In Edit Mode, you can define the hierarchy of the bones. Select the ones you want to follow another (children), and then select the one you want to act as the parent. Press **Ctrl+P**. You see two options: Connected, which joins the tail of the parent with the head of the children; and Keep Offset, which parents them while keeping them disconnected.

  To remove the connection between an object and its parent, select the object you want to set free and press **Alt+P**. You see two options: Clear Parent, which removes the relationship with the selected bone's parent; and Disconnect, which separates the head from the tail but preserves the relationship.

- If you select one or more bones, you can roll them by pressing **Ctrl+R** to control orientation. Pressing **Ctrl+N** gives you several automatic orientation options. Active Bone is a useful option, as it aligns the orientation of all selected bones to the active bone (the last one you selected); this option is handy for orienting the bones of chains such as fingers, arms, and legs.

- If you select two bone tips and press **F**, Blender creates a new bone to fill the gap. This process is similar to how the Make Edge modeling tool creates an edge to connect two vertices in a mesh. Keep in mind that only the bone's head is connected to its parent; its tail will be free, and you have to parent the tail with the next bone to weld the bones.

- If you select one or more bones, pressing **W** opens the Specials menu, where you can choose the Subdivide option to divide bones into shorter ones. You can set the number of divisions on the Tools Region's Operator panel.

- You can select two connected bones and merge them by pressing **Alt+M**.

- If you want a chain to work in the opposite direction, you can switch the direction of a bone by pressing **Alt+F**. This keyboard shortcut switches the head and tail of a bone, changing the direction of the hierarchy.

- If you have undesired bones in your skeleton, delete them by pressing **X**.

- As always, you can hide and unhide bones by pressing **H** and **Alt+H** to display only the ones you're working with or to hide some bones that are in the way. **Shift+H** hides everything except the currently selected bones.

Working in Object, Edit, and Pose Modes

The interaction modes for armatures are different from those for other objects. It's important to understand what you can do in each of the modes:

- **Object Mode:** The full rig is inside the armature object, so in Object Mode, you can move it around, rotate it, or scale it to change the size of your character. As the rig is inside this object, the scale of the object won't affect it or cause issues in its contents (bones).

- **Edit Mode:** In Edit Mode, you have access to the bones. You can build your character's skeleton, define the structure's shape, and do parenting to define bone hierarchies. The position of bones in the Edit Mode is the default pose of the bones in other modes.

- **Pose Mode:** When the hierarchy and the bones are in place in Edit Mode, you should go to Pose Mode to add constraints to the bones, move everything around as needed, pose your character, and set keyframes to create animation.

In Object Mode, you don't have access to the individual bones or controls; you can only transform the rig as a whole. In Edit Mode, you can modify the bones' position, size, and orientation to fit your character and also define the hierarchy. Finally, in Pose Mode, you can add constraints to the skeleton so that it works as you expect, and then you can pose it. While you're setting up the rig, you'll be jumping a lot between Edit Mode and Pose Mode to create and adjust bones while you add and tweak the constraints.

When you're in Pose Mode, selected bones are shown in blue as a reminder that you're in that mode.

Adding Constraints

Constraints make your rig work. You could say that constraints make bones react to other bones. If you move a bone, you provoke a certain action in another part of the rig. Throughout the rest of this chapter, you use several constraints in Jim's rig, but for now, I describe how they work and how to add them to your bones.

First, you need to know that most constraints have a target, which means that they're applied to a bone but target another bone to create the constraint between them. If you use the Track To constraint for an eye, for example, you apply the constraint to the eye and select the bone that you want the eye to look at as the target.

Caution

You can apply constraints to any object in your scene, but understand the difference between object constraints and bone constraints. If you're in Object Mode and add a constraint, that constraint affects the entire armature. If you're in Pose Mode, Blender displays a different tab: Bone Constraints. The Object Constraints tab has a chain as its icon, and the Bone Constraints tab shows a smaller chain near a bone.

You can add constraints in two ways when you're in Pose Mode:

- Select the bone to which you want to add the constraint. In the Bone Constraints tab of the Properties Editor, click the Add Bone Constraint button, and select the constraint type you want to add. The constraint is added to the list of constraints, affecting the selected bone in a way similar to what modifiers do. Inside the constraint panel, there is a field for the Target. Enter the name of the armature, and a new field for the bone's name will show up where you should insert the name of the bone you want to have as the target for the constraint.

- A faster method is to select the target bone first and then select the one to which you want to add the constraint while holding down **Shift**. Press **Shift+Ctrl+C** to open a menu and add constraints (or go to the Armature menu on the header and choose the constraints). This way, when you add a constraint, it automatically picks the first selected bone as a target and you won't have to add it manually in the Constraints panel.

Tip

When you have to insert the name of an object into a field, start typing the name, and a list appears, displaying the names of objects that start with the letters you typed. (Keeping your objects named correctly can help a lot!) If you don't type anything but click the text field, you see a list of all the objects that fall into the selectable object category for that specific field. Also, to select an object or bone, place the mouse cursor over its name field, press **Ctrl+C** to copy it, select the object with the constraint, go to the desired field, place the mouse cursor on top of it, and press **Ctrl+V** to paste it.

Eyedropper

In the most recent versions of Blender, the eyedropper tool has been added. In image-editing software, the eyedropper is a common tool used for clicking a pixel and selecting that pixel's color. In Blender, the eyedropper is now used to quickly select objects in different menus. When you add a modifier or constraint that requires a secondary object to work with, for example, you don't need to know the name, type it, or select it from the list; you click the eyedropper to the left of the text field and then click the object inside 3D View. Blender picks that object and introduces it into the text field for you.

Although the eyedropper tool is available for bone constraints, its behavior is a bit tricky. You can use it to pick the armature's name (Object), but the eyedropper won't work with bones, which you have to select from a list or type yourself.

Rigging Your Character

Now that you know how to manipulate bones, you're ready to create Jim's rig!

Creating the Base Bone Structure

To start, create the base skeleton. In this case, because the model is symmetrical, you have to create only one of the halves. Later, when you add all the constraints, you can mirror that half to the other side, carrying constraints with it; otherwise, you have to add the constraints to the other side manually. Figure 11.2 shows what the base skeleton looks like. Pay attention to the names of the bones, as you use them in the following sections.

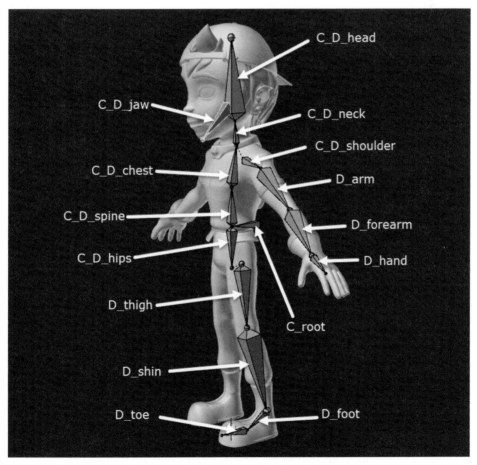

Figure 11.2   The base skeleton, with only the left side created so that those parts can be mirrored to the right side later

Here are some things that may help you create this base structure:

- In the Armature tab of the Properties Editor, find the Display panel, and activate the X-Ray option. This option always displays the bones on top, even if they are inside the mesh, which makes it easier to see what you're doing while keeping the mesh visible behind so that you can align the bones to it.

- Don't create things like the fingers yet—only the base structure. Later, you add all the needed details part by part.

- Naming bones is essential when you're working on a rig so that when you add constraints later, you know which bones you're referring to. (It's a lot easier to find a bone called D_hand than a bone called bone.064.) Also, pay attention to the fact that all the bones in this structure will have the D_ prefix, which is a nice way to organize the bone names inside your rig.

> **Tip**
>
> You can use prefixes to help yourself recognize the type of bone. D_name would be a bone that is part of the main structure that will deform the mesh, C_name would be a controller bone, and H_name would be a helper bone. Also, some of the bones may be used for deformation as well as for control, such as the bones in the spine. Those bones use two prefixes: C_D_name. Using this naming convention helps you when you search for a bone in a list, as all bones will be organized by type in the list that shows up when you enter just the prefix!

- Keep an eye on the hierarchy. C_D_hips and C_D_spine have to be children of C_root. D_shoulder has to be a child of C_D_chest. D_thigh has to be a child of C_D_hips and C_D_jaw needs to be a child of C_D_head. If the hierarchy is correct, and you go to the Pose Mode to test it, everything in the rig should follow the C_root control. If you don't parent bones correctly, when you move part of the rig, other parts may be left in place.

- To create the arms, for example, you can extrude the bones from the chest to the shoulder. When you have the arm bones in place, you can delete the bone between the chest and the shoulder (or leave it if you want to). You can use the same technique for the legs.

> **Tip**
>
> When you're testing the bone structure in Pose Mode, it's very easy to reset the bone's default pose (the one defined in Edit Mode). In the Armature menu of the 3D View header, you find the Clear Transform option, which gives you different ways of resetting the pose. Otherwise, you can reset the movement by pressing **Alt+G**, reset the rotations by pressing **Alt+R**, and reset the scale by pressing **Alt+S**.

- To organize your scene, in Object Mode, select the armature, and call it Jim_rig. Press **M**, and from the squares in the pop-up menu (layers), select a different layer from the model so that you can quickly show and hide the model or the armature separately whenever you need to focus on one of them alone.

Rigging the Eyes

In this section, you move to the eyes. You use a Track To constraint to control where the eyes are looking. Figure 11.3 shows the eye rig. Again, for now, you're working only on the left side of the rig.

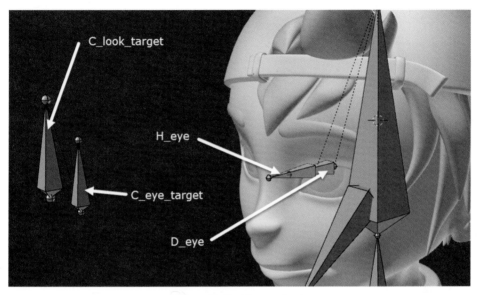

Figure 11.3   The eye's rig

You need to create the bone that moves the eye's model, which can be a little tricky in this case, as you have an eye that is being deformed by the Lattice modifier. In normal models, the eye would be a perfect sphere, so you'd have a single bone with its head in the center of the eye, but in this case, you use two different bones. Follow these steps:

1. Select the eye's mesh, enter Edit Mode, select the central loop, and press **Shift+S** to move the 3D cursor to its center. Exit Edit Mode, and you see that the 3D cursor is not centered in the eye at all. That doesn't matter, because the eye will be rotated from there before the deformation by the Lattice modifier takes place. The tricky thing about this eye is that it has two versions: the original one (the one that you must rig) and the one you see (after the Lattice modifier deforms it).

2. Go to Edit Mode in the armature, and create a bone in that place. Duplicate that bone, and move the new one to the approximate point from which the deformed eye will rotate. This bone is needed because later, you use it to deform the eyelids slightly when you rotate the eye to create a more organic effect. The first bone is a helper, there only to rotate the eye (the eye being just a sphere without deformations, it only needs to be parented to the eye bone without an Armature modifier or weights),

and the second one is a deformer, as it deforms the eyelids. These two bones should be parented to the C_D_head bone so that when you move the head, they follow it.

3. Duplicate one of those bones, and move it in front of the head. You need to end up with two new bones: one in the center that controls where the two eyes look, and a second one in front of the eye. C_eye_target is parented to C_look target, so when you move the latter, the first one follows it. This techniques allows you to make Jim look where you want and control each eye's movement independently.

> **Tip**
>
> To make sure that a bone is in the center (X=0), you can insert the values manually into the Properties Region's Transform panel.

4. To add the constraints, select C_eye_target. Hold down **Shift**, and select H_eye. Press **Ctrl+Shift+C**, and select the Track To constraint. Automatically, the first selected bone becomes the target of the constraint you applied to H_eye. Now if you move C_look_target, C_eye_target should follow, and H_eye should reorient itself so that it's always looking at the target.

5. Repeat the process from Step 1 with D_eye.

Rigging the Leg

Rigging the legs is a little trickier, but I hope that you'll learn a lot of new things in the process! Figure 11.4 shows the steps of the process, and the instructions follow.

Inverse Kinematics

Before you start following the steps, you should know what inverse kinematics (IK) is. Usually, when you create a bone structure such as the leg, if you try to pose the structure, you have to rotate each bone, and its children follow it. For the leg, you should rotate the thigh first, followed by the ankle and then the foot. This way of working is called forward kinematics (FK), but for the legs or parts of the rig that need to touch surfaces (such as the feet), IK is a much more convenient option. IK works the opposite way, so to pose the leg, you have only to move the foot; the knee flexes to fit that pose. This feature is useful because when you move the character's torso, the legs are automatically flexing and moving to make the feet stand on the floor. Now you can use IK to rig Jim's leg!

Use IK to rig Jim's leg by following these steps:

1. Extrude a bone from the knee joint and another one from the heel joint. Press **Alt+P** to clear the bones' parents and disconnect them from the rest of the leg. Select the new bone, and move it forward a little so that it's in front of the leg at a distance that allows free movement of the knee without touching it. (The bone should be right in front of the knee, aligned.)

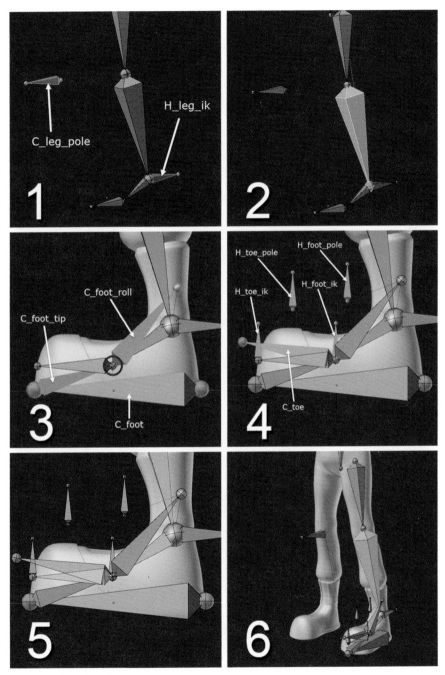

Figure 11.4   Rigging the leg with inverse kinematics

2. In Pose Mode, select H_leg_ik, which is the target of the IK chain. Holding down **Shift**, select D_shin. Add a constraint by pressing **Shift+Ctrl+C** and selecting Inverse Kinematics, or press **Shift+I** to apply IK directly. Go to the Bone Constraints tab of the Properties Editor, and tweak a couple of IK constraint values.

   The first value is Chain Length. By default, IK goes up to the root of the hierarchy (which in this case is the C_root bone). Set the Chain Length value to 2 so that IK works up to two bones in the hierarchy, which in this case are the shin and the thigh. At this point, if you move the C_root bone or the H_leg_ik bone, you see the effect of IK.

   Next, give this IK a pole. IK makes the bones of the leg flex in a plane, and the pole defines that plane, so you can use the pole to orient the leg. In the Pole Target field, enter the rig's name (in this case, Jim_rig), and the bone field appears. In the field, enter the name of the pole bone (in this case, C_leg_pole). Move C_leg_pole sideways, and you see its effect on the direction in which the knee bends.

   > **Caution**
   >
   > Due to the orientation of the bones, sometimes when you apply a pole to an IK chain, they get rotated. You can compensate with the Pole Angle value of the IK constraint. Usually, if bones are correctly aligned, round values such as 90, -90, and 180 are enough to correct orientation.

3. Create a new bone chain aligned with the foot. (Create a bone and then extrude to create two more.) The first bone starts from the heel; use the 3D model as a reference, as these bones define the pivot points for rotating the foot. The second bone starts from the toe tip, and the third one starts from the toe articulation. The point circled in red in Figure 11.4 is where all those joints are aligned to prevent sliding when you rotate those bones later. These three bones control the foot movement, so you can rotate the foot from the heel or the tip and roll it in a way similar to human walking. The H_leg_ik bone must be a child of C_foot_roll, so the IK target follows the last bone of the chain you just created.

4. The foot needs IKs as well so that it's under control while you use the IK leg; otherwise, it will rotate uncontrollably. Having IKs set up with their defined poles fixes rotation. Create a new bone from the toe articulation, and call it C_toe. This bone will control the toe when it's not touching the ground. From that articulation and from the tail of the D_toe bone, extrude a couple of bones, and disconnect them; they'll be the targets of the IKs you'll use in the foot. Duplicate those two targets, and move them up so that they act as the poles for the foot IKs.

   Be sure to parent these bones correctly. The IK target and pole of D_foot are children of C_foot_roll, the IK target and pole of D_toe are children of C_toe, and C_toe is a child of C_foot_tip. This arrangement may sound tricky, but when you have it working, you'll understand why everything needs to be this way.

5. In Pose Mode, add the IK constraints for D_foot and D_toe. Use the targets and poles you created in Step 4 for that purpose, and set the Chain Length values to 1.

This setting will make the IKs work only in the bones that have the constraint assigned and control their rotations thanks to the poles, but the IK's effect will not climb up through the bone hierarchy.

6. In Pose Mode, move and rotate the controller bones (the ones prefixed with C_) to see how the deform bones move naturally following the controllers. When you rotate C_foot_tip, the entire foot rotates around the tip, and when you rotate C_foot_roll, the heel raises while the toe stays in place—very useful when you're making your character walk. With C_foot, you can move the entire foot around, and with C_toe, you can rotate the toe alone if needed (usually when the foot is not touching the ground). Jim's leg is rigged!

Rigging the Torso and Head

In this section, you move up the character and set up the torso. This task is really simple, but it helps you understand the power of constraints. Follow these steps:

1. Select the C_D_spine bone; then hold down **Shift**, and select the C_D_chest bone. Add a Copy Rotation constraint to the latter. Don't worry if the bone gets messed up when you apply the constraint; it's not set up yet. Set the two Space fields to Local Space (so that the constraint affects the local spaces from the target and the current bone). Now if you rotate C_D_spine, the chest bone rotates as well. Usually, you rotate the spine as a whole, so this step sometimes saves you from having to rotate the chest as well. In the constraint, enable the Offset option to manually rotate the chest. Blender adds the rotation to the current rotation generated by the constraint. (Otherwise, the constraint overrides rotation, and it's blocked for manual transforms.). Also, set the Influence parameter to define how much of the target's rotation this bone will copy.

2. Select the bone C_D_head, and in the Bone tab of the Properties Editor, find the Relations panel. Disable Inherit Rotation so that the head doesn't keep the rotation from its parent (the neck). Now when you rotate the body, the head is aligned, which is a more natural behavior.

3. Sometimes, you want the head to follow the neck's rotation, so add a Child Of constraint to the head, for which the target is the neck bone. You may have to click the Set Inverse button to make this setup work correctly. With the influence of this constraint, you can control the amount of rotation of the neck that carries over to the head, giving you more control of what you want to do. Keep in mind that you can animate the influence and change it along an animation. You learn about animation in Chapter 12, "Animating Your Character."

Rigging the Arm

The arms are easy enough. Usually, they're animated with IK just as the legs are, but as the hands are not always touching a surface, you may prefer to use them with FK instead. For that purpose, you can use a technique called IK/FK Blend, which is a rig made of three chains: the IK arm, the FK arm, and the deform arm. The latter chain uses Copy Rotation constraints to blend its rotations between IK and FK. You're going to build only the IK one in this book, but I encourage you to look into the subject if you like rigging and want a little challenge. Figure 11.5 shows the resulting rig for the arm.

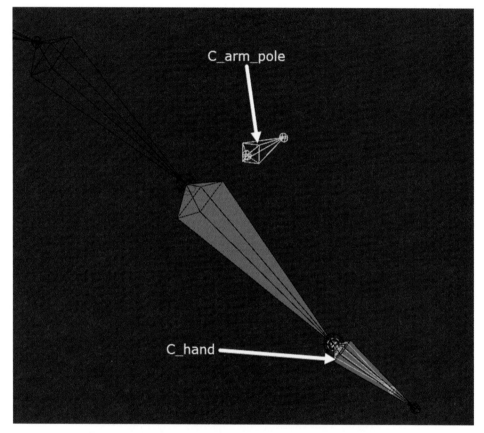

Figure 11.5   The arm's IK rig in Wireframe display mode so
that you can see the IK target in the hand

Follow these steps to create the arm's rig:

1. In Edit Mode, extrude a new bone from the elbow, clear its relationship with the arm bones (**Alt+P**), and move it back. This bone is the pole for the arm's IK.

2. Duplicate the D_hand bone, disconnect it (**Alt+P**), and scale it down. Using the 3D cursor (**Shift+S**), move the head of the new bone to the wrist joint. This bone serves as the IK target for the arm and also controls the hand's rotation. The bone is scaled down so that it doesn't completely overlap with D_hand, as the bones are in

the same position. Making the bone smaller or bigger lets you see it in Wireframe display mode (**Z**) and makes it easier to select. Add an IK constraint, using the new bone for the hand (C_hand) as its target and C_arm_pole as the IK pole.

3. Select the D_hand bone. On the Bone tab of the Properties Editor, deactivate the Inherit Rotation option in the Relations panel (as you did for the head bone). Add a Copy Rotation constraint to the bone, using C_hand as its target. Now when you move C_hand, you control the arm's IK, and when you rotate it, you rotate the hand's bone as well.

Rigging the Hand

It's time to create the rig for Jim's fingers (see Figure 11.6).

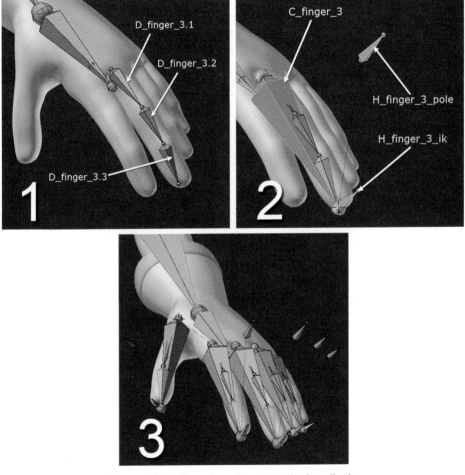

Figure 11.6   The steps to create the hand's rig

Follow these steps:

1. Create the bones for a single finger and give them intuitive names. In Figure 11.6, I used names like D_finger_3.1 to describe the finger position and the articulation number. A tricky thing about fingers is the bone orientation. You can select one of the bones, orient it correctly by rolling it (**Ctrl+R**), and then select the other bones of that finger, with the one you rolled being the active selection. Press **Ctrl+N**, and select the Active Bone option to cause the roll of the selected bones to fit the active bone's roll. When you have the rotations set up, select the first bone of the finger chain, and make it a child of the hand bone.

2. Create a bone with its head and tail aligned to the beginning and end of the finger chain; this bone controls the entire finger. At its tip, extrude a new bone to act as the IK target. Duplicate that target, and move it up to be used as the pole for the finger's IK. In Edit Mode, make the C_finger_3 bone a child of the hand, and make the IK target and pole children of C_finger_3. Apply an IK with those targets and poles to the D_finger_3.3 bone. Remember to set IK Chain Length to 3 so that it goes up through the finger bones only. Try the finger rig now, and you see that you need to use only the C_finger_3 bone to control it. Rotate the bone to rotate the finger, and scale it up and down to flex the finger. Now you have one finger set up.

3. Duplicate the finger in Edit Mode, and place copies of it in the rest of the finger spaces; be sure to align and name them properly. For the thumb, you may want to delete the first articulation and use only two. Keep in mind that you need to realign the C_finger_1 bone to the deform bones.

> **Tip**
>
> Aligning the fingers may be difficult, as the pole is not always aligned in a single axis. In such a case, put the pole in place in Pose Mode until the finger bones are in line with the model. Then select the bones you tweaked in Pose Mode, and go to the 3D View header. In the Pose menu, look for the Apply option, and choose Apply Pose As Rest Pose. Alternatively, press **Ctrl+A** in 3D View and select the same option. This option transfers the current transforms of the bones in Pose Mode to Edit Mode.

Mirroring the Rig

You have one side rigged, so now you must duplicate it on the other side.

Before mirroring, you need to know that later, you'll be able to copy poses and paste them mirrored. Blender knows how to do this by recognizing the names of the bones. Each bone has a name and a suffix that tells Blender whether that bone is in the left side or on the right side. Here is an example:

- **Right:** C_hand.R. The .R suffix tells Blender that this bone is on the right side.
- **Left:** C_hand.L. The .L suffix tells Blender that this bone is on the left side.

- **Center:** C_D_spine. When the name has no suffix, Blender knows that the bone is in the center.

This naming convention serves Blender to translate the pose from one bone to the same bone on the other side of the rig. When you're painting the weights for the skinning, you can mirror those weights to the other side as well.

Naming Bones Automatically

Blender has tools that add suffixes to the bones' names automatically. Select all the bones in Edit or Pose Mode by pressing **A**, and from the Armature or Pose menu (depending on the interaction mode you're working in) of the 3D View header, choose the option AutoName Left/Right. This option detects the bones that are on the positive and negative sides of the X axis and names them accordingly, which is why it's important to center your character on the X axis.

Then go to the bones that are in the center, and check their names. Sometimes, the bones are not exactly at X=0, so they get suffixes as well. For these bones, check their names, and delete the suffixes.

Mirroring Bones

The bones now have names, and if you worked on the left side of the rig, all the bones (except the ones in the center) have a .L suffix in their names. Follow these steps to mirror those bones:

1. In Edit Mode, select the bones in the left side (you can use a Box Selection by pressing **B** to avoid the ones in the center).

2. Press **Shift+D** to duplicate them, and right-click to cancel the movement.

3. Place the 3D cursor on the center of the scene by pressing **Shift+C**, and switch the pivot point to the 3D cursor by pressing **.** (period).

4. Press **Ctrl+M** to mirror the selected bones, and press **X** to mirror them in the X axis. Press Enter to accept.

5. The bones are mirrored, but they have names like C_hand.L.001. (Don't worry. This is what Blender does when duplicating an object; it automatically renames the object so that you don't have two objects with the same name.) With the left-side bones selected, go to the Armature or Pose menu of the 3D View header, and choose the Flip Names option. This option converts those duplicated names from the left side to appear as right side, such as C_hand.L.001 to C_hand.R.

Adjusting Bones

Mirroring bones is very cool and can save you tons of work, adding constraints and repetitive tasks for both sides of the rig, but unfortunately, it has some side effects.

When you mirror bones, some of them may get rotated in a weird way as an effect of inverting their X axis, and you'll have to fix these rotations manually. Even though that's *not* very cool, it's usually less work than creating both sides manually!

Here are some tips you can use to adjust everything after mirroring:

- In the Armature tab's Display panel, enable the Axes option to display the orientations of bones in 3D View. Using this helpful feature, you can compare the orientations on the right and left sides to see whether some of them are off. To adjust rotation, press **Ctrl+R** to roll the bones in Edit Mode.

- Some IK constraints may be off as well, and you probably need to change their pole angle values. Alternatively, you can change the orientation in Pose Mode and then apply that orientation as a rest pose (**Ctrl+A**) to transfer the changes to the bones in Edit Mode.

- A good way to see whether your rig is working properly is to test how it supports mirroring poses. If something is wrong, when you mirror a pose, the bone on the other side takes the rotation differently, and the pose won't look the same. Figure 11.7 shows the Copy and Paste options for poses.

Pose your character in Pose Mode, select all bones, click the Copy Pose button, and then click the Paste Mirrored button. If something doesn't work properly, go back to Edit Mode and adjust the rolling of problematic bones by pressing **Ctrl+R**.

Copy Pose ─┐   ┌─Paste Mirrored
                                    Pose

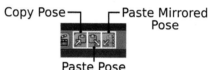

Paste Pose

Figure 11.7   You can copy and paste poses by clicking these buttons
on the 3D View header when you're working in Pose Mode.

Organizing the Rig

Your character's rig works, but you can organize it to increase usability. Two ways to do this are to use bone groups and bone layers.

Bone Groups

Bone groups let you organize your bones with colors and also allow quick group selections. You can have different colors for different type of bones, such as Deform, Control, and Helpers groups. Figure 11.8 shows the Bone Groups panel on the Armature tab of the Properties Editor.

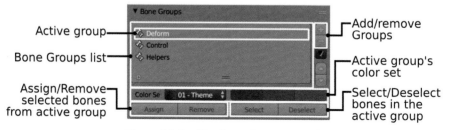

Figure 11.8   The Bone Groups panel

From the Bone Groups panel, you can add groups to the list, and when you click Assign, the selected bones become part of the active bone group (the one highlighted in the list). You can select a color set for that group or create your own color set by clicking the colors of that panel.

Do this to assign every bone in the rig to the appropriate group. Note that some bones are part of several groups, such as the spine and the chest, which are meant to deform the mesh but are controllers as well. Place those bones in the Control bone group so that just by looking at the color, you know that you can control them. Unfortunately, the same bone can't be part of multiple bone groups. Figure 11.9 shows how your rig should look after all the work you've done.

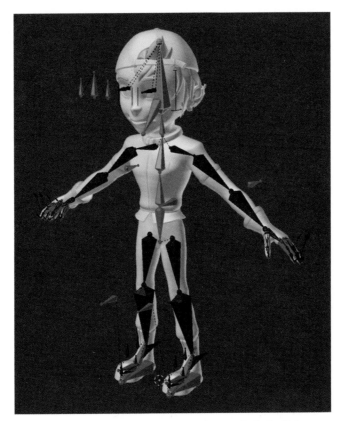

Figure 11.9   Jim's rig is looking better little by little.

Bone Layers

Jim's rig is looking much more usable, but it still has a lot of bones that are not supposed to move (such as the helpers). To hide them, use bone layers.

Bone layers are similar to scene layers, but they work only inside the armature. On the Armature tab, the Skeleton panel has four sets of little squares. The first two sets, in the

Layers section, are the layers themselves. The other two sets, in the Protected Layers section, allow you to mark specific layers as protected to prevent other users of the rig from manipulating them when linking the character. (I talk about linking near the end of this chapter).

When you're in Edit or Pose Mode, you can select one or more bones and press **M** to access the Bone Layers panel, which is similar to Scene Layers for organizing objects. When you press **M**, a pop up menu with little squares appears; each of the squares is a layer. Select a square, or select more than one by pressing **Shift+LMB**, as the same bone can be a part of more than one layer, to add that bone to the appropriate layer(s).

When you have bones added to layers, you can show or hide layers from the Armature tab. Left-click layers to show or hide them. Hold down the **Shift** key while you click to show or hide more than one layer.

Assign bones to layers depending on their purpose. In Jim's rig, you can add the deformer bones to one layer, helpers to another, and controllers to a third. Bones that are both deformers and controllers can be part of both layers.

What you'll get from setting up bones in layers is that later, you can show or hide only the ones you need. When you're going to work on the skinning, for example, you can show only the deformer bones so that the rest of them are not in the way. When the rig is finished, you can hide the deformer and helper bones so that only the ones you should move to control the rig are visible. In other words, work is easier because you see only what you need to see.

Later, you create the facial rig. You can store it on a different layer, which allows you to work on the full character pose first; then you can show the facial rig and focus on the facial expressions. This way, the facial rig won't be unnecessarily showing all the time, as it can confuse you or you might move something accidentally when you're working on the body pose.

Skinning

Skinning is the process of telling Blender how bones have to deform the meshes. To do that, you use vertex weights. Each bone has an internal weight over the vertices to define how vertices follow the movement of bones. To see how weights work, consider a simple example.

Understanding Vertex Weights

In this section, you see a simple example of how weights work in a mesh. Take a look at Figure 11.10. The first image is a simple model: a cylinder with two bones inside it. The second image shows the weight of the bone at the top. Red means 100 percent influence, and dark blue means 0 percent influence; all the colors in between (orange, yellow, and green) indicate amounts of effect between 0 and 100 percent. The third image shows what happens to the model when you rotate the bone. The parts in red follow the bone's movement completely, and the parts with less influence average their movement among the bones that affect them.

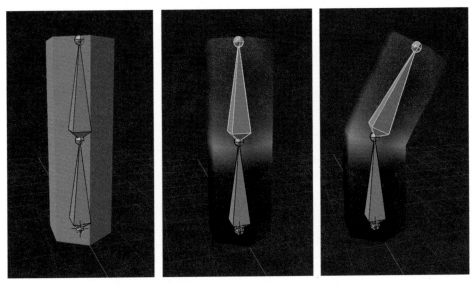

Figure 11.10   How weight affects meshes when you transform bones

Setting Up the Model for Skinning

You need to set up several things up before you start setting the weights of the bones.

Models

The following procedures may help you navigate your scene and make the process easier:

- Apply every Mirror and Shrinkwrap modifier to objects so that they don't interfere when you weight the meshes.

- When you apply the Mirror modifier, some objects (such as the details of the arms, gloves, or boots) need to be separated so that each side of the object is a separate object. In Edit Mode, select the faces on one of the sides and press **P** to separate the current selection into a different object.

- Press **Ctrl+A** to apply the location, rotation, and scale of every mesh (except the lattices of the eyes, in case you scaled them when you made the deformations, because they depend on that scale to cause the deformations). This action prevents bad things from happening when you link everything to the skeleton. If you scaled the objects, for example, you may find issues later. When you apply the transforms, keep in mind that some things may go wrong. If an object gets darkened or looks weird, switch to Edit Mode, select everything, and press **Ctrl+N** to reset the normals. Also, the objects that use modifiers (such as Solidify) may have to be revised, as their thickness depends directly on their scale, so when you apply the scale, the thickness value may be affected.

- The eyebrows should be part of the face model so that they're easier to tweak when you create facial expressions. You can move them together with the face vertices by using the Proportional Editing tool. When joining the eyebrows to the face (**Ctrl+J**), you end up with a single mesh, in which the eyebrows have a different material applied to them.

- Name every model (if you haven't already) so that you can recognize objects by their names. This practice is useful at this stage and later in the process.

Deformer Bones

The rig has a lot of bones, and you need to tell Blender which ones will actually deform the meshes. By default, all the bones deform them.

On the Bone tab of the Properties Editor is the Deform panel, where you set up the envelopes and some features of the bone deformations. If you don't want a bone to deform the mesh, just disable that option. Disabling options for every bone would be very slow, however, so here's a faster way:

1. In Edit or Pose Mode, select every bone. With all the layers enabled (all the bones visible), press **Alt+W** to display the Bone Settings options. Alternatively, you can find those options in the Armature/Pose menu of the 3D View header, in the Bone Settings section.

2. Click the Deform option of the Bone Settings menu to deselect everything. Or select some bones and make sure that the Deform option is disabled.

3. In the Armature Layers panel, turn on only the layer for the deform bones. Select all those bones, press **Shift+W**, and select the Deform option a second time. Now those bones have been enabled as deformers, and all the rest (control and help bones) will not affect the mesh.

This method is pretty quick, right? Layers and groups allow you to quickly select bones and change the settings for only the ones you need.

Bone Settings

Pressing **Alt+W** is the same as pressing **Shift+W** to display the Bone Settings menu, so what's the difference? The Alt key is usually used to remove given effects inside Blender. **Shift + W** switches the mode, so if you have the Deform option enabled, the option is disabled, and the other way around. Pressing **Alt+W**, on the other hand, only disables the option, so if you want to make sure that the option is disabled, press **Alt+W**.

Adding an Armature Modifier

The Armature modifier tells the mesh to be deformed by the bones of an armature. As with constraints, you have two ways to add an Armature modifier to your mesh:

- Select the mesh, go to the Modifiers tab of the Properties Editor, and add an Armature modifier. In the Armature field of the modifier, type the name of the armature you want to use to deform the model—in this case, Jim_rig.

- Select the mesh, select a bone or armature while holding down **Shift**, and press **Ctrl+P** to parent. When you parent a mesh to an armature, Blender shows you several options, some of which are Armature options. Automatic Weights usually is the best choice (unless you have set up envelopes for the bones and such, but I don't cover that topic here). These options add an Armature modifier and set the selected skeleton to act as the deformer. Different options set the skeleton differently. Automatic Weights, for example, detects the bones closest to the vertices and automatically assigns weights based on that distance. (You can control how those automatic weights react by setting up the bone envelopes accordingly, but I don't go that far here).

Caution

If you previously added a Subdivision Surface modifier to your models, when you add an Armature modifier, it works on top of the Subdivision Surface, which reduces performance and makes weighting more difficult because it has to affect all the polygons generated by the Subdivision Surface. Move the modifier up through the modifiers stack until it's placed before the Subdivision Surface modifier. (Subdivision Surface should be the last one, at the bottom.)

Defining Weights

Before you start setting up the bone weights over the model, you may want to change the display of the armature to Stick (on the Display panel of the Armature tab) so that it doesn't block the view of the mesh and shows only the layer with the deform bones. It is unlikely that you disabled the X-Ray option to always see the bones on top of the mesh, but if you did, enable it again to make the bone-selection process much easier.

Weight Painting

Weight painting is probably the fastest way to assign bone weights to your model. To enter Weight Paint Mode, go to the Interaction Mode selector on the 3D View header, and select Weight Paint. You see the model in blue, yellow, green, and red; the colors represent the weights of the selected bone. You can also switch to this mode by pressing **Ctrl+Tab**.

Weight Paint Mode (see Figure 11.11) is similar to Texture Paint Mode; the painting tools and options are on the left side of the Tools Region.

When you add an Armature modifier to a mesh by using the Automatic Weights option, vertex groups are created in the mesh. Blender creates one group for each bone, and the groups have the same names as the bones so you can recognize them. Each of those vertex groups stores the vertex weights that define the influence of each bone of the armature.

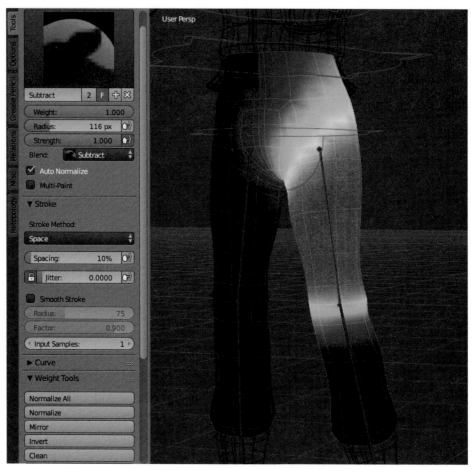

Figure 11.11   Weight Paint Mode's interface

Here is some information about how to work in Weight Paint Mode:

- On the left side of the Tools Region, you find a series of settings that control the brush and options while you work in Weight Paint Mode. At the top are brush types: Add, Subtract, Draw, Blur, and so on. Each brush has a different effect on the weights when you paint.

- You can paint by left-clicking and dragging over the mesh's vertices.

- You can also set the size, strength, and the weight of the brush. As in Texture Paint Mode, you can change the size and strength of the brush by pressing **F** and **Shift+F** in 3D View.

- You can paint by pressing **LMB**, but pressing **RMB** allows you to select other meshes so that you can jump among them and paint their weights. If the meshes were not in Weight Paint Mode the last time you had them selected, you switch to Object Mode when you select one of those other meshes. Press **Ctrl+Tab** to switch to Weight Paint Mode.

- An alternative way to select the bone weight that you want to paint is to go to the Mesh tab of the Properties Editor. In the Vertex Groups panel, select the desired bone from the list. (Notice how useful it is to name bones adequately!)

> **Tip**
> Selecting the vertex groups from a list is not the fastest method, though. Select the armature, and make sure that you're in Pose Mode. Now select the mesh. If you have the deform bones visible in the armature, you can select the bones by pressing **RMB** while you paint weights. When you select a bone, you see its influence on the vertices, and its vertex group is selected.

- When you select bones to paint their weights with **RMB**, you have even more control. While weight painting, press **G**, **R**, or **S** to move, rotate, or scale the bone. This method allows you to move the character while you paint and test whether the weights behave as you expect. (From time to time, you may want to reset bones to their original positions. Press **A** to select all the bones, or select the ones you want to reset; then press **Alt+G**, **Alt+R**, or **Alt+S** to reset location, rotation, or scale.)

  You can even take this process further by creating animations (see Chapter 12, "Animating Your Character") that move the bones you're weighting so that you can see how they behave when you drag the cursor in the timeline across the animation.

- The Options tab of the Tools Region has some features that you may find useful. One of these features is the X-Mirror option. If your mesh is the same on both sides of the X axis, you're in luck! X-Mirror mirrors the weights you paint on one side to the other, in their correspondent bones. This option works properly only if your bones are correctly named with their left and right suffixes, of course.

- The Blur brush is handy. Paint basic weights first, and where you need them to be softer in articulations, use the Blur brush to paint the weight borders. Keep in mind that this brush blurs the weights of the vertices inside the brush size, so you may need to make it bigger to use it properly.

> **Tip**
> It's usually easiest to see what you're doing with weights when you're in Wireframe display mode (**Z**). You see everything in wireframes except for the object you had selected when you jumped to Weight Paint Mode, which you see in shadeless colors representing the weights.

Weight Values

Weight painting is generally easy but can be tricky sometimes. In complex parts of the model or in areas where you need specific weights, it's better to add values.

In the Vertex Groups panel on the Mesh tab (the one with a little triangle and its vertices) of the Properties Editor are options that let you do this. Just follow these steps:

1. In Edit Mode, select the vertices that you want to weight precisely.

2. Go to the Vertex Groups panel, find the group with the name of the bone to which you want to add the weight, and left-click to select it. If you click the little + button at the bottom of the list (you can find it on every list in Blender), you can filter and search groups by their name, so type the name and press Enter to display only the groups that have those letters in their name. (This is yet another case in which naming stuff is useful!)

3. Below the list are a few options, very similar to the ones in the Bone Groups panel. You can set the weight value and click Assign to set that weight to the active vertices for the selected bone/vertex group.

Another way to adjust vertex weights is to select one or more vertices in Edit Mode, and if they have weights assigned, a Vertex Weights panel appears in the Properties Editor. Tweak the weight values for each vertex group, copy weights from the active vertex, and paste those weights into the rest of the selected vertices.

Mirroring Weights

The gloves and the boots are the same mesh but different objects on opposite sides, affected by different bones. You have several ways to make weight painting faster, such as weighting only one side. Weighting both sides manually takes longer (especially for a complex model such as the hands), and you may end up with different deformations between one side and the other. Two tricks that you can use are mirroring weights before painting and mirroring weights after painting.

Mirroring Before

I recommend that you mirror the mesh before weight painting. If you're working on a mirrored mesh, enable the X-Mirror option before you start painting, because once weights are painted, fixing things is tedious and slow, requiring you to paint both sides separately.

If possible, join both sides. You might join the two gloves in a single mesh (or apply Mirror modifiers). Activate the X-Mirror option, and paint the weights on one side. Blender should reflect those weights on the other side.

When you're done defining weights, separate the meshes again so that they become different objects. The meshes keep their weights.

Mirroring After

If you forget to mirror before and have already painted the weights for one of the gloves, for example, here is what you can do to mirror the weights after painting:

1. Delete the glove that you haven't weighted.

2. Select the gloves you weighted, and duplicate it by pressing **Shift+D**. Right-click to cancel the transform after duplication. Set the 3D cursor in the center by pressing **Shift+C**. Press **Ctrl+M** to mirror the glove, and press **X** to mirror it on the X axis. Press **Enter** to confirm.

3. In the Vertex Groups panel, delete the vertex groups from the new side, and replace the names with the ones on the other side. You may want to look at this tricky step in detail. This example uses only one bone, and the one that was painted is on the left side.

   a. Find all the vertex groups on the right side (the ones that you need now) whose names end with .R. (You can find them by typing .R in the list filter.) The one you want to mirror is the D_hand.L bone weight. You have to delete D_hand.R.

   b. Double-click D_hand.L, and rename it D_hand.R. Now the current weights in that vertex group are affected by the right bone instead of the left one.

   c. Repeat the entire process with all the bones you need to mirror.

Knowing What Objects Don't Need Weights

That's right—the objects that are not going to be deformed don't need to be weighted! You can just parent those objects to a bone. As an example, the hair, cap, teeth, and tongue would only need to be parented to their respective bones, without an Armature modifier or weights, as they don't need deformations. The tongue could be deformable, but in this exercise, to keep it simple, it just stays there. The eyes should be parented to the H_eye bones, not the D_eye bones (which are meant to deform the eyelids), as they also won't need deformations—only rotations following the H_eye bones.

To parent an object to a bone, make sure that you're in Pose Mode in the armature. Select the object, hold down **Shift**, and select the bone you want to serve as parent. Press **Ctrl+P** to do the parenting. Instead of selecting the Automatic Weights option, select the Bone option.

Posing Jim

After you've weighted all the models that need deformations, you'll be able to pose Jim. Here are some things to keep in mind as you're weighting your character (and afterward):

- The jawbone should open the mouth (moving the bottom lips) and should move the bottom teeth and the tongue with it.

- The clothing details of the arms, for example, can be deformed by bones, but you can just parent them to the arm bones. During design, the details were strategically placed there because in those positions, only one bone would affect them, so parenting them should be enough.

- The arms and legs usually show a tricky effect when rotating: the so-called twisting effect. When you twist your hand, for example, you affect the forearm—an effect that isn't contemplated in simple rigs. A cool way you can achieve the twisting effect in Blender is to use bendy bones.

  On the Bone tab of the Properties Editor is the Bendy Bones panel, where you can increase the number of segments to make the bone flexible and create a curve between a parent and its child. If you set Easing to 0, the segments won't be curved—only twisted along the original bone orientation. If you want to see the segments at work, change the display mode to B-Bones on the Armature tab. This method won't create perfect deformations, but it emulates the twisting effect in the forearms, which would take a more complex rig and way more weighting time to create manually.

  Bendy bones divide a bone into segments, so even though it acts as a single bone, it's divided internally to create the deformations that a chain of bones would have. This feature is really useful!

Creating the Facial Rig

Only the facial rig is missing, which allows Jim to express himself and smile at you. For that, you use shape keys. *Shape keys* are different statuses of the same model in which you can store different vertices' positions. One shape might be Jim's smile. Later, you'd be able to move the vertices from their neutral position to the smile position by sliding a bar from 0 to 100 percent, so you'd clearly see the transition. After you have those shapes modeled, you create a few new bones and learn how to use them to control those shapes. In the end, you will be able to control Jim's expressions with just a few bones.

Modeling Shapes

The first step in building Jim's facial rig is modeling the needed shape keys. You need to isolate different parts of the face and create different shape keys for each of them. Here are a few examples of the shape keys you can create: smile, blink, frown, mouth open, eyebrows up, and eyebrows down.

For each of those expressions (except the ones that affect both parts of the model), you have to create two shape keys—one for each side of the face. You need the left and right eyelids to blink, for example. For Jim, things are pretty simple, as you don't need him to make dramatic facial movements, just some basic things such as smiling and blinking, so you can keep the shape keys to a minimum. If you want to create a really nice facial rig, you need a lot of shapes and even bones to aid the facial deformations and make them more accurate. Figure 11.12 shows the Shape Keys panel on the Mesh tab of the Properties Editor.

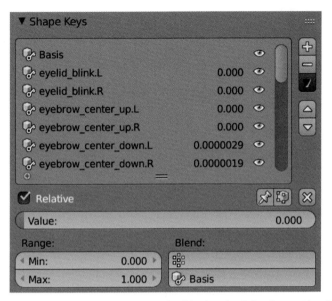

Figure 11.12   Shape Keys panel on the Mesh tab of the Properties Editor, where you can add, remove, and tweak shape keys

Creating Shape Keys

Here is how shape keys work. You start with the one called Basis. Basis is the base shape key, on which the rest build; Basis is the model itself. Click the **+** button to add a shape. Double-click a shape key to rename it. Suppose that you're going to create the smile shape. Name it something similar to mouth_smile.L (the left side of the mouth that will be smiling). With that shape selected, if you switch to Edit Mode, you can adjust the model to make it smile on the left side of the mouth (Proportional editing is useful in this stage.) When you exit Edit Mode, the model jumps back to its original shape, and you don't see the smile because the smile shape is at 0 percent effect at the moment. Near the shape's name is a number that you can drag left and right to increase or decrease its value. Also, you can select the shape and drag the Value slider below the list.

The shape key's value can extrapolate the position farther than the original shape key. If you set the value to 2, for example, the shape key can continue the movement of the vertices until they reach the double of the effect that you originally modeled.

The idea is that you have different shape keys for each part of the face that you can mix to create facial expressions. Happiness, for example, is a smile, with the lips a little open, the eyes semiclosed, cheeks lifted, and eyebrows lifted as well. The mix of those shape keys helps you create the happiness expression on the face. Figure 11.13 shows different expressions on Jim's face created by mixing some basic shape keys.

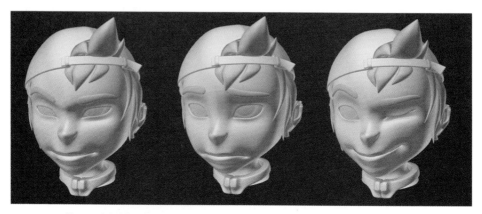

Figure 11.13   Jim's shape keys in action. Isolated parts of the face
are moving together to create full-face expressions.

Mirroring Shapes

You need some shape keys to isolate one side of the face from the other, such as a right-eye blink and a left-eye blink. If your character's face is symmetrical, modeling the shapes for each side is tedious, and the shapes may be different. To mirror shapes, follow these steps:

1. Create one side's shape key, such as the left-eye blink.
2. Exit Edit Mode, and set the left-eye blink shape key's value to 100 percent.
3. Click the button with a down triangle down near the + and − buttons to add shapes to and remove shapes from the list. Select the New Shape from Mix option to create a new shape with the vertex positions, including the values of current shapes. Rename the resulting shape for the other side.
4. Click the same button again, and select the option Mirror Shape to translate the vertex positions to the other side of the mesh.

Creating the Face Rig

You have many ways to create the facial rig: using bones to deform the face parts, using Lattice or Mesh Deform modifiers to deform the face, and so on. In this section, you create some bones to act as controllers that let you manipulate expressions from 3D View. This way, you won't have to tweak the shape keys in the Shapes panel one by one.

Depending on how you want to control your character expressions, you need different types of controls. In this section, you make a few bones in front of the face, each of which will control a few shapes. The bone for the mouth is set up so that when it's scaled up, the mouth opens. The ones for the eyebrows control the lifting of the eyebrows when you change their position. You have to think of these controls as intuitive (later, custom shapes make them even more intuitive), so they should make sense. Imagine that if you move one of the controls up, something in the face should move up; having a different effect would be counterintuitive. In Figure 11.14, you see the bones that control Jim's basic expressions. A more complex model with more shapes (to make him talk, for example) would need more controls.

Figure 11.14   These bones are responsible for controlling Jim's facial expressions.

Parent those bones to the head bone, and make sure that they're in the Control bone group. Also, you can put them on a new layer to separate them from the rest of the bones so that you can hide the facial controllers while you're working on the body. You can also name them with a different prefix, such as CF_cheek.L (Control Facial).

Using Drivers to Control the Face Shapes

Now you need to tell Blender how those bones and their properties will control the shape keys' values. For that purpose, you use drivers. This topic is quite technical and advanced, so you only get your feet wet in this section, but I encourage you to look into the topic and create more complex things with drivers.

Divide your interface, and switch to the Graph Editor. In the header of the Graph Editor is an option that lets you switch between F-Curves and Drivers. Select Drivers. (You learn about F-Curves, which are used for animation, in Chapter 12, "Animating Your Character.")

Creating Drivers

At this point, the Drivers interface is empty, as you have no drivers in your scene. Creating drivers is easy. Find the parameter you want to control, such as the Value parameter of one of the shapes in Jim's face, and right-click it. In the resulting menu, where you see the option Add Driver, choose Manually Create Later (Single). When you do, the parameter becomes uncontrollable from the interface (the driver overrides it) and turns violet so that you know that it is being controlled by a driver.

Setting Up a Driver

In this section, you set up the driver to make the eye blink when you scale down a bone. Then you use the same method for the rest of the shapes and control bones. Follow these steps:

1. In the left region of the Graph Editor, expand the list of the properties that have drivers. (See Figure 11.15.)

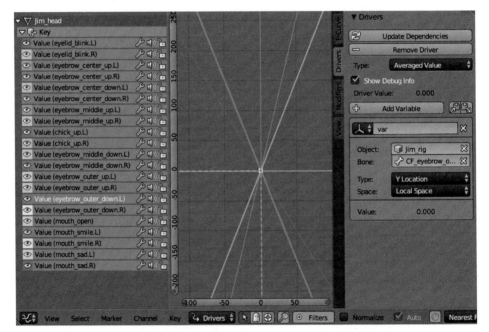

Figure 11.15   Graph Editor, showing the Drivers settings

2. Click the property to which you want to add a driver, and press the **N** key with your mouse over the Graph Editor to display the Properties Region. You see the parameters you need to tweak.

3. On the Drivers tab, set the Driver Type to Averaged Value, as you won't be scripting now. This option makes an average of the variables. (You use only one variable, but you can add more and complicate this process to extreme levels.)

4. In the variables field is a variable called var by default. Change its name if you want to use several variables and still be able to recognize them.

5. In the object name field, type the name of the armature. Another field shows where you can type the name of the bone you want to use to drive this property (the value of a shape key).

6. Select the type of transform of the bone that you want to drive the property. You want to control the eye-blink shape with the Z scale. (The axis doesn't matter, as you want the driver to work when you scale the bone on every axis.) Set Space to Local Space so that the driver depends on the local position of the bones. The bones will be moving around with the head, so selecting World Space isn't a good idea.

7. Make sure that everything works properly. At the top of the Drivers panel are two buttons: Update Dependencies and Remove Driver. To make sure that the driver has been updated with the changes you've made, click Update Dependencies. Then go to 3D View and try the controller out. It should be working, but the eye is closed, and it opens as you scale the object down. To make the animation intuitive, you want the eye to open and close when you scale the bone down.

8. In the Properties Region, find the Modifiers tab. (Yes, drivers can have modifiers!) The diagonal lines in Figure 11.15 (shown earlier in this section) represent the effects of each driver, and by modifying those lines, you change the effects to be faster, slower, and so on.

   Add a Generator modifier. By tweaking the two values inside the Generator, you can control the driver F-Curve and, hence, the effect of the bone over the shape key. To keep things simple, with the first value, you can set the starting point of the F-Curve; with the second value, you can set the inclination of the F-Curve, which defines the speed of the effect. (If you have to move the bone a lot to increase the shape key's value, increasing the speed will compensate.) If you want to reverse the movement, use negative values. Click Update Dependencies as you change those values to see their effects, and try the bones in 3D View.

9. Repeat this entire process with every controller and every shape.

Tip

When you have some drivers already set up, you'll probably find that you have to create new ones that are similar to those for other objects, bones, shape keys, and so on. Right-click a property with a driver, and choose Copy Driver from the menu that appears. Go to the property to which you want to add the new driver, right-click the property, and choose Paste Driver from the menu. Now you only need to go to the new driver and tweak its parameters to set it up for the new property.

Creating Custom Shapes

The rig is finished, but it's not looking very good. To make it better-looking, simpler, and easier to use, add custom shapes to the bones (see Figure 11.16). You can use any model or curve as a custom shape for the bones.

Figure 11.16   Using custom shapes for Jim's rig

Select a bone in Pose Mode. On the Bone tab of the Properties Editor, the Display panel has a Custom Bone field. In that field, type the name of the shape (any object) you want to use instead of the bone. This shape is only aesthetical; it has no influence on the functionality of the bone. You see another option to enable wireframes, which shows only the edges of the selected as a custom shape.

Following is the usual procedure for using custom shapes:

1. Create a shape such as a plane or a circle, and name it. (An S_ prefix will help you recognize a shape.)

2. Select the bone, and apply the new object as a custom shape.

3. Go back to the object; enter Edit Mode; and tweak, scale, and rotate the shape until you're happy with it.

4. Repeat the process from Step 1 for every controller bone.

Making Final Retouches

You can still do plenty of things to improve your rig, but this one is pretty complete. One thing you can do to make it much more comfortable to use is lock the transforms that you shouldn't be using for bones. This action has two functions: preventing accidental transforms (such as scaling a bone that shouldn't be scaled or rotating a bone that is meant only to be translated) and helping you see what you can do with each bone.

Take the foot roll as an example. The foot is supposed to rotate in a single axis; the others make the foot look wrong, and it's not meant to be moved or scaled. The Properties Region of 3D View has a lock icon below the Transform panel, next to the axis. If you click that lock icon, you won't be able to transform the bone on that axis (which disappears from the manipulators, helping you see what you can do with it).

Also, the bones that you have to rotate at some point can rotate with an XYZ Euler method. In the same Transform panel of the Properties Region, switch the rotation type from Quaternion to XYZ Euler. (The effect is easier to understand when you're using animation curves, as you'll have three controllable curves instead of four abstract ones.)

You see Jim posing for you in Figure 11.17.

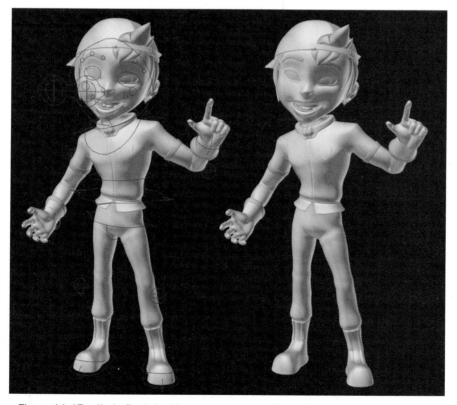

Figure 11.17   Jim's final rig. Now you can pose him and make him do cool stuff!

Reusing Your Character in Different Scenes

In this last section, I talk about linking, appending, and other interesting ways to reuse your character in other scenes or files.

Library Linking

Library Linking is the process through which you link objects from one scene to another. Why would you want to do that? Suppose that you're working on a film, and several animators are working on different shots at the same time. The same character needs to be in more than one scene, maybe interacting with other characters. You need to prepare your model so that it can be easily loaded into other scenes.

Linking and appending are the two ways in which you can bring objects from a .blend file into another.

Linking

Linking an object from one scene to another is easy. Choose Link from the File menu. Then you can navigate to another .blend file in your hard drive and access its contents. You can select anything from the contents: objects, meshes, lamps, materials, node trees, groups, scenes, and so on. When you've selected one or multiple elements, click Link. Those elements are brought into your current scene.

Linking brings the objects or other .blend file contents into your current .blend file, but it keeps a link to the original. You won't be able to modify those contents in the current file; you can only place them in the scene. To modify them, you have to go to the original .blend file and perform the desired changes. When you save the files and load the new one again, the changes are reflected in every scene in which that original object has been linked.

Suppose that you have a character, and you're working on some shots in which the character is involved. You have some animations done, and you suddenly decide that you want to change the character's hair color. Making this change file by file would be tedious and problematic. (It's just a color change, but imagine doing something more complex.)

This process is super-easy when you use links. Change the character in the original file, and when you save the file, the rest of the files that have this linked character reflect those changes automatically.

Appending

Appending is similar to linking but does not keep the link with the original contents. It creates a new copy of the elements in the current scene. You have complete access to this copy and can modify it as you want.

Linking and appending have advantages and disadvantages. Depending on the project and the specific case, you may be more interested in using one or the other. Choose wisely.

Working with Groups

Whether you're working with links or appending, you should use groups instead of objects. Following are a couple of reasons why working with groups is better:

- When you work with a group, all objects in the group are linked or appended. If you use objects instead, you have to select all of them, which makes it tricky to work with complex models made up of many objects. With a group, you have to select just one!

- If you work with objects and add a new one to your character (scenery, a stone in the floor, or a wardrobe, for example), you have to go through all the scenes in which the character is linked and link the new object. With groups, you just add the object to the character's group and save the file, and you're done, as the contents of the group are updated.

Follow these steps if you want to turn your character into a group:

1. Select all the objects, the armature, and anything else that is part of the character. (Remember to unhide hidden objects and layers.)
2. Press **Ctrl+G** to create a new group out of the selected objects.
3. Open the Operator menu of the Tools Region (or press **F6**), access the text field, and type a name for the group.

That's it! The next time you want to link or append a group, when you navigate to the .blend file, enter the Groups folder inside the .blend file's contents, and the character's group will be there waiting for you.

> **Note**
>
> A simple way to know whether an object is a part of a group is to pay attention to its outline when you select it. If the object is part of a group, its outline is green.

What if you want to add objects to or subtract objects from your group? Access the Object tab of the Properties Editor. The Group options on this tab control the groups to which an object belongs. You can remove the selected object from the group by clicking the X button, or you can add the object to an existing group. Alternatively, to remove an object from a group, select it, press **Ctrl+Alt+G**, and select the group from which you want to remove it.

Protecting Layers

In the Armature options of a skeleton in the Properties Editor, you see a Protected Layers section. In this section, you can mark some layers as selected to prevent modification of those layers when you link the character in another file. This option doesn't lock the bones so they can't be modified, but they are reset to their original states when the file reloads.

You can add layers such as the helper bones and the deform bones, which you don't want the animator (or yourself) to mess up accidentally. This feature is a layer of security for your rig.

Using Proxies to Animate a Linked Character

When you link a character to a different scene, something interesting happens: You can't modify linked objects except in the original scene from which they're linked. Armatures are exceptions, precisely to enable you to keep your character linked while you pose the rig and create animations.

Armatures can be modified when they're linked in a scene thanks to proxies. A *proxy* is a copy of the rig that allows you only to pose it. You can't enter Edit Mode and modify the shape or hierarchy of the bones, for example.

To create a proxy, select the linked character, press **Ctrl+Alt+P**, and select the armature from the list of objects that pops up. Then you'll be able to pose the copy of the rig, and the rest of the objects will follow.

Using Dupli Visibility

When you use proxies and linked groups, an interesting option to keep in mind is Dupli Visibility, which controls the visibility of different layers in a duplicate of the group (such as in a link).

You can access this options from the Groups menu on the Object tab of the Properties Editor. Below the name of the group to which the selected object belongs, you see the Dupli Visibility section, which has two groups of squares (layers).

By default, all the layers are enabled, so everything that you link from the group is visible. You can disable some layers, though. This feature is extremely useful for rigs.

When you create a proxy, the rig is duplicated, so you see two rigs overlapped in the same position, which may look a bit confusing. In the Dupli Visibility layers, disable the one that contains your character's rig. When you link the character from now on, the rig is invisible, but it becomes visible when you create a proxy.

Summary

Surely this chapter showed you that rigging is the most technical, complex part of the character-creation process. It takes time, and it can be frustrating, such as when the rig doesn't behave as you expect. There are quicker ways to create rigs, such as the Rigify add-on, which generates a very cool rig automatically based on the proportions you set for your character. But you should create at least a few rigs yourself so that you can understand the process. Sometimes, you need rigs for simple things, and it's not always possible to use an automatically generated rig. You may be working on something that's not a character, or maybe the character is very strange. In those cases, this knowledge is useful. Furthermore, you learned how to create a group with your character, link it to other scenes, and reuse it efficiently. Jim is much closer to being alive!

Exercises

1. Why is a rig so important for your character?
2. What is an armature?
3. What are vertex weights?
4. What is the difference between forward kinematics (FK) and inverse kinematics (IK)?
5. What are constraints used for?
6. Why are drivers useful?

12

Animating Your Character

Your character comes to life through animation. Animation is the process in which you make your character move along time. To animate characters convincingly, you have to study the principles of motion, such as action and reaction, and you need to understand how weight affects the way a character moves. Animation is a wide subject, with plenty of resources, books, and courses available. In this chapter, you learn the basics of the Blender animation system. You find out what tools are at your disposal, and you learn how to use keyframes and the animation editors that help you during this stage.

Inserting Keyframes

A *keyframe* is a specific stored value in different parameters of objects at a given point in time. If you want to make an object move from A to B, each one of those positions is a keyframe, and Blender automatically interpolates the movement between those keyframes. In this section, I describe some ways of adding keyframes in Blender.

Using the Manual Method

Inserting keyframes manually is the most basic way to add keyframes to your objects. Set the frame in the timeline to define the time at which you want to save that specific position, select your object or objects, and press **I**. A menu appears, letting you choose from among the channels and transform properties of that object so that you can record a keyframe in the desired channels. You can set a keyframe just for the location (Loc), for example, or for the rotation (Rot). To keep matters simple, choose LocRotScale to set a keyframe for the three transform types, which is what you usually want to do.

Using the Automatic Method

In the Timeline Editor, at the bottom of the default interface, you can define the duration of the animation, play it, scroll through it, and so on. A little button with a red circle is similar to the Record button on old cassette players. If you click this button, you enable the Auto Keyframing option.

When this option is enabled, every time you change something, a keyframe is saved for it automatically in the current frame. This option is really useful when you're animating, as it lets you insert keyframes by moving things and saves you the time it would take to insert keyframes manually. You have to be very careful with Auto Keyframing, however, because if you forget that it's turned on, you might save keyframes when you don't want to.

Using Keying Sets

Using keying sets may be the most comfortable way to add keyframes. You can select a keying set in the field right next to the Auto Keyframing button (the field that has a key icon on it). When you pick a keying set, you don't need to select the channels in which you want to set a keyframe each time you press **I**. Blender automatically keyframes the channels you selected in your keying set.

If you select the LocRotScale keying set, for example, when you press **I**, Blender automatically adds a keyframe to the three channels; you don't need to confirm manually each time. Also, a keying set called Whole Character saves a keyframe for the full rig when you press **I**. You don't even need to select the other bones, which is very handy!

Animating Properties in the Menus

Animating a property is simple. (Yes, you can animate properties; almost everything in Blender can be animated, such as the number of subdivisions in a modifier, the color of a material, or the influence of a constraint on an object.) Place the mouse cursor over the property value field, and press **I**. Blender stores a keyframe for that property in the current frame. That property's field is yellow in the frames where Blender has stored keyframes and green in the rest of the frames, just to let you know that the property owns an animation.

Working with Animation Editors

Several editors help you manipulate an animation, from moving through the animation's time (as in the Timeline) to editing the animation curves to tell Blender how you want it to interpolate the movement between two keyframes. You can even mix animations as though you're editing video! Figure 12.1 shows the editors.

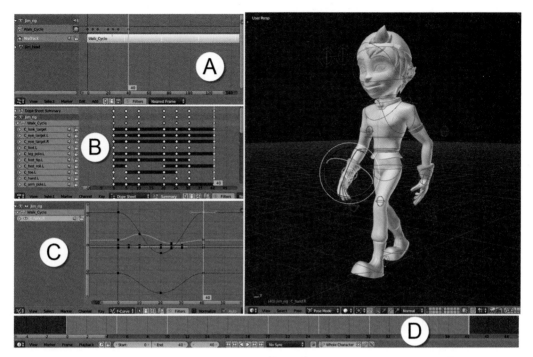

Figure 12.1   Non-Linear Animation (A), Dope Sheet (B), Graph (C), and Timeline (D) editors

Timeline

The Timeline is the most basic animation editor, showing the time and displaying keyframes on the selected objects as yellow vertical lines. You can change the current frame and scrub through the animation by pressing and dragging **LMB** and positioning the green cursor along the Timeline.

In the Timeline, you can also set the start and end frames of the animation, Press **S** to set the current frame as the start frame, and press **E** to set the current frame as the end. Also, you can type frame numbers in the Start and End fields of the Timeline's header.

Also on the header are controls for playing the animation, jumping to the start or end, and jumping to the next or previous keyframe. Here are some shortcuts you can use in 3D View (or any other editor to control time):

- Press **Alt+A** to play the animation. Press **Alt+A** again to pause it. Press **Esc** to stop it and go to the frame from which you started playing.
- To quickly select the frame range you want to play, press **P** and then click and drag the box to cover the desired range.
- Press the **Left** or **Right** arrow key to move to the previous or next frame. Press the **Up** or **Down** arrow key to jump to the next or previous keyframe.

Dope Sheet

Pretty basic, the Dope Sheet editor shows keyframes on objects (the left side of the Dope Sheet lists the objects in the scene) as yellow diamond shapes in a timeline. This editor lets you move keyframes so that you can adjust the timing of your animation.

You can use basic keyboard shortcuts such as **G** to move keys and **S** to scale them, or press **Shift** while you right-click the keys to select several at the same time. Press **B** to box-select a group of keyframes. Press **Shift+D** to duplicate keyframes.

Enable the Summary option on the Dope Sheet's header to display another line at the top that shows all the keys for every object in the list.

The Dope Sheet has different modes, and the header features a mode selector. By default, Dope Sheet is selected to allow you to access objects' keyframes. Other options are Action Editor, Mask, which allows you to access masks' animations (created in the Movie Clip Editor and used in the compositor), Shape Keys, and Grease Pencil. An object can store different animations (actions), and in the Action Editor, you can select which one to play. This editor also lets you name the actions; later, you can mix these actions in the Non-Linear Animation Editor (explained later in this section). If you work on videogames, you probably know that a character can have different animations, such as walking, running, remaining idle, and picking up an object. You can use those actions in the same scene and switch among them, create new ones, and edit existing ones, thanks to the Action Editor.

You could say that the Dope Sheet is a general editor, displaying all the animations going on in the scene. The Action Editor works with a specific animation of a specific object—especially useful with armatures, allowing you to store different animations for your characters.

Tip

If you come from other software that lets you manipulate the keyframes from the timeline, you can replace the Timeline in Blender with a Dope Sheet. Enable the Summary option so that you can see all the keyframes at the top of the editor, and you're all set. This feature is what's cool about the versatility of Blender's interface!

Graph Editor

The Graph Editor is the scariest thing you'll see in animation. Seriously, it's not that complicated, but the first time you see the animation curves without a proper understanding of how they work, they can look complex and frightening.

In the Graph Editor, you can edit the animation curves, also called *F-Curves* in Blender. Animation curves are pretty simple.

When you create two keyframes, Blender automatically creates an interpolation between them. The curves define how the interpolation happens, and you can control the curves to change the interpolation in case you're not happy with the default behavior.

Each transform or property has an F-Curve on each axis. Suppose that you want to make an object fly from point A to point B. Figure 12.2 shows what would happen with different curve configurations.

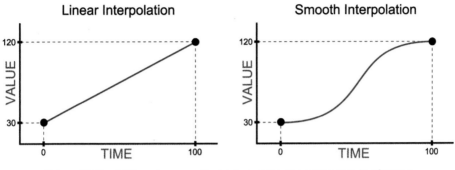

Figure 12.2   Different curves that interpolate the same two keyframes

Figure 12.2 shows two keyframes. The position of a keyframe horizontally defines its time, and its vertical position sets its value. In the figure, the first keyframe sets a value of 30 in frame 0. The second keyframe has a value of 120 in frame 100.

The image on the left represents a linear interpolation, which tells Blender to increase the value from 30 to 120 between frames 0 and 100 at a constant speed.

The image on the right shows a smooth interpolation. Blender starts increasing the value slowly and then accelerates; it starts decreasing slowly before reaching the value of 120 at frame 100.

As you can see in the figures, these two different movements between the same keyframes are defined by the animation curves.

In the Graph Editor, you can manipulate the curves. Move, rotate, or scale keyframes by pressing **G**, **R**, and **S**. You can duplicate keyframes by pressing **Shift+D**.

To change the interpolation of a keyframe, select it, and press **V**. (You can do the same thing in the Dope Sheet, but the difference is more visual in the Graph Editor.) A menu appears, displaying options that allow you to set the interpolation and the handle type of that keyframe.

You can tweak handles by right-clicking and dragging. Modify the curvature of the interpolations to control how the animation accelerates, decelerates, and at which rate. Another way to tweak handles is to select a keyframe and then rotate or scale it, which changes the behavior of the keyframe's handles.

Tip

The Editing tab of User Preferences has an option that allows you to set how your keyframe interpolations are adjusted by default when you create them. You can find the Interpolation option in the New F-Curve Defaults section.

Non-Linear Animation (NLA)

The Non-Linear Animation (NLA) Editor is interesting. It works similarly to a video editor. You can use it to load strips, mix them, layer them, make them longer or shorter, and so on, but instead of videos, you'll be using animations!

You can load actions that you saved in the Action Editor (a mode of the Dope Sheet, discussed earlier in this chapter) and mix them to build a bigger animation. Later in this chapter, in the "Repeating the Animation" section, you use this editor to repeat a walk cycle constantly. Instead of animating Jim taking 10 steps, you animate a cycle of two steps (one for each leg), and with the NLA Editor, you can repeat that action for as long as necessary.

Suppose that you have another action of Jim running. You could add that action to the NLA Editor as another strip by pressing **Shift+A**; then you could mix the action with the walk-cycle animation so that Jim goes progressively from walking to running.

Another option is to add tweaks to an animation as though they were layers. You could have an animation with Jim turning his head, looking to the sides. You could add the secondary animation over the walking animation so that Jim could walk and move his head at the same time. Think of the possibilities!

Common Controls and Tips

All these editors have some controls in common. You can move or duplicate things in these editors the same way that you do in other Blender editors (by pressing **G** and dragging your mouse to move or pressing **Shift+D** to duplicate). You find other similarities for navigation:

- **MMB**-click and drag to pan so that you can see other parts of the charts.
- Press **Home** to adjust zoom so that Blender shows the entire animation time range.
- Press **Ctrl+MMB** and drag your mouse to zoom. In some editors, you can zoom only horizontally, but in the Graph Editor, you can zoom horizontally and vertically. You can also zoom in and out by using the scroll wheel.
- Press **P** and drag the resulting box to define the start and end frames of the animation.
- Press **Alt** and use the scroll wheel to go to the next or previous keyframe, which is a fast way to scrub through your animation (in small steps).

Here are some options that can make it easier to work with these editors:

- On the header of most of the animation editors is a button that shows a mouse cursor. If you enable that option, you see the keyframes of only selected objects, which can prevent you from going crazy looking at dozens (or hundreds) of curves or keyframes at the same time. This option helps you recognize what you're seeing in those editors.

- Choose Only Selected Curves Keyframes from the View menu on the header in Graph Editor. This option displays only the keyframes of the curves from properties you select on the list, preventing you from selecting or accidentally moving keyframes of other curves that are overlapping with the one you want to adjust.

- The Graph Editor's header also has a Normalize option. When you're working with curves that have different value ranges, navigation can be hard, as you have to zoom in and out continually to see what you need to see. When Normalize is enabled, all the curves are adjusted to fit inside a 0-to-1 range for easier tweaking. This change is visual only; it doesn't affect the real values of the curves.

Frames Per Second

I recommend that you set the frames per second (fps) at which you want your animation to play. Blender's default setting is 24, used in many formats, but depending on your country, this rate may vary. (In the United States, the typical fps rate for TV broadcasting is 29.97; in Europe, the typical rate is 25 fps.) Or you may want to select a different frame rate for artistic reasons; using 10 fps, for example, can help you mimic a stop-motion animation. Whatever rate choose, you should set it before you start working on your animation. Otherwise, if you change the fps rate later, playback speed will vary, and you'll probably have to adjust the timing of your animation. You can change the frame rate in the Dimensions panel of the Properties Editor's Render tab. I recommend you use 25 fps with the animations for the project in this book, as the videos in which Jim will be composed in Chapter 14, "Lighting, Compositing, and Rendering," have been recorded at 25 fps.

Animating a Walk Cycle

In this section, I guide you step by step through the process of creating of a basic walking animation. Make Jim come alive!

Tip

When you animate, you should have a good performance in 3D View so that you can see your animation smoothly while you work. Blender has an interesting option called Simplify; look for it on the Scene tab of the Properties Editor. If you enable Simplify, you can select the maximum number of subdivisions for every object in the scene, both in 3D View and during render. In this exercise, the model probably uses two to three levels of subdivision, which is nice for a final render, but the effect on performance can be big, making the animation drop frames and play slower than it should. You can change the Simplify value to 1 or 0 while you work on the animation and leave it at 2 or 3 for the render. You can set these parameters in the Subdivision Surface modifier that you add to each of the objects. Simplify, however, acts on all the modifiers of the scene at the same time, making it very valuable when you have many objects, because tweaking those parameters one by one would be time-consuming.

Creating an Action

The walking animation is a cycle, meaning that you have to animate only one step that will be repeated. (The step occurs in a static place, so the character won't move across space; that movement will be animated later.) As you'll be repeating the step by using the NLA Editor, you need to create an action that you can load later.

Each object has different actions, so make sure that you have the rig selected in Pose Mode before you create an action. (If you are in Object Mode, Blender creates an action for the container, not for the individual bones, which is what you need.)

Open the Dope Sheet, and switch to Action Editor mode. If you haven't animated anything yet, the header has a field in which you can create a new action. Click the New button, and this action is called (surprise!) Action. Rename the action something intuitive, such as Walk_Cycle. Now every keyframe you set for the bones in the rig is part of the Walk_Cycle action.

Caution

If you create more than one action, remember that Blender deletes datablocks that are not in use when you close the program. Each object can use only a single action at a time. If you want to make sure that the rest of them are saved, click the F button next to their names so that they have a fake user. This action prevents Blender from deleting them when you exit because they are technically in use.

Creating the Poses for the Walk Cycle

To make Jim walk, you must define the basic poses for the character that form the motion of walking. There are two contact poses—the moments in which a character touches the floor with its feet. There are two other poses when the character has one foot on the floor and the other one is in the air. Those four positions define the basic walk movement.

You must create a motion that can be repeated, which means that the animation needs to end in the same position as the one in which it starts. This type of animation is called a *loop*. Figure 12.3 shows the main poses and a couple of additional ones to refine the movement. Notice that after those poses is another one that's equal to the first one (pose 7). This pose is added so that the animation's end fits with its start, so that the loop can be repeated.

Figure 12.3 represents several things:

- Poses 1, 3, 4, and 6 (marked as yellow keys) are the main poses. Poses 2 and 5 (marked as blue keys) are extra poses to better define the movement, and pose 7 is the same as pose 1.

- Actually, you need to create only three poses: 1, 2, and 3! Poses 4, 5, and 6 are nothing more than mirrored versions of poses 1, 2, and 3. Pose 7 is a copy of pose 1. Being able to copy and paste poses makes the process a lot easier and faster.

- Poses 1, 4, and 7 are the contact poses, in which the foot that goes forward touches the ground. Poses 3 and 6 are the intermediate poses between two contacts to set the moments in which Jim is standing on a single leg.

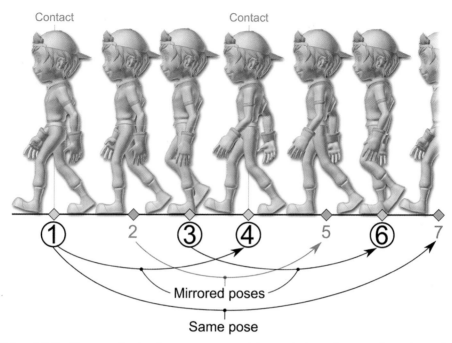

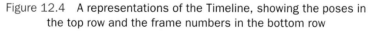

Figure 12.3   Here are the basic poses you need to create to make your character walk.

Before diving into the animation process, take a look at the timing, which defines the speed of the animation (see Figure 12.4).

Figure 12.4   A representations of the Timeline, showing the poses in the top row and the frame numbers in the bottom row

Figure 12.4 shows the frame numbers at which you should create the poses for the animation. Keep in mind that regardless of the frame number in which you create a keyframe, you can always rework the timing later, using one of the animator editors (the Dope Sheet is especially useful for retiming keyframes), and make Jim walk faster or slower. What you can see is that a main pose happens every 10 frames.

Follow this easy process to create the walking animation:

1. Set your animation to start at frame 0 and end at frame 40.

2. Pose your character in frame 0 with the first contact pose. Set a keyframe in all the bones of the rig. (You can select any bone, select Whole Character Keying Set, and press **I**.)

3. Select all the bones (**A**), and copy this pose by clicking the Copy Pose button on the header or by pressing **Ctrl+C**. Go to frame 20, and paste the mirrored pose by pressing the Paste Inverted Pose button on the header or by pressing **Shift+Ctrl+V**. Set a keyframe. Move the timeline to frame 40, and paste the pose normally (**Ctrl+V**). Set another keyframe. Now you have all your contact poses in place. You create those keyframes first because now if you go to frame 10, you have an intermediate pose almost ready.

4. Pose the character so that he looks better, and make sure that the pose of his feet is good to go (one foot on the floor and the other one passing through the air). Insert a keyframe, copy this pose, and paste it mirrored in frame 30. Set another keyframe.

5. A few frames after the contact poses (poses 1 and 4), adjust the poses to make the foot in front step on the ground completely, and keep elevating the foot from the tip while the foot keeps sliding back. This simple pose gives the walk cycle a more natural look.

6. Play the animation to see how it looks, adjust the poses, and copy them to the other moments of the animation that are similar. If you want to make everything smoother, you can tweak the animation curves in the Graph Editor. If some curve looks rigid, adjust it while you play the animation to get instant feedback.

Repeating the Animation

Jim is walking in place but taking only one step. Before you make Jim move through space, you have to repeat the animation so that he performs more steps. You can accomplish this task in several ways. You could duplicate all the poses in the Dope Sheet to add another step after the first one. But in this section, you use the NLA Editor. Follow these steps:

1. Open the NLA Editor, which looks similar to Figure 12.5. The editor displays a horizontal line with the name of your current action (inside the rig's name, which is the object that performs the action). The action's keyframes are displayed in the editor, along with a button with two arrows pointing down.

Figure 12.5   The NLA Editor when you open it

2. You have two ways to proceed.

The first option is to click the X button in the action's name inside the Action Editor (make sure that you click the F near it first) so that Jim stops performing that action and frees the NLA Editor to do its job. Go to the NLA Editor, press **Shift+A**, and select the Walk_Cycle action to add it as a strip.

The second option, which is much easier and faster, is to click the double-arrow button for the Walk_Cycle action in the NLA Editor. This option turns the action into a strip and performs the actions in the first option automatically. Now you can move that strip to change the time at which the animation happens. You can even scale by pressing **S** to make the action faster or slower, or duplicate it to add more steps (see Figure 12.6).

Figure 12.6   The NLA Editor with the Walk_Cycle
action as a strip, ready to be edited

3. You could duplicate the Walk_Cycle strip to add more steps to your animation, but here's a more elegant method. Press **N** in the NLA Editor to open the Properties Region. In the Action Clip panel, cut frames at the start or end of the animation. Set the end as frame 39 instead of frame 40 so that pose 1 doesn't repeat in two frames; this setting makes the transition more natural when you repeat it. Then, in the same panel, change the scale of the strip and the number of repetitions. Set the repetitions to something like 5 or 6 so that you have enough steps in the animation. Then you can play with the scale of the strip to make the animation faster or slower as needed.

As you can see, using the NLA Editor is a very easy way of controlling actions instead of dealing with a lot of keyframes to achieve the same result. This chapter is only an introduction, but you can do all sorts of cool things in this editor, such as overlapping actions or creating transitions between actions.

Walking Along a Path

Jim is taking a lot of steps now, but he's not moving in space. Follow these steps to use a constraint so that he follows a path while he walks:

1. Press **Shift+A**, and choose a Path object from the Curve category of the Add menu.

2. In Edit Mode, edit the points of the curve to describe the path you want Jim to walk. In this case, the path should be a straight line. Delete all the points of the curve except the start and end ones. Place the start vertex at the origin of the scene, where Jim is, and the end vertex aligned in the Y axis.

3. Select Jim's rig in Object Mode to apply a constraint to it. On the Constraints tab of the Properties Editor, add a Follow Path constraint.

4. From the Follow Path constraint menu, choose the path you just created. If the path doesn't work automatically when you play the animation, click the Animate Path button. If you want a curved path, enable the Follow option so that the character turns with the path.

5. Select the path, and on the Curve tab of the Properties Editor, in the Path Animation panel, adjust the number of frames that Jim uses to go from the start to the end of the path. Also adjust the length of the curve and the speed of the walking cycle until you get a nice result and Jim's feet slide over the floor as little as possible. (You can activate the grid on the floor and add more lines to it in the Display panel of the Properties Region in 3D View to get a reference on how Jim is moving over the floor, as you see in Figure 12.7.) You can also use the 3D cursor to mark where the heel steps in space, giving you a reference point for correcting the sliding of the feet.

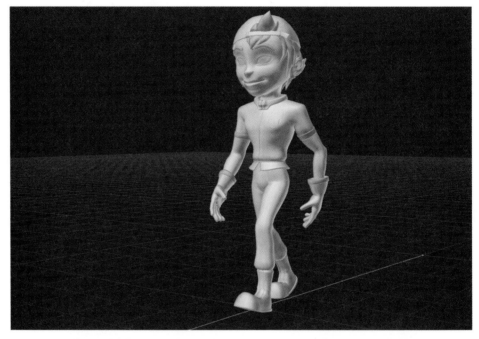

Figure 12.7   Jim walking along the path on the floor. He is alive!

Summary

Animation is a complex thing. Creating believable movements for your characters is tricky and requires a lot of knowledge, experience, and dedication. I hope that this chapter showed you the basics and opened your desire to learn more.

Now you have a walking, finished character. And you started this book with little or no idea of how Blender works! In Chapter 13, "Camera Tracking in Blender," you keep doing cool things.

Exercises

1. What is a keyframe?
2. What animation editors are available in Blender?
3. What are animation curves used for?
4. When would you use actions in Blender? What's the advantage of using them?
5. Which constraint type would you use to move an object along a curve?

VI

Getting the Final Result

13 Camera Tracking in Blender

14 Lighting, Compositing, and Rendering

Camera Tracking in Blender

When you want to mix your 3D objects into a real-world video, you need a camera in the 3D world that moves exactly the same way as the camera that filmed the real-world footage so that the 3D objects fit perfectly into the scene. *Camera tracking* is the process that allows you to track features in the real video to give Blender information about the changes in perspective so that it can generate a 3D camera that mimics the movement of the real one. Until very recently, you needed expensive specialized software for this purpose. Now Blender provides an efficient alternative, and the best thing about it is that you don't need to import/export scenes or use any other software; everything you need is already inside Blender! In this chapter, you learn the basics of camera tracking in Blender.

Understanding Camera Tracking

Before you start the process of tracking, it's important that you understand how it works:

1. First, you load a video and track its features by using the tracking tools in Blender. Good features are typically details in the video that are highly visible and static relative to the world and have a high contrast or distinct shapes, enabling Blender to recognize them easily from one frame to the next. Tracking uses these features to establish which way the objects in the video are moving relative to the frame. This process is generally done frame by frame, but sometimes it can be faster; Blender also provides some automatic tools that try to do most of the work, so you have to manually track only those areas and moments for which the algorithm can't figure out the movement.

2. Next, when you have enough tracked markers in the video, you input the camera settings to tell Blender the type of camera and lens you used to film the video. If you don't know exactly what lens you used, Blender can estimate the settings and give you something pretty close to those that you used.

3. You have to solve the camera's movement. At this stage, Blender analyzes the points you tracked through the video, and by comparing their movements in different frames, it reconstructs the camera's perspective and determines where the 3D camera should be on each frame. You end up with a 3D camera that moves exactly the same way as the real camera you used.

4. Finally, you align the 3D camera and adjust it to your scene so that its orientation is correct and your 3D objects fits within the real-world footage.

Shooting Video for Easy Tracking

Sometimes, when you have a video that you need to track, the level of difficulty directly depends on how the video was shot. If the video wasn't shot with some basic considerations in mind, you'll probably have a hard time tracking it. The video may not contain enough clearly visible features that you can use to track it, for example, or it may be very blurry or fast-moving. Keep in mind that a movie may have a lot of these tricky shots to track, but also realize that people who have significant experience and use expensive software put in a lot of effort (and sometimes even perform manual magic) to make the 3D camera fit perfectly with the camera that took the real footage. If you want to create your own videos and prevent your shots from being difficult to track, you just need to know how the tracker works.

Camera tracking uses what is called *perspective shift* or *parallax effect* to detect the perspective and depth in your footage. Suppose that you are inside a train, and you look out a window. The objects close to you appear to move really fast, and the objects farther away, such as clouds, are almost stationary. This situation is what perspective shift is all about: An object that is close to the camera shifts its perspective faster than one that is far away.

Knowing this, you can understand that a video in which you move the camera to show that perspective shift helps Blender determine where the markers are. If that shift doesn't fit the idea you have for the shot, don't worry! You can shoot some video reference frames that capture perspective shift before shooting the actual video; then you can use the frames of the reference footage to show Blender the correct perspective, and the rest of the video will incorporate that perspective. This technique gives you good results when you're working with a video that has minimal perspective shift. When you finally edit the video, you can cut out those reference frames at the beginning, of course.

Here are some other useful tips on shooting a video for tracking:

- Because of perspective shift, it helps to have tracking features in both the foreground and the background to give Blender a good reference of the real scene's depth.

- Make sure that the video has enough recognizable features that you will be able to track throughout the video. (High-contrast elements with 90-degree corners offer the best results for tracking.) The more often a feature appears during the video, the more stable the camera motion's solution will be. If you feel that the video doesn't have a lot of features, place something in the scene that can help you—a little stone here, a piece of paper there. Just add things that will help you later and won't distract the viewer. An alternative is to add physical markers (usually, small designs that contain contrasting shapes or corners that you can print and place in your scene during filming). This technique can be tricky, however, because you have to remove the markers later in postproduction, so it's best to place only small, unobtrusive objects in strategic positions.

- Avoid zooming if possible, because changes in the lens while shooting the footage can compromise the tracking and make it much trickier. You can always fake the zooming in postproduction (at the expense of some image quality) by making the image bigger.

- Try to prevent very fast movement that might blur the image. If you have blurry footage, chances are that you'll have to track it almost completely manually, and the tracking probably won't be very precise because you won't be able to see the tracking features clearly. Use some kind of camera stabilization if possible. A simple weight under the camera can help a great deal!

- Shooting a good-quality video makes tracking a lot easier. If the video has compression artifacts or low resolution, small (and even big) features change a lot from one frame to the next, making things very difficult for Blender's automatic tracker, and you'll have to do a lot of manual work.

- To track the camera movement, you can use only features that are static. Don't use things that move as features to track, because they can break Blender's perspective analysis. Keep this fact in mind when you plan how to shoot the scene to make sure that you have enough static features to track. Remember that the more features you track, the more stable and closer to the real footage the 3D camera movement will be.

- If possible, take note of the focal length and other camera parameters you used while shooting the video footage. That information will help Blender solve the 3D camera's motion.

Using the Movie Clip Editor

Camera tracking happens inside the Movie Clip Editor. Work on a Blender area in the Movie Clip Editor by selecting that editor type on the area's header. Figure 13.1 shows the editor.

You may not understand anything about the Movie Clip Editor right now, but don't worry. Here is a quick and simple explanation of the Movie Clip Editor:

- **Tools Region (A):** Here, you find options for creating new markers and for tracking and solving the camera's movement. Press **T** to show and hide this region.
- **Movie Clip (B):** This area is the real footage you've shot and is where you can track features by using markers. The integrated and tracking specialized timeline at the bottom lets you work with this editor full-screen.
- **Properties Region (C):** In this section of the editor are the settings of the selected marker, together with display and camera parameters. Press **N** to show and hide this region.

You learn more about the part of the editor throughout this chapter.

Figure 13.1   The Movie Clip Editor is where you perform camera tracking.

Tracking the Camera

In this section, you learn how to load video footage, track moving points in the image, and generate the 3D camera movement that simulates the movement of the real camera. For now, you need to see only the Movie Clip Editor, so you may want to make it full-screen by pressing **Shift+Space** or **Ctrl+Up**.

Loading Your Footage

You can't track your footage if you have no footage, of course, so first, you must load it. You have different ways to load your footage, but the process is basically the same as loading images in the UV/Image Editor:

- You can press **Alt+O** and select your footage.
- You can click and drag the footage from your operating-system folder into the Movie Clip Editor.
- You can choose the Open Clip option from the Clip menu on the header.
- You can click the big Open button on the header.

After you load your footage, you can scrub through it by using the timeline at the bottom of the editor, just above the header. When you're tracking, you don't use anything other than the Movie Clip Editor to scrub through the footage.

Left-clicking and dragging the green numbered cursor on the timeline changes the current frame and displays the frame number. The timeline also has two horizontal lines, one blue and one yellow; the blue line is for the footage. As you play the video (**Alt+A**), Blender caches the frames, so next time you play the video, the frames load a lot faster. I recommend that you play the entire video to cache it completely before you start tracking, which makes the process faster. Alternatively, if you click the Prefetch button at the top of the Tools Region (or press **P**), Blender automatically caches the video without playing it. The blue line is lighter in the parts that are cached, you'll know which parts you've cached and which you haven't.

> **Tip**
>
> By default, Blender uses only 1GB of RAM to cache your footage. If you're working with a big video or full HD, 1GB may not be enough to cache all the frames. On the System tab of the User Preferences (**Ctrl+Alt+U**), you find a Sequencer/Clip Editor section where you can increase the amount of memory to be used for caching videos. A value of 8000 (8GB) is enough for most videos (depending on their length, resolution, and format, of course). Also, your machine needs to have enough RAM for this purpose.

The yellow line is for the markers. When a tracker is at work, moving and following a feature, Blender displays a muted yellow line. In the frames where you add manual keyframes to the track, the line is brighter yellow, so you'll know which parts of the footage have keyframes that were added manually and which parts were tracked automatically.

Video Resolution and FPS

When you load a video, keep in mind that resolution and the fps rate will be those that you set up in the Properties Editor. On the Render tab (the tab with a camera icon), select the proper size and frame rate in the Dimensions panel. The downloadable videos provided with this book (inside the Resources folder) are 1920 × 1080 and 25 fps.

Studying the Anatomy of a Marker

Markers (also called trackers) are the main tools you use to track features in your footage, so before you start tracking, you need to understand what a marker is and what its parts do (see Figure 13.2):

- **Pattern:** The pattern is the main part of the marker—the area of the image in one frame that Blender (or you, manually) will look for in the next frame to track it. Usually, you should use a feature of the footage that is easy to recognize as the pattern's center: a high-contrast area or a specific shape that is unique in the image. You can move the marker, rotate it, and scale it as always by pressing **G**, **R**, and **S** (and combine them with **Shift** to enable precision transforms). Also, the Track panel of the Properties Region displays an image that shows the selected marker's pattern, so you can clearly see the pattern that the selected marker will be looking for in the next frame.

- **Search area:** This area is where Blender looks for the pattern defined in the pattern area in the next frame. (This area is not visible by default; you need to enable it in the Marker Display panel of the Properties Region if you want to see it.) The faster the movement of the image, the bigger the search area needs to be, because if the pattern in the next frame falls outside the search area, Blender won't find it. The bigger the search area, however, the slower automatic tracking becomes. You can change the size of this area or its position by left-clicking and dragging its top-left and bottom-right marked corners.

- **Pattern orientation:** You can rotate the pattern (or distort it by dragging its corners) to make tracking it easier. If you do, you also have options to track the pattern's rotation or perspective, which can be very useful at times. In this example, though, you work only with the markers' locations. When you left-click and drag the little square at the end of the short line, you can rotate or scale the pattern (or press **R** and **S** when you select the marker).

- **Tracked frames:** When you're tracking, the marker shows a red and a blue line, both with dots across them. The track is always in the current frame's position; the blue line shows the trajectory and positions of the next frames (if tracked), and the red line displays the tracked positions in the previous frames. These lines can help you compare different markers' movements to determine whether one of them is clearly off.

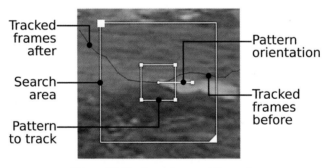

Figure 13.2   A marker and its parts

Tracking Features in the Footage

Now that you know the basics, you can explore the marker settings.

You can modify the tracking settings for markers in two places: the Properties Region and the Tools Region. The settings in the Properties Region affect the selected marker's tracking settings, and the settings in the Tools Region are the parameters that Blender applies by default when you create trackers.

Tracking settings include options and values that control things such as the color channel the settings will be tracking, the pattern and search size, and whether the marker will track location (you'll use this option in an upcoming example), as well as rotation, scale, and perspective of the features.

The Match Type option is very important. You can set it to match the keyframe or the previous frame. The Keyframe setting tells Blender to look in every frame for a feature similar to the one you set in the last manual keyframe for the marker. The Previous Frame setting looks for a feature similar to the one in the last tracked frame. Usually, you want to use Previous Frame, as a tracking feature can change slightly throughout the video (because of perspective), so it's better for the tracker to adapt to that small change that happens frame by frame. Otherwise, at some point, the feature will be very different from its appearance in the previous manual keyframe, and the tracker will stop working.

Now it's time to start tracking. Here are the steps you need to follow to track features:

1. First, create a marker. On the Marker tab of the Tools Region, click the Add button; then left-click the footage where you want to create the marker.

   Tip

   A quicker way to create markers is to press **Ctrl+LMB** where you want to place the new marker.

2. Adjust the marker so that the pattern area fits the feature you want to follow (maybe a corner or a spot). Scale the marker up or down by pressing **S** to adjust it to the feature's size. In the Track panel at the top of the Properties Region, look at the zoomed version of the pattern defined by the marker to make sure that it's placed correctly.

3. Track that feature along the footage by using the Track Forward and Track Backward features. In the Track panel of the Tools Region, launch automatic tracking or press **Ctrl+T** to track forward or **Shift+Ctrl+T** to track backward.

4. Track frame by frame by pressing **Alt+Right** and **Alt+Left**. Press **L** to center the view on the selected marker. In the Marker Display panel of the Properties Region, set the options that control what you want to see on the screen (such as the marker search area). This technique is useful for finding out whether the marker is stable.

   Tip

   Sometimes, a feature won't be visible. Suppose that you're tracking a window in a building in the background, and it's obscured in some frames by a post in the foreground. You can stop tracking, skip some frames, and start tracking when the feature becomes visible again. Blender evaluates a marker only while it has tracking keyframes (manual or automatic), so if you skip some frames without tracking the marker, it will be treated as disabled for those frames. You can also manually force the marker to be disabled or enabled at a specific frame by clicking the button with an eye icon in the Track panel (on top of the pattern preview) of the Properties Region.

5. Track the markers one at a time to make sure that tracking is progressing correctly. It's possible to track multiple markers at the same time. Keep in mind, however, that you can't focus on more than one marker at a time to make sure that the track is stable, so I recommend that you track markers one by one, especially for tricky features that may cause problems.

6. When a marker is correctly tracked in all parts of the footage where the feature that the marker is following appears, lock it to prevent accidental moves or tracks. The Track panel of the Properties Region has two icons: an eye and a lock. The eye icon enables and disables the tracker, and the lock icon makes it impossible to adjust the marker until you unlock it. You can also lock the selected trackers by pressing **Ctrl+L** and unlock them by pressing **Alt+L**.

> ### Tip
>
> When you press **Ctrl+T** or **Shift+Ctrl+T** to automatically track with a marker, tracking is very fast (depending on your computer and the complexity/size of the pattern Blender is searching for) and almost impossible to follow. Sometimes, that high-speed tracking feature is good because Blender completes the tracking quickly and stops only when tracking fails. In some situations, however, even though tracking doesn't fail, it's not correct because it slides little by little on the feature, meaning that the track won't be exact.
>
> To better monitor tracking, go to the Tracking Settings panel of the Properties Region, and set the Speed option to Realtime or slower. This way, even though Blender can track the feature faster, it tracks it at normal speed so that you can see what's going on throughout the process. You can also set a frame limit so that the automatic tracking stops after a certain number of frames, giving you time to react if something goes wrong. A good value for this option is 20 to 30 frames.
>
> You can also press **L** when you're tracking to enable the Locked to Selection option (in the Display panel of the Properties Region). When this option is turned on, the camera is centered on the marker, and only the background video moves, making it much easier to see whether the tracker is stable and avoid having to pan the view around all the time.

7. Repeat the entire process from Step 1 for as many features as you can. Try to have a minimum of 8 to 10 tracked markers in every frame. Press **M** to mute the video (press it again to unmute) and play the video to see only the markers moving against a black background.

8. Make sure that no markers are going crazy or moving weirdly compared with others. If a marker is not right, don't worry; you can come back and adjust it at any time if the camera solution fails.

Configuring Camera Settings

Before you solve the camera motion, you need to tell Blender your camera parameters. Knowing the lens you used as well as other camera settings makes it easier for Blender to calculate perspective. In the Properties Region's Camera and Lens panels, you can input information about the focal length you used to film the footage, as well as the camera sensor.

If you don't know this information, no problem. Blender has a tool called Refine that estimates that information for those situations. You use this tool in the next section, which covers solving camera motion.

Solving Camera Motion

In the Tools Region, jump to the Solve tab, which has options for solving the camera motion that will ultimately be in your 3D scene. You might use the Tripod option, for example. If you filmed from a tripod, your footage won't have much perspective information, so Blender calculates the camera rotation only if you enable this option.

Keyframes selection is also important. Blender needs to select two frames of the footage that will serve as a base for calculating the perspective in the rest of the frames. Those two frames should include fairly different perspectives but have a significant number of markers in common. This way, Blender compares the perspective shift of those markers between the two frames and uses that information as a guide. When you activate the Keyframe option, Blender selects those two frames for you, or you can enter them yourself as keyframes A and B.

The Refine option is useful when you don't have information about the camera's focal length or distortion values (the K1, K2, and K3 parameters). If you enable one of those options for Refine, Blender estimates those values for you.

When you've made the appropriate selections, click the Solve Camera Motion button, and look at the header, which displays the error margin at the right end, after all the buttons (see Figure 13.3). Blender detects the difference between the 3D camera's and the real camera's perspective information, which it determined from the markers. A tracking solve error of 0 would be perfect tracking, but perfect tracking never happens; a small amount of error always occurs. Usually, tracking is acceptable if the tracking solve error value is less than 3. The camera can have a slide effect at times (noticeable when you place the 3D objects on the real footage), and a tracking solve error value of 1 is pretty good; a value of less than 0.4 or 0.3 is considered to be a very good tracking.

Figure 13.3   The solution's solve-error value, shown
on the Movie Clip Editor's header

Applying Tracked Motion to the Camera

If you go to the 3D scene, you probably see nothing going on, because you still have to do one thing to make the scene work. Here are the steps to follow:

1. Select the camera, and on the Constraints tab of the Properties Editor, add a Camera Solver constraint.

2. Enable the active clip or select the clip's name from the list. Now you should see the camera and a set of little points in the scene. Each one of those points represents a marker in the Movie Clip Editor.

3. Scrub through the timeline. You see the camera moving (see Figure 13.4).

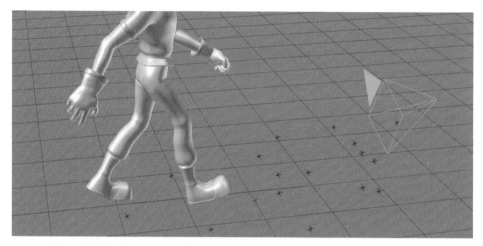

Figure 13.4   Camera motion exists, but you still need to align the camera
so that the 3D scene is in place over the real footage.

Adjusting Camera Motion

Now you just need to align the camera. The Movie Clip Editor offers you a couple of tools for this purpose, but you can also align the camera manually. Follow these steps to use the Movie Clip Editor to align camera motion:

1. Select three markers in the footage that are placed on the floor. In the Orientation panel of the Solve tab, click the Floor button. Blender aligns the camera and all the markers in such a way that those three markers are on the floor, completely horizontal.

2. To define the scale of the scene, select two markers in the 3D scene. (It's best if you know the distance between them in the real scene, but at least make a guess.) In the Orientation panel of the Solve tab, in the Distance field, type the distance between the two selected markers in the real scene. Click Set Scale. The camera with all the markers scales to reflect that measurement.

3. Click Set As Background in the Scene Setup panel, which is on the Solve tab in the Tools Region. Blender applies the current footage to the Camera view as a background. Press **NumPad 0** to look at the scene from the active camera.

4. Align the camera manually until your 3D objects fit in the background footage where you want them. A good way to do this is to place the 3D cursor in the origin of the scene (or where a 3D object such as the character is placed on the floor) and then rotate, move, and scale the camera and tracking points from the 3D cursor until the camera is aligned (see Figure 13.5).

Figure 13.5   The camera is aligned, and Jim is standing on the floor of the real footage.

Tip

At this point, you could click the Setup Tracking Scene button (below under the Set As Background button) in the Movie Clip Editor. This option creates the nodes in the compositor, as well as the render layers and anything else you need to make the character cast shadows on the floor. You learn how to do all these things manually in Chapter 14, "Lighting, Compositing, and Rendering," so that you understand the process and can adjust it as you want.

Testing Camera Tracking

Press **Alt+A** in 3D View to see whether the camera tracking works. The camera alignment may need some adjustments, or the camera may not be moving accurately. In that case, go back to the Movie Clip Editor and look for the frames in which the camera movement fails. Maybe a marker is moving strangely or is jumping from one point to another. Maybe those frames don't have enough markers and you need to add more to make the frames more stable.

In any case, the process is as simple as retouching those markers or adding new ones (or even deleting a marker that you feel is moving in a weird way compared with the others or that is following a moving feature that confuses Blender). Solve the camera motion again, and realign the camera in the scene. Just keep trying until you get the camera motion to work, and don't give up!

Summary

Camera tracking can be fast and simple or tricky and frustrating. Every shot presents its own challenges, but this chapter gives you an idea of how the process works so that you can do basic camera tracking for your own projects. Keep in mind that filming an easy-to-track video depends greatly on your experience with tracking. Keep practicing, tracking as many videos as you can, and eventually, you'll understand what makes a video easy or difficult to track.

This chapter is just the tip of the iceberg in terms of what you can do with the Movie Clip Editor. You can include lens distortions, use tracking to stabilize footage, or even track objects in the video and translate their movements to objects in the 3D scene. (Some people even manage to use the tracking tools to capture facial expressions.) I hope that this chapter showed you basic tips that will encourage you to keep learning and to look for more information on the subject. In any case, you're close to finishing the project!

Exercises

1. Record some video, and track the camera.
2. Track the camera in a video shot with a tripod to understand how the footage looks when the camera motion is solved.

14

Lighting, Compositing, and Rendering

Welcome to the final stage of the project! In this chapter, you light your scene to match the real footage, learn how to set everything up so that you can composite your scene with nodes, and launch the final render. Node compositing can be a little tricky to understand when you see it for the first time, but when you finish compositing a few scenes with nodes, you'll like it a lot. Compositing is an important, decisive part of the process, because during compositing, you tweak your scene and take it from a raw render to a nice-looking final render. You can retouch colors, add effects, mix elements, and do anything else you want.

Lighting Your Scene

The first step, whether you're using Blender Render or Cycles, is adding lights to your scene so that in the compositing stage, you have shadows to work with. When you work on an animated 3D video, you can decide how you want your lights to light the scene, but when you're trying to mix a 3D object into real footage, you must make your 3D scene lighting fit with the real scene lighting.

Analyzing the Real Footage

Before you add lights, carefully analyze the real footage into which you want to fit your 3D scene. Take a look at the shadows; they tell you where the light is coming from, as well as its intensity. Pay attention to how diffuse or sharp the shadows are. The color of the lights in the scene is also very important.

In the footage you'll be using in this chapter, the sky is cloudy, and the clouds act as a huge light diffuser, making shadows nearly nonexistent. Clouds let light pass through them, but water particles make light bounce inside them in all directions, causing random lighting orientation. The layer of clouds makes light come from all directions. When you're outside on a cloudy day, you don't see many shadows—only subtle smooth shadows where two objects touch (see Figure 14.1).

Figure 14.1   If the footage has shadows, they provide light angle, direction,
and intensity. In this footage, though, the cloudy sky makes
light bounce everywhere, and shadows nearly disappear.

Creating and Testing Lights

When you know about the lights and shadows in real footage, you can start creating
lights in your 3D scene. Again, the light settings are slightly different between Blender
Render and Cycles. The illumination you have to achieve is similar, though. Here are
the things you need to add lights to a scene:

- **Floor:** You need to create a plane for the floor to receive shadows on the ground.
  For now, create a plane and adjust it to fit the area Jim is walking on and to be wide
  enough to receive his shadows.

- **Sun light:** If the real footage has marked shadows, you need a directional sun
  light that mimics the direction of the main light in the original scene. Just press
  Shift+A and create a sun lamp. Align it, taking into account how the shadows
  are projected.

  Next, adjust the softness of the shadows to fit the shadows in the footage. In
  Cycles, you tweak the Size value on the Lamp tab of the Properties Editor. In
  Blender Render, you enable raytrace shadows, increase samples, and tweak the
  soft size, also on the Lamp tab.

  The footage you're using here has no defined shadows, so use the Ambient Occlusion
  setting to imitate those soft shadows.

> **Tip**
>
> You can divide your screen to have a rendered preview of your scene on one side
> and the footage in the Movie Clip Editor on the other side.

- **Environmental light:** This light is useful for lighting the parts of the scene that are totally dark, as complete darkness doesn't happen in reality; there's always a bit of light, even in shadows, because light bounces. In this example, you use this light as your main light source; you need light coming from all directions, as the scene is a cloudy day.

In Cycles, go to the World tab of the Properties Editor and tweak the strength. Enable Nodes if they are still disabled. Keep in mind that environmental light has to be very subtle. For now, don't worry whether the general lighting completely fits with the colors in the real footage, as you'll tweak everything later in the node compositor.

In Blender Render, also on the World tab, enable Environment Lighting, and set a small value for the Energy parameter (0.35 or so) to prevent areas in the shadow from looking absolutely black. If you want to use another color, change Environment Lighting from White to Sky Color, and in the World panel, change Horizon Color.

Note

At this point, everything is pretty much guesswork. But don't worry if you don't get everything perfect on the first try. Later, in the compositor, you'll see much more clearly whether your lighting fits the lighting in the real footage, and if it doesn't, you can always adjust it and render again until the footage looks nice. Remember that making something cool is not a one-way street. At some point, you'll need to go back and forth until you reach the result you like.

Using the Node Editor

In this section, you work on the compositing. First, however, I briefly show you how to use the Node Editor and discuss what nodes are and how they work. After this introduction, you'll be ready to carry on with some basic compositing.

Compositing

Usually, a scene doesn't come out as you need it in the raw render, so you need to process it to make it look good. Sometimes, you need to render different elements on different layers and then compose them together in the compositing stage. Maybe you just want to place something in a photo or real-world footage, so you need to mix those images with your render and tweak colors to make them fit. You can do such things in imaging software, such as Adobe Photoshop or GIMP, but you can do them in Blender as well.

You have two main ways to do compositing:

- Do the compositing before the rendering. You take a test render, composite it in the Node Editor, and then launch the final render (even an animation) with the effects of the compositor applied. For this purpose, you use the scene render as an input.

■ Do the raw render of elements and then load those image sequences or videos into the compositor to tweak them. Suppose that you want to color-correct a video. Just load the video into the compositor, color-correct it, and render it. You don't need to touch 3D View and definitely don't need to render a scene again for such small retouches.

Understanding Nodes

When you take a simple render (a raw render, with no compositing involved), your scene is the input, and the output is the same as the input. When you enable the use of nodes, the input and the output are connected, but you can add nodes between them that apply effects and changes over the input before it reaches the output, thereby modifying the final result. The modifications can be as simple as color corrections or as complex as adding visual effects or mixing renders.

Figure 14.2 shows how a basic node tree can evolve as you add nodes.

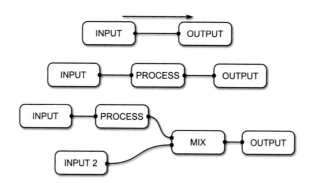

Figure 14.2   Three node trees, which could be the same in different stages of their evolution: a basic setup, which you get when you enable node editing (top); a modification added to the input before it reaches the output (middle); and a second input mixed into the result (bottom)

A node tree is processed from left to right. A connection from another node comes into the current node, which modifies the input with its properties (a color correction, for example) and outputs the result that gets plugged into another node.

You can always add nodes between other nodes. Consider the third example in Figure 14.2. Each of the inputs might be a different render of a different layer of the scene. The first input has a process going on before it's mixed with the second input; that process could be a color correction, for example. Suppose that you want to make your entire render look more reddish or have more contrast. You could add a color-correction node between the Mix node and the output to affect all the previous nodes after the mix happens.

If you still don't get how nodes work, you just need to get your hands on them to understand their inner workings. As you continue this chapter and create your first node tree, you see the result with your own eyes and understand how your changes affect the result.

Studying the Anatomy of a Node

Before you start using the Node Editor, you need to know the parts of a node. Figure 14.3 dissects an RGB Curves node, which you use to make color corrections in the nodes you connect to its input. (The colors of the Node Editor were changed in User Preferences to improve readability, so yours will look different.)

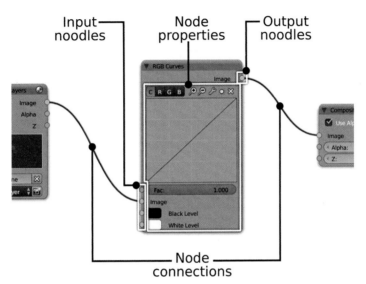

Figure 14.3   The main parts of a node: noodles, connections, inputs, properties, and outputs.

- **Noodles:** *Noodles* are the little colored dots on the left and right sides of a node. They support the connections. The ones on the left are inputs, and the ones on the right are outputs. The color tells you what each connector is for. Gray is for values (or grayscale images), yellow is for RGB (red, green, blue) images, and blue is for vectors (three values: X, Y, Z). A given type of output should always be connected to the same color input of the next node, and you can use some Converter nodes to convert the output to a different type if you need to. Some types are converted automatically if you connect them. An RGB output converts to grayscale when it's connected to a gray input, and RGB values turn into XYZ values when you connect a yellow output to a blue one (and vice versa). Next to those noodles is text that tells you what that noodle should receive (if it is an input) or what it's generating (if it is an output).

- **Node properties:** Each node has different properties and is used for different purposes. You find all the properties inside the node itself.

- **Node connections:** A node does nothing by itself. Every node needs other nodes to work, which is why nodes are connected. The way and order in which you connect nodes define the result.

Blender has a lot of node types but only three main node structures: input nodes, output nodes, and modifiers. You can identify these structures because the input nodes own only output noodles, which is why they generate or load something, such as an image, a render, or an RGB color. The output nodes are not expected to be modified after they do their jobs, so they only receive input connections, which export or display the result. The modifiers are in the middle; they modify and mix inputs before they reach the outputs.

Using the Node Editor

In this section, you learn the basic controls of the Node Editor, as well as how to create and interact with nodes, connect them, and so on. Figure 14.4 shows the Node Editor.

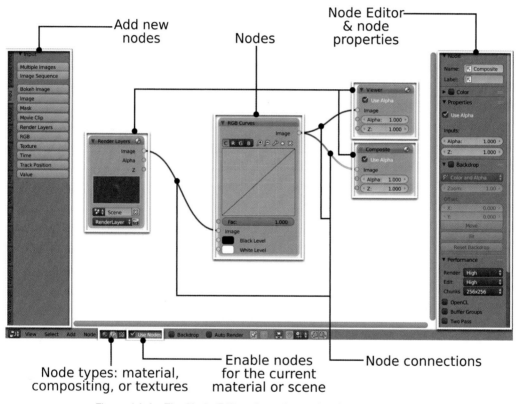

Figure 14.4   The Node Editor, featuring a simple node setup to show what nodes and their connections look like

Getting Started with the Node Editor

When you open the Node Editor, keep in mind that it's used for different things in Blender: materials creation, compositing, and texture creation. To use this editor for compositing, you need to select Compositing Mode by clicking the Compositing Node type button on the header.

When you're in Compositing Mode in the Node Editor, you still don't see anything. Before you start using nodes, you need to enable them in your scene. Enable the Use Nodes option on the header, and Blender displays basic node setup: the render plugged to a Composite node. Nothing interesting is going on right now; the render goes out of Blender as it's generated.

The editor is ready for you to start playing with nodes. If you launch a render now, it uses the node tree you have in the editor. If you need to launch a raw render without using the nodes, disable the Use Nodes option.

Navigation is pretty straightforward, as it uses Blender's standard controls. Press **MMB** to pan, and use the scroll wheel or press **Ctrl+MMB** to zoom in and out.

Creating Nodes

You have three ways to create nodes in the Node Editor:

- **Tools Region:** The Tools Region of the Node Editor (**T**) has a panel for each type of node. Expand the panels, click the node you want, move your mouse to the desired position, and left-click to place the node there.
- **Add menu:** On the Node Editor header, choose the type of node you want from the Add menu. Left-click the node, move the mouse to the desired position, and left-click again to place the node there.
- **Shift+A:** If you press **Shift+A** inside the Node Editor, the Add menu appears at the mouse cursor's position. Click the node type you want, drag it with your mouse, and left-click to drop the node in that place.

Tip

When you place a new node, if you drag it over a connection between two nodes, Blender highlights the connection, and when you drop the node, Blender automatically connects it between those nodes. This feature is a big time-saver!

Connecting and Manipulating Nodes

The core of working with nodes is connecting them to make them interact. It's also important to know how to move nodes so that your node tree is always organized. Otherwise, you can end up with a lot of overlapping nodes, which makes your work harder, as it becomes difficult to find specific nodes and understand their purposes. Here are some common controls that you use to manipulate the Node Editor:

- You can select nodes by pressing **LMB** and **RMB**. Drag nodes by left- or right-clicking.
- If you select several nodes by pressing **B** (Box Selection) or **Shift**-clicking, you can move them, rotate them, and scale them by pressing **G**, **R**, and **S**.
- Right-click and drag in an empty space to perform a box selection.
- To connect nodes, left-click and drag from an output noodle of a node to the desired input noodle of another node.

- If a node has multiple input noodles, and you want to switch a connection among them, left-click and drag from one noodle to the other.

- To remove a connection, left-click the input noodle and drag it to an empty space.

- To remove one or more connections quickly, press **Ctrl+LMB** and drag a line over the connections you want to cut. When you release **LMB**, Blender removes the connections under the cutting line.

- Select one or more nodes and press **M** to mute them. This method is a nice way to see in the preview how a node changes the image. Nodes become red when they're muted. Press **M** again to enable the nodes again.

- You can duplicate nodes or groups of connected nodes by pressing **Shift+D**.

- You can press **H** when you select a node to collapse it if you don't need to access its properties so that it takes less space. Press **H** again to expand the node.

- Detach a node and leave the connection between the previous and next nodes intact by holding down **Alt** while dragging the node.

- Select one or more nodes, and press **X** to remove them. Press **Ctrl+X** to delete them, keeping the connections between the previous and next nodes.

Previewing the Result

You don't need to work blindly. You can have an image showing real-time updates of what you're doing in the Node Editor. To enable a preview, create a Viewer node inside the Output nodes group. Add the node to your workspace, and connect the output of the node you want to preview to the input of the Viewer node.

An even faster method is to press **Shift+Ctrl** and left-click the node you want to preview. This method automatically creates a Viewer node and connects it to a specific node. Pressing **Shift+Ctrl+LMB** on any other node connects that node to the Viewer node so you can switch the point of the node tree you want to preview really fast.

The Viewer node displays a preview of the node that is connected as an input.

Once you have a Viewer node in your node tree, you have two options for previewing your work in the compositor:

- **Backdrop:** In the Node Editor, enable the Backdrop option. Blender shows the resulting image behind your node tree, in the background of the Node Editor workspace. Press **Alt+MMB** to pan, **V** to zoom out, and **Alt+V** to zoom in.

- **UV/Image Editor:** Although the backdrop allows you see everything in the same window, it can be very distracting, and the nodes on top of the image don't always let you see what's going on (especially in a complex tree). In such a case, or if you want to see the result on a secondary monitor, you have a nice way to preview your work. Open the UV/Image Editor, and select the Viewer output from the images list on the header. You see the Viewer node preview as though it were an image in the UV/Image Editor.

> **Note**
>
> Don't forget that to see what you're doing in the compositor, you have to have rendered your scene (unless you're working with already-rendered images or tweaking a video instead of the current 3D scene). If you render your scene, close Blender, and open the scene again. The renders need to be made again, as they are only temporary. Keep that fact in mind, especially when you're working on big, complex scenes that take a long time to render. You can always save the render in an image file and work on the compositing with that file; then, when you're done, you can replace the image file with a Render Layers node.

Compositing Your Scene in Blender Render

In this section, you see how to do the compositing in Blender Render. The compositing in the Node Editor works identically in Blender Render and Cycles, but the materials are different, so a couple of things will change in compositing as well.

Setting Up the Scene

You need to know what you need before you start compositing. One thing stands out immediately: You need the floor to go away but you need to keep the shadows that it receives from the character so that you can composite on top of the real footage.

This process is simple in Blender Render. A material option allows you to have an object that only receives shadows; so the object would be transparent, except for those areas of the object that have shadows cast on them. Follow these steps:

1. Create a new material for the floor. In the Shadows panel of the Properties Editor, on the Material tab, enable Shadows Only.

2. In the Shadows Only section, choose Shadow and Shading (instead of Shadows and Distance) from the drop-down list.

3. Launch a render. You see that the floor is not rendered, but Jim's shadows are there.

4. On the World tab of the Properties Editor, enable Ambient Occlusion, and set it to Multiply mode. In the Gather panel, increase Samples to around 10 or more so that the ambient occlusion has more quality and less noise.

5. Enable Environment Lighting on the World tab to make light come from all directions around the scene.

You could take a render now and put the footage in the back, and the job would be done. But I complicate the process a little more in the following sections so that you'll have more control and deeper experience in compositing with nodes.

Setting Up Render Layers

In this section, you separate Jim from his shadow. How are you supposed to do that? It's simple enough: Render Layers allow you to separate elements on different layers so that you can composite them later on.

First, you need Jim and the floor to exist on different layers of the scene. If you've followed the instructions in this book to the letter, Jim is on one layer and his rig is on another one. Perfect. Select the floor, press **M**, and select a third layer for the floor. Jim could be on the first layer, and the floor could be on the second one. In Object Mode, you can select the visible layers in the scene from the 3D View header; press **Shift** while you left-click several layers to see multiple players.

Now go to the Render Layers tab of the Properties Editor (see Figure 14.5).

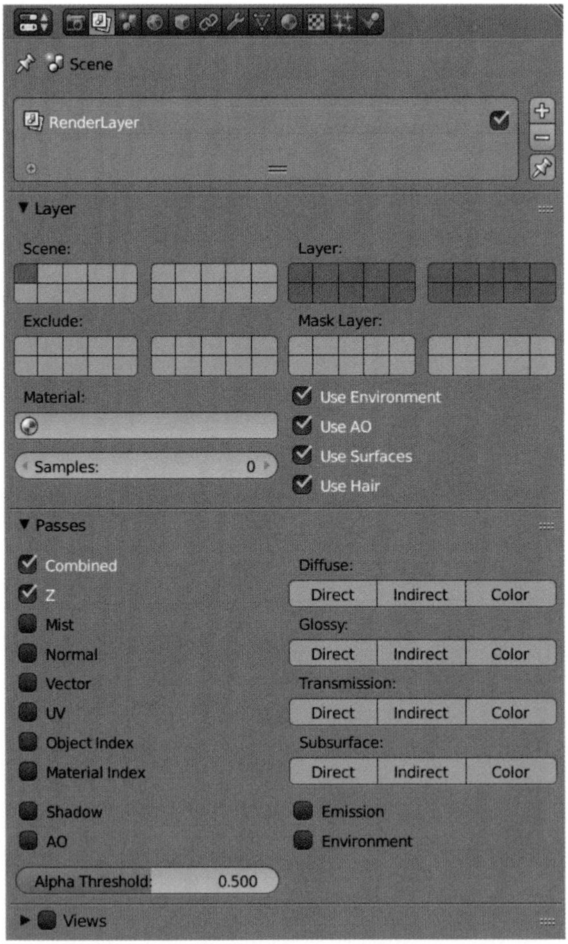

Figure 14.5   The Render Layers tab, where you can set
the elements to be rendered separately

On this tab, you can create new render layers and define which layers are going to be rendered on a specific render layer. Also, in the Passes panel, you can select the passes (channels) of the layer that you want to render separately so that you can access passes individually from the compositor. (By default, Blender combines them.) You can render the Ambient Occlusion, Diffuse, and Specular passes, for example, and they become outputs in the Render Layer node so that you can work separately with those passes in the compositor. A Specular pass, for example, gives you only the shines of the scene, which can be very useful for creating glares that could be mixed over the original render. You have a lot of possibilities, but as this chapter is just an introduction to the technique, you do only a couple of things. Follow these steps:

1. Create two render layers, and name them Jim and Floor Shadows.

2. For each one of them, select the layers that should be rendered for each render layer in the Layer section of the Layers panel (see Figure 14.6).

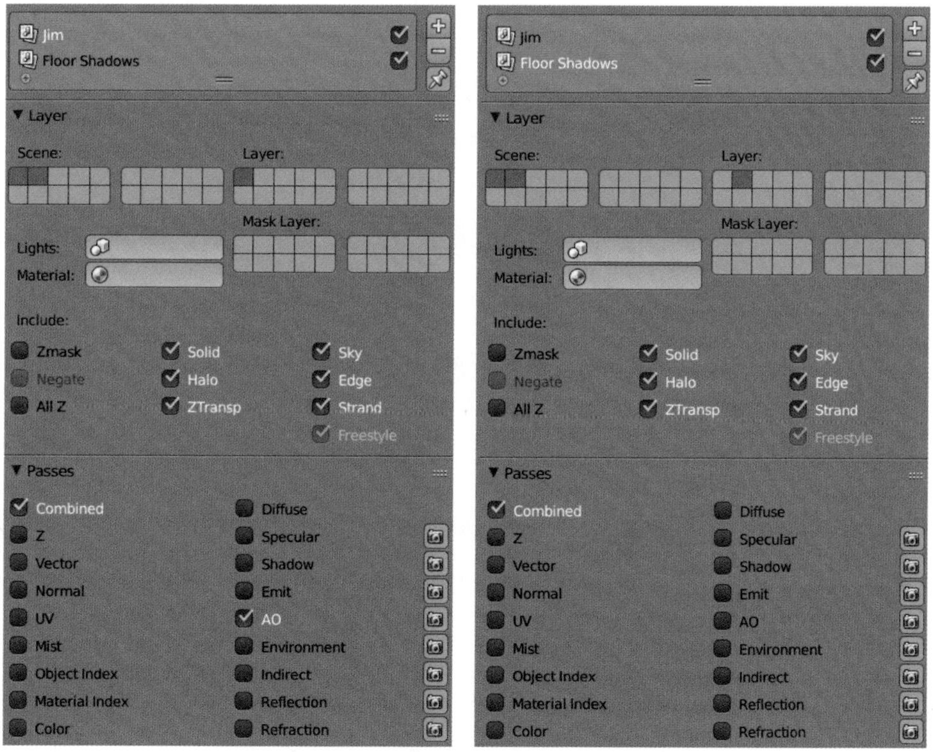

Figure 14.6   The settings for the two render layers: the layer for Jim (left) and the layer for the floor (right)

3. For Jim's render layer, enable the Ambient Occlusion pass, which will serve later to make Jim's soft shadows more visible and add a bit more contrast to the shapes. Environment lighting makes the scene look flat, so this setting helps bring some of the character's volume back. If you launch a render now, you see the sky color behind Jim and the shadow.

4. Go to the Render tab of the Properties Editor, and in the Shading panel, set Alpha to Transparent. Now the background of the renders is transparent, allowing you to insert your footage there.

Compositing Nodes

This process can be difficult to understand, so look at the finished node tree with numbered nodes in Figure 14.7. (If you want to see the full node tree with no numbers, go to the end of this section.) You need to press F12 and render a frame with the render layers set up so that you can load them in the Node Editor; if these layers are not rendered, you see nothing.

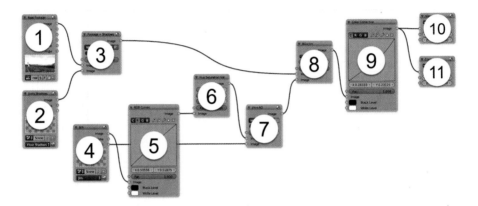

Figure 14.7   The node tree, numbered so that you can follow the instructions

Here's the step-by-step process:

1. Start with a Render Layer and a Composite (Output) node. Move the composite all the way to the right, as the output nodes should be at the end of the tree. (The Composite node is 11 in Figure 14.7.) Create a Movie Clip node (from the Input category), and select the clip that you loaded in the Movie Clip Editor for tracking.

2. At the bottom of the Render Layer node (which is an input node, as it takes the render of the scene and inserts it into the Node Editor), from the drop-down list, choose the render layer you want to show in that node: the Floor Shadows render layer.

3. Create a Mix node in the Color category to merge the shadows over the floor of the real footage. Next to the blending mode's drop-down list (which is set to Mix by default), enable the alpha channel of the second input (the shadows, which include transparency). Connect the Movie Clip in the first Image input of the Mix node (background) and the shadows' Render Layer node to the second Image input (foreground). Blender displays the shadows on top of the real footage's floor.

4. Create a new Render Layers node, and select the Jim render layer on it.

5. Create an RGB Curves node (in the Color category). Connect the Image output from the Jim Render Layer to the Image input of the RGB Curves node. After you mix Jim on top of the background, you can come to this RGB Curves node and correct the colors to make Jim's colors fit the background's real footage.

> **Note**
>
> Curves allow you to correct colors. If you're not familiar with curves from image-editing software, they can be tricky to understand, so here is a very brief explanation. You can modify the master color of an image or each of the RGB channels. The master (C) controls brightness and contrast, and the RGB channels define the amount of each color in the image and its contrast. When you click the curve, you add points to it. When modifying the curve's shape, you add or subtract color in that part of the spectrum; left is dark and right is bright. If you set the curve higher to the right, you increase the color in the bright values. If you decrease the curve on the left, you make the dark tones even darker. I hope that this explanation and playing around with curves will help you understand what they do.

6. Connect the output of the RGB Curves to a Hue Saturation Value node (also from the Color category). This node provides an extra layer of color correction over the RGB Curves. Specifically, this node is useful for increasing or decreasing the saturation of Jim's colors to fit the background if needed.

7. Add Jim's ambient occlusion (AO) on top of the original Jim to increase the soft shadows a bit and generate some contrast in the character. (A great benefit of nodes is that you can reuse them and connect them to multiple nodes at the same time.) Create another Mix node, and set it to Multiply blending mode. (Multiply merges the two images that you connect to the node in such a way that the second input's white areas become transparent and dark areas darken the image in the back.) Connect the Hue Saturation Value node (6) to the Mix first input (background)—the color-corrected Jim—and connect the AO output of Jim's Render Layers node (4) to the second Image input (foreground), so that the soft shadows from the AO are on top of Jim. Now tweak the factor of the Mix node to determine how much of those shadows you want. Around 0.5 should be fine.

8. Use an alternative node to mix two images: the Alpha Over node. This node is similar to the Mix node, but it works better when the image in the second input (foreground) has an alpha channel. You use this node to merge the background with its shadows and Jim on top of it. Connect the first Mix node (3) to the background (first Image input of the Alpha Over node) and Jim + AO node (7) in the foreground (second Image input of the Alpha Over node). Finally, Jim is on top of the real video.

> **Note**
>
> At this point, you see the mix of all of the elements, so now is a good time to go back to nodes 5 and 6 (RGB Curves and Hue Saturation Value) and modify Jim's colors a bit to make him fit with the real footage colors if needed. Make sure that the Viewer node is around during the entire process so that you can see what you are doing. The new node should be connected to the same node that is connected to the Composite node so you can see exactly what is going to be in the final output. No surprises!

9. When all the nodes are in place, add an extra RGB Curves node to modify the colors to your liking. This node corrects the colors of the entire node tree. First, correct the elements so that they fit together; then correct them to make the composite look better.

The Composite node is important. Although you don't need it until you're done with the compositing, you must have it if you want the scene to be rendered when nodes are enabled. You get an error if you don't have this node or don't connect any nodes to it.

10. Connect the final node of your composition to the Composite node, which will define what is finally rendered!

Figure 14.8 shows what the node tree should look like at the end of the process.

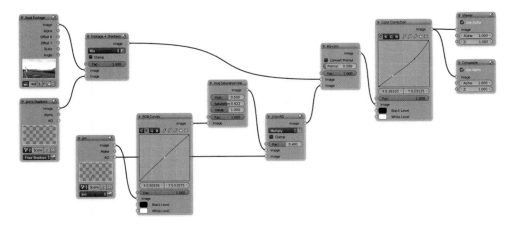

Figure 14.8   Completed node tree with Jim and his shadow composited over the footage

If you want to improve the result, go to the Render tab of the Properties Editor, and enable the Sampled Motion Blur option. This option greatly increases render time, as it renders the same frame as many times as you define in the Motion Samples value. The difference in movement depends on the Shutter value. Blender takes those samples and mixes them in the same render, creating the impression of motion blur—an effect that adds a lot of realism to movement. The more motion samples you use, the better-quality the result, but the more time rendering takes.

Compositing Your Scene in Cycles

Now you know how to do compositing in Blender Render. How do you do compositing in Cycles? The process is similar except for the lack of "shadow catcher" materials (materials that render only the shadows they receive), so you need to use the Shadow pass and do a little trick to get it to work.

Setting Up the Scene

You don't have to do a lot to set up the scene; just add a basic material to the floor. In Blender Render, you set the floor to receive shadows, but as you can't do the same thing in Cycles, the floor shadows effect will have to be set up in the Render Layers. On the Render tab of the Properties Editor, in the Film panel, set the background to Transparent to enable that option.

On the World tab of the Properties Editor, tweak the background color and intensity to generate the lighting for the scene. This setting is similar to environment lighting in Blender Render. Also, you can increase the Render Samples value on the Render tab of the Properties Editor to get better quality.

Setting Up Render Layers

This section is where differences between Blender Render and Cycles start. Place Jim on one layer and the floor on a different layer. Create two render layers: one for Jim and another for the ground plane (see Figure 14.9). For the floor render layer, on the Passes panel, you see a list of the passes that you can enable. Enable AO pass for both layers. In Cycles, you don't have fancy material that catches shadows, so use AO for the same purpose.

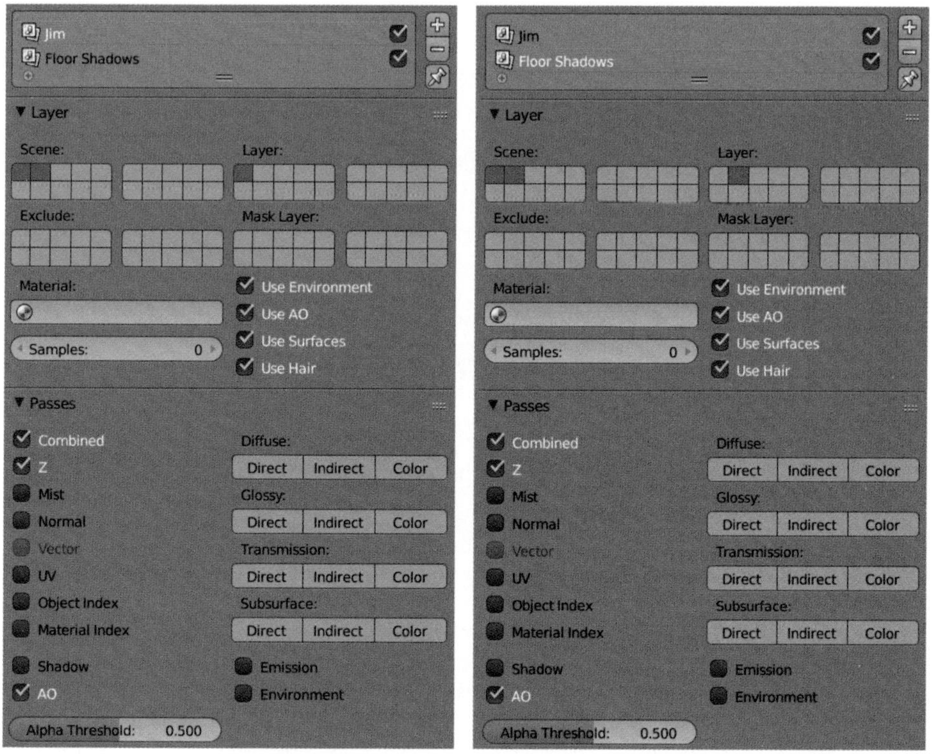

Figure 14.9   Render layers settings in Cycles

Node Compositing

As the compositing process is almost the same in Cycles as it is in Blender Render, this section focuses on the subtle differences in setting up the shadows. Figure 14.10 shows a numbered node tree illustrating how the shadows are done. The full node tree appears at the end of the section to provide a complete reference. Remember that when the shadows are done, the rest is exactly the same as in Blender Render.

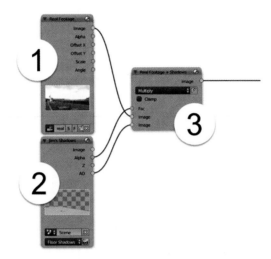

Figure 14.10   The node tree to make the shadows in Cycles composite on top of the footage

To composite the nodes, follow these steps:

1. Load the movie clip.
2. Create a Render Layers node that shows the floor-shadows render layer.
3. Create a Mix node, and set its blending mode to Multiply so that the darker areas of the AO pass are kept on top of the real footage and the white parts become transparent. Connect the movie clip to the first Image input of the Mix node and the AO output of the floor shadows to the second Image input of the Mix node.

> **Note**
>
> You have to use an AO pass to create the shadows, but AO is not a pass with transparency on its own; it's only a grayscale image. The problem is that the areas outside the plane in the AO pass are black, and that darkness is shown over the real footage. An easy solution is to use the factor of the Mix node. The factor allows you to determine the amount of mix that occurs between the two inputs, but instead of just a numerical value, you can connect a grayscale image (such as the floor plane's alpha channel) that defines different values in different parts of the material: White pixels would be 1, and black pixels would be 0, with gray being values in between. Keep in mind that this trick won't work for every scene, but it will do for the one you're working on now.

4. Connect the Alpha output of the Floor Shadows Render Layers node to the factor of the Mix node. As the part of the image occupied by the plane is white and the rest is black, the black area has a Mix factor of 0, which makes that black area of the AO pass transparent.

That's it! The rest of the tree (see Figure 14.11) looks exactly the same as in Blender Render.

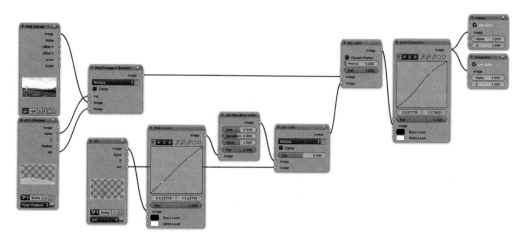

Figure 14.11   Finished node tree for Cycles

If you want to add a natural touch, you can add motion blur in Cycles. On the Render tab of the Properties Editor, search for the Motion Blur panel, enable it, and set a Shutter value. This technique creates a more realistic motion blur than the one in Blender Render; the effect functions as it would for a real camera. Keep in mind that the render time is a bit longer, and you may need more samples to get a better result.

Rendering

Now you need to adjust a couple of settings and launch the final render.

Render Settings

This stage is your final chance to change the render settings (unless you want to render again with different settings later). Make sure that you're happy with your scene, and ensure that the Composite node is connected to the final node of the tree in the Node Editor. Then, on the Render tab of the Properties Editor, set the image resolution. (For this example, use full HD: 1920 × 1080 pixels.)

> **Tip**
>
> Before this point, you usually work with smaller resolutions or fewer samples in Cycles so that you can get faster test renders. Remember to increase the resolution and samples before the final render.

Output

Another important thing is to set up the output folder and format. For a single image, this step is not important, as you can save the image from the UV/Image Editor when the render is done by pressing **F3**. But in animations, when a frame finishes, Blender deletes it from the temporary memory to start rendering the next one.

In the Output panel of the Properties Editor's Render tab, select the format of the exported images and the output folder to which the renders are going to be saved. I recommend choosing PNG format; the quality is better than JPG and not as good as TGA or TIFF, but the output takes less space on your hard drive.

> **Tip**
>
> You can save the animation as a video, but I recommend doing that only for quick render tests. If you expect the render to take a few hours (or even days), it's better to export the animation in an image sequence. What you get, instead of a video, is a series of JPEG, PNG, or TGA images—one for each frame of the animation.
>
> This method has several benefits. If the render fails at some point, you won't lose the rendered frames, whereas with a video, the entire video would be corrupted. Also, videos are usually highly compressed, so with images, you get full quality and then can convert the image sequence to a video quickly, as it's much easier and faster to render images than an entire 3D scene. (You can even do this in Blender, loading the sequence into the Video Sequencer, or as a clip in the compositor and rendering it in a video format.) This way, you have a sequence of uncompressed images and can compress it into a video later.

Final Render

You have only one thing left to do: Click the Render button. On the Render tab, click Render to render a still frame or Animation to render the entire animation.

If you're becoming a pro with Blender, go ahead and use the keyboard shortcuts: **F12** for a still-frame render and **Ctrl+F12** to render the entire animation. Figure 14.12 shows the results in Blender Render and Cycles. The differences are subtle because both engines used basic options.

Figure 14.12   The final results with Jim integrated into the real
footage in Blender Render (left) and Cycles (right)

Summary

Compositing is kind of technical but also leaves room for you to be very creative. I
hope that you understand the basics, know how nodes work, and know why compositing has such a big effect on the final result.

You've come a really long way to get here, and you've completed this sample project.
Congratulations! As you can see, integrating an animated character into a real video is a
lot of work involving a lot of different skills—modeling, texturing, rigging, animation,
compositing, and so on—but all these skills are really fun to use.

Now that you've gotten your feet wet, I encourage you to keep looking into the
parts of the process you've liked the most so far. The goal of this book is to show you
the entire process so that you can decide which area to dedicate time to and determine
whether to specialize in that area. Or you may like the entire process and want to
become a generalist!

Exercises

1. Why is compositing so important?
2. What objects are meant to render only the shadows they receive?
3. What are render layers for?
4. What node would you use to merge images?
5. Which node of your tree should you connect to the Composite node?

VII

Keep Learning

15 Other Blender Features

15

Other Blender Features

You've already seen a lot of what Blender can do, but you've just scratched the surface! Blender has much more to offer than what you've seen in this book. I touched on the basics and covered only a few of the advanced tools and features. In this chapter, I discuss other features that Blender provides in case you're interested in learning more about them.

This chapter is not meant to be a manual or to show you how to use these features. It just describes what tools are at your disposal so you can decide whether you want to learn more about them. You'll have to do some research to find the necessary information.

Particles

Particles are useful when you need to create and animate a lot of objects that behave similarly. Imagine snow, rain, or leaves falling. Instead of animating each snowflake or raindrop individually, create an emitter geometry and, on the Particles tab in the Properties panel, add a particle system to it.

From there, you can set the number of emitted particles, their time range, their behavior, their physics (such as gravity, weight, and friction), and so on. You can also select other objects and set them as obstacles so that particles collide with them. You can create forces such as wind, vortex, and turbulence to make the particles behave in certain ways. You can also use particles to simulate fluid substances.

Hair Simulation

Hair is a subset of particles, as you're actually creating hair particles. If you create a particle system and set it to be a hair emitter, instead of creating normal particles, the system creates a lot of hairs on the desired surface and grows strands from there.

Later, when you have a hair-particle system on the selected object, you're able to switch to Particle Mode in 3D View, which allows you to grow, cut, and comb the hair to create a hairstyle for your character.

When the hair is in place, you can run a simulation to make the hair follow the character's movements and automatically react to gravity and objects that touch it.

This hair-simulation feature is not limited to characters. You can use it to spray a lot of objects over a surface, such as adding trees to a forest or simulating grass in a field.

Cloth Simulation

If you want to create anything from clothes for a character to banners or bedsheets, cloth simulation is the way to go. Don't worry about creating wrinkles or folds manually; on the Physics tab of the Properties Editor, turn the cloth mesh into a Cloth object, and click Play.

You can control the properties of the cloth to make it behave like a specific type of material. You also can set other objects as obstacles, and the cloth will react to them.

Cloth simulation even works in real time, so if you click Play and try to grab the cloth, it reacts to your touch and to the objects that collide with it.

Rigid and Soft Bodies

Similar to the cloth simulation, this feature is for rigid and soft objects. If you need to make a house fall down or destroy a wall, divide the object into pieces, and in the Physics panel, make those pieces rigid bodies. You can bind the objects to one another to define how they behave and limit the range of movements they can perform to simulate the force of gravity on them.

When you need to make an object behave as though it has weight, you can run a rigid-body simulation; Blender simulates gravity and object interactions in a realistic manner for you. Also, you can define other objects as obstacles so that the rigid or soft bodies collide with them.

Soft bodies are similar to rigid ones, except that they can be deformed. Using soft bodies, you can simulate an object behaving like jelly, for example.

Fluids Simulation

You can simulate fluids such as water in a glass or liquids flowing and reacting to other objects. You can let objects fall into a pool and create splashes, as well as many other simulations of a fluid's properties. Just play with the different types of fluid objects to add liquid to the simulation, subtract it, have it collide with other objects, or even use it to form shapes.

Fire and Smoke

Particles are also the basis for fire and smoke, and you can create these effects and preview them in real time in 3D View. (Remember that high-resolution simulations slow your computer a lot). You can adjust parameters for these effects and can control how the fire and smoke behave as well as how they are rendered.

Here's a quick way to create a fire simulation. First, select an object. In the 3D View header's Object menu, look for Quick Effects, and choose Quick Smoke. Go to frame 0 and press **Alt+A** to play the animation and see what happens. You'll need to make additional adjustments to get the simulation to render nicely, but this method is a good starting point.

Grease Pencil

Grease Pencil started as a basic annotation tool that allowed drawing on top of the scene. That tool is very useful for various things: adding information to the file for other team members, making drawings from the director or supervisor to explain changes to be made in a scene, and even drawing the topology on a surface to use it as a reference when doing retopology.

After a few years, however, the tool got some attention from artists and developers, and it has grown a lot. Now it's possible to use Grease Pencil as a proper 2D animation tool in Blender. Search online for Grease Pencil 2.0, and check out some of the animations that have been created with it.

You can quickly play with Grease Pencil by holding down **D** and left-clicking to start drawing; **RMB**-drag to erase. You can retime your Grease Pencil drawings easily by adjusting them in the Dope Sheet editor and choosing Grease Pencil from the Mode drop-down list on the header (which shows Dope Sheet by default).

Pie Menus

You can enable the Pie Menus add-on from User Preferences, as it comes bundled with Blender. This add-on gives some menus a new look and feel, turning them into radial menus from which you can choose options just by dragging your mouse in a given direction. This feature becomes really powerful after you use it for a while and start memorizing the directions for specific options. Then muscle memory will do its thing, and you'll navigate Pie Menus super fast.

Game Engine

Blender has its own game engine. Although some people complain that you can't export the games you create to mobile platforms (at least for now), even more people don't really understand the power of this feature.

The Blender Game Engine is meant to create interactive content, not just games (although some people have managed to create interesting games with it). 3D presentations, for example, are surprisingly exciting options. Suppose that you're an architect, and you've built an interactive walk-through of the building that your client wants to construct. Wouldn't that presentation be useful and valuable? With the Blender Game Engine, those kinds of things are pretty easy to do.

Freestyle Rendering

Freestyle is a set of options available in Blender Render and Cycles that allow for non-photorealistic rendering with cartoon- and anime-type results. This feature can draw the outlines of objects as though your 3D models were inked, for example. You can easily adjust those lines to achieve all kinds of interesting effects, such as a blueprint or sketch effect. Then you can mix those lines on top of a normal render and tweak the render to achieve flat colors if you so desire. I really recommended this feature if you're into motion graphics and 2D art.

Masking, Object Tracking, and Video Stabilization

In this book, you learn how to use the Movie Clip Editor to track the camera motion. Although that function is probably its best-known function, this editor can perform many more tasks. You can use the tracking data to stabilize your footage and make the video look a lot smoother, for example.

You can also track the motion of objects in the video to apply that motion to 3D objects in your scene. You could shoot a video of an actor wearing paper markers, track it, and composite futuristic weapons on top of the markers.

The Movie Clip Editor also gives you the necessary tools to create masks over your footage that you can use later in the compositor. If you want something in the real video to stay in front of the 3D stuff, you can mask it and keep it in front by using the compositor.

Sculpting

Sculpting is one of the most creative ways of modeling. If you like organic modeling, sculpting is something that you really need to check out, especially for creating characters.

In 3D View, just switch to Sculpt Mode and use it as you would with the texture brushes. This mode pushes and pulls geometry in different ways, however, depending on the brush you select. For sculpting, you usually want to use a Multi-Resolution modifier, which is similar to a Subdivision Surface modifier but also stores the details of each subdivision level, allowing you to detail geometry much more accurately.

By combining a Multi-Resolution modifier with Sculpt Mode, you can create extremely detailed organic models in a very artistic way, almost as though you were sculpting with clay, which can be really entertaining.

Another tool to keep in mind when you want to sculpt is Dynamic Mesh. It's not compatible with a Multi-Resolution modifier; instead, it dynamically divides the mesh under the brush as needed. The resulting mesh needs retopology (see the next section) because it can get very dense and triangulated, but in exchange, it gives you a lot of freedom when sculpting, as you won't be limited by the original topology. Also, it divides the mesh locally, meaning that you don't have to subdivide the entire model to add a little localized detail.

Retopology

Retopology is usually the next step after sculpting. It's not a specific tool or set of tools—more like a technique of building new geometry with a good topology on top of other geometry that doesn't have a good topology. Retopology is all about re-creating a shape with a new topology. Some software is designed specifically for retopologizing, and sculpting software offers retopology tools.

You can easily use this technique in Blender, even though it's just normal modeling while snapping to other surfaces. A sculpted mesh usually is heavy, with lots of polygons, and you often start from a basic geometry that doesn't have an optimal topology when the details are in place. Retopology tools help you create the final mesh with a good topology, using the high-resolution mesh as a base for the shape.

Retopology is simple: Just enable the Snapping tool and set it to Snap to Faces. Thereafter, when you adjust geometry and create new vertices, for example, Blender snaps them to the surfaces of other objects, allowing you to re-create their shapes with the desired topology.

Maps Baking

This feature is really cool. If you have lights and shadows in your scene, you can bake that lighting into a texture for the selected object. When you load that texture into the object, it has the lights and shadows projected on it so you can see it in real time, avoiding heavy, long-rendering calculations.

This feature is useful when you want to see an effect in real time while still getting the look of a final render (or just to render a lot faster). With this method, you can make a scene look like a final render by displaying a simple texture that already includes light and shadows.

You can bake details from other objects into the selected one to generate normal maps and displacement maps that you can use later to make the object look as though it has a lot more detail than it actually does.

You can find these tools on the Render tab of the Properties Editor. The setup for maps baking is different in Blender Render and in Cycles, but both engines can bake maps.

Included Add-Ons

In User Preferences is a tab named Add-ons, where you can define which add-ons should be enabled or disabled, and you can install external add-ons. Blender already includes some interesting, useful add-ons that you should check out. Some of these add-ons allow you to create special primitives (stars, pipes, and so on); others enable you to export and import files in different formats. Still other add-ons provide new features or modeling tools. Some of these add-ons may be interesting to you or useful for some specific task you need to do.

Blender includes dozens of add-ons. Check them out, and enable the ones that you'd like to try.

More Add-Ons

If the add-ons included in Blender are not enough for you, or if you're looking for something more specific, you can perform an online search. Many Blender users have developed hundreds (if not thousands) of add-ons for their own needs and shared them with the public so that everyone can take advantage of them.

Since the first edition of this book, an online market has grown; now you can buy Blender resources (models, textures, and so on) online, as well as add-ons. This development opens the possibility for companies and individual developers to make a living by creating and maintaining great add-ons, thereby greatly increasing the quality of these tools.

Better selection tools and options, retopology tools, node improvements, material libraries … anything is possible with add-ons, and some add-ons will make your life a lot easier.

Animation Nodes

If you like nodes, Animation Nodes is an add-on (still in development) that allows you to use nodes created and tailored for animation to procedurally animate objects in Blender. This add-on is useful for creating motion graphics and for replicating, offsetting, and controlling repetitive animations through a lot of objects.

Python Scripting

If the tools that Blender provides are not enough for you, or if you need something specific, you can use Python scripts to develop your own tools. Blender lets you create and run scripts, change how the interface looks, and make your own add-ons to add new functionalities. Head to the Script Editor, and start coding!

Python scripting makes Blender quite customizable and represents an attractive feature for developing tools that achieve specific results.

Summary

Blender is a lot more than meets the eye. This book describes some of the main features and tools available to you, but many more are available.

I hope that you learned a lot from this book and that it helped you understand Blender's basic features so you can get started creating animations. Keep improving your skills and learning more about Blender's advanced features.

Blender is a continually evolving software, and new features are added all the time. You can see this evolution as it happens because the development process is transparent; you don't need to wait until the next version is released to know what will be new.

You should be very proud that you've learned how to create characters in Blender, because that's no simple task. Character creation is very challenging, but now you're on your way to expressing your creativity by using the extensive features of this cutting-edge software!

Index

Numbers

2D
 comparing 2D with 3D drawings, 117
 converting 3D shape into 2D surface. *See* Unwrapping
 converting 3D to. *See* Rendering
 creating textures with 2D image editing software, 188
2D cursor, UV/Image Editor, 164
3D
 comparing 2D with 3D drawings, 117
 converting 3D shape into 2D surface. *See* Unwrapping
 converting to 2D. *See* Rendering
 creating 3D graphics, 3
3D cursor
 creating circle with, 139
 Screw tool, 101
 using, 25–27
3D Cursor Pivot, 26
3D modeling. *See also* Modeling tools
 displaying UV test grid, 172
 separating/connecting UVs, 174–175
 working with vertices, edges, and faces, 79–80
3D View
 accessing Interaction Modes, 38
 accessing unwrapping menus, 166
 in Blender interface, 14
 creating character reference images, 72–74
 creating objects, 31
 displaying UV test grid in 3D model, 172
 editor types and uses, 24
 features, 14–18
 manipulator controls, 33
 navigating, 18–20
 renaming objects, 36
 separating/connecting UVs, 174–175
 setting up reference planes, 115
 setting up shading, 205
 Sync UVs and 3D View, 165
 Texture Paint Mode. *See* Texture Paint Mode
 viewing project, 167
 working with texture brushes, 182–183

A

Action Editor mode, Dope Sheet, 266, 270
Add menu
 creating nodes, 297
 creating objects, 31
 Curve category, 273–274
Add Modifier button, 41
Add-Ons
 Animation Nodes add-on, 318
 available, 317–318
 F2 add-on, 107
 included, 317
 LoopTools, 105–107
 Pie Menus add-on, 315
 setting user preferences, 28
Add shader, shading character with Cycles, 215
Adobe Illustrator, 74
Adobe Photoshop, 186, 188, 190
Advanced shading, Cycles, 217–218
All Transforms, 32
Alpha. *See also* Transparency
 transparency settings, 208, 302
 unwrapping human face, 173
Ambient Occlusion, Properties Editor, 299, 301, 305–307
Animation
 animated films, 58
 character-creation plan, 59
 controls, 268–269
 creating poses for walk cycle, 270–272
 creating walk action, 270
 in Dope Sheet editor, 266
 editors for, 264–265

Animation (*continued*)
  fps (frames per second), 269
  in Graph Editor, 266–267
  inserting keyframes, 263–264
  launching and saving render, 49–50
  in NLA editor, 268
  repeating for walk cycle, 272–273
  summary and exercises, 274–275
  in Timeline, 265
  walking along a path, 273–274
Animation Nodes, 318
Appearance, character design, 63
Appending objects, 258
Areas, 13, 20–21
Armature Options panel, Tools Region, 225
Armature tab, Properties Editor, 230, 240
Armatures. *See also* Rigs/rigging
  defined, 223
  managing datablocks, 36–37
  manipulating bones, 225–227
  overview of, 224
  using Interaction Modes, 38–39
Arms
  adding detail to belt and jacket, 138–139
  blocking shape of, 132–134
  defining, 134–136
  detailing backpack and jacket, 136–138
  modeling, 131–134
  rigging, 235–237
Audio, launching and saving render, 49–50
Auto Save files, 29
AutoMerge feature, 108, 145
Axes (X, Y, Z)
  3D modeling and, 161
  constraining movements, 86, 91–92
  keyboard shortcuts, 34
  manipulators and, 32–33
  mirroring and, 120
  mirroring and adjusting eyes, 120–121
  nodes and, 295
  Shared Vertex options, 165

B

Backdrop option, Node Editor, 298
Background Images panel, 115–116
Backgrounds, 173
Backing up files, 29

Badges, modeling, 156
Bevel tool, 86–87
Bisect tool, 88–89
Black, material channels, 197
.blend
  file format, 29
  linking and appending objects, 258
  packing images, 187
  saving and loading, 49
Blender
  community, 9–10
  downloading and installing, 11
  hardware recommendations, 11–12
  history of, 5–7
  summary and exercises, 10
  what it is, 3–4
Blender Cloud, 8
Blender Foundation, 5, 7–8
Blender Institute, 6
Blender Render
  applying materials, 45, 207–208
  applying textures, 202–205
  compositing in, 299–304
  freestyle rendering, 315–316
  light options, 46
  maps baking, 317
  materials, 198
  overview of, 44
  refining/adjusting materials, 208–210
  rendering in, 48
  setting up materials, 199–202
  shading in, 205–206
  test render in, 211–212
Blocking shapes, 122–124, 132–134
Blur brush, 247
Bone tab, Properties Editor, 235, 250
Bones
  manipulating, 225–227
  mirroring and adjusting, 239–240
  naming anatomically, 239
  rig elements, 223
  rigging, 229–230
Border selection, meshes, 84
Boundary loop selection, 85
Boundary tool, 94–95
Box Center Pivot, using 3D cursor, 26
Box modeling, 113

Box Selections, 25
Branches, 7–8
Bridge Edge Loops tool, 89
Bridge tool, 106
Brushes
    Blur brush, 247
    design methods, 74
    Texture Paint Mode, 182
Bump, material channels, 197

C

Camera
    3D View, 15, 18–19
    positioning, 47–48
Camera panel, Properties Region, 286
Camera tracking
    adjusting camera motion, 288–289
    applying tracked motion to camera,
        287–288
    character-creation plan, 59
    configuring camera settings, 286
    loading footage, 282–283
    marker use in, 283–284
    modifying tracking settings of markers,
        284–286
    in Movie Clip Editor, 281–282
    overview of, 279
    shooting video for, 280–281
    solving/refining camera motion, 287
    summary and exercises, 290
    testing, 289
Cap, modeling, 147–150
Chain
    manipulating bones, 225–227
    rigging arms, 236
    rigging hand, 238
    rigging legs, 234
Chamfers, Bevel tool, 86–87
Channels, for materials, 196–197
Character
    animating. *See* Animation
    character-creation plan, 59–60
    posing, 249–250
    rigging. *See* Rigs/rigging
Character design
    adding color, 70–71
    appearance, 63

base design, 65–67
context, 62
creating character reference images, 72–74
description, 61
details, 68–69
finalizing, 71–72
head, 67–68
methods, 74–75
personality, 62
refining, 69–70
silhouettes, 64–65
style, 63
summary and exercises, 75
Character modeling
    adding detail to belt and jacket, 138–139
    adding ears, 128–129
    applying shading, 216–217
    blocking face shape, 122–124
    building inside of mouth, 130
    choosing modeling methods, 113–114
    creating eyeball, 117–119
    defining eyes, mouth, and nose, 126–128
    defining face shape, 124–126
    defining torso and arms, 134–136
    detailing backpack and jacket, 136–138
    lattices used for deforming eyeball, 119–120
    mesh topology, 111–112
    mirroring and adjusting eyes, 120
    modeling boots, 141–143
    modeling cap, 147–150
    modeling final details, 154–157
    modeling hair, 150–154
    modeling hands, 143–147
    modeling legs, 139–141
    modeling torso and arms, 131–134
    overview of, 111
    setting up reference planes, 114–117
    studying face topology, 121–122
    summary and exercises, 158
    unwrapping human face, 173
    unwrapping other aspects of character,
        176–177
    viewing painted character, 193
Character reference images, 72–74
Checker Deselect tool, 85
Circle tool, LoopTools, 106
Cloth simulation, 314

Clothing, adding to model, 157
Colors
  adding base colors to texture, 189–190
  adding to character design, 70–71
  enabling Specular Color, 210
  material channels, 197
Colors panel, Property Editor, 204
Commercial software, 4–5
Compositing
  in Blender Render, 299–304
  character-creation plan, 60
  connecting/manipulating nodes, 297–298
  creating nodes, 297
  in Cycles, 304–307
  design methods, 75
  overview of, 293–294
  previewing nodes, 298–299
  summary and exercises, 309–310
  understanding nodes, 294–296
  using Node Editor, 296–297
Connect tool, 89–90
Constraints
  adding to eye rig, 232
  adding to leg rig, 234–235
  adding to rigs, 227–228
  adding to torso rig, 235
  Camera Solver, 287
  rig elements, 224
Constraints tab, Properties Editor, 287
Control bones, 223
Controls, animation, 268–269
CPUs (central processing units), 12
CTRL key, for manipulators, 33
Cubes, 15, 167
CUDA graphics cards, 12
Cursors
  2D, 164
  3D, 25–27, 101, 139
Curve category (Add menu), 273–274
Curve tool, LoopTools, 106
Curves, editing animation curves, 266–267
Custom shapes, 224
Cycles
  advanced shading, 217–218
  applying shading to human character, 216–217
  basic shaders, 214–215
  compositing, 304–307

  creating new material, 172
  freestyle rendering, 315–316
  light options, 46–47
  loading textures, 215–216
  maps baking, 317
  materials, 198
  mixing and adding shaders, 215
  overview of, 44
  rendering, 49
  shading, 212–214
  test render in, 219
  using materials, 45–46
Cylinder projections, UV mapping, 167

D
Datablocks, managing, 36–38
Default cube, 3D View, 15
Deform bones, 223, 244
Delete tool, 90–91
Diffuse option, managing materials, 45, 196
Diffuse panel, Properties Editor, 201
Display panel, 164, 240
Dissolve tools, 90–91, 147
Dope Sheet
  animation in, 266
  creating walk action, 270
  editor types and uses, 23
  retiming keyframes, 271
Downloading Blender, 11
Drivers, creating for face shapes, 252
Dupli Visibility, controlling layer visibility, 260
Duplicate
  managing areas, 21
  shaping locks of hair, 151
  working with meshes, 91

E
Ears, 128–129, 155
Eclipse Public License (EPL), 5
Edge flow, 83
Edge menu, 85, 166, 170
Edge Offset tool, 91–92
Edges
  adding natural details to hair, 152
  Bevel tool, 86–87
  border selection, 84

Bridge Edge Loops tool, 89
Connect tool, 89–90
Delete/Dissolve tools, 90–91
Edge Offset tool, 91–92
Extrude tool, 92–93
grow/shrink selection, 84
Intersect options, 87–88
keyboard shortcuts, 81
Knife Project, 96–97
Knife tool, 95–96
limiting selection to visible, 84
linked selections, 83
Make Edge/Face tool, 98
Merge tool, 98–99
in mesh topology, 111–113
proportional editing, 82
Screw tool, 101
selecting, 80
selecting boundary loop and loop
     inner-region, 85
Selection Mode of UV/Image Editor, 165
shortest path selection, 81–82
Slide tool, 102–103
Spin tool, 103–104
Subdivide tool, 105
working with, 79–80
Edit Mode
   adjusting UVs, 179
   applying flat or smooth surfaces, 39–40
   blocking face shape, 122
   creating armatures, 225–226
   creating bone layers, 242
   Deform options, 244
   exporting UVs to image file, 188–189
   interacting with rigs, 227
   limiting selection to visible, 84
   making selections, 81
   managing materials, 44
   marking seams, 170–171
   mirroring bones, 239
   mirroring face shapes, 252
   naming bones anatomically, 239
   rigging eyes, 231–232
   using Interaction Modes with, 38–39
   UV Mapping pop-up menu, 166
   valuing weights, 248
   walking along a path, 273–274

Editing tab, user preferences, 27
Editors. *See also* by individual types
   for animation, 264–267
   navigating user interface, 13
   working with editor types, 21–24
Emission
   managing materials, 45
   material channels, 196
   not supported in Blender Render, 198
Environmental light, 293, 299
EPL (Eclipse Public License), 5
Export UV Layout, UVs menu, 188
Extrude tool, 92–93
Extrusions
   adding detail to belt and jacket, 139
   adding details to cap, 150
   adding ears to face, 128
   adding fingers and wrist to hand, 145
   blocking torso and arms shapes, 132
   detailing backpack and jacket, 136
   modeling boots, 141–143
   modeling legs, 139
   shaping locks of hair, 152
Eyebrows, 154–155
Eyedropper tool, 228
Eyes
   creating eyeball, 117–119
   defining, 126–128
   lattices used for deforming eyeball,
      119–120
   mirroring and adjusting, 120
   modeling, 117
   refining materials, 208–209
   rigging, 231–232

F
F-Curves, 266–267
F2 add-on, 107
Face (human)
   adding ears, 128–129
   blocking shape, 122–124
   building inside of mouth, 130
   creating drivers for face shapes, 253–255
   creating eyeball, 117–119
   creating eyebrows, 154–155
   defining eyes, mouth, and nose, 126–128
   defining face shape, 124–126

Face (human) (*continued*)

    lattices used for deforming eyeball, 119–120

    mirroring and adjusting eyes, 120

    mirroring face shapes, 252

    modeling face shapes, 250–252

    modeling teeth and tongue, 156–157

    rigging, 252–253

    studying face topology, 121–122

    unwrapping, 173

Faces

    Bevel tool, 86–87

    Connect tool, 89–90

    Delete/Dissolve tools, 90–91

    Extrude tool, 92–93

    F2 add-on used with, 107

    Grid Fill tool, 94

    grow/shrink selection, 84

    Inset tool, 94–95

    keyboard shortcuts, 81

    Knife tool, 95–96

    limiting selection to visible, 84

    linked selections, 83

    Make Edge/Face tool, 98

    Merge tool, 98–99

    mesh topology, 112

    Poke tool, 99

    proportional editing, 82

    selecting, 80

    selecting linked flat surfaces, 85

    Selection Mode of UV/Image Editor, 165

    separating/connecting UVs, 174–175

    shortest path selection, 81–82

    Solidify tool, 103

    Spin tool, 103–104

    Split tool, 104–105

    Subdivide tool, 105

    working with, 79–80

Faces menu, 152

File Browser, 21

File formats, 29, 308

File menu, 27, 187

File tab, user preferences, 28

Fill tool, 93–94

Films, project stages and. *See also* Video, 57–58

Fingers, adding to hand, 145–147

Fire simulation, 314

FK (forward kinematics), 232, 235–237

Flat, applying flat surface, 39

Flatten tool, 102, 106

Floor, 292, 299

Fluid simulation, 314

Fly mode, 3D View, 20

Footage. *See* Video

Forums, Blender community, 9

Forward kinematics (FK), 232, 235–237

Fps (frames per second), 269, 283

Freestyle rendering, 315–316

Full Area command, 21

Full Screen command, 21

G

Game Engine, in Blender, 315

General Public License (GPL), 5–6

GIMP image editing software, 186, 188

Glass, managing materials, 46

Global views, 3D View, 19

Glossy, material management, 45

GLSL shading, Shading panel, 205

GPL (General Public License), 5–6

GPU (Graphics Processing Units), 12

Grab

    arranging objects, 35

    defining arms and torso, 134

    keyboard shortcuts, 34

Graph Editor

    animation in, 266–267

    creating drivers for face shapes, 253–255

    editor types and uses, 24

    Normalize option, 269

Graphic cards, 12

Graphics Processing Units (GPU), 12

Grease Pencil, 266, 315

Grid Fill tool, 93–94

Grids, 16, 171–172

Groups, 240–241, 259

Grow/shrink selection, 84

Gstretch tool, LoopTools, 106

H

Hair

    adding natural details to, 152–154

    modeling, 150–151

    shaping locks, 151–152

    simulation, 313

Hands
    adding fingers and wrist, 145–147
    building shape of, 143–145
    rigging, 237–238
Hardware recommendations, 11–12
Head, 67–68, 235
Headers, 17–18, 164
Helper bones, rig elements, 223
Hide and Reveal, Blender options, 108
Hide/Unhide, UVs, 175

I

IK (inverse kinematics)
    rigging arms, 235–237
    rigging hand, 238
    rigging legs, 232–235
Image menu, 187
Images
    creating for UV test grid, 171–172
    creating textures, 188
    exporting UVs to image file, 188–189
    loading textures, 206
    packing, 187
    painting textures, 185–186
    resolution settings, 307
    saving, 187
    texture face, 172
    Texture panel of Property Editor, 204
    textures as, 181
    working with UV/Image Editor, 164
Influence panel, 204, 210
Info Editor, 13, 21
Inkscape, design methods, 74
Input tab, user preferences, 28
Inset tool, 94–95, 134
Installing Blender, 11
Instances, object, 36–37
Interaction modes, 38–39, 227
Interface. See UI (user interface)
Interface option, UV/Image Editor, 164
Interface tab, user preferences, 27
Intersect (Boolean), in meshes, 87–88
Intersect (Knife), in meshes, 88
Inverse kinematics. See IK (inverse kinematics)
Islands, 83, 165
Item panel, Properties Region, 226

J

Join tool
    combining objects in same mesh, 178
    managing areas, 20
    working with meshes, 95

K

Keyboard hardware requirements, 12
Keyboard shortcuts
    accessing modeling tools, 81
    controlling transformations, 34–35
    launching and saving render, 49–50
    for Subdivision Surface modifier, 43
Keyframes
    editing animation curves, 267
    inserting, 263–264
    Match Type option, 285
    retiming, 271
    solving/refining camera motion, 287
Keying sets, 264
Knife Project, 96–97
Knife tool
    adding details to cap, 149
    adding fingers and wrist to hand, 145
    blocking face shape, 124
    creating base of cap, 147
    defining arms and torso, 135–136
    defining face shape, 124–126
    modeling hands, 145
    modeling legs, 140
    working with meshes, 95–96
Krita image editing software, 65, 186, 188

L

Lamps. See also Lights/lighting
    3D View elements, 16
    managing datablocks, 36–37
    turning on, 46–47
Lasso Selections, 25
Lattice tool
    creating face rig, 252
    for deforming geometry, 119–120
    mirroring and adjusting eyes, 120
Layers
    bone layers, 241–242
    protecting, 259–260

Layers (*continued*)
   setting up Render Layers, 299–302, 305
   using with materials, 196
Layers panel, 301
Legs
   modeling boots, 141–143
   modeling shape of, 139–141
   rigging, 232–235
Lens panel, Properties Region, 286
Library Linking, for character reuse, 258
Licenses, open-source, 5
Lights/lighting
   adding to scene, 47
   analyzing footage, 291–292
   Blender Render and Cycles lights, 46–47
   in character-creation plan, 60
   creating and testing lights, 292–293
   creating/testing lights, 292
   creating two suns, 219
   maps baking, 317
   overview of, 291
   setting as Sun type, 211
Linked duplicates, objects, 36–37
Linked flat surfaces, 85
Linked selections, 83
Linking, 258, 260
Live Unwrap tool, 174
LocRotScale, inserting keyframes, 263–264
Loft tool, LoopTools, 106
Logic Editor, 23
Loop animation, 270
Loop Cut and Slide tool
   blocking face shape, 122
   blocking torso and arms shapes, 133
   defining eyes, mouth, and nose, 126
   defining face shape, 125
   modeling legs, 139–141
   working with meshes, 97–98
Loop Inner-Region, selecting, 85
Loops
   adding ears to face, 129
   blocking torso and arms shapes, 134
   building inside of mouth, 130
   defining eyes, mouth, and nose, 126–128
   in meshes, 83–84
   modeling hands, 143–147

   modeling legs, 139–140
   Slide tool, 102–103
LoopTools, 105–107

M
Make Edge/Face tool, 98
Manipulators, controlling transformations, 32–33
Mapping panel, Property Editor, 204, 210
Maps Baking, 317
Mark Seam command, Edge menu, 170
Marker tab, Tools Region, 286
Markers
   in camera tracking, 283–284
   modifying tracking settings, 284–286
   options and settings, 281
   as yellow line in Movie Clip Editor, 283
Marking Seams option, Edge menu, 166
Mask mode, Dope Sheet, 266
Masks/masking, 196, 316
Massachusetts Institute of Technology (MIT), 5
Master version, Blender, 7
Match Type option, keyframes, 285
Material tab, Properties Editor, 195, 199–202, 205–206
Materials
   adding, 46, 195
   advanced shading, 217–218
   applying several materials to single object, 207–208
   applying shading to human character, 216–217
   applying textures, 202–205
   basic Cycles shaders, 214–215
   Blender Render and Cycles, 45–46, 198
   channels for, 196–197
   creating, 172, 299
   final adjustments, 210
   loading textures, 215–216
   managing, 44–45
   managing datablocks, 36–37
   masks and layers and, 196
   mixing and adding shaders, 215
   overview of, 195–196
   painting textures, 185–186
   procedural textures, 198–199

refining, 208–209
separating by, 102
setting up in Blender Render, 199–202
shading in Blender Render, 205–206
shading in Cycles, 212–214
summary and exercises, 220
test render in Blender Render, 211–212
test render in Cycles, 219
textures for controlling material properties,
    209–210
Merge tool, 98–99
Merging vertices, 137
Mesh Deform modifiers, 252
Mesh flow, 83
Mesh Menu, 80
Mesh tab, Properties Editor, 247
Meshes
    Bevel tool, 86–87
    Bisect tool, 88–89
    border selection, 84
    Bridge Edge Loops tool, 89
    for character hair, 66
    combining objects in, 178
    Connect tool, 89–90
    Delete/Dissolve tools, 90–91
    Duplicate tool, 91
    Edge Offset tool, 91–92
    Extrude tool, 92–93
    Fill/Grid Fill tools, 93–94
    Inset tool, 94–95
    Interaction Modes, 38
    Intersect options, 87–88
    islands, 83
    Join tool, 95
    Knife Project, 96–97
    Knife tool, 95–96
    limiting selection to visible, 84
    Loop Cut and Slide tool, 97–98
    loops and rings, 83–84
    Make Edge/Face tool, 98
    managing datablocks, 36–37
    Merge tool, 98–99
    modeling tools for, 86
    Poke tool, 99
    Remove Doubles tool, 100
    Rip/Rip Fill tools, 100–101
    Screw tool, 101

Separate tool, 102
Shrink/Flatten tool, 102
Slide tool, 102–103
Smooth Vertex tool, 103
Solidify tool, 103
Spin tool, 103–104
Split tool, 104–105
Subdivide tool, 105
topology, 111–112
unwrapping and, 161, 169
Mirror Mode, 120–121
Mirror modifier
    adding detail to belt and jacket, 139
    blocking torso and arms shapes, 132
    modeling boots, 141
    setting up model for skinning, 243
Mirror panel, Properties Editor, 201
Mirroring
    adjusting eyes, 120–121
    bones, 239–240
    face shapes, 252
    managing materials, 45
    rig, 238–239
    vertex weights, 248–249
MIT (Massachusetts Institute of Technology), 5
Mix, material management, 46
Mix shader, 215
Modeling
    character-creation plan, 59
    character modeling. See Character modeling
    choosing methods, 113–114
    creating character reference images, 72–74
    design methods, 74
    face shapes, 250–252
    sculpting, 316
Modeling tools
    accessing, 80–81
    Bevel tool, 86–87
    Bisect tool, 88–89
    border selection, 84
    Bridge Edge Loops tool, 89
    Checker Deselect tool, 85
    Connect tool, 89–90
    Delete/Dissolve tools, 90–91
    Duplicate tool, 91
    Edge Offset tool, 91–92
    Extrude tool, 92–93

Modeling tools (*continued*)
 F2 add-on, 107
 Fill/Grid Fill tools, 93–94
 grow/shrink selection, 84
 Inset tool, 94–95
 Intersect options, 87–88
 Join tool, 95
 Knife Project, 96–97
 Knife tool, 95–96
 limiting selection to visible, 84
 linked selections, 83
 Loop Cut and Slide tool, 97–98
 loops and rings, 83–84
 LoopTools, 105–107
 Make Edge/Face tool, 98
 making selections, 81
 Merge tool, 98–99
 for meshes, 86
 overview of, 79
 Poke tool, 99
 proportional editing, 82–83
 Remove Doubles tool, 100
 Rip/Rip Fill tools, 100–101
 Screw tool, 101
 selecting boundary loop and loop
  inner-region, 85
 selecting linked flat surfaces, 85
 selecting similar, 84–85
 Separate tool, 102
 Shrink/Flatten tool, 102
 shortest path selection, 81–82
 Slide tool, 102–103
 Smooth Vertex tool, 103
 Solidify tool, 103
 Spin tool, 103–104
 Split tool, 104–105
 Subdivide tool, 105
 summary and exercises, 109
 tips and tricks, 108–109
 working with vertices, edges, and faces,
  79–80
Modifiers
 adding, 41–42
 adding armature modifier, 244–245
 adding Subdivision Surface modifier to
  object, 42–43
 choosing modeling methods, 114
 copying to other objects, 42

 creating face rig, 252
 design methods, 74–75
 lattices used for deforming eyeball, 119–120
 overview of, 40–41
 setting up model for skinning, 243–244
 unwrapping considerations and, 169
Modifiers tab, Properties Editor, 245
Mouse hardware requirements, 12
Mouth, defining, 126–128
Move, object management, 32
Movie Clip Editor
 adjusting camera motion, 288–289
 camera tracking in, 281–282
 editor types and uses, 23
 loading footage, 282–283
 masking, object tracking, and video
  stabilization, 316
 testing camera tracking, 289
Movies, history of Blender, 6

N
Naming objects, 35–36, 38
NaN (Not a Number), 5
NeoGeo, 5
NLA Editor
 creating walk action, 270
 editor types and uses, 23
 non-linear animation, 268
 repeating animation, 272–273
Node Editor
 compositing, 293–294
 connecting/manipulating nodes, 297–298
 creating nodes, 297
 editor types and uses, 23
 mixing shaders, 198
 previewing nodes, 298–299
 understanding nodes, 294–296
 using, 296–297
Nodes
 anatomy of, 295–296
 Animation Nodes, 318
 compositing in Blender Render, 302–304
 compositing in Cycles, 306–307
 connecting/manipulating, 297–298
 creating, 297
 previewing, 298–299
 understanding, 294
Noodles, in node anatomy, 295

Normal, material channels, 197
Normalize option, Graph Editor, 269
Nose, defining, 126–128
Not a Number (NaN), 5

O

ObData (object data), 36, 38
Object Mode
   interacting with rigs, 227
   Join tool use in, 95
   organizing rigs, 230
   using Interaction Modes, 38
Object tab, Properties Editor, 259
Objects
   adding modifiers, 42–43
   applying several materials to single object, 207–208
   arranging, 35
   copying modifiers, 42
   creating, 31–32
   joining, 95
   knowing which objects don't need weights, 249
   linking and appending, 258
   managing datablocks, 36
   monkey head (Suzanne) test object, 32
   naming, 35–36, 38
   rigid and soft bodies, 314
   selecting, 25
   tracking, 316
Occlusion, 197, 211, 299, 301, 305–307
Opacity, 182, 196
Open Movies, 6, 8
Open-source software (OSS), 3–5
OpenCL graphics cards, 12
Operator menu, Tools Region, 259
Operator panel
   3D View elements, 15
   Bevel tool, 87
   Loop Cut and Slide tool options, 97–98
   modifying objects, 31
   modifying selections, 84
   Remove Doubles tool, 100
   working with armatures, 226
Options tab, Tools Region, 247
Orbit, 3D View, 18
Orphan data, 37

Orthographic views, 3D View, 19
OSS (open-source software), 3–5
Outliner
   editor types and uses, 22
   navigating Blender user interface, 14
   renaming objects, 36
Output options, rendering, 308
Output tab, Properties Editor, 308

P

Packing UVs, 177–179
Paint Mode, UV/Image Editor, 183
Paint Selections, 25
Painting textures. *See* Textures
Pan, 3D View, 18
Parallax effect, in camera tracking, 280
Particles
   fire and smoke simulation, 314
   hair simulation, 313
   overview of, 313
Path object, Curve category of Add menu, 273–274
Personality, character design, 62
Perspective shift, in camera tracking, 280
Perspective views, 3D View, 19
Photographs, project stages, 58
Pie Menus add-on, 315
Pin option, UV/Image Editor, 164
Pipeline, project, 55
Pivot Point, 33, 165
Poke tool, 99
Poly count, in mesh topology, 112
Poly to poly modeling method, 113
Polygons, 112–113
Pose Mode
   adding constraints to leg rig, 234–235
   adding constraints to rigs, 228
   bone layers, 242
   creating custom shapes, 256
   Deform options, 244
   interacting with rigs, 227
   naming bones anatomically, 239
   using Interaction Modes, 39
Poses, 249–250, 270–272
Postproduction
   character-creation plan, 59–60
   project stages, 56

Postproduction (*continued*)
  stages for animated film, 58
  stages for film with visual effects, 57–58
  stages for film without visual effects, 57
  stages for photograph, 58
Predefined views, 3D View, 19
Preferences, user preferences, 27–28
Preproduction
  character-creation plan, 59
  project stages, 55–56
  stages for animated film, 58
  stages for film with visual effects, 57–58
  stages for film without visual effects, 57
  stages for photograph, 58
Preview panel, Property Editor, 204
Previewing render, 47
Procedural textures, 198–199
Production
  character-creation plan, 59
  project stages, 56
  stages for animated film, 58
  stages for film with visual effects, 57–58
  stages for film without visual effects, 57
  stages for photograph, 58
Projects
  3D View, 167
  character-creation plan, 59–60
  stages for animated film, 58
  stages for film with visual effects, 57–58
  stages for film without visual effects, 57
  stages for photograph, 58
  stages of, 55–56
  summary and exercises, 60
Properties
  animating, 264
  node, 295
Properties Editor
  adding materials, 205–206
  adding modifiers, 41
  Armature tab, 230
  Bone tab, 235, 250
  checking object name, 36–37
  Constraints tab, 287
  editor types and uses, 22
  managing materials, 44
  Materials tab, 195, 198–201
  Mesh tab, 247

  Modifiers tab, 245
  navigating Blender user interface, 14
  Object tab, 259
  Output tab, 308
  Protected Layers, 259–260
  renaming objects, 36
  Render Properties, 48
  render tests, 211
  setting image resolution, 307
  setting up reference planes, 115
  Shadows panel, 299
  Texture tab, 198–199
  turning on lights, 46–47
  working with armatures, 226
  World tab, 293
Properties Region
  3D View elements, 16
  Camera and Lens panels, 286
  Item panel, 226
  marker settings, 281
  modifying tracking settings of markers,
    284–286
  setting up reference planes, 115
  Shading panel, 205
  UVs visualization, 173
Proportional editing
  adjusting UVs, 174–175
  blocking face shape, 123
  detailing backpack and jacket, 136
  for modeling, 82–83
  UV/Image Editor, 165
Protected Layers, Properties Editor, 259–260
Proxies, for animating linked character, 260
.psd files, 190
Python console, 21
Python scripting, 318

R
RAM requirements, 12
Raytrace Transparency, 208
Real Time Rendering Mode, 47
Red, green, blue (RGB), material channels,
  197
Reference images, creating, 72–74
Reference planes, for character modeling,
  114–117
Refine option, camera motion, 287

Reflection, material channels, 197
Relations panel, Properties Editor, 235
Relax tool, LoopTools, 107
Remove Doubles tool, 100
Render engines, 44
Render Layers, 289–302, 305
Render panel, 49
Render Properties, 49
Rendering
    in Blender Render, 48
    character-creation plan, 60
    in Cycles, 49
    final results, 308–309
    launching and saving render, 49–50
    output options, 308
    overview of, 48
    previewing, 47
    saving and loading .blend file, 49
    settings, 307
    test render in Blender Render, 211–212
    test render in Cycles, 219
Resize, area management, 21
Resolution
    images, 307
    textures, 184
    video, 283
Retopology modeling method, 113, 316–317
RGB (red, green, blue), material channels, 197
Rigid bodies, 314
Rigs/rigging
    adding armature modifier, 244–245
    adding constraints, 227–228
    arms, 235–237
    bones (skeleton), 229–230
    character-creation plan, 59
    creating custom shapes, 255–256
    creating drivers for face shapes, 253–255
    defining weights, 245–248
    eyes, 231–232
    face, 252–253
    final retouches, 257
    hand, 237–238
    interaction modes, 227
    legs, 232–235
    manipulating bones, 225–227
    mirroring and adjusting bones, 239–240
    mirroring face shapes, 252

    mirroring the rig, 238–239
    mirroring weights, 248–249
    modeling face shapes, 250–252
    naming bones anatomically, 239
    organizing the rig, 240–242
    posing character, 249–250
    process of, 224
    reusing characters, 258–260
    setting up model for skinning, 243–244
    skinning, 242
    summary and exercises, 260–261
    torso and head, 235
    vertex weights in skinning, 242–243
    what it is, 223–224
Rings, in meshes, 83–84
Rip/Rip Fill tools, 100–101
Roosendaal, Ton, 5–7
Rotate
    arranging objects, 35
    Copy Rotation constraint, 235–236
    keyboard shortcuts, 34
    manipulating objects, 32
Roughness/glossiness, material channels, 197

S
Saving files, 29, 49
Scale
    arranging objects, 35
    keyboard shortcuts, 34
    manipulating objects, 32
Scenes, creating
    applying flat or smooth surfaces, 39–40
    arranging objects, 35
    creating objects, 31–32
    interaction modes, 38–39
    keyboard shortcuts, 34–35
    lights and shadows, 46–47
    managing datablocks, 36–38
    managing materials, 44–46
    manipulators, 32–33
    naming objects, 35–36, 38
    positioning camera, 47–48
    rendering, 48–50
    summary and exercises, 51
    using render engines, 44
    working with modifiers, 40–43
Screw tool, 101

Scripts, Python, 318
Sculpt modeling method, 113, 316
Seams
    accessing unwrapping menus, 166
    defining, 168
    marking, 170–171
    working with UV mapping tools, 166–167
Search menu, 80
Select menu
    Checker Deselect tool, 85
    selecting boundary loop and loop
        inner-region, 85
    selection methods, 85–86
Select Split tool, 174–175
Selections
    border selection, 84
    Checker Deselect tool, 85
    grow/shrink selection, 84
    limiting to visible, 84
    linked selections, 83
    loops and rings, 83–84
    making active, 25
    selecting boundary loop and loop
        inner-region, 85
    selecting linked flat surfaces, 85
    selecting objects, 24–25
    selecting similar, 84–85
Separate tool, 102
Shaders/shading
    basic, 214–215
    in Blender Render, 205–206
    character-creation plan, 59
    in Cycles, 212–217
    Cycles materials consisting of, 212
    defined, 195
    mixing and adding, 198, 215
Shading panel, Properties Editor, 201, 205, 209
Shadows
    adding to scene, 46–47
    creating/testing lights, 292
    node compositing, 306–307
    raytrace shadows, 211
    setting up Render Layers, 301
Shadows panel, Properties Editor, 202, 299
Shape keys
    creating, 251–252

creating facial rig, 250
    mirroring face shapes, 252
    modeling face shapes, 250–251
Shape Keys mode, Dope Sheet, 266
Shapes
    creating drivers for face shapes, 252
    custom, 255–256
    mirroring face shapes, 252
    modeling face shapes, 250–252
Shared Vertex, UV/Image Editor, 165
Shrink/Flatten tool, 102
Shortest Path selection, 81–82, 171
Shrink/grow selection, 84
Shrink Wrap modifier, 156, 243
Silhouettes, in character design, 64–65
Skeleton. See Bones
Sketches
    adding color to design, 71
    character details, 69
    creating character reference images,
        73–74
    finalizing character design, 72
    head, 67
    of refined design, 70
    silhouettes, 64–66
Skin modifier, 74–75
Skinning
    adding armature modifier, 244–245
    defining weights, 245–248
    mirroring weights, 248–249
    overview of, 242
    setting up model for, 243–244
    vertex weights in, 242–243
Slide tool, 102–103
Slots tab, Tools Region, 185, 210
Smoke simulation, 314
Smooth Stroke feature, 182, 187
Smooth surface, 39
Smooth Vertex tool, 103, 122–123
Snap menu, 26
Snapping
    Blender options, 108–109
    Snap to Faces, 317
    UV/Image Editor, 165
Soft bodies, 314
Software, commercial vs. open-source, 4–5

Solidify tool
    creating eyebrows, 154–155
    detailing backpack and jacket, 136–137
    shaping locks of hair, 152
    working with meshes, 103
Solve Camera Motion, 287
Solve tab, Tools Region, 287
Space tool, LoopTools, 107
Specials menu
    modeling hands, 144
    Subdivide Smooth tool, 144
    Subdivide tool, 226
Specular option
    adjusting intensity of, 208–209
    enabling Specular Color, 210
    material channels, 197
    material management, 45
Specular panel, Properties Editor, 201
Spheres, 147, 167
Spin tool, 103–104
Splash Screen, 14
Split tool
    area management, 20
    working with meshes, 104–105
Stages, project
    for animated film, 58
    for film with visual effects, 57–58
    for film without visual effects, 57
    overview of, 55–56
    for photograph, 58
Still frames, 49–50
Stitch tool, UVs, 175
Storyboarding, 57
Strand panel, Properties Editor, 202
Style, character design, 63
Subdivide tool
    Specials menu, 226
    Subdivide Smooth, 144
    working with meshes, 105
Subdivision Surface modifier
    adding ears to face, 128–129
    adding to objects, 42–43
    creating eyebrows, 154–155
    defining eyes, mouth, and nose, 126
    density and tension in, 112
    Edge Offset tool, 91–92

modeling badges, 156
working with modifiers, 40
Subsurface Scattering panel, Properties
    Editor, 202
Sun light
    choosing Sun type, 211
    creating/testing lights, 292
    creating two suns, 219
Surface panel, 219
Surfaces, applying flat or smooth, 39–40
Swap, area management, 21
Sync UVs and 3D View, 165, 175
System tab, user preferences, 28

T
Teeth, modeling, 156–157
Test render, 211–212, 219
Texel density, 168
Text Editor, 23
Texture face, UV/Image Editor, 172
Texture Paint Mode
    accessing, 181
    conditions for painting, 184–185
    considerations before painting, 183–184
    limitations of, 186
    overview of, 182–183
    paint slots for, 185–186
Texture tab, Properties Editor, 198, 202–206
Textures
    with 2D image editing software, 188
    adding base colors, 189–190
    adding details, 191
    applying finishing touches, 192
    applying in Blender Render, 202–205
    character-creation plan, 59
    conditions for painting, 184–185
    considerations before painting, 183–184
    controlling material properties, 209–210
    creating, 210
    creating base texture, 186–187
    creating new texture, 206
    exporting UVs to image file, 188–189
    limitations of Texture Paint Mode, 186
    loading in Cycles, 215–216
    loading UVs and base elements, 189
    managing datablocks, 36–37

Textures (*continued*)
    paint slots for, 185–186
    procedural textures, 198–199
    resolution settings, 184
    summary and exercises, 193–194
    texel density, 168
    Texture Paint Mode, 182–183
    viewing painted character in Blender, 193
    workflows for painting, 181
Themes, user preferences, 28
Timeline
    animation in, 265
    editor types and uses, 24
    navigating Blender user interface, 14
Tongue, modeling, 156–157
Tools Region
    3D View elements, 14
    accessing Knife Project from, 96
    accessing LoopTools, 105
    accessing modeling tools, 80
    accessing unwrapping menus, 166
    applying flat or smooth surfaces, 39–40
    Armature Options panel, 225
    Bisect tool, 88–89
    creating objects, 31
    marker options, 281
    Marker tab, 286
    Missing UVs message, 184
    modifying tracking settings of markers,
        284–286
    navigating Blender user interface, 14
    node panels, 297
    Operator menu, 259
    Options tab, 247
    Slots tab, 185
    Solve tab, 287
    Texture Paint Mode and, 182
Topology
    mesh topology, 111–113
    studying face topology, 121–122
Torso
    adding detail to belt and jacket, 138–139
    blocking shape of, 132–134
    defining, 134–136
    detailing backpack and jacket, 136–138
    modeling, 131–134
    rigging, 235
Transform Orientation manipulator, 33

Transformations
    keyboard shortcuts, 34
    manipulators controlling, 32–33
    numerically precise, 34–35
Transparency
    alpha settings, 302
    material channels, 196
    material management, 45
    Raytrace Transparency, 208
    unwrapping human face, 173
Transparency panel, Properties Editor, 201

U
UI (user interface)
    3D View features, 14–18
    making selection active, 25
    managing areas, 20–21
    navigating, 13–14
    navigating 3D View, 18–20
    selecting objects, 24–25
    setting preferences, 27–28
    summary and exercises, 29
    using 3D cursor, 25–27
    working with editor types, 21–24
Unwrapping
    accessing unwrapping menus, 166
    adjusting UVs, 174–175
    in Blender, 162
    character-creation plan, 59
    considerations before, 169
    creating/displaying UV test grid, 171–172
    defining seams, 168
    face of character, 173
    Live Unwrap tool, 174
    marking seams, 170–171
    navigating UV/Image Editor, 166
    other aspects of character, 176–177
    overview of, 161–162
    reviewing UVs (human face), 175–176
    summary and exercises, 179–180
    texture workflows and, 188
    using UV/Image Editor, 177–179
    working with UV mapping tools, 166–167
User interface. *See* UI (user interface)
User Preferences
    add-ons, 317–318
    editor types and uses, 22
    setting, 27–28

UV/Image Editor
  adjusting UVs, 163–165
  editor types and uses, 23
  exporting UVs to image file, 188–189
  Live Unwrap tool, 174
  navigating, 166
  packing UVs, 179
  Paint Mode, 183
  previewing nodes, 298
  saving images, 187
  unwrapping human face, 173
  unwrapping in Blender, 162
  viewing rendering, 50
UV mapping. *See* Unwrapping
UV Mapping menu, 166–167
UVs
  adjusting, 163–165, 174–175
  creating/displaying test grid, 171–172
  creating sphere, 147
  Current UV Map, 165
  defining seams, 168
  exporting to image file, 188–189
  Live Unwrap tool, 174
  loading for base texture, 189
  marking seams, 170–171
  Missing UVs message, 184
  overview of, 161–162
  packing, 177–179
  painting textures, 181
  reviewing, 175–176
  separating/connecting, 174–175
  setting coordinates to, 210
  Texture Paint Mode and, 186
  unwrapping, 162, 169, 173
  working with UV mapping tools, 1
    66–167
UVs menu, Export UV Layout, 188

V
Vector imaging, design methods, 74
Vertex Groups panel, Properties Editor,
  247–248
Vertex weights
  defining, 245–247
  knowing which objects don't need weights,
    249
  mirroring, 248–249

  overview of, 242–243
  weight values, 248
Vertices
  adding natural details to hair, 152
  adjusting UVs and, 174
  Bevel tool, 86–87
  blocking torso and arms shapes, 134
  Connect tool, 89–90
  defining face shape, 124–126
  Delete/Dissolve tools, 90–91
  Extrude tool, 92–93
  grow/shrink selection, 84
  keyboard shortcuts, 81
  limiting selection to visible, 84
  linked selections, 83
  Make Edge/Face tool, 98
  Merge tool, 98–99
  merging, 137
  Poke tool, 99
  proportional editing, 82
  Remove Doubles tool, 100
  Rip/Rip Fill tools, 100–101
  Screw tool, 101
  selecting, 80
  Selection Mode of UV/Image Editor, 165
  Shrink/Flatten tool, 102
  shortest path selection, 81–82
  Slide tool, 102–103
  Smooth Vertex tool, 103, 122–123
  Spin tool, 103–104
  unwrapping and, 161
  UVs and, 161–162
  working with, 79–80
  working with F2 add-on, 107
Video
  analyze footage for lighting, 291–292
  loading footage, 282–283
  modifying tracking settings of markers,
    284–286
  recording character-creation plan, 59
  resolution and fps, 283
  shooting for camera tracking, 280–281
  stabilization, 316
  understanding camera tracking, 279
Video Sequences Editor, 23
View name, 3D View, 14
Visual effects, 57–58

W

Walk cycle (animation example)
   creating poses for, 270–272
   creating walk action, 270
   repeating animation, 272–273
   walking along a path, 273–274
Walk mode, 3D View, 19
Websites, Blender community, 9
Weight Paint Mode, 245–247
Weights. *See* Vertex weights
White material channel, 197
Wireframe display mode, 84

Work Mode menu, UV/Image Editor,
   164
Workflows, 55, 181
World tab, Properties Editor, 293
Wrist, adding to hand, 145–147

X

XYZ axes. *See* Axes (X, Y, Z)
XYZ Euler method, 257

Z

Zoom, 3D View, 19